MW01004003

The Majority Press
**THE PHILOSOPHY AND OPINIONS
OF MARCUS GARVEY
Or, Africa for the Africans**

THE NEW MARCUS GARVEY LIBRARY

A Series of Original Works by TONY MARTIN and Important Writings by MARCUS GARVEY

THE PHILOSOPHY AND OPINIONS OF MARCUS GARVEY

or

Africa for the Africans
Volumes I and II

Compiled by
AMY JACQUES GARVEY

New Preface by **TONY MARTIN**

The New Marcus Garvey Library, No. 9

THE MAJORITY PRESS
P.O. Box 538
Dover, Mass. 02030, U.S.A.

Library of Congress Cataloging in Publication Data

Garvey, Marcus, 1887-1940.
    The philosophy and opinions of Marcus Garvey, or, Africa for the Africans.

    (The New Marcus Garvey library ; no. 9)
    Reprint. Originally published: Philosophy and opinions of Marcus Garvey. Universal Pub. House, 1923-1925. With new pref.
    1. Afro-Americans--Collected works. I. Garvey, Amy Jacques. II. Title. III. Title: Africa for the Africans. IV. Series.
E185.97.G3A25 1986 973'.0496073 86-18031
ISBN 0-912469-24-2 (pbk.)

First published in 1923 and 1925.

First Majority Press edition, 1986.

25 24 23 22 21 20 19 18 17 16

The Majority Press
P.O. Box 538
Dover, Massachusetts 02030

Printed in the United States of America

Preface to The Majority Press Centennial Edition

The Philosophy and Opinions of Marcus Garvey, or, Africa for the Africans is an unusual work. Begun as the private compilation of a devoted wife, it was transformed, under the pressure of circumstances into a celebrated apologia for a great leader.

The history and contents of the book are a metaphor on the Black experience of the last five hundred years. Careful perusal of these pages reveals much more than the dreams and achievements and the trials and tribulations of the most successful Pan-African movement of all time. They reveal much also of the strengths and hopes, of the failures and frustrations besetting scattered Africa in its tedious meanderings out of the quagmire of slavery and subjugation.

The Black struggle in the western world, like all struggles of oppressed peoples everywhere, has produced leaders of exceptional ability and unswerving dedication to a cause. In these pages we see the singleness of purpose, the breadth of vision, the belief in the righteousness of his work, the boldness born of conviction, that made Marcus Garvey both the most loved and the most feared and hated Black man of his time. Qualities like these in leaders from Toussaint L'Ouverture to Nat Turner to Martin Luther King, Jr. and Malcolm X have always helped sustain this struggle when the need was greatest.

The price for such leadership has always been too high. All of the names enumerated above suffered martyrdom. Marcus Garvey escaped the assassin's bullet only to be jailed, deported, hounded and harassed. A significant portion of these two volumes is taken up with the successful judicial and extra-judicial efforts to railroad him to prison for crimes he was not guilty of.

The commitment of exceptional leaders has, over the years, been matched by the loyalty of masses of people energized by the hope of freedom, justice and equality. In these pages we catch glimpses, through text and photos, of the multitudes who followed Garvey and believed in him.

The loyalty of the masses has, unhappily, all too often been offset by the treachery of the fainthearted. Garvey's struggle was not exempt from the universal phenomenon of Judases, Quislings and traitors. "The Negro," he was moved to declare, "is his own greatest enemy." So here, too, we see ample evidence of the enemies from within, as they collaborate with the enemies without to effect Garvey's downfall and, with it, the hopes and aspirations of millions of their own kind.

In the unrelenting hostility of the larger world, too, we see in Garvey's experience a metaphor for the experience of scattered Africa. The larger world has not usually viewed with equanimity movements that would bring dignity to the sons and daughters of slaves. J. Edgar Hoover of the Justice Department plotted Garvey's undoing in 1919 even as, near half a century later and as head of the Federal Bureau of Investigation, he orchestrated the campaign of dirty tricks against Martin Luther King, Jr. and Malcolm X.

In death, as in life, the story of Marcus Garvey and *The Philosophy and Opinions* continued to reflect the generality of Black history in microcosm. The movement declined and the volumes went out of print. The man and his writings remained alive in the memories of many humble folk. For long dreary years, Mrs. Amy Jacques Garvey stood almost alone against the near successful attempt in the halls of academia and in the larger society generally, to consign Garvey's memory to oblivion. She desired to reprint the volumes but could not afford to do so. At least two small concerns essayed limited editions, but in quantities insufficient to have significant impact. Established publishers refused Mrs. Garvey's requests to reissue the work. Then came the Black Power revolution and with it the unseemly haste of mainstream publishing houses to capitalize on the new found interest in things Black. By the late 1960's, three of the more substantial houses had competing editions in print.

Whether in or out of print, *The Philosophy and Opinions* has exercised an enduring fascination on large numbers of people. A 1934 advertisement called it "the textbook of Negro inspiration." It is biblical in its scope. It contains the history of a people, from their glorious days in the Nile Valley, to slavery in the West, to the stirrings of hope in the twentieth century. The dramas that unfold in its pages are timeless as the hills. They are the stories of good versus evil, of heroism in the face of fearful odds. There is tragedy here, as the hero marches to inevitable doom, but unbowed and triumphant.

In Garvey's prose there is all the grandeur of the prophet's voice declaiming from the mountaintops. His language is ringingly rhetorical, and several of these writings were in fact designed for oral presentation. And thinly concealed beneath the prosaic veneer of his oratory there lurks always the hint of poetic eloquence. His aphorisms and longer compositions alike resound with a beauty that compels frequent rereading. "Men who are in earnest are not afraid of consequences; Africa for the Africans, those at home and those abroad; whatsoever man has done, man can do" -- these are among the often quoted expressions that resonate from these pages. "Look for me in the whirlwind or the storm," says Garvey in another much quoted and often recited passage; "look for me all around you, for with God's grace, I shall come and bring with me countless millions of Black slaves who have died in America and the West Indies and the millions in Africa to aid you in the fight for Liberty, Freedom and Life."

As we approach the 1987 celebration of the centennial of Marcus Garvey's birth, the time seems appropriate for the United States and Jamaican governments to declare null and void the legal proceedings that unjustly sent him to jail in both countries. Nor should a mere "pardon" suffice, presupposing as it does, the presence of guilt to begin with. "You will see that from the start we tried to dignify our race," Garvey says to a New York jury from these pages; "If I am to be condemned for that I am satisfied." But those who celebrate the man's centennial ought not to be satisfied with anything less than a complete restoration of his good name.

Tony Martin
Wellesley, Massachusetts
June 14, 1986

VOLUME I

AMY JACQUES-GARVEY

Dedicated To
THE TRUE AND LOYAL MEMBERS OF
THE UNIVERSAL NEGRO IMPROVEMENT
ASSOCIATION
In The Cause Of
AFRICAN REDEMPTION

PREFACE

This Volume is compiled from the speeches and articles delivered and written by Marcus Garvey from time to time.

My purpose for compiling same primarily, was not for publication, but rather to keep as a personal record of the opinions and sayings of my husband during his career as the Leader of that portion of the human family known as the Negro Race. However, on second thought, I decided to publish this volume in order to give to the public an opportunity of studying and forming an opinion of him; not from inflated and misleading newspaper and magazine articles, but from expressions of thoughts enunciated by him in defence of his oppressed and struggling race; so that by his own words he may be judged, and Negroes the world over may be informed and inspired, for truth, brought to light, forces conviction, and a state of conviction inspires action.

The history of contact between the white and black races for the last three hundred years or more, records only a series of pillages, wholesale murders, atrocious brutalities, industrial exploitation, disfranchisement of the one on the other; the strong against the weak; but the sun of evolution is gradually rising, shedding its light between the clouds of misery and oppression, and quickening and animating to racial consciousness and eventual national independence black men and women the world over.

It is human, therefore, that few of us within the Negro race can comprehend this transcendent period. We all suffer in a more or less degree; we all feel this awakened spirit of true manhood and womanhood; but it is given to few the vision of leadership—it is an inspiration—it is a quality born in man. Therefore in the course of leadership it is natural that one should meet opposition because of ignorance, lack of knowledge and sympathy of the opposition in understanding fully the spirit of leadership.

With the dawn of this new era, which precedes the Day of National Independence for Negroes, it is well for all members of the race to understand their leadership; know what its essentials, its principles are, and help it to attain its goal and liberate a race in the truest sense of the word.

In Chapter 1 of this volume. I have endeavored to place before my readers gems of expression convincing in their truths.

Chapter 2 deals with definitions and expositions of various interesting themes.

Chapters 3 and 4 contain a collection of brief essays on subjects affecting world conditions generally and Negroes in particular.

In Chapter 5 I have reproduced what I consider two of the best speeches of my husband.

It is my sincere hope and desire that this small volume will help to disseminate among the members of my race everywhere the true knowledge of their past history, the struggles and strivings of the present leadership, and the glorious future of national independence in a free and redeemed Africa, acheived through organized purpose and organized action.

AMY JACQUES-GARVEY

New York City,

February, 23rd., 1923.

CONTENTS

CHAPTER I

CHAPTER II

CHAPTER III

Philosophy and Opinions

OF

MARCUS GARVEY

CHAPTER 1

HISTORY is the land-mark by which we are directed into the true course of life.

The history of a movement, the history of a nation, the history of a race is the guide-post of that movement's destiny, that nation's destiny, that race's destiny.

What you do to-day that is worthwhile, inspires others to act at some future time.

———o———

CHANCE has never yet satisfied the hope of a suffering people.

Action, self-reliance, the vision of self and the future have been the only means by which the oppressed have seen and realized the light of their own freedom.

———o———

LIFE is that existence that is given to man to live for a purpose, to live to his own satisfaction and pleasure, providing he forgets not the God who created him and who expects a spiritual obedience and observation of the moral laws that He has inspired.

———o———

There is nothing in the world common to man, that man cannot do.

———o———

The ends you serve that are selfish will take you no further than yourself; but the ends you serve that are for all, in common, will take you even into eternity.

———o———

It is only the belief and the confidence we have in a God why man is able to understand his own social institutions, and move and live like a rational human being.

Take away the highest ideal—FAITH and CONFIDENCE IN A GOD—and mankind at large is reduced to savagery and the race destroyed.

———o———

A race without authority and pwoer, is a race without respect.

———o———

CRITICISM is an opinion for good or ill, generally indulged in by the fellow who knows more than any one else, yet the biggest fool. There is no criticism that calls not forth yet another. The last critic is the biggest fool of all, for the world starts and ends with him. He is the source of all knowledge, yet knows nothing, for there is not a word one finds to use that there is not another that hath the same meaning, then wherefore do we criticise?

FEAR is a state of nervousness fit for children and not men. When man fears a creature like himself he offends God, in whose image and likeness he is created. Man being created equal tears not man but God. To fear is to lose control of one's nerves, one's will—to flutter, like a dying fowl, losing consciousness, yet, alive.

————o————

AMBITION is the desire to go forward and improve one's condition. It is a burning flame that lights up the life of the individual and makes him see himself in another state. To be ambitious is to be great in mind and soul. To want that which is worth while and strive for it. To go on without looking back, reaching to that which gives satisfaction. To be humanly ambitious is to take in the world which is the province of man; to be divinely ambitious is to offend God by rivalling him in His infinite Majesty.

————o————

ADMIRATION is a form of appreciation that is sometimes mistaken for something else. There may be something about you that suggests good fellowship when kept at a distance, but in closer contact would not be tolerated, otherwise it would be love.

————o————

RELIGION is one's opinion and belief in some ethical truth. To be a Christian is to have the religion of Christ, and so to be a believer of Mohammed is to be a Mohammedan but there are so many religions that every man seems to be a religion unto himself. No two persons think alike, even if they outwardly profess the same faith, so we have as many religions in Christianity as we have believers.

DEATH is the end of all life in the individual or the thing; if physical, the crumbling of the body into dust from whence it came. He who lives not uprightly, dies completely in the crumbling of the physical body, but he who lives well, transforms himself from that which is mortal, to immortal.

————o————

FAITHFULNESS is actuated by a state of heart and mind in the individual that changes not. No one is wholly faithful to a cause or an object, except his heart and mind remain firm without change or doubt. If one's attitude or conduct changes toward an object, then one has lost in one's faithfulness. It is a wholeness of belief overshadowing all suspicion, all doubt, admitting of no question; to serve without regret or disgust, to obligate one's self to that which is promised or expected, to keep to our word and do our duty well. There are but few faithful people now-a-days.

————o————

PROHIBITION—is to abstain from intoxicating liquor, as it makes us morbid and sometimes drunk. But we get drunk every day, nevertheless, not so much by the strength of what we sip from the cup, but that which we eat, the water we drink, and the air we inhale, which at fermentation conspire at eventide to make us so drunk and tired that we lose control of ourselves and fall asleep. Everybody is a drunkard, and if we were to enforce real prohibition we should all be dead.

————o————

There is no strength but that which is destructive, because man has lost his virtues, and only respects force, which he himself cannot counteract.

This is the day of racial activity, when each and every group of this great human family must exercise its own initiative and influence in its own protection, therefore, Negroes should be more determined to-day than they have ever been, because the mighty forces of the world are operating against non-organized groups of peoples, who are not ambitious enough to protect their own interests.

————o————

Wake up Ethiopia! Wake up Africa! Let us work towards the one glorious end of a free, redeemed and mighty nation. Let Africa be a bright star among the constellation of nations.

————o————

A man's bread and butter is only insured when he works for it.

————o————

The world has now reached the stage when humanity is really at the parting of the ways. It is a question of "MAN MIND THYSELF."

————o————

The political readjustment of the world means that those who are not sufficiently able, not sufficiently prepared, will be at the mercy of the organized classes for another one or two hundred years.

————o————

The only protection against INJUSTICE in man is POWER —Physical, financial and scientific.

————o————

The masses make the nation and the race. If the masses are illiterate, that is the judgment passed on the race by those who are critical of its existencce.

The function of the Press is public service without prejudice or partiality, to convey the truth as it is seen and understood without favoritism or bias.

———o———

EDUCATION is the medium by which a people are prepared for the creation of their own particular civilization, and the advancement and glory of their own race.

———o———

NATIONHOOD is the only means by which modern civilization can completely protect itself.

Independence of nationality, independence of government, is the means of protecting not only the individual, but the group.

Nationhood is the highest ideal of all peoples.

———o———

The evolutionary scale that weighs nations and races, balances alike for all peoples; hence we feel sure that some day the balance will register a change for the Negro.

———o———

If we are to believe the Divine injunction, we must realize that the time is coming when every man and every race must return to its own "vine and fig tree."

———o———

Let Africa be our guiding Star—OUR STAR OF DESTINY.

———o———

So many of us find excuses to get out of the Negro Race, because we are led to believe that the race is unworthy—that it has not accomplished anything. Cowards that we are! It is we who are unworthy, because we are not contributing to the uplift and up-building of this noble race.

How dare any one tell us that Africa cannot be redeemed, when we have 400,000,000 men and women with warm blood coursing through their veins?

The power that holds Africa is not Divine. The power that holds Africa is human, and it is recognized that whatsoever man has done, man can do.

———o———

We of the Negro Race are moving from one state of organization to another, and we shall so continue until we have thoroughly lifted ourselves into the organization of GOVERNMENT.

———o———

Be as proud of your race today as our fathers were in the days of yore. We have a beautiful history, and we shall create another in the future that will astonish the world.

———o———

WOMAN

What the night is to the day, is woman to man. The period of change that brings us light out of darkness, darkness out of light, and semi-light out of darkness are like the changes we find in woman day by day.

She makes one happy, then miserable. You are to her kind, then unkind. Constant yet inconstant. Thus we have WOMAN. No real man can do without her.

———o———

LOVE

A happy but miserable state in which man finds himself from time to time; sometimes he believes he is happy by loving, then suddenly he finds how miserable he is. It is all joy, it sweetens life, but it does not last. It comes and goes, but when it is active, there is no greater virtue, because it makes one supremely happy.

We cannot hold our love, but there is one love that never changeth or is mistaken, and that is God's. The longer we hold our love, the nearer we approach like unto our Creator.

The whole world is run on bluff. No race, no nation, no man has any divine right to take advantage of others. Why allow the other fellow to bluff you?

Every student of Political Science, every student of Economics knows, that the race can only be saved through a solid industrial foundation. That the race can only be saved through political independence. Take away industry from a race; take away political freedom from a race, and you have a group of slaves.

Peoples everywhere are travelling toward industrial opportunities and greater political freedom. As a race oppressed, it is for us to prepare ourselves that at any time the great change in industrial freedom and political liberty comes about, we may be able to enter into the new era as partakers of the joys to be inherited.

Lagging behind in the van of civilization will not prove our higher abilities. Being subservient to the will and caprice of progressive races will not prove anything superior in us. Being satisfied to drink of the dregs from the cup of human progress will not demonstrate our fitness as a people to exist alongside of others, but when of our own intiative we strike out to build industries, governments, and ultimately empires, then and only then will we as a race prove to our Creator and to man in general that we are fit to survive and capable of shaping our own destiny.

————o————

The world ought to know that it could not keep 400,000,000 Negroes down forever.

There is always a turning point in the destiny of every race, every nation, of all peoples, and we have come now to the turning point of the Negro, where we have changed from the old cringing weakling, and transformed into full-grown men, demanding our portion as MEN.

————o————

I am not one of those Christians who believe that the Bible can solve all the problems of humanity.

The Bible is good in its place, but we are men. We are the creatures of God. We have sinned against Him, therefore it takes more than the Bible to keep us in our places.

Man is becoming so vile that to-day we cannot afford to convert him with moral, ethical, physical truths alone, but with that which is more effective—implements of destruction.

————o————

LEADERSHIP means everything—PAIN, BLOOD, DEATH.

————o————

To be proseprous in whatever we do is the sign of TRUE WEALTH. We may be wealthy in not only having money, but in spirit and health. It is the most helpful agency toward a self—satisfying life. One lives, in an age like this, nearer perfection by being wealthy than by being poor. To the contended soul, wealth is the stepping stone to prefection; to the miser it is the nearest avenue to hell. I would prefer to be honestly wealthy, than miserably poor.

To be free from temptation of other people's property is to reflect the HONESTY of our own souls. There are but few really honest people, in that between the thought and the deed we make ourselves dishonest. The fellow who steals, acts dishonestly. We can steal in thought as well as in deed, therefore to be honest is a virtue that but few indulge. To be honest is to be satisfied, having all, wanting nothing. If you find yourself in such a state then you are honest, if not the temptation of your soul is bound to make you dishonest. This applies to the king and the peasant alike.

———o———

All peoples are strugglnig to blast a way through the industrial monopoly of races and nations, but the Negro as a whole has failed to grasp its true significance and seems to delight in filling only that place created for him by the white man.

———o———

The Negro who lives on the patronage of philanthropists is the most dangerous member of our society, because he is willing to turn back the clock of progress when his benefactors ask him so to do.

———o———

No race in the world is so just as to give others, for the asking, a square deal in things economic, political and social.

———o———

Men who are in earnest are not afraid of conseqeunces.

———o———

No one knows when the hour of Africa's Redemption cometh. It is in the wind. It is coming. One day, like a storm, it will be here. When that day comes all Africa will stand together.

Any sane man, race or nation that desires freedom must first of all think in terms of blood. Why, even the Heavenly Father tells us that "without the shedding of blood there can be no remission of sins?" Then how in the name of God, with history before us, do we expect to redeem Africa without preparing ourselves—some of us to die.

———o———

I pray God that we shall never use our physical prowess to oppress the human race, but we will use our strength, physically, morally and otherwise to preserve humanity and civilization.

———o———

For over three hundred years the white man has been our oppressor, and he naturally is not going to liberate us to the higher freedom—the truer liberty—the truer Democracy. We have to liberate ourselves.

———o———

Every man has a right to his own opinion. Every race has a right to its own action; therefore let no man persuade you against your will, let no other race influence you against your own.

———o———

The greatest weapon used against the Negro is DISORGANIZATION.

———o———

If you have no confidence in self you are twice defeated in the race of life. With confidence you have won even before you have started.

———o———

At no time within the last five hundred years can one point to a single instance of the Negro as a race of haters.

The Negro has loved even under severest punishment. In slavery the Negro loved his master, he safe-guarded his home even when he further planned to enslave him. We are not a race of Haters, but Lovers of humanity's Cause.

———o———

Mob violence and injustice have never helped a race or a nation, and because of this knowledge as gathered from the events of ages, we as a people in this new age desire to love all mankind, not in the social sense, but in keeping with the Divine Injunction "MAN LOVE THY BROTHER."

———o———

PREPAREDNESS is the watch-word of this age. For us as a race to remain, as we have been in the past—divided among ourselves, parochializing, insularizing and nationalizing our activities as subjects and citizens of the many alien races and governments under which we live—is but to hold ourselves in readiness for that great catastrophe that is bound to come—that of racial extermination, at the hands of the stronger race—the race that will be fit to survive.

———o———

Humanity takes revenging crime from one age to the next, according to the growth and development of the race so afflicted.

But the perpetuation of crime through revenge and retaliation will not save the human race.

———o———

Europe is bankrupt today, and every nation within her bounds is endeavoring to find new openings, new fields for exploitation—that exploitation that will bring to them the resources, the revenue and the power necessary for their rehabilitation and well-being.

We are living in a strenuous, active age, when men see, not through the spectacles of sympathy, but demand that each and every one measures up in proportion to the world's demand for service.

————o————

The attitude of the white race is to subjugate, to exploit, and if necessary exterminate the weaker peoples with whom they come in contact.

They subjugate first, if the weaker peoples will stand for it; then exploit, and if they will not stand for SUBJUGATION nor EXPLOITATION, the other recourse is EXTERMINATION.

————o————

If the Negro is not careful he will drink in all the poison of modern civilization and die from the effects of it.

————o————

There can be no peace among men and nations, so long as the strong continues to oppress the weak, so long as injustice is done to other peoples, just so long will we have cause for war, and make a lasting peace an impossibility.

————o————

Hungry men have no respect for law, authority or human life.

————o————

I am not opposed to the white race as charged by my enemies. I have no time to hate any one. All my time is devoted to the up-building and developement of the Negro Race.

————o————

When nations outgrow their national limits, they make war and conquer other people's territory so as to have an outlet for their surplus populations.

————————

The world does not count races and nations that have nothing.

Point me to a weak nation and I will show you a people oppressed, abused, taken advantage of by others.

Show me a weak race and I will show you a people reduced to serfdom, peonage and slavery.

Show me a well organized nation, and I will show you a people and a nation respected by the world.

———o———

The battles of the future, whether they be physical or mental, will be fought on scientific lines, and the race that is able to produce the highest scientific development, is the race that will ultimately rule.

———o———

Let us prepare TODAY. For the TOMORROWS in the lives of the nations will be so eventful that Negroes everywhere will be called upon to play their part in the survival of the fittest human group.

———o———

Let us in shaping our own Destiny set before us the qualities of human JUSTICE, LOVE, CHARITY, MERCY AND EQUITY. Upon such foundation let us build a race, and I feel that the God who is Divine, the Almighty Creator of the world, shall forever bless this race of ours, and who to tell that we shall not teach men the way to life, liberty and true human happiness?

———o———

Day by day we hear the cry of "AFRICA FOR THE AFRICANS." This cry has become a positive, determined one. It is a cry that is raised simultaneously the world over, because of the universal oppression that affects the Negro.

———o———

All of us may not live to see the higher accomplishment of an African Empire—so strong and powerful, as to compel the respect of mankind, but we in our life-time can so work and act as to make the dream a possibility within another generation.

CHAPTER II

PROPAGANDA

We are living in a civilization that is highly developed. We are living in a world that is scientifically arranged in which everything done by those who control is done through system; proper arrangement, proper organization, and among some of the organized methods used to control the world is the thing known and called "PROPAGANDA."

Propaganda has done more to defeat the good intentions of races and nations than even open warfare.

Propaganda is a method or medium used by organized peoples to convert others against their will.

We of the Negro race are suffering more than any other race in the world from propaganda—Propaganda to destroy our hopes, our ambitions and our confidence in self.

———o———

SLAVERY

Slavery is a condition imposed upon individuals or races not sufficiently able to protect or defend themselves, and so long as a race or people expose themselves to the danger of being weak, no one can tell when they will be reduced to slavery.

When a man is a slave he has no liberty of action; no freedom of will, he is bound and controlled by the will and act of others; as of the individual, so of the race.

15

Slavery is not a condition confined to any one age or race of people. Slavery has been since man in the different distribution of himself, scattered here, there and everywhere, has grown and developed, wherein one race will become strong and the other race remains weak. The strong race has always reduced the weak to slavery. It has been so in ages past, it is so now in certain parts of the world, and will be so until the end of time.

The great British nation was once a race of slaves. In their own country they were not respected because the Romans went there, brutalized and captured them, took them over to Rome and kept them in slavery. They were not respected in Rome because they were regarded as a slave race. But the Briton did not always remain a slave. As a freed man he went back to his country (Britain) and built up a civilization of his own, and by his self-reliance and initiative he forced the respect of mankind and maintains it until today.

———o———

FORCE

The powers opposed to Negro progress will not be influenced in the slighest by mere verbal protests on our part. They realize only too well that protests of this kind contain nothing but the breath expended in making them.

They also realize that their success in enslaving and dominating the darker portion of humanity was due solely to the element of FORCE employed (in the majority of cases this was accomplished by force of arms.)

Pressure of course may assert itself in other forms, but in the last analysis whatever influence is brought to bear against the powers opposed to Negro progress must contain the element of FORCE in order to accomplish its purpose, since it is apparent that this is the only element they recognize.

EDUCATION

To be learned in all that is worth while knowing. Not to be crammed with the subject matter of the book or the philosophy of the class room, but to store away in your head such facts as you need for the daily application of life, so that you may the better in all things understand your fellowmen, and interpret your relationship to your Creator.

You can be educated in soul, vision and feeling, as well as in mind. To see your enemy and know him is a part of the complete education of man; to spiritually regulate one's self is another form of the higher education that fits man for a nobler place in life, and still, to approach your brother by the feeling of your own humanity, is an education that softens the ills of the world and makes us kind indeed.

Many a man was educated outside the school room. It is something you let out, not completely take in. You are part of it, for it is natural; it is dormant simply because you will not develop it, but God creates every man with it knowingly or unknowingly to him who possesses it—that's the difference. Develop yours and you become as great and full of knowledge as the other fellow without even entering the class room.

———o———

MISCEGENATION

Some of the men of the Negro race aggravate the race question because they force the white man to conclude that to educate a black man, to give him opportunities, is but to fit him to be a competitor for the hand of his woman; hence the eternal race question.

But not all black men are willing to commit race suicide and to abhor their race for the companionship of another. There are hundreds of millions of us black men who are proud of our skins and to us the African Empire will not be a Utopia, neither will it be dangerous nor fail to serve our best interests, because we realize that like the leopard we cannot change our skins.

The men of the highest morals, highest character and noblest pride are to be found among the masses of the Negro race who love their women with as much devotion as white men love theirs.

------o------

PREJUDICE

Prejudice of the white race against the black race is not so much because of color as of condition; because as a race, to them, we have accomplished nothing; we have built no nation, no government; because we are dependent for our economic and political existence.

You can never curb the prejudice of the one race or nation against the other by law. It must be regulated by one's own feeling, one's own will, and if one's feeling and will rebel against you no law in the world can curb it.

Prejudice can be actuated by different reasons. Sometimes the reason is economic, and sometimes political. You can only obstruct it by progress and force.

------o------

RADICALISM

"Radical" is a label that is always applied to people who are endeavoring to get freedom.

Jesus Christ was the greatest radical the world ever saw. He came and saw a world of sin and his program was to inspire it with spiritual feeling. He was therefore a radical.

George Washington was dubbed a radical when he took up his sword to fight his way to liberty in America one hundred and forty years ago.

All men who call themselves reformers are perforce radicals. They cannot be anything else, because they are revolting against the conditions that exist.

Conditions as they exist reveal a conservative state, and if you desire to change these conditions you must be a radical.

I am, therefore, satisfied to be the same kind of radical, if through radicalism I can free Africa..

GOVERNMENT

Government is not infallible. Government is only an executive control, a centralized authority for the purpose of expressing the will of the people.

Before you have a government you must have the people. Without the people there can be no government. The government must be, therefore, an expression of the will of the people.

EVOLUTION AND THE RESULT

Evolution brings us changes that sometimes make us fail to recognize ourselves even after a lapse of centuries.

When the great white race of today had no civilization of its own, when white men lived in caves and were counted as savages, this race of ours boasted of a wonderful civilization on the Banks of the Nile.

It may sound good for some Negroes to say that they were born here or there, and they do not intend to go anywhere else but where they saw the light of day. But let me say to you men, the world is small and humanity in the many and various race groups, is growing larger every day.

A race that was ten millions fifty years ago is today sixty millions. A race that was thirty millions fifty years ago is today ninety millions; how many will they be tomorrow and the world is not growing larger?

What will happen through the multiplication of all these various race groups, of those who are in power, of those who are strong, those who have at their command the forces of nature, through which they can exploit the weak and ultimately exterminate them? What will happen to you, the weak and unprepared, when the strong becomes more numerous even though the world remains at its present size?

Ah, if you will but think down the future and compare the possibilities of that future with the happenings of the past you will come to the conclusion that there is no other salvation for the Negro but through a free and independent Africa.

Whilst geographically speaking the world has ever been in its natural divisions as we know it, and see it, yet, politically speaking, the world has changed, and is still changing. Yesterday we had the Roman Empire, we had the Grecian Empire, we had even before the Carthaginian, the Assyrian and the Babylonian empires. What has become of them? They have gone into the oblivion of the past, because of human progress, because of the development of certain races as aginst the stagnation of others; but even yesterday we also had the great German Empire; we had the Russian Empire; we had the Empire of Austria and Hungary. Where are they now? They too, are travelling toward the oblivion of the past. Today we have the great French Empire, the British Empire and other great commonwealths. Will they stand?

Ah, methinks not, because evolution and human progress bring changes, and in the changes no man can tell what will happen tomorrow as against what exists today. Therefore, I say to the four hundred million Negroes of the world, prepare yourselves for the higher life, the life of liberty, industrially, educationally, socially and politically.

———o———

POVERTY

A hellish state to be in. It is no virtue. It is a crime.

To be poor, is to be hungry without possible hope of food; to be sick without hope of medicine; to be tired and sleepy without a place to lay one's head; to be naked without the hope of clothing; to be despised and comfortless. To be poor is to be a fit subject for crime and hell.

The hungry man steals bread and thereby breaks the eighth commandment; by his state he breaks all the laws of God and man and becomes an outcast. In thought and deed he covets his neighbor's goods; comfortless as he is he seeks his neighbor's wife; to him there is no other course but sin and death. That is the way of poverty. No one wants to be poor.

———o———

POWER

Power is the only argument that satisfies man.

Except the individual, the race or the nation has POWER that is exclusive, it means that that individual, race or nation will be bound by the will of the other who possesses this great qualification.

It is the physical and pugilistic power of Harry Wills that makes white men afraid to fight him.

It was the industrial and scientific power of the Teutonic race that kept it for years as dictator of the economic and scientific policies of Europe.

It is the naval and political power of Great Britain that keeps her mistress of the seas.

It is the commercial and financial power of the United States of America that makes her the greatest banker in the world. Hence it is advisable for the Negro to get power of every kind. POWER in education, science, industry, politics and higher government. That kind of power that will stand out signally, so that other races and nations can see, and if they will not see, then FEEL.

Man is not satisfied or moved by prayers or petitions, but every man is moved by that power of authority which forces him to do even against his will.

UNIVERSAL SUSPICION

Humanity everywhere is struggling toward political freedom and economic opportunity. In this struggle we are confronted with the rivalry of the keenest minds of the age; each race and nation seeking to present its best to the world.

So much is expected of each by the different rivals, that it becomes impossible to reach an amicable settlement and to establish universal confidence.

It can be plainly seen that no one race or nation trusts the other. There is a UNIVERSAL SUSPICION that hovers over the conduct of every great leader representative of his race or nation. It is this suspicion that limited the Washington Four pact Treaty; it is this suspicon that caused the failure of the Genoa Conference; it is this suspicion that is going to wreck ultimately many of the nations and empires of today, thereby throwing into obscurity many of the races that now dominate the affairs of men. We as a race, are called upon to play our part, and we must do it well.

In the spread of this universal suspicion that causes nation to distrust nation, and race to distrust race, we also have our distrust which makes it impossible for us to believe in anyone else but ourselves.

DISSERTATION ON MAN

Man is the individual who is able to shape his own character, master his own will, direct his own life and shape his own ends.

When God breathed into the nostrils of man the breath of life, made him a living soul, and bestowed upon him the authority of "Lord of Creation," He never intended that that individual should descend to the level of a peon, a serf, or a slave, but that he should be always man in the fullest possession of his senses, and with the truest knowledge of himself.

But how changed has man become since creation!" We find him today divided into different classes—the helpless imbecile, the dependent slave, the servant and the master. These different classes God never created. He created MAN. But this individual has so retrograded, as to make it impossible to find him—a real man.

As far as the Negro race is concerned, we can find but few real men to measure up to the higher purpose of the creation, and because of this lack of manhood in the race, we have stagnated for centuries and now find ourselves at the foot of the great human ladder.

After the creation, and after man was given possession of the world, the Creator relinquished all authority to his lord, except that which was spiritual. All that authority which meant the regulation of human affairs, human society, and human happiness was given to man by the Creator, and man, therefore, became master of his own destiny, and architect of his own fate.

In process of time we find that only a certain type of man

has been able to make good in God's creation. We find them building nations, governments and empires, as also great monuments of commerce, industry and education (these men realizing the power given them exerted every bit of it to their own good and to their posterity's) while, on the other hand, 400,000,000 Negroes who claim the common Fatherhood of God and the Brotherhood of Man, have fallen back so completely, as to make us today the serfs and slaves of those who fully know themselves and have taken control of the world, which was given to all in common by the Creator.

I desire to impress upon the 400,000,000 members of my race that our failings in the past, present and of the future will be through our failures to know ourselves and to realize the true functions of man on this mundane sphere.

RACE ASSIMILATION

Some Negro leaders have advanced the belief that in another few years the white people will make up their minds to assimilate their black populations; thereby sinking all racial prejudice in the welcoming of the black race into the social companionship of the white. Such leaders further believe that by the amalgamation of black and white, a new type will spring up, and that type will become the American and West Indian of the future.

This belief is preposterous. I believe that white men should be white, yellow men should be yellow, and black men should be black in the great panorama of races, until each and every race by its own initiative lifts itself up to the common standard of humanity, as to compel the respect and appreciation of all, and so make it possible for each one to stretch out the hand of welcome without being able to be prejudiced against the other because of any inferior and unfortunate condition.

The white man of America will not, to any organized extent, assimilate the Negro, because in so doing, he feels that he will be committing racial suicide. This he is not prepared to do. It is true he illegitimately carries on a system of assimilation; but such assimilation, as practised, is one that he is not prepared to support because he becomes prejudiced against his own offspring, if that offspring is the product of black and white; hence, to the white man the question of racial differences is eternal. So long as Negroes occupy an inferior position among the races and nations of the world, just so long will others be prejudiced against them, because it will be profitable for them to keep up their system of superiority. But when the Negro by his own initiative lifts himself from his low state to the highest human standard he will be in a position to stop begging and praying, and demand a place that no individual, race or nation will be able to deny him.

CHRISTIANITY

A form of religion practised by the millions, but as misunderstood, and unreal to the majority as gravitation is to the untutored savage. We profess to live in the atmosphere of Christianity, yet our acts are as barbarous as if we never knew Christ. He taught us to love, yet we hate; to forgive, yet we revenge; to be merciful, yet we condemn and punish, and still we are Christians.

If hell is what we are taught it is, then there will be more Christians there than days in all creation. To be a true Christian one must be like Christ and practice Christianity, not as the Bishop does, but as he says, for if our lives were to be patterned after the other fellow's all of us, Bishop, Priest and Layman would ultimately meet around the furnace of hell, and none of us, because of our sins, would see salvation.

THE FUNCTION OF MAN

God placed man on earth as the lord of Creation. The elements—all nature are at his command—it is for him to harness them subdue them and use them.

Edison harnessed electricity. Today the world reflects the brilliancy of his grand illumination.

Stephenson, through experiments, has given us the use of the steam engine, and today the railroad train flies across the country at a speed of sixty miles an hour.

Marconi conquered the currents of the air and today we have wireless telegraphy that flashes news across the continents with a rapidity never yet known to man.

All this reveals to us that man is the supreme lord of creation, that in man lies the power of mastery, a mastery of self, a mastery of all things created, bowing only to the Almighty Architect in those things that are spiritual, in those things that are divine.

TRAITORS

In the fight to reach the top the oppressed have always been encumbered by the traitors of their own race, made up of those of little faith and those who are generally susceptible to bribery for the selling out of the rights of their own people.

As Negroes, we are not entirely free of such an encumbrance. To be outspoken, I believe we are more encumbered in this way than any other race in the world, because of the lack of training and preparation for fitting us for our place in the world among nations and races.

The traitor of other races is generally confined to the mediocre or irresponsible individual, but, unfortunately, the traitors among the Negro race are generally to be found among the men highest placed in education and society, the fellows who call themselves leaders.

For us to examine ourselves thoroughly as a people we will find that we have more traitors than leaders, because nearly everyone who essays to lead the race at this time does so by first establishing himself as the pet of some philanthropist of another race, to whom he will go and debase his race in the worst form, humiliate his own manhood, and thereby win the sympathy of the "great benefactor", who will dictate to him what he should do in the leadership of the Negro race. It is generally "You must go out and teach your people to be meek and humble; tell them to be good servants, loyal and obedient to their masters. If you will teach them such a doctrine you can always depend on me to give you $1,000 a year or $5,000 a year for the support of yourself, the newspaper or the institution you represent. I will always recommend you to my friends as a good fellow who is all right," With this advice and prospect of patronage the average Negro leader goes out to lead the unfortunate mass. These leaders tell us how good Mr. So and So is, how many good friends we have in the opposite race, and that if we leave everything to them all will work out well.

This is the kind of leadership we have been having for the last fifty years. It is nothing else but treachery and treason of the worst kind. The man who will compromise the attitude of his country is a traitor, and even so the man who will compromise the rights of his race can be classified in no other way than that of a traitor also.

Not until we settle down as four hundred million people and let the men who have placed themselves in the lead of us realize that we are disgusted and dissatisfied, and that we shall have a leadership of our own and stick by it when we get it, will we be able to lift ourselves from this mire of degradation to the heights of prosperity, human liberty and human appreciation.

CHAPTER III

PRESENT DAY CIVILIZATION

We are circumvented today by environments more dangerous than those which circumvented other peoples in any other age. We are face to face with environments in a civilization that is highly developed; a civilization that is competing with itself for its own destruction; a civilization that cannot last, because it has no spiritual foundation; a civilization that is vicious, crafty, dishonest, immoral, irreligious and corrupt.

We see a small percentage of the world's populace feeling happy and contented with this civilization that man has evolved, and we see the masses of the human race on the other hand dissatisfied and discontented with the civilization of today—the arrangement of human society. Those masses are determined to destroy the systems that hold up such a society and prop such a civilization.

As by indication, the fall will come. A fall that will cause the universal wreck of the civilization that we now see, and in this civilization the Negro is called upon to play his part. He is called upon to evolve a national ideal, based upon freedom, human liberty and true democracy.

DIVINE APPORTIONMENT OF EARTH

God Almighty created all men equal, whether they be white, yellow or black, and for any race to admit that it cannot do what others have done, is to hurl an insult at the Almighty who created all races equal, in the beginning.

The white man has no right of way to this green earth, neither the yellow man. All of us were created lords of the creation, and whether we be white, yellow, brown or black Nature intended a place for each and every one.

If Europe is for the white man, if Asia is for brown and yellow men, then surely Africa is for the black man. The great white man has fought for the preservation of Europe, the great yellow and brown races are fighting for the preservation of Asia, and four hundred million Negroes shall shed, if needs be, the last drop of their blood for the redemption of Africa and the emancipation of the race everywhere.

————o————

UNIVERSAL UNREST IN 1922

The human race is universally disturbed because of the many injustices inflicted upon the masses by the dominant powers. The privileged classes have for centuries dominated the will of the masses, and as it would appear, have ground out of the toiling millions the last drop of sweat. These millions are now in rebellion. They are striking everywhere—in England, France, Germany, America and other parts of the world. Those who are not on strike are shaking their fists in bloody revolution as a protest against the industrial and political systems of the day.

In this big noise for world readjustment in the affairs of the human race, four hundred million Negroes cry out for better consideration and for justice.

WORLD DISARMAMENT

Present day statesmen are making the biggest blunder of the age if they believe that there can be any peace without equity and justice to all mankind.

Any attempt at disarmament when half the world oppresses the other half is but a farce, because the oppressed will make their oppressors get armed sooner or later.

------o------

CAUSE OF WARS

The world is not yet perfect. It is in chaos; yes, in confusion and out of this confusion will come many more upheavals that will shake its very foundation. Fool not yourselves that the conferences that have been held, and will be held in the future, are sufficient to settle the disgruntled state of the world, the dissatisfied condition of humanity. They have not gone down to the root of all evils that give cause to the great discontent, they will never be able to establish a permanent peace and present to us a settled world.

The history of the past teaches us that we have had many wars, each more deadly, each more catastrophic, and even as the war of 1914-18 was the most deadly we have experienced for ages, so in the very near future we shall see the most bloody conflict ever waged by man. Whether it is to be a war of the races or of the nations, no one can tell, but so long as this injustice continues; so long as the strong continues to oppress the weak; so long as the powerful nations arrange among themselves to oppress the weaker ones, and to keep the more unfortunate of humanity in serfdom, and to rob and exploit them, so long will the cause of war be fed with the fuel of revenge, of hatred, and of discontent.

WORLD READJUSTMENT

The political re-adjustment of the world means this-that every race must find a home; hence the great cry of Palestine for the Jews—Ireland for the Irish,—India for the Indians and simultaneously Negroes are raising the cry of "AFRICA FOR THE AFRICANS", those at home and those abroad.

It is a cry for political re-adjustment along natural lines, and this re-adjustment has come out of the war of 1914-18, because, we, as Negroes, realize that if (with our knowledge and experience of western civilization) we allow the world to adjust itself politically without taking thought for ourselves, we would be lost to the world in another few decades.

———o———

THE FALL OF GOVERNMENTS

The fall of nations and empires has always come about first by the disorganized spirit,—the disorganized sentiment of those who make up the nation or the empire.

The one class opposing, fighting against the other, the other class seeking to deprive them of the essentials of life which are necessary for the good and well-being of all.

The class that ruled in the past and the class that rules now in government, are the people who have always provoked the spirit of those who are ruled. Hence you have social revolutions, civil strifes, which ultimately result in the downfall of the empire or the nation. What has happened in the past will happen again. I am not attempting to prophesy the destruction of any of the now existing empires or nations, but the empires and nations themselves are going to their own ruin.

In Europe **we** hear of great industrial unrests. **Laborers** uniting themselves and marching to the representatives of governments asking for better conditions to alleviate their suffering. Instead of the representatives seeking to pacify and satisfy those who are in need, the representatives of such governments adopt a strongarmed policy to prosecute and persecute those who suffer and appeal for aid from the nation or the empire. What happens? The dissatisfied who are driven away by the majesty of the law, go back to those who suffer with them and scatter throughout the nation or the empire the spirit of dissatisfaction that ultimately breaks out in civil strife, social disorder, which in turn brings the downfall of the nation or the empire.

People who rule (being selected by the masses of their own) forget when they come into power that they have an obligation to those who placed them in authority and through selfishness arrogate to themselves all that is good within the nation to the exclusion of those who suffer and to the exclusion of those who placed them in their positions of trust. HENCE MONOPOLY—industrial, commercial and economic—which places power in the hands of the select few, and through the selfishness of administration by the few they cause the majority of the masses to exist always in want. Through this want, a spirit of disssatisfaction springs up among the people, and they, in their passion, seeking to correct the evil, tear down governments.

GREAT IDEALS KNOW NO NATIONALITY

My enemies in America have done much to hold me up to public contempt and ridicule, but have failed. They believe that the only resort is to stir up national prejudice against me, in that I was not born within the borders of the United States of America.

I am not in the least concerned about such a propaganda, because I have travelled the length and breath of America and I have discovered that among the fifteen million of my race, only those who have exploited and lived off the ignorance of the masses are concerned with where I was born. The masses of the people are looking for leadership, they desire sincere, honest guidance in racial affairs. As proof of this I may mention, that the largest number of members in the Universal Negro Improvement Association (of which I am President-General) are to be found in America, and are native born Americans. I know these people so well and I love them so well, that I would not for one minute think that they would fall for such an insidious propaganda.

All intelligent people know that one's nationality has nothing to do with great ideals and great principles. If because I am a Jamaican the Negro should not accept the principle of race rights and liberty, or the ideal of a free and independent race; then you may well say that because Jesus was a Nazarene the outside world should not accept His Doctrine of Christianity, because He was an "alien."

Because Martin Luther was born in Germany, the world should not accept the doctrine of Protestantism.

Because Alexander Hamilton and Lafayette were not born in America, Americans should not accept and appreciate the benefits they bestowed upon the nation.

Because Marconi was an Italian, we of the new world should not make use of wireless telegraphy. Again I say, great principles, great ideals know no nationality.

I know no national boundary where the Negro is concerned. The whole world is my province until Africa is free.

————o————

PURPOSE OF CREATION

The man or woman who has no confidence in self is an unfortunate being, and is really a misfit in creation.

God Almighty created each and every one of us for a place in the world, and for the least of us to think that we were created only to be what we are and not what we can make ourselves, is to impute an improper motive to the Creator for creating us.

God Almighty created us all to be free. That the Negro race became a race of slaves was not the fault of God Almighty, the Divine Master, it was the fault of the race.

Sloth, neglect, indifference caused us to be slaves.

Confidence, conviction, action will cause us to be free men to-day.

————o————

PURITY OF RACE

I believe in a pure black race just as how all self-respecting whites believe in a pure white race, as far as that can be.

I am conscious of the fact that slavery brought upon us the curse of many colors within the Negro race, but that is no reason why we of ourselves should perpetuate the evil; hence instead of encouraging a wholesale bastardy in the race, we feel that we should now set out to create a race type and standard of our own which could not, in the future, be stigmatized by bastardy, but could be recognized and respected as the true race type anteceding even our own time.

MAN KNOW THYSELF

For man to know himself is for him to feel that for him there is no human master. For him Nature is his servant, and whatsoever he wills in Nature, that shall be his reward. If he wills to be a pigmy, a serf or a slave, that shall he be. If he wills to be a real man in possession of the things common to man, then he shall be his own sovereign.

When man fails to grasp his authority he sinks to the level of the lower animals, and whatsoever the real man bids him do, even as if it were of the lower animals, that much shall he do. If he says "go." He goes. If he says "come," he comes. By this command he performs the functions of life even as by a similar command the mule, the horse, the cow perform the will of their masters.

For the last four hundred years the Negro has been in the position of being commanded even as the lower animals are controlled. Our race has been without a will; without a purpose of its own, for all this length of time. Because of that we have developed few men who are able to understand the strenuousness of the age in which we live.

Where can we find in this race of ours real men. Men of character, men of purpose, men of confidence, men of faith, men who really know themselves? I have come across so many weaklings who profess to be leaders, and in the test I have found them but the slaves of a nobler class. They perform the will of their masters without question.

To me, a man has no master but God. Man in his authority is a sovereign lord. As for the individual man, so of the individual race. This feeling makes man so courageous, so bold, as to make it impossible for his brother to intrude upon his rights. So few of us can understand what it takes to make a man—the man who will never say die; the man who will never give up; the man who will never depend upon others to do for him what he ought to do for himself; the man who will not blame God, who will not blame Nature, who will not blame Fate for his condition; but the man who will go out and make conditions to suit himself. Oh, how disgusting life becomes when on every hand you hear people (who bear your image, who bear your resemblance) telling you that they cannot make it, that Fate is against them, that they cannot get a chance. If 400,000,000 Negroes can only get to know thesmelves, to know that in them is a sovereign power, is an authority that is absolute, then in the next twenty-four hours we would have a new race, we would have a nation, an empire,—resurrected, not from the will of others to see us rise,—but from our own determination to rise, irrespective of what the world thinks.

A SOLUTION FOR WORLD PEACE—1922.

We hear a great deal of talk about world peace today. Wilson of America, Lloyd George of England, Clemenceau of France a few years ago prophesied at Versailles a reign of peace. Up to the present many of the leading statesmen of the world have pledged themselves to a program of world peace. Many conferences have been held (political as well as industrial) for the purpose of settling the question of peace; but up to now none of them has laid the foundation for a real peace, for a lasting peace.

The peace of the world cannot be settled by political conferences, or by industrial conferences only. If we are to have a world peace it will only come when a great inter-racial conferenc is called. When Jew will meet Gentile; when Anglo-Saxon will meet Teuton; when the great Caucasian family will meet the Mongolian, and when all will meet the Negro, and then and there straighten out the differences that have kept us apart for hundreds of years, and will continue to keep us apart until Doom's Day, if something is not done to create better racial understanding.

If white men continue to exploit yellow men, if white men continue to exploit black and brown men, if yellow men continue to exploit brown and black men, then all we can look forward to is a reign of wars and rumors of wars. So long as Anglo-Saxons oppress Indians; so long as the French exploit the black race; so long as the Russian murders the Jew, so long will the cause for war be found, and so long will man continue to fight and kill his brother.

If England wants peace, if France wants peace, I suggest to them to pack up their bag and baggage and clear out of Africa, because Africa in the future will be to them what Europe has been for the last three hundred years—a hot bed of wars, political intrigues and upheavals,—and Europe has changed many a time politically. Once the great Napolean ruled, the Czars ruled and but recently the German Eagle was the symbol of fear. To-day England stands out as the most brilliant star in the European political constellation. But what of tomorrow? Africa with her threatened upheaval will produce the same conditions in another century as Europe has done in the past. Can we not see that we are marching headlong into the abyss of eternal destruction? Can we not realize that we are not laying the foundation of peace? Can we not realize that we are but provoking the sleeping passions of the races? How long do you believe that four-hundred million Negroes will allow themselves to be exploited by alien races, robbed and murdered? Just so long until the truth is brought home to them, and then when the sleeping giant awakens, even like Samson, he may bring down the pillars of the temple.

The war of 1914-18 has created a new sentiment throughout the world. Once upon a time weaker peoples were afraid of expressing themselves, of giving vent to their feelings, but today no oppressd race or nation is afraid of speaking out in the cause of liberty. Egypt has spoken, Ireland has spoken, Poland has spoken and Poland is free, Egypt is free, Ireland is also free. Africa is now speaking, and if for seven-hundred and fifty years Irishmen found perseverance enough to have carried the cause of freedom on and on until they won, then four hundred million Negroes are prepared to carry on the fight for African liberty even if it takes us to the seat of the Most High, yes if it takes us until judgment day, we shall fight the cause on and on without relenting. The world may scoff at us, the world may deride us, but there have been many surprises for the world before, and there will be many more. Englishmen scoffed at the Colonists when they agitated for independence in America, but their scoffs and derisions did not prevent George Washington from giving us the glorious Stars and Stripes. Men laughed at the propaganda of Tolstoi. The Czar himself impugned the idea of a more liberal Russia, but today Lenine and Trotszky rule. Yes, the Louis's laughed at the propaganda of the Liberals of France, but the French Monarchy is no more. Today Frenchmen take pride in the new democracy of France; so that others may laugh at us today because we are agitating the question of a free and independent Africa, but tomorrow, who knows, Africa will loom up as the greatest Republic in the world.

GOD AS A WAR LORD

God is a bold Sovereign—A Warrior Lord. The God we worship and adore is a God of War as well as a God of Peace. He does not allow anything to interfere with His power and authority.

The greatest battle ever fought was not between the Kaiser of Germany on the one hand and the Allied Powers on the other, it was between Almighty God on the one hand and Lucifer the Archangel on the other.

When Lucifer challenged God's power in Heaven and marshalled his forces on the plains of Paradise, the God we worship and adore also marshalled His forces, His Archangels, His Cherubims and His Seraphims, and in battle array He placed Himself before them with the royal standard of Heaven. He faced the opposing general Lucifer with his hordes on the battle plains of Heaven and there the great war began. The whole universe shook as the battle raged between the two opposing forces, and as God the Creator gained the upper hand of Lucifer, what did He do? Did He hoist the white flag of peace? No, God Almighty, God the Omnipotent took hold of Lucifer and flung him from the heights of Heaven to the depths of hell, thereby proving that He is a God of war as well as a God of peace. And when anyone transgresses His power He goes to war in defence of His rights.

Man is only a little lower than the angels; the angels are only a little lower than the creator, but the Creator, has bequeathed to angels and to men the same principles, the same policies that govern Him as God. And even as he goes to war in defense of His rights, so man goes to war in defense of his rights.

I believe with Napoleon. When some one asked him "On what side is God?" he replied. "God is on the side of the strongest battalion." Napolean was right. He had a true concept of God. God is really on the side of the strongest peoples because God made all men equal and He never gave superior power to any one class or group of people over another, and any one who can get the advantage over another is pleasing God, because that is the servant who has taken care of God's command in exercising authority over the world.

---o---

THE IMAGE OF GOD

If the white man has the idea of a white God, let him worship his God as he desires. If the yellow man's God is of his race let him worship his God as he sees fit. We, as Negroes, have found a new ideal. Whilst our God has no color, yet it is human to see everything through one's own spectacles, and since the white people have seen their God through white spectacles, we have only now started out (late though it be) to see our God through our own spectacles. The God of Isaac and the God of Jacob let Him exist for the race that believes in the God of Isaac and the God of Jacob. We Negroes believe in the God of Ethiopia, the everlasting God—God the Father, God the Son and God the Holy Ghost, the One God of all ages. That is the God in whom we believe, but we shall worship Him through the spectacles of Ethiopia.

CHAPTER IV

THE SLAVE TRADE

Three hundred years ago no Negroes were to be found in this Western Hemisphere, we were to be found exclusively in Africa. Just about that time a large number of white people (called Colonists) settled in America. They desired laborers to help them in the country's development. They turned to Asia and were unable to use the yellow man. At that time a man named John Hawkins (afterwards knighted) asked permission of Queen Elizabeth of England to take the blacks from Africa into her colonies of America and the West Indies and use them in their development. The Queen asked, "what consideration will you give them?" Hawkins said "They will be civilized and Christianized in the Colonies, for in their own country they are savages and barbarians."

Under these pretenses the British Queen signed a charter empowering John Hawkins and others to remove from Africa millions of our fore-parents—men, women and children—who were sold in the slave markets of the Southern States of America and the West Indies. Parents were separated from children, husbands from wives· All scattered in this Western Hemisphere to work in the cottonfields of the Southern States of America and the sugar plantations of the West Indies.

The Negroes who were sold in the West Indies remained as slaves for two hundred and thirty years and those sold in America for two hundred and fifty years. The West Indian Negroes were emancipated eighty five years ago by Queen Victoria of England,

and the American Negroes fifty eight years ago by Abraham Lincoln.

We-the Negroes in this Western Hemisphere are descendants of those Africans who were enslaved and transported to these shores, where they suffered, bled and died to make us what we are today—Civilized, Christian free men.   Shouldwe not, therefore, turn our eyes towards Africa, our ancestral home and free it from the thraldom of alien oppression and exploitation?

NEGROES' STATUS UNDER ALIEN GOVERNMENTS

Within modern times the Negro race has not had any real statesmen, and the masses of our people have always accepted the intentions and actions of the statesmen and leaders of other races as being directed in our interest as a group in conjunction with the interests of others. Such a feeling on our part caused us to believe that the Constitution of the United States was written for Negroes, as well as the Constitutions of England, France, Italy, Germany and other countries where Negroes happen to have their present domicile, either as citizens or as subjects.

That we suffer so much today under whatsoever flag we live is proof positive that constitutions and laws, when framed by the early advocates of human liberty, never included and were never intended for us as a people. It is only a question of sheer accident that we happen to be fellow citizens today with the decendants of those who, through their advocacy, laid the foundation for human rights.

So this brings us to the point where, as a people, we can expect very little from the efforts of present day statesmen of other races, in that their plans, (as far as advantages to be derived therefrom are concerned) are laid only in the interests of their own people and not in the interest of Negroes; hence it is imperative that Negroes as a people evolve just at this time a statesmanship sufficiently able to cope with the designs and movements that are being made that will (except we prevent it) ultimately mean our doom and destruction.

THE NEGRO AS AN INDUSTRIAL MAKE-SHIFT

The Negro's prosperity today, limited as it is, is based upon the foundation laid by an alien race that is not disposed to go out of its way to prepare for the economic existence of anyone else but itself; therefore our present prosperity as far as employment goes, is purely accidental. It is as accidental to-day as it was during the war of 1914-18 when colored men were employed in different occupations, not because they were wanted, but because they were filling the places of men of other races who were not available at that time. Negroes are still filling places, and as time goes on and the age grows older our occupations will be gone from us, because those for whom we filled the places will soon appear, and as they do we shall gradually find our places among the millions of permanent unemployed. The thing for the Negro to do therefore, is to adjust his own economic present, in readiness for the future.

A race that is solely dependent upon another for its economic existence sooner or later dies. As we have in the past been living upon the mercies shown us by others, and by the chances obtainable, and have suffered therefrom, so will we in the future suffer if an effort is not made now to adjust our own affairs.

LACK OF CO-OPERATION IN THE NEGRO RACE

It is so hard, so difficult to find men who will stick to a purpose ,who will maintain a principle for the worth of that principle, for the good of that purpose, and if there is a race that needs such men in the world today, God Almighty knows it is the race of which I am a member.

The race needs men of vision and ability. Men of character and above all men of honesty, and that is so hard to find.

The greatest stumbling block in the way of progress in the race has invariably come from within the race itself. The monkey wrench of destruction as thrown into the cog of Negro Progress, is not thrown so much by the outsider as by the very fellow who is in our fold, and who should be the first to grease the wheel of progress rather than seeking to impede it.

But notwithstanding the lack of sympathetic co-operation, I have one consolation—That I cannot get away from the race, and so long as I am in the race and since I have sense and judgment enough to know what affects the race affects me, it is my duty to help the race to clear itself of those things that affect us in common.

WHITE MAN'S SOLUTION FOR THE NEGRO PROBLEM IN AMERICA

Immediately after the signing of the Emancipation Proclamation in America, the white man started to think how he could solve the new problem of the Negro.

He saw that the Negro could not be slaughtered by wholesale killing in that it would be a blot on American civilization, he therefore had to resort to some means of solving the problem, which meant the extinction of the Negro in America.

The plan he decided on was as follows:

"Now that America is undeveloped and we have but 34,000,000 in population (30,000,000 being white and 4,000,000 black) a number not large enough to develop the country as we want it, we will use the 4,000,000 blacks until we have built up the country, sufficiently and when we no longer need their labor, we will throw them off and let them starve economically and die of themselves, or emigrate elsewhere, we care not where. Then no one can accuse us of being inhuman to the Negro as we shall not have massacred him."

A hearty welcome is extended to white people from all parts of the world to come to and settle in America. They come in by the thousands every month. Why? The idea is to build up a vast white population in America, so as to make the white people independent of Negro labor; thereby depriving them of the means of livelihood, the wherewithal to buy bread, which means that in a short while they will die of starvation.

Those of us who study industrial conditions among the race must have noticed that Negroes in America have been thrown out of jobs that they occupied formerly, and their positions taken by

European Immigrants. Now if the white people have not reached the apex of their intention industrially, as far as the development of the country is concerned, and they have exhibited such a degree of prejudice since they started their plan; how much more prejudiced will they not become in the next one hundred years when their population will be doubled by emigration and birthrate? This is the problem the Negro has to face in America.

THE TRUE SOLUTION OF THE NEGRO PROBLEM—1922

As far as Negroes are concerned, in America we have the problem of lynching,peonage and dis-franchisement.

In the West Indies, South and Central America we have the problem of peonage, serfdom, industrial and political governmental inequality.

In Africa we have, not only peonage and serfdom, but outright slavery, racial exploitation and alien political monopoly.

We cannot allow a continuation of these crimes against our race. As four hundred million men, women and children, worthy of the existence given us by the Divine Creator, we are determined to solve our own problem, by redeeming our Motherland Africa from the hands of alien exploiters and found there a government, a nation of our own, strong enough to lend protection to the members of our race scattered all over the world, and to compel the respect of the nations and races of the earth.

Do they lynch Englishmen, Frenchmen, Germans or Japanese? No. And Why? Because these people are represented by great governments, mighty nations and empires, strongly organized. Yes, and ever ready to shed the last drop of blood and spend the last penny in the national treasury to protect the honor and integrity of a citizen outraged anywhere.

Until the Negro reaches this point of national independence, all he does as a race will count for naught, because the prejudice that will stand out against him even with his ballot in his hand, with his industrial progress to show, will be of such an overwhelmning nature as to perpetuate mob violence and mob rule, from which he will suffer, and which he will not be able to stop with his industrial wealth and with his ballot.

You may argue that he can use his industrial wealth and his ballot to force the government to recognize him, but he must understand that the government is the people. That the majority of the people dictate the policy of governments, and if the majority are against a measure, a thing, or a race, then the government is impotent to protect that measure, thing or race.

If the Negro were to live in this Western Hemisphere for another five hundred years he would still be outnumbered by other races who are prejudiced against him. He cannot resort to the government for protection for government will be in the hands of the majority of the people who are prejudiced against him, hence for the Negro to depend on the ballot and his industrial progress alone, will be hopeless as it does not help him when he is lynched, burned, jim-crowed and segregated. The future of the Negro therefore, outside of Africa, spells ruin and disaster.

WHITE PROPAGANDA ABOUT AFRICA

This propaganda of dis-associating Western Negroes from Africa is not a new one. For many years white propagandists have been printing tons of literature to impress scattered Ethiopia, especially that portion within their civilization, with the idea that Africa is a despised place, inhabited by savages, and cannibals, where no civilized human being should go, especially black civilized human beings. This propaganda is promulgated for the cause that is being realized today. That cause is COLONIAL EXPANSION for the white nations of the world.

At the present time the world is not producing enough food to feed all its inhabitants. The strong are fed and the weak starve. That is why there are famines in certain countries, even though those countries produce certain things for human consumption. The strong go there and take the food and send it home just as how Great Britain and France go into Africa, take out the products and ship them away to feed Europeans and leave Africans to starve. The strong will always live at the expense of the weak.

This rush for territory, this encroachment on lands, is only a desire of the strong races, especially the white race, to get hold of those portions and bits of land necessary for their economic existence, knowing well, that, in another two hundred years, there will not be enough supplies in the world for all of its inhabitants. The weaker peoples must die . At present Negroes are the weakest people and if we do not get power and strength now we shall be doomed to extermination.

THE THREE STAGES OF THE NEGRO IN CONTACT WITH THE WHITE MAN

I believe, as far as the Negro is concerned politically, that there are three stages relating to our contact with the white man:

The First Stage in the life of the Negro in this Western Hemisphere was the stage when the white man shackled us in Africa and brought us here and kept us for two hundred and fifty years. During this period we worked and received no recompense, no pay for our labor, and we were satisfied because of the white man's Christian teaching "Learn to labor and to wait."

The Second Stage was the thing called Emancipation, which we have enjoyed for fifty-eight years. This stage came when they gave us partial freedom, and a petty existence by way of wages, and we were satisfied during that stage to do just what they told us to do. We worked for small wages and voted Republican Democratic and so forth, until after fifty-eight years we discovered that a change was necessary.

Now we have entered into the **Third Stage** of our existence, wherein we say to the white man "After two hundred and fifty years of slavery and fifty eight years of partial freedom under your leadership we are going to try but fifty years under our own direction.

This new stage calls for all the manhood within the race and means that we must throw off all the conditions that affected us in the first and second stages, and go out and do—acquit ourselves like men in the economic, industrial and political arena.

BOOKER T. WASHINGTON'S PROGRAM

The world held up the great Sage of Tuskegee—Booker T. Washington—as the only leader for the race. They looked forward to him and his teachings as the leadership for all times, not calculating that the industrially educated Negro would himself evolve a new ideal, after having been trained by the Sage of Tuskegee.

The world satisfied itself to believe that succeeding Negro leaders would follow absolutely the teachings of Washington. Unfortunately the world is having a rude awakening, in that we are evolving a new ideal. The new ideal includes the program of Booker T. Washington and has gone much further.

Things have changed wonderfully since Washington came on the scene. His vision was industrial opportunity for the Negro, but the Sage of Tuskegee has passed off the stage of life and left behind a new problem—a problem that must be solved, not by the industrial leader only, but by the political and military leaders as well.

If Washington had lived he would have had to change his program. No leader can successfully lead this race of ours without giving an interpretation of the awakened spirit of the New Negro, who does not seek industrial opportunity alone, but a political voice. The world is amazed at the desire of the New Negro, for with his strong voice he is demanling a place in the affairs of men.

BELIEF THAT RACE PROBLEM WILL ADJUST ITSELF A FALLACY

Some of our leaders in the Negro race flatter themselves into believing that the problem of black and white in America will work itself out, and that all the Negro has to do is to be humble, submissive and obedient, and everything will work out well in the "Sweet bye and bye". But the keen student will observe this,—that a terrible mistake was made between forty and fifty years ago when black men were elected to legislative assemblies all over the country, especially in the southern states and even at the National Capitol when representatives of this race occupied seats in Congress. The mistake was made as far as the white people were concerned. There was a state of dis-organization in the Nation, and in that state certain things happened by mere chance. In the chance, dozens of black men became Senators and Congressmen. This opened up to the eyes of the white nation the possibility of the black man governing the white man in these United States of America—the possibility of the black man making laws to govern the white man? This possibility drove them almost to madness, in suddenly rejecting the spirit of the constitution and the Declaration of Lincoln that "all men are created equal", hence a determination was arrived at, that never again would it be possible for the race of slaves to govern the race of masters within these United States of America.

Some of us believe that this slave race of ours will live in the United States of America and in the future again become law makers for the white race (our slave masters of sixty years ago). Nothing of the kind has happened in all human history. There is not one instance where a slave race living in the same country (within the same bounds as the race of masters that enslaved them and being in numbers less than the race of masters) has ever yet ruled and governed the masters. It has never been so in history, and it will never be so in the future. The hidden spirit of America is determined that it shall never be, caring not what hopes and promises we get.

But history has recorded where a race of slaves through evolution, through progress, has risen to the heights where they ruled and dominated those who once enslaved them, but that race of slaves has always had to betake itself to other habitats (usually their own native land) and there, apart from those who once enslaved them, developed a power of their own, a strength of their own, and in the higher development of that strength, and of that power, they. like others, have made conquests, and the conquests sometimes have enabled them to enslave those who once enslaved them. So for us to encourage the idea that one day Negroes will rise to the highest in the administration of this white government, is only encouraging a vain hope.

The only wise thing for us as ambitious Negroes to do, is to organize the world over, and build up for the race a mighty nation of our own in Africa. And this race of ours that can not get recognition and respect in the country where we were slaves, by using our own ability, power and genius, would develop for ourselves in another country in our habitat a nation of our own, and be able to send back from that country,—from that native habitat—to the country where we were once enslaved, representatives of our race, that would get as much respect as any other ambassadors from any other race or nation.

EXAMPLES OF WHITE CHRISTIAN CONTROL OF AFRICA

The world has seen many fair examples of white Christian control of Africa:

The outrages of Leopold of Belgium, when he butchered thousands of our defenceless brothers and sisters in the Belgian Congo, and robbed them of their rubber.

The natives of Kenya South East Africa armed with sticks and stones rebelled against the injustices and brutality of the English, and were hewn down by machine guns, because they did not supply the demands of the invaders.

The Hottentots of South West Africa in rebellion against similar brutality and exploitation, using spears and leather shields to protect themselves, were bombed from aeroplanes by the Christian? whites.

The above are but few examples of the many atrocities committed on our defenceless brothers and sisters in Africa by white exploiters and invaders. Surely the introduction of chemical gas among the natives of Africa would place them in a better position to handle "the alien disturbers of African peace."

It strikes me that with all the civilization this Western Hemis phere affords, Negroes ought to take better advantage of the cause of higher education. We could make of ourselves better mechanics and scientists, and in cases where we can help our brothers in Africa by making use of the knowledge we possess, it would be but our duty. If Africa is to be redeemed the Western Negro will have to make a valuable contribution along technical and scientific lines.

THE THOUGHT BEHIND THEIR DEEDS

Behind the murder of millions of Negroes annually in Africa is the well organized system of exploitation by the alien intruders who desire to rob Africa of every bit of its wealth for the satisfaction of their race and the upkeep of their bankrupt European countries.

If we of the Western World take no interest in the higher development of the African natives, it will mean that in another hundred years historians and writers will tell us that the black man once inhabited Africa, just as the North American Indian once inhabited America. But those of us who lead are well versed in Western civilization and are determined that the black man shall not be a creature of the past, but a full-fledged man of the present and a power to be reckoned with in the future.

———o———

SIMILARITY OF PERSECUTION

Christ came into the world centuries ago to redeem lost mankind. From the age of twelve to His Crucifixion He taught the doctrine of salvation without fear of the great and mighty ones of His day. But His fellow Jews became jealous of His success and sought means to get rid of Him. They argued among themselves saying, "How can we do it. We have no power, no judges, and if we lay hands upon Him, He will have us apprehended by the Roman authorities. The best thing we can do is to frame him up". So they made certain statements to the Roman Government which had Jesus incarcerated, while His brother Jews shouted with joy as they had accomplished their desire.

When Jesus was brought to trial Pontius Pilate, the Governor, did not care to send Him to prison as He had not interfered with the honor and reputation of any Roman citizen, and the Romans were not jealous of the work of this Jew. But the Jews who were jealous of Christ said, "This man is preaching against Caesar and the State; He is preaching the doctrine of rebellion among the peaceful Jews and citizens of the State; if you do not convict this man, you are not a friend of Caesar". **Pilate being thus forced against his will, was compelled to decide against Jesus, even though he knew that Jesus had done no wrong.**

After He was condemned Pilate still hoped to get his conscience clear by letting Jesus go, in that he Pilate was empowered to release one criminal on Feast Day. When the time came for the condemned men to be crucified Pilate asked them to choose between Barrabas, the robber and Jesus whom they called the King of the Jews, and they cried, "Crucify Jesus and let Barrabas go". Pilate said, "What evil hath he done", but they cried the more "Crucify him".

So we have a relative position at this time. Selfish, jealous Negroes know they can do nothing to impede the progress of the Universal Negro Improvement Association, and if left alone we will go on organizing Negroes throughout the world, so they say: "We cannot handle Garvey and his Organization, as we have no power, let us go to the State and Federal authorities, and frame him up, let us say he is an anarchist, a seditionist and is speaking against the government". Like the Jews of old, they cry "Crucify him," or rather, "Send him to prison, deport him."

During Christ's sojourn on earth He taught many lessons, among them: "Blessed are they which are persecuted for righteousness' sake, for theirs is the kingdom of heaven." This declaration has inspired men through all ages to make their sacrifice in the cause of human liberty.

When we recount the many noble deeds of the heroes and martyrs of the various nations and races of the world, who have sacrificed their lives in the cause of freedom, we will readily realize that this declaration of Christ has proved itself true. Through the sacrifice of Jesus and the yielding up of His life on Calvary's Cross, the world today has caught an inspiration that will live forever. In the time when He taught His doctrine few men believed in and followed Him, but after the lapse of centuries we find that Christianity has become the greatest moral force in the world. As with Christianity, so with every great human Movement taught under similar circumstances.

May we not say to ourselves that the doctrine Jesus taught—that of redeeming mankind—is the doctrine we ourselves must teach in the redemption of our struggling race? Let us therefore cling fast to the great ideal we have before us. This time it is not the ideal of redeeming the world, such as was the ideal of Jesus, but it is the ideal of redeeming and saving 400,000,000 souls who have suffered for centuries from the persecution of alien races. As Christ by His teachings, His sufferings and His death, triumphed over His foes, through the resurrection, so do we hope that out of our sufferings and persecutions of today we will triumph in the resurrection of our newborn race.

SHALL THE NEGRO BE EXTERMINATED?

The Negro now stands at the cross roads of human destiny. He is at the place where he must either step forward or backward. If he goes backward he dies; if he goes forward it will be with the hope of a greater life. Those of us who have developed our minds scientifically are compelled, by duty, to step out among the millions of the unthinking masses and convince them of the seriousness of the age in which we live.

From Adam and Eve

We are either on the way to a higher racial existence or racial extermination. This much is known and realized by every thoughtful race and nation; hence, we have the death struggle of the different races of Europe and Asia in the scramble of the survival of the fittest race.

As we look at things we see that the great world in which we live has undergone much change since the time of the creation. When God created the world, and all therein, He handed His authority over to the two beings He created in His own image; namely, Adam and Eve. From the time of Adam and Eve the human race has multiplied by leaps and bounds. Where we once had two persons to exercise authority over the world, we to-day have one billion five hundred millions claiming authority and possession of the same world that was once the property of the two.

The Tragedy of Race Extinction

When the Colonists of America desired possession of the land they saw that a weak aboriginal race was in their way. What did they do? They got hold of them, killed them, and buried them underground. This is a fair indication of what will happen to the weaker peoples of the world in another two or three hundred years when the stronger races will have developed themselves to the position of complete mastery of all things material. They will not then as they have not in the past, allow a weak and defenceless race to stand in their way, especially if in their doing so they will endanger their happiness, their comfort and their pleasures. These are the things that strike the thoughtful Negro as being dangerous, and these are the things that cause us who make up the Universal Negro Improvement Association to be fighting tenaciously for the purpose of building up a strong Negro race, so as to make it impossible for us to be exterminated in the future to make room for the stronger races, even as the North American Indian has been exterminated to make room for the great white man on this North American continent.

The illiterate and shallow-minded Negro who can see no farther than his nose is now the greatest stumbling block in the way of the race. He tells us that we must be satisfied with our condition; that we must not think of building up a nation of our own, that we must not seek to organize ourselves racially, but that we must depend upon the good feeling of the other fellow for the solution of the problem that now confronts us. This is a dangerous policy and it is my duty to warn the four hundred million Negroes of the world against this kind of a leadership—a leadership that will try to make Negroes believe that all will be well without their taking upon themselves the task of bettering their condition politically, industrially, educationally and otherwise.

The time has come for those of us who have the vision of the future to inspire our people to a closer kinship, to a closer love of self, because it is only through this appreciation of self will we be able to rise to that higher life that will make us not an extinct race in the future, but a race of men fit to survive.

The Price of leadership

Those of us who are blazing the way in this new propaganda of the Universal Negro Improvement Association to enlighten our people everywhere are at times very much annoyed and discouraged by the acts of our own people in that consciously or unconsciously they do so many things to hurt our deeper feeling of loyalty and love for the race. But what can we do? Can we forsake them because they hurt our feelings? Surely not. Painful though it may be to be interfered with and handicapped in the performance of the higher sense of duty, yet we must, martyr-like, make up our minds and our hearts to pay the price of leadership. We must be sympathetic, we must be forgiving, we must really have forbearance, so that when the ignorant and illiterate fellow who happens to be a member of your own race stands up to block the passage of some cause that you believe would be to his benefit and to yours as a people you will be able to overlook him, even though he fosters his opposition with the greatest amount of insult to your intelligence and to your dignity.

The excuse that some of our most brilliant men give for not identifying themselves with race movements is, that they cannot tolerate the interference of the illiterate Negro, who, being a member of the same organization will attempt to dictate what you should do in the interest of the race, when his act is based upon no deeper judgment than his like or dislike for the person he is opposing, or the satisfaction it would give him to embarrass the person he feels like opposing. Many an able leader is lost to his race because of this fear, and sometimes we must admit the reasonableness of this argument; but as I have said leadership means martyrdom, leadership means sacrifice, leadership means giving up one's personality, giving up of everything for the cause that is worth while. It is only because of that feeling that I personally continue to lead the Universal Negro Improvement Association, because like every other leader, I have had to encounter the opposition, the jealousy, the plotting of men who take advantage of the situation, simply because they happen to be members of the organization, and that we may have to depend upon their vote one way or the other for the good of the cause. Not that some of us care one row of pins about what the other fellow thinks, but when it is considered that we can only achieve success through

harmony and unity, then it can be realized how much one has to
sacrifice as a leader for getting that harmony that is necessary
to bring about the results that are desired.

The White Race

We desire harmony and unity to-day more than ever, because
it is only through the bringing together of the four hundred
million Negroes into one mighty bond that we can successfully
pilot our way through the avenues of opposition and the oceans
of difficulties that seem to confront us.   When it is considered
that the great white race is making a herculean struggle to become the only surviving race of the centuries, and when it is
further considered that the great yellow race under the leadership
of Japan is making a like struggle, then more than ever the seriousness of the situation can be realized as far as our race is concerned.   If we sit supinely by and allow the great white race to
lift itself in numbers and in power, it will mean that in another
five hundred years this full grown race of white men will in turn
exterminate the weaker race of black men for the purpose of finding enough room on this limited mundane sphere to accommodate
that race which will have numerically multiplied itself into many
billions.   This is the danger point.   What will become of the
Negro in another five hundred years if he does not organize now
to develop and to protect himself?   The answer is that he will
be exterminated for the purpose of making room for the other
races that will be strong enough to hold their own against the
opposition of all and sundry.

An appeal to the Intelligentsia

The leadership of the Negro of to-day must be able to locate
the race, and not only for to-day but for all times.   It is in the
desire to locate the Negro in a position of prosperity and happi
ness in the future that the Universal Negro Improvement Association is making this great fight for the race's emancipation
everywhere and the founding of a great African government.

Every sober-minded Negro will see immediately the reason why we should support a movement of this kind. If we will survive then it must be done through our own effort, through our own energy. No race of weaklings can survive in the days of tomorrow, because they will be hard and strenuous days fraught with many difficulties.

I appeal to the higher intelligence as well as to the illiterate groups of our race. We must work together. Those of us who are better positioned intellectually must exercise forbearance with the illiterate and help them to see the right. If we happen to be members of the same organization, and the illiterate man tries to embarras you, do not become disgusted, but remember that he does it because he does not know better, and it is your duty to forbear and forgive because the ends that we serve are not of self, but for the higher development of the entire race. It is on this score, it is on this belief, that I make the sacrifice of self to help this downtrodden race of mine. Nevertheless, I say there is a limit to human patience, and we should not continue to provoke the other fellow against his human feelings for in doing so we may be but bringing down upon our own heads the pillars of the temple

AFRICA FOR THE AFRICANS

For five years the Universal Negro Improvement Association has been advocating the cause of Africa for the Africans—that is, that the Negro peoples of the world should concentrate upon the object of building up for themselves a great nation in Africa.

When we started our propaganda toward this end several of the so-called intellectual Negroes who have been bamboozling the race for over half a century said that we were crazy, that the Negro peoples of the western world were not interested in Africa and could not live in Africa. One editor and leader went so far as to say at his so-called Pan-African Congress that American Negroes could not live in Africa, because the climate was too hot. All kinds of arguments have been adduced by these Negro intellectuals against the colonization of Africa by the black race. Some said that the black man would ultimately work out his existence alongside of the white man in countries founded and established by the latter. Therefore, it was not necessary for Negroes to seek an independent nationality of their own. The old time stories of "African fever," "African bad climate," "African mosquitos," "African savages," have been repeated by these "brainless intellectuals" of ours as a scare against our people in America and the West Indies taking a kindly interest in the new program of building a racial empire of our own in our Motherland. Now that years have rolled by and the Universal Negro Improvement Association has made the circuit of the world with its propaganda, we find eminent statesmen and leaders of the white race coming out boldly advocating the cause of colonizing Africa with the Negroes of the western world. A year ago Senator MacCullum of the Mississippi Legislature introduced a resolution in the House for the purpose of petitioning the Congress of the United States of America and the President to use their good influence in securing from the Allies sufficient territory in Africa in liquidation of the war debt, which territory should be used for the establishing of an independent nation for American Negroes. About the same time Senator France of Maryland gave expression to a similar desire in the Senate of the United States. During a speech on the "Soldiers' Bonus." He said: "We owe a big debt to Africa and one which we have too long ignored. I need not enlarge upon our peculiar interest in the obligation to the people of Africa. Thousands of Americans have for years been contributing to the missionary work which has been carried out by the noble men and women who have been sent out in that field by the churches of America."

Germany To The Front

This reveals a real change on the part of prominent statesmen in their attitude on the African question. Then comes another suggestion from Germany, for which Dr. Heinrich Schnee, a former Governor of German East Africa, is author. This German statesman suggests in an interview given out in Berlin, and published in New York, that America takes over the mandatories of Great Britain and France in Africa for the colonization of American Negroes. Speaking on the matter, he says "As regards the attempt to colonize Africa with the surplus American colored population, this would in a long way settle the vexed problem, and under the plan such as Senator France has outlined, might enable France and Great Britain to discharge their duties to the United States, and simultaneously ease the burden of German reparations which is paralyzing economic life."

With expressions as above quoted from prominent world statesmen, and from the demands made by such men as Senators France and McCullum, it is clear that the question of African nationality is not a far-fetched one, but is as reasonable and feasible as was the idea of an American nationality.

A "Program" At Last

I trust that the Negro peoples of the world are now convinced that the work of the Universal Negro Improvement Association is not a visionary one, but very practical, and that it is not so far fetched, but can be realized in a short while if the entire race will only co-operate and work toward the desired end. Now that the work of our organization has started to bear fruit we find that some of these "doubting Thomases" of three and four years ago are endeavoring to mix themselvves up with the popular idea of rehabilitating Africa in the interest of the Negro They are now advancing spurious "programs" and in a short while will endeavor to force themselves upon the public as advocates and leaders of the African idea.

It is felt that those who have followed the career of the Universal Negro Improvement Association will not allow themselves to be deceived by these Negro opportunists who have always sought to live off the ideas of other people.

The Dream Of A Negro Empire

It is only a question of a few more years when Africa will be completely colonized by Negroes, as Europe is by the white race. What we want is an independent African nationality, and if America is to help the Negro peoples of the world establish such a nationality, then we welcome the assistance.

It is hoped that when the time comes for American and West Indian Negroes to settle in Africa, they will realize their responsibility and their duty. It will not be to go to Africa for the purpose of exercising an over-lordship over the natives, but it shall be the purpose of the Universal Negro Improvement Association to have established in Africa that brotherly co-operation which will make the interests of the African native and the American and West Indian Negro one and the same, that is to say, we shall enter into a common partnership to build up Africa in the interests of our race.

Oneness Of Interests

Everybody knows that there is absolutely no difference between the native African and the American and West Indian Negroes, in that we are descendants from one common family stock. It is only a matter of accident that we have been divided and kept apart for over three hundred years, but it is felt that when the time has come for us to get back together, we shall do so in the spirit of brotherly love, and any Negro who expects that he will be assisted here, there or anywhere by the Universal Negro Improvement Association to exercise a haughty superiority over the fellows of his own race, makes a tremenduous mistake. Such men had better remain where they are and not attempt to become in any way interested in the higher development of Africa.

The Negro has had enough of the vaunted practice of race superiority as inflicted upon him by others, therefore he is not prepared to tolerate a similar assumption on the part of his own people. In America and the West Indies, we have Negroes who believe themselves so much above their fellows as to cause them to think that any readjustment in the affairs of the race should be placed in their hands for them to exercise a kind of an autocratic and despotic control as others have done to us for centuries. Again I say, it would be advisable for such Negroes to take their hands and minds off the now popular idea of colonizing Africa in the interest of the Negro race, because their being identified with this new program will not in any way help us because of the existing feeling among Negroes everywhere not to tolerate the infliction of race or class superiority upon them, as is the desire of the self-appointed and self-created race leadership that we have been having for the last fifty years.

The Basis Of An African Aristocracy.

The masses of Negroes in America, the West Indies, South and Central America are in sympathetic accord with the aspirations of the native Africans. We desire to help them build up Africa as a Negro Empire, where every black man, whether he was born in Africa or in the Western world, will have the opportunity to develop on his own lines under the protection of the most favorable democratic institutions.

It will be useless, as before stated, for bombastic Negroes to leave America and the West Indies to go to Africa, thinking that they will have privileged positions to inflict upon the race that bastard aristocracy that they have tried to maintain in this Western world at the expense of the masses. Africa shall develop an aristocracy of its own, but it shall be based upon service and loyalty to race. Let all Negroes work toward that end. I feel that it is only a question of a few more years before our program will be accepted not only by the few statesmen of America who are now interested in it, but by the strong statesmen of the world, as the only solution to the great race problem. There is no other way to avoid the threatening war of the races that is bound to engulf all mankind, which has been prophesied by the world's greatest thinkers; there is no better method than by apportioning every race to its own habitat.

The time has really come for the Asiatics to govern themselves in Asia, as the Europeans are in Europe and the Western world, so also is it wise for the Africans to govern themselves at home, and thereby bring peace and satisfaction to the entire human family.

THE FUTURE AS I SEE IT

It comes to the individual, the race, the nation, once in a life time to decide upon the course to be pursued as a career. The hour has now struck for the individual Negro as well as the entire race to decide the course that will be pursued in the interest of our own liberty.

We who make up the Universal Negro Improvement Association have decided that we shall go forward, upward and onward toward the great goal of human liberty. We have determined among ourselves that all barriers placed in the way of our progress must be removed, must be cleared away for we desire to see the light of a brighter day.

The Negro is Ready

The Universal Negro Improvement Association for five years has been proclaiming to the world the readiness of the Negro to carve out a pathway for himself in the course of life. Men of other races and nations have become alarmed at this attitude of the Negro in his desire to do things for himself and by himself. This alarm has become so universal that organizations have been brought into being here, there and everywhere for the purpose of deterring and obstructing this forward move of our race. Propaganda has been waged here, there and everywhere for the purpose of misinterpreting the intention of this organization; some have said that this organization seeks to create discord and discontent among the races; some say we are organized for the purpose of hating other people. Every sensible, sane and honest-minded person knows that the Universal Negro Improvement Association has no such intention. We are organized for the absolute purpose of bettering our condition, industrially, commercially, socially, religiously and politically. We are organized not to hate other men, but to lift ourselves, and to demand respect of all humanity. We have a program that we believe to be righteous; we believe it to be just, and we have made up our minds to lay down ourselves on the altar of sacrifice for the realization of this great hope of ours, based upon the foundation of righteousness.   We declare to the world that Africa must be free, that the entire Negro race must be emancipated from industrial bondage, peonage and serfdom; we make no compromise, we make no apology in this our declaration.   We do not desire to create offense on the part of other races, but we are determined that we shall be heard, that we shall be given the rights to which we are entitled.

The Propaganda Of Our Enemies

For the purpose of creating doubts about the work of the Universal Negro Improvement Association, many attempts have been made to cast shadow and gloom over our work.   They have even written the most uncharitable things about our organization; they have spoken so unkindly of our effort, but what do we care? They spoke unkindly and uncharitably about all the reform movements that have helped in the betterment of humanity.   They maligned the great movement of the Christian religion; they maligned the great liberation movements of America, of France, of England, of Russia; can we expect, then, to escape being maligned in this, our desire for the liberation of Africa and the freedom of four hundred million Negroes of the world?

We have unscrupulous men and organizations working in opposition to us.   Some trying to capitalize the new spirit that has come to the Negro to make profit out of it to their own selfish benefit; some are trying to set back the Negro from seeing the hope of his own liberty, and thereby poisoning our people's mind against the motives of our organization; but every sensible far-seeing Negro in this enlightened age knows what propaganda means.   It is the medium of discrediting that which you are opposed to, so that the propaganda of our enemies will be of little avail as soon as we are rendered able to carry to our peoples scattered throughout the world the true message of our great orgagnization.

"Crocodiles" As Friends

Men of the Negro race, let me say to you that a greater future is in store for us; we have no cause to lose hope, to become faint-hearted. We must realize that upon ourselves depend our destiny, our future; we must carve out that future, that destiny, and we who make up the Universal Negro Improvement Association have pledged ourselves that nothing in the world shall stand in our way, nothing in the world shall discourage us, but opposition shall make us work harder, shall bring us closer together so that as one man the millions of us will march on toward that goal that we have set for ourselves. The new Negro shall not be deceived. The new Negro refuses to take advice from anyone who has not felt with him, and suffered with him. We have suffered for three hundred years, therefore we feel that the time has come when only those who have suffered with us can interpret our feelings and our spirit. It takes the slave to interpret the feelings of the slave; it takes the unfortunate man to interpret the spirit of his unfortunate brother; and so it takes the suffering Negro to interpret the spirit of his comrade. It is strange that so many people are interested in the Negro now, willing to advise him how to act, and what organizations he should join, yet nobody was interested in the Negro to the extent of not making him a slave for two hundred and fifty years, reducing him to industrial peonage and serfdom after he was freed; it is strange that the same people can be so interested in the Negro now, as to tell him what organization he should follow and what leader he should support.

Whilst we are bordering on a future of brighter things, we are also at our danger period, when we must either accept the right philosophy, or go down by following deceptive propaganda which has hemmed us in for many centuries.

Deceiving The People

There is many a leader of our race who tells us that everything is well, and that all things will work out themselves and that a better day is coming. Yes, all of us know that a better day is coming; we all know that one day we will go home to Paradise, but whilst we are hoping by our Christian virtues to have an entry into Paradise we also realize that we are living on earth, and that the things that are practised in Paradise are not practiced here. You have to treat this world as the world treats you; we are living in a temporal, material age, an age of activity, an age of racial, national selfishness. What else can you expect but to give back to the world what the world gives to you, and we are calling upon the four hundred million Negroes of the world to take a decided stand, a determined stand, that we shall occupy a firm position; that position shall be an emancipated race and a free nation of our own. We are determined that we shall have a free country; we are determined that we shall have a flag; we are determined that we shall have a government second to none in the world.

An Eye For An Eye

Men may spurn the idea, they may scoff at it; the metropolitan press of this country may deride us; yes, white men may laugh at the idea of Negroes talking about government; but let me tell you there is going to be a government, and let me say to you also that whatsoever you give, in like measure it shall be returned to you. The world is sinful, and therefore man believes in the doctrine of an eye for an eye, a tooth for a tooth. Everybody believes that revenge is God's, but at the same time we are men, and revenge sometimes springs up, even in the most Christian heart.

Why should man write down a history that will react against him? Why should man perpetrate deeds of wickedness upon his brother which will return to him in like measure? Yes, the Germans maltreated the French in the Franco-Prussian war of 1870, but the French got even with the Germans in 1918. It is history, and history will repeat itself. Beat the Negro, brutalize the Negro, kill the Negro, burn the Negro, imprison the Negro, scoff at the Negro, deride the Negro, it may come back to you one of these fine days, because the supreme destiny of man is in the hands of God. God is no respecter of persons, whether that person be white, yellow or black. Today the one race is up, to-morrow it has fallen; today the Negro seems to be the footstool of the other races and nations of the world; tomorrow the Negro may occupy the highest rung of the great human ladder.

But, when we come to consider the history of man, was not the Negro a power, was he not great once? Yes, honest students of history can recall the day when Egypt, Ethiopia and Timbuctoo towered in their civilizations, towered above Europe, towered above Asia. When Europe was inhabited by a race of cannibals, a race of savages, naked men, heathens and pagans, Africa was peopled with a race of cultured black men, who were masters in art, science and literature; men who were cultured and refined; men who, it was said, were like the gods. Even the great poets of old sang in beautiful sonnets of the delight it afforded the gods to be in companionship with the Ethiopians. Why, then, should we lose hope? Black men, you were once great; you shall be great again. Lose not courage, lose not faith, go forward. The thing to do is to get organized; keep separated and you will be exploited, you will be robbed, you will be killed. Get organized, and you will compel the world to respect you. If the world fails to give you consideration, because you are black men, because you are Negroes, four hundred millions of you shall, through organization, shake the pillars of the universe and bring down creation, even as Samson brought down the temple upon his head and upon the heads of the Philistines.

An Inspiring Vision

So Negroes, I say, through the Universal Negro Improvement Association, that there is much to live for. I have a vision of the future, and I see before me a picture of a redeemed Africa, with her dotted cities, with her beautiful civilization, with her millions of happy children, going to and fro. Why should I lose hope, why should I give up and take a back place in this age of progress? Remember that you are men, that God created you Lords of this creation. Lift up yourselves, men, take yourselves out of the mire and hitch your hopes to the stars; yes, rise as high as the very stars themselves. Let no man pull you down, let no man destroy your ambition, because man is but your companion, your equal; man is your brother; he is not your lord; he is not your sovereign master.

We of the Universal Negro Improvement Association feel happy; we are cheerful. Let them connive to destroy us; let them organize to destroy us; we shall fight the more. Ask me personally the cause of my success, and I say opposition; oppose me, and I fight the more, and if you want to find out the sterling worth of the Negro, oppose him, and under the leadership of the Universal Negro Improvement Association he shall fight his way to victory, and in the days to come, and I believe not far distant, Africa shall reflect a splendid demonstration of the worth of the Negro, of the determination of the Negro, to set himself free and to establish a government of his own.

CHAPTER V

SPEECH DELIVERED ON EMANCIPATION DAY AT LIBERTY HALL, NEW YORK CITY, N. Y. U. S. A.

January 1, 1922

Fifty-nine years ago Abraham Lincoln signed the Emancipation Proclamation declaring four million Negroes in this country free. Several years prior to that Queen Victoria of England signed the Emancipation Proclamation that set at liberty hundreds of thousands of West Indian Negro slaves.

West Indian Negroes celebrate their emancipation on the first day of August of every year. The American Negroes celebrate their emancipation on the first of January of every year. Tonight we are here to celebrate the emancipation of the slaves in this country.

We are the descendants of the men and women who suffered in this country for two hundred and fifty years under that barbarous, that brutal institution known as slavery. You who have not lost trace of your history will recall the fact that over three hundred years ago your fore-bears were taken from the great Continent of Africa and brought here for the purpose of using them as slaves. Without mercy, without any sympathy they worked our fore-bears. They suffered, they bled, they died. But with their sufferings, with their blood, which they shed in their death, they had a hope that one day their posterity would be free, and we are assembled here tonight as the children of their hope.

I trust each and every one of you therefore will realize that

you have a duty which is incumbent upon you; a duty that you
must perform, because our fore-bears who suffered, who bled,
who died had hopes that are not yet completely realized. They
hoped that we as their children would be free, but they also
hoped that their country from whence they came would also be
free to their children, their grand-children and great grand-
children at some future time. It is for the freedom of that
country—that Motherland of ours—that four and a half million
Negroes, as members of the Universal Negro Improvement Association, are laboring today.

This race of ours gave civilization, gave art, gave science;
gave literature to the world. But it has been the way with races
and nations. The one race stands out prominently in the one
century or in the one age; and in another century or age it
passes off the stage of action, and another race takes its place.
The Negro once occupied a high position in the world, scientifically, artistically and commercially, but in the balancing of the
great scale of evolution, we lost our place and some one, other
than ourselves occupies the stand we once held.

God never intended that man should enslave his fellow, and
the price of such a sin or such a violation of Heaven's law must be
paid by every one. As for me, because of the blessed past, because of the history that I know, so long as there is within me
the breath of life and the spirit of God, I shall struggle on and urge
others of our race to struggle on to see that justice is done to the
black peoples of the world. Yes, we appreciate the sorrows of the
past, and we are going to work in the present that the sorrows
of our generation shall not be perpetuated in the future. On
the contrary, we shall strive that by our labors, succeeding
generations of our own shall call us blessed, even as we call
the generation of the past blessed today. And they indeed
were blest. They were blest with a patience not yet known to
man. A patience that enabled them to endure the tortures and

the sufferings of slavery for two hundred and fifty years. Why?
Was it because they loved slavery so? No. It was because
they loved this generation more-Isn't it wonderful. Transcendent? What then are you going to do to show your appreciation of this love, what gratitude are you going to manifest in return for what they have done for you? As for me, knowing the
sufferings of my fore-fathers I shall give back to Africa that
liberty that she once enjoyed hundreds of years ago, before her
own sons and daughters were taken from her shores and brought
in chains to this Western World.

No better gift can I give in honor of the memory of the love
of my fore-parents for me, and in gratitude of the sufferings they
endured that I might be free; no grander gift can I bear to the
sacred memory of the generation past than a free and a redeemed
Africa—a monument for all eternity—for all times.

As by the action of the world, as by the conduct of all the
races and nations it is apparent that not one of them has the
sense of justice, the sense of love, the sense of equity, the sense
of charity, that would make men happy, and make God satisfied.
It is apparent that it is left to the Negro to play such a part in
human affairs-for when we look to the Anglo-Saxon we see
him full of greed, avarice, no mercy, no love, no charity. We
go from the white man to the yellow man, and we see the same
unenviable characteristics in the Japanese. Therefore we must
believe that the Psalmist had great hopes of this race of ours
when he prophesied "Princes shall come out of Egypt and
Ethiopia shall stretch forth her hands unto God"

If humanity is regarded as made up of the children of God
and God loves all humanity (we all know that) then God will be
more pleased with that race that protects all humanity than with
the race that outrages the children of God.

And so tonight we celebrate this anniversary of our emancipation, we do it not with regret, on the contrary we do it with an

abiding confidence, a hope and faith in ourselves and in our God. And the faith that we have is a faith that will ultimately take us back to that ancient place, that ancient position that we once occupied, when Ethiopia was in her glory.

CHRISTMAS MESSAGE TO THE NEGRO PEOPLES OF THE WORLD.

December 1921

Fellow men of the Negro Race,

Greeting:—

To us is born this day the Child Jesus—the Christ. The Shepherds and wise men are now wending their way toward Bethlehem, there to behold the Wonder of God. Because, there, in a manger, is to be found the Baby Christ who is to be the Redeemer of the world.

And so our thoughts go back for more than nineteen hundred years. We hear the shout "Hosanna in the Highest, blessed is He that cometh in the name of the Lord."

With all the preparation the human race has made to welcome into the world the Christ who is to redeem us, we find ourselves still in confusion, still fighting, still exploiting, still merciless in our onslaught one upon the other. But on this Christmas morn may we not all members and brothers of the great human family, forget our differences, and in one glorious chorus sing out to the world "Peace, perfect peace?".

Christ died to free Mankind.

When we come to consider the Brotherhood of Man and the Fatherhood of God, and that this Child of our own flesh, yet spirit of the Great Creator has been sent to link us nearer to our common Father, will we not admit of the reason that there should be but very little differences between us? What will we gain fighting the battle of man against man? Absolutely nothing but death; and was not this Child Jesus sent into this world to teach us the new life, the life of Love, of Charity, the Life of Mercy? What greater example do we desire than that which He gave in His own Life? He suffered, He died that others might be free. Yet even with the great object of the Cross before us, even though He died on Mount Calvary to make us free; even though He overcame death, the grave and hell to demonstrate to us the new life possible to each and every one, we have not yet turned from the path of sin to enter into the glory of His Eternal Kingdom.

The Spirit of Christmas

Instead of planning a career of sin on this Christmas Morn, may we not lift our thoughts to that grand and noble Father who gave to us on this day His Royal Son, whom He has made our brother, and ask Him to bless each and every one of us that our hearts may be touched with the true spirit of the first Christmas morn? That first day in the stable at Bethlehem was a beacon of a new born hope, for with the birth of the Prince of Peace there came to us an age of spiritual grace, which in its course sought to link man nearer to his God, and coming down the ages for more than nineteen hundred years, we have tried to preach Him as He appeared to us in His innocence, His Love and in His Charity.

Christ labored for thirty three years to teach us the way to glory, but in His career man, his brother sought the life that he could not give; he persecuted Him, he derided Him, he jeered Him and at last he crucified Him. But when that which was physical in the Christ died, the spiritual continued, and from earth betook its flight to heaven, there, probably, for all eternity, to look down upon the sinful, wicked world, and still to shower upon us blessings that we really need.

We shall never succeed in taking the Spirit of Christ out of the world, because in some of us, still, there is that spark of love, charity, and mercy that links us to our God. But may we not ask the Great Omnipotent, the Great Creator, our Eternal Father to send once more into the world, just at this time and oh, how we pray that it be on this Christmas morn, our brother

Christ, so that He may calm the raging storm and in truth pour out His benediction upon a corrupt world, a soulless human race, and make us subjects fit for Eternal Life?

Hail! the New born King

As with the angels let us sing, "Hail the New Born King, the Prince of Peace, Hail to the Son of Righteousness, for with Thee there is life, without Thee there is death". For as thou died upon Calvary's mount to make us better, to redeem us from our sins, may we not hope for a continuance of that love even for today? and knowing Thee in Thy bountiful love for all mankind, may we not further ask that Thy Spirit lighten up our hearts and bring to us by the touch of Thy grace, the knowledge of the Everlasting Brotherhood of Man, and the Eternal Fatherhood of God?

As the angels now rejoice in heaven over this new birth, so we rejoice on earth, four hundred millions of us, who are members of this Negro race, feeling that Thou art our King, that Thou art our Savior, that thou shalt be our Emanuel. We love Thee because Thou art the Son of God. We praise, worship and adore Thee because Thou art the Prince of Peace.

The Prince of Peace Our Guide to-day.

Let others in their sin, in their wickedness seek after the infant Life that Thou gavest to all mankind. We in our simplicity shall find refuge for Thee even in the land of Egypt. Yes, the world of sinful, wicked men cried out "Crucify Him! Crucify Him! But Lord because Thou art our Master, because Thou art our Prince of Peace, because Thou art our Redeemer, we shall render unto Thee all help possible, even in bearing the Cross up the heights of Calvary, for in life Thou hast been our friend; in death we know Thou shalt remember us, and now that Thou art sitting at the right hand of God, the Father, now that Thou hast conquered death, the grave and hell, surely in Thy mercy Thou shalt remember us. So today even though hundreds of years have rolled by since Thy crucifixion, we know that there is in Thine heart, there is in Thy soul a warm spot for the Sons and Daughters of Africa whose forebears bore the cross for Thee up the heights of Calvary to Thy crufixion.

We sing and shout with the angels; we ring our joy bells; we blow our horns in praise because Thou art indeed the Jesus, the Christ, the Emanuel to us, the Son of Righteousness, the Prince of Peace.

As sons and daughters of Africa, may not four hundred millions of us the world over on this Christmas morn pray for the redemption of that Motherland which sheltered our Blessed Redeemer when the wild, wicked men of the world sought His life; in the same manner wild, wicked men seek the lives of Negroes today, and burn, lynch and kill them because they have not the strength that makes man mighty. But with the Almighty Power of God and with the guidance and mercy of our Blessed Lord we feel that one day Ethiopia shall stretch forth her hand, and whether it be at the second coming or before, we shall all sing our Hosannas, shout our praises to God for freedom, for liberty, for life.

> "For Christ is born of Mary,
>   And gathered all above
> While mortals sleep, the angels keep
>   Their watch of wondering love.
> O morning stars, together
>   Proclaim the holy birth,
> And praises sing to God our King,
>   And peace to men on earth."

THE RESURRECTION OF THE NEGRO

Easter Sunday Sermon Delivered at Liberty Hall, New York City, N. Y. April 16th, 1922.

The Lord is risen! A little over nineteen hundred years ago a man came to this world called JESUS. He was sent here for the propagation of a cause—that of saving fallen humanity. When He came the world refused to hear Him; the world rejected Him; the world persecuted Him; men crucified Him. A couple days ago He was nailed to the cross of Calvary; He died; He was buried. To-day He is risen; risen the spiritual leader of creation; risen as the first fruit of them that slept. To-day that crucified Lord, that crucified Christ sees the affairs of man from His own spiritual throne on high.

After hundreds of years have rolled by, the doctrine He taught has become the accepted religion of hundreds of millions of human beings. He in His resurrection triumphed over death and the grave; He by His resurrection convinced humanity that His cause was spiritual. The world felt the truth about Jesus too late to have accepted His doctrine in His lifetime. But what was done to Jesus in His lifetime is just what is done to all reformers and reform movements. He came to change the spiritual attitude of man toward his brother. That was regarded in His day as an irregularity, even as it is regarded to-day. The one who attempts to bring about changes in the order of human society becomes a dangerous imposter upon society, and to those who control the systems of the day.

The desire to enslave others.

It has been an historic attitude of man to keep his brother in slavery—in subjection for the purpose of exploitation. When Jesus came the privileged few were taking advantage of the unfortunate masses. Because the teaching of Jesus sought to equalize the spiritual and even the temporal rights of man, those who held authority, sway and dominion sought His liberty by prosecution, sought His life by death. He was called to yield up that life for the cause He loved—because He was indeed a true reformer.

The Example Set by Christ

The example set by our Lord and Master nineteen hundred years ago is but the example that every reformer must make up his mind to follow if we are indeed to serve those to whom we minister. Service to humanity means sacrifice. That has been demonstrated by our blessed Lord and Redeemer whose resurrection we commemorate this day. As Christ triumphed nearly two thousand years ago over death and the grave, as He was risen from the dead, so do I hope that 400,000,000 Negroes of to-day will triumph over the slavishness of the past, intellectually, physically, morally and even religiously; that on this anniversary of our risen Lord, we ourselves will be risen from the slumber of the ages; risen in thought to higher ideals, to a loftier purpose, to a truer conception of life.

The Hope of the U. N. I. A.

It is the hope of the Universal Negro Improvement Association that the 400,000,000 Negroes of the world will get to realize that we are about to live a new life—a risen life—a life of knowing ourselves.

How many of us know ourselves? How many of us understand ourselves? The major number of us for ages have failed to recognize in ourselves the absolute masters of our own destiny—the absolute directors and creators of our own fate.

To-day as we think of our risen Lord may we not also think of the life He gave to us—the life that made us His instruments, His children—The life that He gave to us to make us possessors of the land that He himself created through His Father? How many of us can reach out to that higher life; that higher purpose; that creative world that says to you you are a man, a sovereign, a lord—lord of the creation? On this beautiful spring day, may we not realize that God made Nature for us; God has given it to us as our province, our dominion? May we not realize that God has created no superior being to us in this world, but Himself? May we not know that we are the true lords and creators of our own fate and of our own physical destiny?

The work of the Universal Negro Improvement Association for the past four and a half years has been that of guiding us to realize that there should be a resurrection in us, and if at no other time I trust that at this Easter-tide we will realize that there is a great need for a resurrection—a resurrection from the lethargy of the past—the sleep of the past—from that feeling that made us accept the idea and opinion that God intended that we should occupy an inferior place in the world.

No Superiority or Inferiority

Men and women of Liberty Hall, men and women of my race, do you know that the God we love, the God we adore, the God who sent His Son to this world nearly two thousand years ago never created an inferior man? That God we love, that God we worship and adore has created man in His own image, equal in every respect, wheresoever he may be; let him be white; let him be yellow; let him be red; let him be black; God has created him the equal of his brother. He is such a loving God. He is such a merciful God. He is such a God that He is no respecter of persons, that He would not in His great love create a superior race and an inferior one. The God that you worship is a God that expects you to be the equal of other men. The God that I adore is such a God and He could be no other.

Some of us seem to accept the fatalist position, the fatalist attitude, that God accorded to us a certain position and condition, and therefore there is no need trying to be otherwise. The moment you accept such an attitude, the moment you accept such an opinion, the moment you harbor such an idea, you hurl an insult at the great God who created you, because you question Him for His love, you question Him for His mercy. God has created man, and has placed him in this world as the lord of the creation, as the sovereign of everything that you see, let it be land, let it be sea, let it be the lakes, rivers and everything therein. All that you see in creation, all that you see in the world, was created by God for the use of man, and you four hundred million black souls have as much right to your possession in this world as any other race.

Created in the image of the same God we have the same common rights, and to-day I trust that there will be a spiritual and material resurrection among Negroes everywhere; that you will lift yourselves from the doubts of the past; that you will lift yourselves from the slumbers of the past, that you will lift yourselves from the lethargy of the past, and strike out in this new life—in this resurrected life—to see things as they are.

See life as Others see It.

The Universal Negro Improvement Association desires that the four hundred million members of our race see life as the other races see it. The great white race sees life in a attitude of sovereignty; the great yellow race sees life in a similar way, that is to say that man, let him be white or yellow, sees that he is master and owner and possessor of everything that God has created in this world, and given to us in Nature; and that is why by knowing himself, by understanding himself, and by understanding his God, man has gone, throughout the length and breadth of this world, conquering the very elements, harnessing Nature and making a servant of everything that God placed within his reach.

As he has done that for thousands of years pleasing God and justifying his existence, so we are appealing to the members of our race to do that now in this risen life, and if you have never made up your minds before I trust on this Easter Sunday you will do so.

Masters of your own Destiny

I repeat that God created you masters of your own destiny, masters of your own fate, and you can pay no higher tribute to your Divine Master than function as man, as He created you.

The highest compliment we can pay to our Creator; the highest respect we can pay to our risen Lord and Savior, is that of feeling that He has created us as His masterpiece; His perfect instruments of His own existence, because in us is reflected the very being of God. When it is said that we are created in His own image, we ourselves reflect His greatness, we ourselves reflect the part of God the Father, God the Son, and God the Holy Ghost, and when we allow ourselves to be subjected and create others as our superior, we hurl an insult at our Creator who made us in the fullness of ourselves.

I trust that you will so live to-day as to realize that you are masters of your own destiny, masters of your fate; if there is anything you want in this world it is for you to strike out with confidence and faith in self and reach for it, because God has created it for your happiness wheresoever you may find it in nature. Nature is bountiful; nature is resourceful, and nature is willing to obey the command of man—Man the sovereign lord; man who is supposed to hold dominion and take possession of this great world of ours.

The difference Between Strong and weak Races.

The difference between the strong and weak races is that the strong races seem to know themselves; seem to discover themselves; seem to realize and know fully that there is but a link between them and the Creator; that above them there is no other but God and anything that bears human form is but their equal in standing and to that form there should be no obeisance; there should be no regard for superiority. Because of that feeling they have been able to hold their own in this world; they have been able to take care of the situation as it confronts them in nature; but because of our lack of faith and confidence in ourselves we have caused others created in a like image to ourselves, to take advantage of us for hundreds of years.

For hundreds of years we have been the footstool of other races and nations of the earth simply because we have failed to realize to recognize and know ourselves as other men have known themselves and felt that there is nothing in the world that is above them except the influence of God.

The understanding that others have gotten out of life is the same understanding that 400,000,000 Negroes must get out of this existence of ours. I pray that a new inspiration will come to us as a race; that we will think of nature as our servant; that we will think of man as our partner through life, and go through the length and breadth of this world achieving and doing as other men, as other nations and other races.

SPEECH DELIVERED AT LIBERTY HALL N. Y. C. DURING SECOND INTERNATIONAL CONVENTION OF NEGROES AUGUST 1921

Four years ago, realizing the oppression and the hardships from which we suffered, we organized ourselves into an organization for the purpose of bettering our condition, and founding a government of our own. The four years of organization have brought good results, in that from an obscure, despised race we have grown into a mighty power, a mighty force whose influence is being felt throughout the length and breadth of the world. The Universal Negro Improvement Association existed but in name four years ago, today it is known as the greatest moving force among Negroes. We have accomplished this through unity of effort and unity of purpose, it is a fair demonstration of what we will be able to accomplish in the very near future, when the millions who are outside the pale of the Universal Negro Improvement Association will have linked themselves up with us.

By our success of the last four years we will be able to estimate the grander success of a free and redeemed Africa. In climbing the heights to where we are today, we have had to surmount difficulties, we have had to climb over obstacles, but the obstacles were stepping stones to the future greatness of this Cause we represent. Day by day we are writing a new history, recording new deeds of valor performed by this race of ours. It is true that the world has not yet valued us at our true worth but we are climbing up so fast and with such force that every day the world is changing its attitude towards us. Wheresoever you turn your eyes today you will find the moving influence of the Universal Negro Improvement Association among Negroes from all corners of the globe. We hear among Negroes the cry of "Africa for the Africans". This cry has become a positive, determined one. It is a cry that is raised simultaneously the world over because of the universal oppression that affects the Negro. You who are congregated here tonight as Delegates representing the hundreds of branches of the Universal Negro Improvement Association in different parts of the world will realize that we in New York are positive in this great desire of a free and redeemed Africa. We have established this Liberty Hall as the centre from which we send out the sparks of liberty to the four corners of the globe, and if you have caught the spark in your section, we want you to keep it a-burning for the great Cause we represent.

There is a mad rush among races everywhere towards national independence. Everywhre we hear the cry of liberty, of freedom, and a demand for democracy. In our corner of the world we are raising the cry for liberty, freedom and democracy. Men who have raised the cry for freedom and liberty in ages past have always made up their minds to die for the realization of the dream. We who are assembled in this Convention as Delegates representing the Negroes of the world give out the same spirit that the fathers of liberty in this country gave out over one hundred years ago. We give out a spirit that knows no compromise, a spirit that refuses to turn back, a spirit that says "Liberty or Death", and in prosecution of this great ideal—the ideal of a free and redeemed Africa, men may scorn, men may spurn us, and may say that we are on the wrong side of life, but let me tell you that way in which you are travelling is just the way all peoples who are free have travelled in the past. If you want liberty you yourselves must strike the blow. If you must be free you must become so through your own effort, through your own initiative. Those who have discouraged you in the past are those who have enslaved you for centuries and it is not expected that they will admit that you have a right to strike out at this late hour for freedom, liberty and democracy.

At no time in the history of the world, for the last five hundred years, was there ever a serious attempt made to free Negroes.

We have been camouflaged into believing that we were made free by Abraham Lincoln. That we were made free by Victoria of England, but up to now we are still slaves, we are industrial slaves, we are social slaves, we are political slaves, and the new Negro desires a freedom that has no boundary, no limit. We desire a freedom that will lift us to the common standard of all men, whether they be white men of Europe or yellow men of Asia, therefore, in our desire to lift ourselves to that standard we shall stop at nothing until there is a free and redeemed Africa.

I understand that just at this time while we are endeavoring to create public opinion and public sentiment in favor of a free Africa, that others of our race are being subsidized to turn the attention of the world toward a different desire on the part of Negroes, but let me tell you that we who make up this Organization know no turning back, we have pledged ourselves even unto the last drop of our sacred blood that Africa must be free. The enemy may argue with you to show you the impossibility of a free and redeemed Africa, but I want you to take as your argument the thirteen colonies of America, that once owed their sovereignity to great Britain, that sovereignity has been destroyed to make a United States of America. George Washington was not God Almighty. He was a man like any Negro in this building, and if he and his associates were able to make a free America, we too can make a free Africa. Hampden, Gladstone, Pitt and Disraeli were not the representatives of God in the person of Jesus Christ. They were but men, but in their time they worked for the expansion of the British Empire, and today they boast of a British Empire upon which "the sun never sets." As Pitt and Gladstone were able to work for the expansion of the British Empire, so you and I can work for the expansion of a great African Empire Voltaire and Mirabeau were not Jesus Christs, they were but men like ourselves. They worked and overturned the French Monarchy. They worked for the Democracy which France now enjoys, and if they were able to do that, we are able to work for a democracy in Africa. Lenine and Trotzky were not Jesus Christs, but they were able to overthrow the despotism of Russia, and today they have given to the world a Social Republic, the first of its kind. If Lenine and Trotzky were able to do that for Russia, you and I can do that for Africa. Therefore, let no man, let no power on earth, turn you from this sacred cause of liberty. I prefer to die at this moment rather than not to work for the freedom of Africa. If liberty is good for certain sets of humanity it is good for all. Black men, Colored men, Negroes have as much right to be free as any other race that God Almighty ever created, and we desire freedom that is unfettered, freedom that is unlimited, freedom that will give us a chance and opportunity to rise to the fullest of our ambition and that we cannot get in countries where other men rule and dominate.

We have reached the time when every minute, every second must count for something done, something achieved in the cause of Africa. We need the freedom of Africa now, therefore, we desire the kind of leadership that will give it to us as quickly as possible. You will realize that not only individuals, but governments are using their influence against us. But what do we care about the unrighteous influence of any government? Our cause is based upon righteousness. And anything that is not righteous we have no respect for, because God Almighty is our leader and Jesus Christ our standard bearer. We rely on them for that kind of leadership that will make us free, for it is the same God who inspired the Psalmist to write "Princes shall come out of Egypt and Ethiopia shall stretch out her hands unto God". At this moment methinks I see Ethiopia stretching forth her hands unto God, and methinks I see the Angel of God taking up the standard of the Red, the Black and the Green, and saying "Men of the Negro Race, Men of Ethiopia, follow me". Tonight we are following. We are following 400,000,000 strong. We are following with a determination that we must be free before the wreck of matter, before the crash of worlds.

It falls to our lot to tear off the shackles that bind Mother Africa. Can you do it? You did it in the Revolutionary War. You did it in the Civil War; You did it at the Battles of the Marne and Verdun; You did it in Mesopotamia. You can do it marching up the battle heights of Africa. Let the world know that 400,000,000 Negroes are prepared to die or live as free men. Despise us as much as you care. Ignore us as much as you care. We are coming 400,000,000 strong. We are coming with our woes behind us, with the memory of suffering behind us—woes and suffering of three hundred years—they shall be our inspiration. My bulwark of strength in the conflict for freedom in Africa, will be the three hundred years of persecution and hardship left behind in this Western Hemisphere. The more I remember the suffering of my fore-fathers, the more I remember the lynchings and burnings in the Soutnern States of America, the more I will fight on even though the battle seems doubtful. Tell me that I must turn back, and I laugh you to scorn. Go on! Go on! Climb ye the heights of liberty and cease not in well doing until you have planted the banner of the Red, the Black and the Green on the hilltops of Africa.

STATEMENT ON ARREST
January, 1922

I believe that true justice is to be found in the conscience of the people, and when one is deprived of it by the machinations and designs of the corrupt, there can be no better tribunal of appeal than that of public opinion, which gives voice to conscience and that is why I now appeal to the conscience of the American people for justice.

I believe that all races have their peculiar characteristics, the Jew fights the Jew, the Irish fights the Irish, the Italian fights the Italian, and so we have the Negro fighting the Negro. As a Negro schooled in the academy of adversity, with the majority of my race, I have ever had a whole-souled desire to work for the race's uplift. Recently out of slavery, we have had but a meagre chance to rise to the higher heights of human development as a people. At Emancipation we were flung upon the civilized world without a program. Unlike the Irish and the Jew we had no national aspiration of our own. We were left to the tender mercies of philanthropists and humanitarians who helped us to the best of their ability.

In the Negro's struggle to get somewhere every member of the race took a selfish course all his own. There was no group program or group interest. The only cause that held us together as a people was RELIGION. During the days of slavery Religion was the only consolation of the Negro, and then it was given to him by his masters. Immediately after the Emancipation, when the Negro was thrown back upon his own resources, the illiterate race preacher took charge of us, and with the eye of selfishness he exploited the zeal of the religious. Our emotions were worked upon by our illiterate preacher-leaders of the early days.

The masses of us having found new employment for which we received pay, were able to contribute to the partial upkeep of our own church life, thus making it profitable for the preachers of our race to exploit us in the name of God, without giving us a program by which we could redeem ourselves.

After the illiterate preacher-leader, came the illiterate race-politician who also had no program for the higher temporal development of the race. He, like the preacher, had his selfish plans of using and feeding upon the emotions of the people. These two illiterate parasites, who extracted all that was worth while from the people travelled hand in hand until we reached the first mile stone of higher intelligence, then the illiterate preacher and politician had to give way to a more intelligent class, who, unfortunately, with only a few exceptions, scattered here and there, followed and are still following in the footsteps of the old preachers and politicians to plunder and exploit the masses, because they had no vision.

And now I come to the source of my troubles, in fighting the battles of the masses. I come to the people in the role of the reformer and say to them, "Awake! the day is upon you, go forth in the name of the race and build yourselves a nation, redeem your country Africa, the land from whence you came and prove yourselves men worthy of the recognition of others".

This is the offence I have committed against the selfish Negro preachers and politicians who have for more than half a century waxed fat at the expense of the people. The shout goes up, "We cannot allow Garvey to preach his reformation and expose us to the people. The people will become too wise. We will lose our standing among them and they will not support us. We must "get" Garvey. We must discredit him before the people. We cannot do it ourselves, because we have no power. We will frame him up; we will lay traps for him; we will state all manner of charges against him to the various departments of government so that the government will prosecute him for us."

Such have been the ravings, machinations and designs of a certain class of Negro politicians and preachers against me because of my reform work of three and a half years among my people that has over four million followers.

Jews, Irish and Reformers of all races have had their troubles and trials with their own people, so I am satisfied to bear the persecution of my own that they might be free.

I trust no one from the people would believe that I could be so mean as to defraud a fellow Negro, either directly or indirectly. I have an ideal that is far above money, and that is to see my people really free.

Others of my race oppose me because they fear my influence among the people, and they judge me from their own corrupt, selfish consciences. There is an old adage that says, ''A thief does not like to see another man carrying a long bag'', and thus the dishonest ones of our preachers and politicians believing that I am of their stamp, try to embarras me by framing me up with the law.

I have had to dismiss from the employ of the Association, and caused the arrest of many dishonest preachers and politicians, and now their fraternities are out for revenge.

Poor misguided mortals! How can they, when the conscience and soul of a man cannot be incriminated from without?

The Negro Ministry needs purging and with the help of God and the people, we shall in a short while, show to the world a new race by the purification of those who lead.

I desire to say that I have a great amount of confidence in several of the preachers and politicians of my race today, but the great majority need purging, because among them we have gamblers, thieves, rogues, vagabonds and these are the ones who are fighting me at this time.

CLOSING REGRET

There has never been a Movement where the Leader has not suffered for the Cause, and not received the ingratitude of the people. I, like the rest, am prepared for the consequence.

NOTE

The UNIVERSAL NEGRO IMPROVEMENT ASSOCIATION referred to in this volume is an Organization of which Marcus Garvey is Founder and President-General. The American Headquarters of this Organization is situated at 56 West 135th Street, New York City, New York, U. S. A.

The following preamble to the constitution, of the Organization, was written by the Founder and speaks for itself:—

The Universal Negro Improvement Association and African Communities' League is a social, friendly, humanitarian, charitable, educational, institutional, constructive and expansive society, and is founded by persons, desiring to the utmost, to work for the general uplift of the Negro peoples of the world. And the members pledge themselves to do all in their power to conserve the rights of their noble race and to respect the rights of all mankind, believing always in the Brotherhood of Man and the Fatherhood of God. The motto of the organization is: "One God! One Aim! One Destiny!" Therefore, let justice be done to all mankind, realizing that if the strong oppresses the weak confusion and discontent will ever mark the path of man, but with love, faith and charity towards all the reign of peace and plenty will be heralded into the world and the generations of men shall be called Blessed.

1925

VOLUME II

MARCUS GARVEY, D. C. L.
in robe of office as President General Universal Negro Improvement Association.

A REQUEST

Not to be read with the eye or mind of prejudice, but with a righteous desire to find the truth, and to help in the friendly and peaceful solution of a grave world problem for the betterment of humanity.

PREFACE

Less than a decade ago Marcus Garvey appeared in Harlem —that crowded section of New York city which has been termed the "Mecca" of the Negroes of the world. Coming unheralded, like John the Baptist, he brought a message which carried conviction to all open-minded listeners. For many years previous Garvey had studied the hard lot of his race everywhere on God's earth. He had witnessed their political and economic oppression and noted the sufferings and discriminations which they experienced. He had himself drunk to the dregs of this bitter cup. As to Moses of old, so to Garvey, there came a clear call to duty and leadership. As a member of a race free from the spirit of retaliation and vindictiveness, with the desire to treat all mankind as brothers without regard to differences in creed, race or country, this young man, while respecting the rights and admiring the progress of alien people, resolved to make the material, political, social and spiritual development of his blood-kin wherever found, and the fostering within them of the spirit of self-reliance, and self-determination, the sole consecrated purpose of his life, to the end that the Negro might eventually take his God-given place in the fraternity of man. Whatever successes Garvey has achieved, whatever efforts have failed of fruition, all were conceived and undertaken in the sincere and honest determination to attain for his race this great goal.

Not long ago Bishop Bratton, the white Episcopal Bishop of Mississippi, wrote a book dealing with the Negro under the title "WANTED LEADERS." The following is a statement of this friendly author: "The Negro has had, and still has, the tremendous task laid upon him of making the place which is his in life; and of taking it, not because he demanded it, but because he has successfully made that place. In general, he who has to DEMAND his place has never earned it. In general, too, he who has MADE a place has deserved it, and in the long run, it will be accorded him."

This is Garvey's philosophy in a nutshell as the unbiased and discriminating reader will discern in this collection of addresses and documents, by which the man must be judged rather than by the opinions of his adversaries or the miscarriage of any of his subsidiary undertakings. Garvey knew full well that the Negro had to **make** his place. Other leaders had either **demanded** or **begged,** but this new leader, the very type which the race wanted according to Bishop Bratton, came preaching to the Negro the necessity of making a place for himself which the world would be compelled to recognize and therefore to accord him.

Advocating and promoting racial organization, racial solidarity and racial self-government, he stimulated in Negroes both in this country and abroad, the spirit of nationalism and the desire for a republic of their own in their ancestral homeland. Millions enlisted under the banner of Marcus Garvey shouting the slogan "Africa for the Africans."

His phenomenal success, as well as his philosophy expressed in his vivid speeches which were broadcast throughout civilization, challenged the attention of those alien nations which dominate Africa and the antagonism of jealous and hostile Negro leaders in the United States of America. Demetrius of Ephesus, when he saw his occupation as a maker of gods threatened by the preaching of St. Paul against idolatry, called a convention of his fellow silversmiths to conspire against the great Apostle whose success would result not only in the cessation of the worship of the goddess Diana but the annihilation of the craft which had brought them wealth. These evil fellows led a mob through the streets of the city, and threw Ephesus into such confusion that the municipal authorities were compelled to take action, resulting in the departure of St. Paul to other parts. The professional Negro leaders of America have duplicated in many ways the strategy of Demetrius. No invective was too violent to express their censure, sarcasm and abuse; no shaft of contempt, ridicule or vilification too sharp to hurl at Garvey; no name in the lexicon too bad to be applied to him. He was called fool, fanatic, freak, deceiver, agitator and described as black, ugly, and an emissary of the Ku Klux Klan. "Garvey must go" was their war cry, and after pursuing various subterranean devices they succeeded in bringing about his imprisonment and are still hoping for his subsequent deportation from America.

Whether Garvey be in prison or out of prison, whether Garvey be living or dead, his vision of a free Africa, in which Negroes shall enjoy nationhood in governments of their own, shall one day become a reality. The Almighty Ruler of men and nations has predestined and spoken it, and Marcus Garvey is but the herald of a free and restored Africa. Newspaper reporters of both races treated Garvey's philosophy and preachments with levity, magnifying and exaggerating his commercial reverses. They intentionally or unintentionally hailed him as the Moses of a wholesale "Back to Africa" pilgrimage, a scheme which Mr. Garvey has never advocated nor planned. It is to be noted, however, that many publicists of the white race are approaching the viewpoint of Garvey and suggesting to America that she give aid and fostering oversight to the attainment of the aims of the Negroes within her borders, who desire to enjoy liberty in a government of their own in Africa.

Marcus Garvey's place in Negro history is secure for all time, despite his misfortunes which have been brought about both by opposition from without and treachery from within the camp. This man has felt the pulse of his people, and inspired them with race consciousness and hope in their future destiny more than any other leader, past or present. The great movement of which he has been the creator will "go on forever" like Tennyson's Brook until it reaches its consummation, for it is, in reality, a spiritual movement. Whether Garvey be in the flesh or in the spirit, the soul of the movement which he has fanned into flame, and the spiritual yearnings of his legions of converts will not be extinguished. Shed of its present physical habiliments the soul will be reincarnated and "go marching on."

To his followers Marcus Garvey is more than a leader. To them he is the outstanding prophet as well as the trail-blazer of the universal freedom of a noble race. Outsiders fail to understand the psychology of the disciples of Garvey, but the writer of this Preface (who is not ashamed to acknowledge that he is an open follower of this great teacher, rather than one of the numerous Nicodemuses who are secret disciples for fear of criticism or opposition) finds the reason for our devotion in the conviction that no man has spoken to us like this man, inculcating pride and nobility of race and pointing out to a downtrodden and discouraged people their Star of Destiny. This writer deems it an honor to prepare the foreword for this volume and seizes the opportunity to plead before the bar of an enlightened and fair-minded public opinion for Marcus Garvey, a man greatly misunderstood in his plans for reformation. For, let it be known and acknowledged, Garvey is no idle dreamer, no empty visionary, no frenzied enthusiast, but rather a true reformer to whom it has been permitted to arouse his people from a condition of apathy growing out of hopelessness and through good report or ill to suffer persecution, yea martyrdom for his race and the cause of truth, justice and liberty.

It is not Garvey who is being weighed in the balance of the world's judgment, but his race, and particularly his jealous and unworthy rivals who conspired against him. The Greeks gave Socrates, the greatest of their philosophers, the cup of hemlock.

The Bohemians burned John Huss, their pioneer reformer, at the stake. Luther, Savonarola and others suffered imprisonment and hardships for the truth's sake, but they were God's noblemen. So with Marcus Garvey, a man of intellectual power and penetrating vision; a man who discovered the only solution of the problem confronting the Negro people the world over; and had the courage to preach the new gospel of salvation from permanent economic and political servitude. Disgruntled leaders who delight in the fleshpots of Egypt or accept gratefully, the crumbs which fall from the political master's table, while secretly protesting against the injustices of the color-line, concentrated their attack upon Garvey for proclaiming this a white man's country with a white man's government in which the black man's place is strictly limited and clearly defined, and beyond which it has been declared he "shall not pass."

While in theory they have vehemently denied this doctrine of Garvey, they have been compelled to accept it in practice, vainly hoping for the political and social millennium in America, when they shall hold the highest offices of State and enjoy the fullest privileges of society. But because Garvey believes with all his soul, and preaches with all his fervid eloquence the doctrine of racial integrity to be secured and maintained in a Negro country and government free from the pollution of miscegenation, his rivals who claim that at all hazards they must fight on American soil for their social, political and economic rights, have heaped opprobrium upon him.

Marcus Garvey in prison, with a conscience untainted from the guilt of fraud to deceive and prey upon his own people for personal gain, poor in pocket, although he has handled millions of dollars, eagerly and willingly contributed by his followers, suffers gladly with determined soul and unbroken spirit. No trace of cowardice has been found in him, even by his bitterest foes, for it is his courage to proclaim his convictions and to attempt the realization of his vision which has removed him from the sphere of his activities. Consecration of a great cause still leads to Calvary, but Calvary is not the scene of the final act of a people's redemption or of a reformer's victory. "Via Crucis" is still the path to permanent achievement, glory and honor. Garvey's work shall endure throughout the ages. His dream of "Africa for the Africans" shall surely be fulfilled.

GEORGE ALEXANDER McGUIRE,
Archbishop and Primate
of the African Orthodox Church.

New York City,
October 28, 1925.

Mrs. Amy Jacques-Garvey,
New York,

My darling Wife:

To you I have entrusted the accompanying manuscripts and other documents, articles and speeches, requesting that you publish same in book form for the information of the Negro race and those concerned, so that the public may be able to judge, impartially, the issues involved.

I request you to do this because of my implicit confidence in you, and my firm belief that you will not alter, change or distort anything that I have said contained therein.

With this belief in you I commit my thoughts, opinions, and the facts and circumstances surrounding my trial and persecution to your hands, feeling that you will, on these instructions publish them letter for letter and word for word.

With loving and affectionate confidence.

Your husband,

Marcus Garvey

Atlanta, Ga.,
May, 1925—

I have, at all times, endeavored to serve him who serves and suffers for his race; the compilation of this volume is but a slight effort in that direction. It is an honor and a pleasure to earn the confidence of one who has been, and is, so signally faithful to his sacred trust.

Amy Jacques-Garvey.

New York
October, 1925

AMY JACQUES-GARVEY

CONTENTS

PART I.

PART II.

PART III.

FULL PAGE ILLUSTRATIONS

The Philosophy and Opinions

of

MARCUS GARVEY

or

Africa for the Africans

PART I

AN APPEAL TO THE SOUL OF WHITE AMERICA

(Written October 2, 1923)

Blessed are the peacemakers; for they shall be called the children of God. Matt. V. 9.

Surely the soul of liberal, philanthropic, liberty-loving, white America is not dead.

It is true that the glamor of materialism has, to a great degree, destroyed the innocence and purity of the national conscience, but, still, beyond our politics, beyond our soulless industrialism, there is a deep feeling of human sympathy that touches the soul of white America, upon which the unfortunate and sorrowful can always depend for sympathy, help and action.

It is to that feeling that I appeal for four hundred million Negroes of the world, and fifteen millions of America in particular.

There is no real white man in America, who does not desire a solution of the Negro problem. Each thoughtful citizen has probably his own idea of how the vexed question of races should be settled. To some the Negro could be gotten rid of by wholesale butchery, by lynching, by economic starvation, by a return to slavery, and legalized oppression, while others would have the problem solved by seeing the race all herded together and kept somewhere among themselves; but a few—those in whom they have an interest—should be allowed to live around as the wards of a mistaken philanthropy; yet, none so generous as to desire to see the Negro elevated to a standard of real progress and prosperity, welded into a homogeneous whole, creating of themselves a mighty nation, with proper systems of government, civilization and culture, to mark them admissible to the fraternities of nations and races without any disadvantage.

I do not desire to offend the finer feelings and sensibilities of those white friends of the race who really believe that they are kind and considerate to us as a people; but I feel it my duty to make a real appeal to conscience and not to belief. Conscience is solid, convicting and permanently demonstrative; belief is only a matter of opinion, changeable by superior reasoning. Once the belief was that it was fit and proper to hold the Negro as a slave, and in this the bishop, priest and layman agreed. Later on, they changed their belief or opinion, but at all times, the conscience of certain people dictated to them that it was wrong and inhuman to hold human beings as slaves. It is to such a conscience in white America that I am addressing myself.

Negroes are human beings—the peculiar and strange opinions of writers, ethnologists, philosophers, scientists and anthropologists notwithstanding. They have feelings, souls, passions, ambitions, desires, just as other men, hence they **must** be considered.

Has white America really considered the Negro in the light of permanent human progress? The answer is NO.

Men and women of the white race, do you know what is going to happen if you do not think and act now? One of two things. You are either going to deceive and keep the Negro in your midst until you have perfectly completed your wonderful American civilization with its progress of art, science, industry and politics, and then, jealous of your own success and achievements in those directions, and with the greater jealousy of seeing your race pure and unmixed, cast him off to die in the whirlpool of economic starvation, thus getting rid of another race that was not intelligent enough to live, or, you simply mean by the largeness of your hearts to assimilate fifteen million Negroes into the social fraternity of an American race, that will neither be white nor black! Don't be alarmed! We must prevent both consequences. No real race loving white man wants to destroy the purity of his race, and no real Negro conscious of himself, wants to die, hence there is room for an understanding, and an adjustment. And that is just what we seek.

Let white and black stop deceiving themselves. Let the white race stop thinking that all black men are dogs and not to be considered as human beings. Let foolish Negro agitators and so-called reformers, encouraged by deceptive or unthinking white associates, stop preaching and advocating the doctrine of "social equality," meaning thereby the social intermingling of both races, intermarriages, and general social co-relationship. The two extremes will get us nowhere, other than breeding hate, and encouraging discord, which will eventually end disastrously to the weaker race.

Some Negroes, in the quest of position and honor, have been admitted to the full enjoyment of their constitutional rights. Thus we have some of our men filling high and responsible government positions, others, on their own account, have established themselves in the professions, commerce and industry. This, the casual onlooker, and even the men themselves, will say carries a guarantee and hope of social equality, and permanent racial progress. But this is the mistake. There is no progress of the Negro in America that is permanent, so long as we have with us the monster evil—prejudice.

Prejudice we shall always have between black and white, so long as the latter believes that the former is intruding upon their rights. So long as white laborers believe that black laborers are taking and holding their jobs, so long as white artisans believe that black artisans are performing the work that they should do; so long as white men and women believe that black men and women are filling the positions that they covet; so long as white political leaders and statesmen believe that black politicians and statesmen are seeking the same positions in the nation's government; so long as white men believe that black men want to associate with, and marry white women, then we will ever have prejudice, and not only prejudice, but riots, lynchings, burnings, and God to tell what next will follow!

It is this danger that drives me mad. It must be prevented. We cannot allow white and black to drift along unthinkingly toward this great gulf and danger, that is nationally ahead of us. It is because of this that I speak, and now call upon the soul of great white America to help.

It is no use putting off. The work must be done, and it must be started now.

Some people have misunderstood me. Some don't want to

understand me.   But I must explain myself for the good of the
world and humanity.

Those of the Negro race who preach social equality, and who
are working for an American race that will, in complexion, be
neither white nor black, have tried to misinterpret me to the
white public, and create prejudice against my work.   The white
public, not stopping to analyze and question the motive behind
criticisms and attacks, aimed against new leaders and their movements, condemn without even giving a chance to the criticised, to
be heard.   Those of my own race who oppose me because I
refuse to endorse their program of social arrogance and social
equality, gloat over the fact that by their misrepresentation and
underhand methods, they were able to have me convicted and
imprisoned for crime which they calculate will so discredit me
as to destroy the movement that I represent, in opposition to
their program of a new American race; but we will not now consider the opposition to a program or a movement, but state the
facts as they are, and let deep souled white America pass its
own judgment.

In another one hundred years white America will have doubled
its population; in another two hundred years it will have trebled
itself.   The keen student must realize that the centuries ahead
will bring us an over-crowded country; opportunities, as the
population grows larger, will be fewer; the competition
for bread between the people of their own class will become
keener, and so much more so will there be no room for two competitive races, the one strong, and the other weak.   To imagine
Negroes as district attorneys, judges, senators, congressmen,
assemblymen, aldermen, government clerks and officials, artisans
and laborers at work, while millions of white men starve, is to
have before you the bloody picture of wholesale mob violence
that I fear, and against which I am working.

No preaching, no praying, no presidential edict will control
the passion of hungry unreasoning men of prejudice when the
hour comes.   It will not come, I pray, in our generation, but it is
of the future that I think and for which I work.

A generation of ambitious Negro men and women, out from
the best colleges, universities and institutions, capable of filling
the highest and best positions in the nation, in industry, commerce, society and politics!   Can you keep them back?   If you
do so they will agitate and throw your constitution in your faces.
Can you stand before civilization and deny the truth of your constitution?   What are you going to do then?   You who are just
will open the door of opportunity and say to all and sundry,

"Enter in." But, ladies and gentlemen, what about the mob, that starving crowd of your own race? Will they stand by, suffer and starve, and allow an opposite, competitive race to prosper in the midst of their distress? If you can conjure these things up in your mind, then you have the vision of the race problem of the future in America.

There is but one solution, and that is to provide an outlet for Negro energy, ambition, and passion, away from the attractions of white opportunity and surround the race with opportunities of its own. If this is not done, and if the foundation for same is not laid now, then the consequence will be sorrowful for the weaker race, and disgraceful to our ideals of justice, and shocking to our civilization.

The Negro must have a country and a nation of his own. If you laugh at the idea, then you are selfish and wicked, for you and your children do not intend that the Negro shall discommode you in yours. If you do not want him to have a country and a nation of his own; if you do not intend to give him equal opportunities in yours. then it is plain to see that you mean that he must die, even as the Indian, to make room for your generations.

Why should the Negro die? Has he not served America and the world? Has he not borne the burden of civilization in this Western world for three hundred years? Has he not contributed of his best to America? Surely all this stands to his credit. But there will not be enough room and the one answer is "find a place." We have found a place; it is Africa, and as black men for three centuries have helped white men build America, surely generous and grateful white men will help black men build Africa.

And why shouldn't Africa and America travel down the ages as protectors of human rights and guardians of democracy? Why shouldn't black men help white men secure and establish universal peace? We can only have peace when we are just to all mankind; and for that peace, and for the reign of universal love, I now appeal to the soul of white America. Let the Negroes have a government of their own. Don't encourage them to believe that they will become social equals and leaders of the whites in America, without first on their own account proving to the world that they are capable of evolving a civilization of their own. The white race can best help the Negro by telling him the truth and not by flattering him into believing that he is as good as any white man without first proving the racial, national, constructive metal of which he is made.

Stop flattering the Negro about social equality, and tell him to go to work and build for himself. Help him in the direction of doing for himself, and let him know that self-progress brings its own reward.

I appeal to the considerate and thoughtful conscience of white America not to condemn the cry of the Universal Negro Improvement Association for a nation in Africa for Negroes, but to give us a chance to explain ourselves to the world. White America is too big, and when informed and touched, too liberal, to turn down the cry of the awakened Negro for "a place in the sun."

RACIAL REFORMS AND REFORMERS

Who thinks of the poor but the poor? The rich and self-satisfied are too busily engaged in the enjoyment of their own pleasures, and the patronage of their own class, to halt, to any great extent, to give the underdogs of human society a thought that would help them rise above their condition.

The missionary work that is being done to lift the unfortunate to the height of a new social order is surrounded with hypocrisy and professionalism; hence, its usefulness is not seen or felt among those to be served.

As in the struggle to lift the unfortunate poor we have no real, honest effort; so, in the struggle of race to find a place in the affairs of the world, we get very little, if any, sympathy and encouragement from the progressive and successful.

There is a vast difference between the white and black races. The two are at extremes. One is dazzlingly prosperous and progressive; the other is abjectly poor and backward.

The fight is to lift the backward and non-progressive to the common standard of progress and civilization; but, apparently, no appreciable number of the prosperous and progressive desire this change. The selfishness of class and monopoly of standing seem to dictate a prejudice of race that creates a barrier to the accepted Christian belief that all men are brothers, and a God is our common Father.

In this conflict of life each human being finds a calling. Some of us are called to be preachers, ministers of the Gospel, politicians, statesmen, industrialists, teachers, philosophers, laborers and reformers. To the reformer, above all, falls the duty or obligation of improving human society, not to the good of the selfish few, but to the benefit of the greatest number.

Persecution of Reformers

The history of the world and of the human race tells us the story of the reformer, of his trials, persecution and suffering in his efforts to reach the heart of man, in creating there a common sympathy for his brother. If it was not a Christ, it was a St. Augustine, a Luther or a Caesar, Alfred the Great, Garibaldi, Lincoln or a McSwiney. But all down the line of human progress we have met the man ready to suffer and to die to make others free while a light-hearted, selfish populace laughs at him and passes by the effort.

Twentieth century humanity and civilization have not changed much, except to their discredit, since the time of Christ, Caesar and Lincoln. Christ sought to help and save a world of human souls, and His fellows nailed Him to a cross; Caesar, in the fullness of his human love and his patriotism to Rome, fought for the elevation of his countrymen, and the ascendency of his country, but there was one to strike him even to the fall at the base of Pompey's statue; Lincoln, as stated, had a burning love for all humanity, not desiring to see half slave and half free, but all free, for the practice of which love he was downed by an assassin, and withal we have not gone far in solving the peace of the world. We are still in chaos. We are still drifing toward the universal pit of destruction, and that is why we need reformers now, those who are not afraid to suffer and die for a cause; men, despite the opposition of an organized social system, of a malicious and malignant school of oppression, who will stand up for the good of the larger humanity, and tell the world of its mistakes and blunders.

Revenge Guiding Force of Human Destruction

And it is here that we must call the attention of the white race to the wrong and injury that they are inflicting upon the rest of the world. It is all well for those who revel in their immediate power to turn a deaf ear to the cries of the suffering races, to oppress, exploit, and even murder them, but what of the consequence?

We live not by ourselves. It is either Providence, God, the First Cause or Nature—any one you wish to call it—that will call us to our judgment, not so much in the world to come, as in the retribution of our own lives; and when that time comes what will the white, once powerful and oppressive race say if another should be lifted to power and supported there by the Grace of Divine Authority?

History, religious and profane, have so many beautiful lessons to teach that none of us should doubt the wonders of God or Nature. In the one age or period the one race or people rule and triumph, while the other stalks under the heel of oppression— the Jews in Egypt, the Britons in Rome, the Negroes in America —to say nothing of the rest in Europe and Asia who have had similar experiences. What do we gather therefrom, but the spirit of revenge, a spirit that has traveled up to the twentieth century and which seems to be the guiding force of human destruction?

Why we have not gone farther in our civilization is because we are still fearful and suspicious of each other. We have done each other so many wrongs and inflicted so many injuries and injustices that we are just afraid to loosen up, believing that the other fellow's time will come. It is natural, because of sin, for the robber to protect his loot; so do we find reason for even the powerful races to still crush and grind the less fortunate. The murderer has to continue murdering so as to protect his own life, but generally there is a hangman; so in the eternal fitness of things all human power hath an end, today for me, tomorrow for thee.

Good Will to All Will Save World

Realizing all that has been written is reason why the world's greatest reformers strive to make a human race with love and sympathies, not having the one group, whether white or black, hating the other, but living in peace, good will and brotherly love without endangering the rights of either. It is such a reformation that will save the world; not the building of battleships, guns, aeroplanes or the invention of deadly gas, but a reasonable coming together of the human groups that will rescue us from our human doom.

If the great statesmen and religious leaders of the world would only forget the selfishness of their own races, and call their conferences and give out their edicts not from the Anglo-Saxon, Teutonic, Celtic or Anglo-American point of view, but from the viewpoint of all humanity considered, then we would indeed come face to face with a new world evolving a new civilization.

Friends, white cannot prosper to the disadvantage of black. Yellow cannot prosper to the disadvantage of brown, for in so doing we but pile up confusion and remorse for our children. This is history; it tells the tales of the past, it will of the future. Then why not make the future right?

Few the reformers are who struggle for such an ideal. Here and there a white man and a woman, a yellow, brown and black man, while the great army of selfish pleasure-seekers and their slaves march on to their doom. Gandhi in prison, a George V. in his castle; a Congo native massacred; an Albert of Belgium drinking his wine; a Senegalese Negro kicked on the plantation of his master; a Poincare driving in his landau in the Champs d'-Elysees; a Negro lynched in Georgia; a Wilson, Harding or Coolidge talking about a world court or league; a Chinaman shot down at Shantung and the Emperor of Japan drinking tea in his palace at Tokio; a Jew murdered on the borders of Eastern Europe, and His Holiness the Pope seeing no further than the Vatican, will not save the human race. But that lonely man or woman, of whatsoever race, who cries out for justice to all humanity, including Europe with its whites, Asia with its browns and yellows, Africa with its blacks, and America and the rest of the world with their mixed populations, will, even though there be persecution and injustice done to him, bring succor and aid,

late though it be, to the rest of us mortals that we may see everlasting life.

Black Reform

There is a fraternity of humanitarians, unknown though it be,
that is working for a true solution of our human problems. Wil-
berforce, Clarkston, Buxton, Lovejoy, John Brown, white though
they were, had the vision of the future of men. They worked for
the freedom of black humanity, therefore, in the midst of our
sorrow and in the racial thought of revenge come up the spirits
of such great humanitarians that silence the tongue of evil; as
in the white race, so among the blacks, our beautiful spirits stand
out, for wasn't there a Douglass, a Washington and even the
typical Uncle Tom?

We hope that the humanitarians of today of all races will
continue to work in furtherance of that ideal—justice, liberty,
freedom and true human independence, knowing thereby no color
or no race.

The Negro of the world, and America in particular, needs a
national homeland with opportunities and privileges like all other
peoples. If we work and fight for this why should others jeer
and laugh at us? Why should they say that we are "ignorant"
and "benighted"? Was it ignorance to free Britain from the
grasp of the invader? Was it ignorance to free America from
the heel of the oppressor? Was it ignorance to liberate France
from the yoke of the tyrant? Surely not. Then why is it ignorant
for Negroes to work for the restoration of their country, Africa?

Broad and liberal-minded white men, although surrounded by
the selfishness of a material environment, will not condemn and
persecute the work of even black reform, but for justice's sake
give unto each and everyone his due.

THE CRIME OF INJUSTICE
(Written from The Tombs Prison, August 2, 1923)

There is no crime like that of injustice, and it is the cause that will ultimately bring about the ruin of the world.

Men in all ages have demonstrated against this evil, the responsibility for which has caused so many human changes. When we think of the injustice of Henry to John, we, without much difficulty, find the reason of the latter for practicing his revenge upon the former. And so, right through the affairs of the human race, we can trace the cause for the perpetuation of revenge one upon the other. But the crime is not traceable to individuals only, but to races and nations as well.

The history of the world will show that most, if not all, of the differences between races and nations have been caused through the infliction of injustice of the one race or nation upon the other.

In the family life the son will avenge the injury done to the father by the neighbor, and so on we go to the third, fourth and fifth generations. In the national life the free and developed nation will revenge the crime of the other when it finds itself strong enough to do so, as in the case of France now revenging Germany for the war of 1870, and so of the Germans revenging the French, or the French revenging the English, of the slave revenging his master.

Those who desire the peace of the world and the permanent settlement of all our human ills should not seek to do so by mere economic and political conferences, but first by the establishment of real justice to all men. Not the justice that is based upon the like or dislike of the individual, race or nation, but justice for justice's sake!

There are but few, if any, of the people of the world who have and practise the true sense of justice.

If we were permitted to see ourselves as we administer justice to others, we would be surprised to realize, if we believe ourselves Christians, how near we approach hell in the exhibition of our supposed good virtues.

The World of Wrong
The world is full of wrong and injustice, the continuation of which will change our civilization and life beyond present recognition. We will go from Czarism, Kaiserism, Monarchism, Republicanism, Sovietism to God knows what; all for the chance of getting "justice." But, although the world in its political and social

systems changes to meet the justice of man, we will find ourselves farther and farther from the ideal.

If we take the political and social systems of England we will find the people divided into many classes, each fighting against the other, under the belief that the crime of injustice is practised against it; and so also of France, Italy and America.

As we witness the struggle of injustice among the classes, so do we have it among the races. No one will gainsay the fact that the injustice of the one race to the Japanese makes them resentful, restless and revengeful, and the same injustice to the Indian and the Negro will ultimately drive them to a union of spirit that may yet develop a new civilization and a new ideal.

As Negroes, no one suffers from the infliction of injustice more than we do. It is practised against us in every walk of life—politically, socially, industrially, educationally, commercially, judicially, and even religiously.

For three hundred years the Negro has cried out against the crime of injustice, and he is no nearer being heard today on his own account than when he first raised his voice. In the general order of things the weak suffers most from the crime of injustice. The strong man will be unjust to the weak, and the strong nation will in like manner oppress the less fortunate. The whole situation, it seems, therefore, hangs on the developed strength of the individual, race or nation. It is the realization of this that causes the Universal Negro Improvement Association to preach the propaganda of "coming together" among Negroes.

If we must have justice, we must be strong; if we must be strong, we must come together; if we must come together, we can only do so through the system of organization.

When the Britons were weak and scattered, they received no justice. When the French were weak and divided, they suffered in the same manner; but with unity, strength was developed, and with strength came national, racial justice. When we can successfully bring together the majority of the four hundred million Negroes of the world, we will have not only racial, collective and individual justice, but national justice as well.

The best that we can do is to work and pray for the hastening of the time when we, too, will have become a united and strong people, able, by our force of character and achievement, to demand not sympathy but justice from all men, races and nations. Let us not waste time in breathless appeals to the strong while we are weak, but lend our time, energy and effort to the accumulation of strength among ourselves by which we will voluntarily attract the attention of others.

Jack Johnson, Harry Wills and Firpo attract the attention of other men because they have developed their bodies and muscles to protect themselves against the attack of their rivals. England, France, Italy, Japan and America attract the attention of other nations because of their powerful military and naval strength; and so the Negro can only arrest the attention of the rest of mankind in the quest for justice, for fair play, when we can produce to the world the "real stuff" that makes man feel, if he doesn't hear.

There can be no argument against the Negro's acquisition of strength and power. This is needed, not only in our racial life but in our national life. We must have a country—and government—of our own. We must make our own impression upon a world of injustice and convince men by the same means or methods of reasoning as others by their strength do.

No Justice But Strength

Don't be deceived; there is no justice but strength. In other words, in our material civilization might is right, and if you must be heard and respected you have to accumulate, nationally, in Africa, those resources that will compel unjust man to think twice before he acts.

Our consolation should be, however, that each and every race will have its day; and there is no doubt that the Negro's day is drawing near. We may not trust to the abnormal strength and progress of others to believe that the world and humanity are settled, for in the twinkling of an eye all creation can pass away, and men, races and nations be no more. In a short hour Pompeii fell, and in a shorter time still Germany was crushed beyond the hope of immediate resurrection, to say nothing of ancient Greece and Rome. What has happened in the past to other races and nations will happen again, so let us work and pray, for surely our day of triumph and authority to mete out justice will come and Africa may yet teach the higher principles of justice, love and mercy, yea, true brotherhood.

Some of us become at times drunk with our power and authority, and, in the fullness of our narrow conceit, wreak our vengeance upon others under the guise of justice. Oh, how wanton is man! Irresponsible in his conceit! Vain in the realization of his power! Even vicious to the point of vengeance! But we glory in the fact that he is only man, and in the natural course of life will pass away, the wretch, with injustice written upon his soul, like the dog, to be unwept and unmourned, in the higher spiritual sense; to be another subject of hell, perdition and the dust from which no pleasant memory springs.

Some of us think that we live only in the physical; but are we not really conscious of a higher life? If there is, and there is, then why die like the dog? Why not die like a Christ, a John the Baptist, a St. Augustine, a Caesar, at the base of Pompey's statue, a Joan of Arc, with the fagots around her; a Robert Emmet, with his head upon the block; a Terrence MacSwiney, in Mountjoy jail. Oh, what honor and glory we give to man for the service he renders unselfishly to his brother! With what disgust we curse the wretch who lives for self, and for those of his kind around him; yes, he who has no knowledge of truth, whose soul is filled with corruption, bribery and injustice!

Negroes, shall we not choose between right and wrong? Shall we not pattern the lives of those men, races and nations that have prospered by justice? Surely we shall, for in so doing we will have removed ourselves from the curse of a heartless, sinful, unjust world to a new temporal sphere, where man will live in peace and die in the consciousness of a new resurrection.

Such will be Africa's day, when a new light will encircle the earth, and black men lift their hands to their God and Princes come out of our country. For this we will not give up hope, but fight and struggle on, until the Angel of Peace and Love appears.

WORLD MATERIALISM

The wonderful force of organization is today making itself felt in every branch of human effort. Whether in industry, society, politics or war it is the force of organization that tells; hence, I can advise no better step toward racial salvation than organization among us.

We have been harassed, trampled upon, and made little of, because of our unfortunate condition of disorganization. The disorganization of our race for hundreds of years made us easy prey to those who sought profit out of human slavery, and with a similar disorganization we are bound to lose out in the great scramble of life for the survival of the fittest group.

The Universal Negro Improvement Association is a movement that seeks unlimited racial union and co-operation. We desire to draw humanity closer together than it has been before, for we realize that with East pulling against West, North pulling against South, there will be nothing left to us but utter ruin.

We can well imagine ourselves as one great united people, having one aim, believing in one God and having one destiny. To see four hundred millions of us standing together as one man is the desire of those of us who lead the Universal Negro Improvement Association.

It is true that twentieth century materialism has so scattered the interests of races and nations that the realization of human ideals becomes more remote, but we dare not sink or destroy holy principles because of the wantonness and soullessness of our age. Time cannot save itself; it is for us to save and redeem Time; hence, the work that lies before us is not so much to identify ourselves with the scattered purpose and greed of others, but to create for ourselves a central ideal and make our lives conform to it in the singling out of a racial life that shall know no end.

It is unfortunate that we should find ourselves at this time the only disorganized group. Others have had the advantage of organization for centuries, so what seems to them unnecessary, from a racial point of view, becomes necessary to us, who have had to labor all along under the disadvantage of being scattered without a racial aim or purpose.

No race or people can well survive without an aim or purpose. We must know beforehand the purpose of our existence. Our racial program of today is a united, emancipated and improved people.

We need improvement in every line—socially, religiously, industrially, educationally and politically. We need the creation of a common standard among ourselves that will fit us for companionship and equitable competition with others.

Man and God to Settle the World

The world is not in the disposition to divide the spoils of materialism, but on the contrary every group is seeking the aggrandizement of self at the expense of those who have lost or who ignore the trend of human effort in the direction of self-preservation.

The Negro, surrounded as he is, has no other alternative than going forward in the atmosphere of racial self-interest, working for the generation of the present and providing for those of our posterity. In the service of race the Universal Negro Improvement Association finds its program, and for its advocacy or promotion we offer no apology.

It is foolish for us to believe that the world can settle itself on chance. It is for man and God to settle the world. God acts indifferently and His plan and purpose is generally worked out through the agency of human action. In His directed, inspired prophecy He promised that Ethiopia's day would come, not by the world changing towards us, but by our stretching out our hands unto Him. It doesn't mean the mere physical test, but the universal and independent effort to surround ourselves with the full glory of man.

No human apologies are needed for the moving or going forward of any people, so none will expect that we will apologize for the efforts we are making to unite our race the world over, and the creating for ourselves of a political superstate wherein we will find the representation and protection that will make us secure in the selfish adjustment of a material world.

Go ahead, Negroes, and organize yourselves! You are serving your race and guaranteeing to posterity of our own an existence which otherwise will be denied them.

Ignore the traps of persuasion, advice and alien leadership. No one can be as true to you as you can be to yourself. To suggest that there is no need for Negro racial organization in a well-planned and arranged civilization like that of the twentieth century is but to, by the game of deception, lay the trap for the destruction of a people whose knowledge of life is incomplete, owing to their misunderstanding of man's purpose in creation.

Vision of New Life

With the vision of a new life the Universal Negro Improvement Association shall direct the course of the four hundred million members of our race, enemies from within and from without notwithstanding.

The campaign of abuse against your leaders and their imprisonment is but a part of the plan to harass and discourage you on the way towards destiny. But no sober-minded Negro will allow himself to be fooled by the design of the wicked. The wicked we have always had, and will ever have. The wicked and unjust have opposed reforms in every age and under all circumstances. They crucified a Christ and drove His apostles from pillar to post. They made, by their wicked acts, martyrs of those who have lived and died for a principle and an idea; so let them go on. They, too, in this age shall drink the bitter dregs of sorrow and remorse, even as succeeding generations of those who crucified Christ and persecuted His disciples have become the cursed creatures of righteousness. Let our traitors sell themselves to the propaganda of the enemy who seeks to destroy the race! They, too, like the character of old, will find no use for the bits of silver.

Let us pray for our enemies, whosoever they be! Let us all over the world pray daily for God's handling of our enemies! Pray hard and earnestly, at least twice a day, for God's dealing with our enemies. At twelve o'clock midday and twelve o'clock midnight let us in silent prayer for thirty seconds send up our supplications and appeal to God for the correction of those who oppose us even against His divine will that we should stretch out our hands unto Him.

Surely God will answer our prayers against the wicked and unjust and strengthen us for the great work that must be done in His name and to His glory. Remember, our duty is to be firm in the Faith.

Personally, I am glad to suffer for the cause. My contribution to the race and to Africa is small, but it is gladly given without any regrets. Some of us will contribute through our ability and our lives, others through service of other kind; but whatever it be, let us give it freely.

Do not falter or faint by the wayside, but let us, with confidence in ourselves and our God go forth in the call for service to our race and to Ethiopia.

WHO AND WHAT IS A NEGRO?
(Written April 16, 1923)

The New York World under date of January 15, 1923, published a statement of Drs. Clark Wissler and Franz Boaz (the latter a professor of anthropology at Columbia University), confirming the statement of the French that Moroccan and Algerian troops used in the invasion of Germany were not to be classified as Negroes, because they were not of that race. How the French and these gentlemen arrive at such a conclusion is marvelous to understand, but I feel it is the old-time method of depriving the Negro of anything that would tend to make him recognized in any useful occupation or activity.

The custom of these anthropologists is: whenever a black man, whether he be Moroccan, Algerian, Senegalese or what not, accomplishes anything of importance, he is no longer a Negro. The question, therefore, suggests itself, "Who and what is a Negro?" The answer is, "A Negro is a person of dark complexion or race, who has not accomplished anything and to whom others are not obligated for any useful service." If the Moroccans and Algerians were not needed by France at this time to augment their occupation of Germany or to save the French nation from extinction, they would have been called Negroes as usual, but now that they have rendered themselves useful to the higher appreciation of France they are no longer members of the Negro race, but can be classified among a higher type as made out by the two professors above mentioned. Whether these professors or France desire to make the Moroccans other than Negroes we are satisfied that their propaganda before has made these people to understand that their destiny is linked up with all other men of color throughout the world, and now that the hundreds of millions of darker peoples are looking toward one common union and destiny through the effort of universal co-operation, we have no fear that the Moroccans and Algerians will take care of the situation in France and Germany peculiar to the interest of Negroes throughout the world.

Let us not be flattered by white anthropologists and statesmen who, from time to time, because of our success here, there or anywhere, try to make out that we are no longer members of the Negro race. If we were Negroes when we were down under the heel of oppression then we will be Negroes when we are up and liberated from such thraldom.

The Moroccans and Algerians have a splendid opportunity of proving the real worth of the Negro in Europe, and who to tell that one day Africa will colonize Europe, even as Europe has been endeavoring to colonize the world for hundreds of years.

Negroes Robbed of Their History

The white world has always tried to rob and discredit us of our history. They tell us that Tut-Ankh-Amen, a King of Egypt, who reigned about the year 1350 B. C. (before Christ), was not a Negro, that the ancient civilization of Egypt and the Pharaohs was not of our race, but that does not make the truth unreal. Every student of history, of impartial mind, knows that the Negro once ruled the world, when white men were savages and barbarians living in caves; that thousands of Negro professors at that time taught in the universities in Alexandria, then the seat of learning; that ancient Egypt gave to the world civilization and that Greece and Rome have robbed Egypt of her arts and letters, and taken all the credit to themselves. It is not surprising, however, that white men should resort to every means to keep Negroes in ignorance of their history, it would be a great shock to their pride to admit to the world today that 3,000 years ago black men excelled in government and were the founders and teachers of art, science and literature. The power and sway we once held passed away, but now in the twentieth century we are about to see a return of it in the rebuilding of Africa; yes, a new civilization, a new culture, shall spring up from among our people, and the Nile shall once more flow through the land of science, of art, and of literature, wherein will live black men of the highest learning and the highest accomplishments.

Professor George A. Kersnor, head of the Harvard-Boston expedition to the Egyptian Soudan, returned to America early in 1923 and, after describing the genius of the Ethiopians and their high culture during the period of 750 B. C. to 350 A. D. in middle Africa, he declared the Ethiopians were not African Negroes. He described them as dark colored races . . . showing a mixture of black blood. Imagine a dark colored man in middle Africa being anything else but a Negro. Some white men, whether they be professors or what not, certainly have a wide stretch of imagination. The above statements of the professors support my contention at all times that the prejudice against us as Negroes is not because of color, but because of our condition. If black men throughout the world as a race will render themselves so independent and useful as to be sought out by other race groups it will simply mean that all the problems of race will be smashed to pieces and the Negro would be regarded like anybody else—a man to be respected and admired.

The Hybrids of South Africa

More than a year ago the natives of South Africa started to press the limited white population to the wall in the demand of "Africa for the Africans." The prejudiced Boers and others were willing then to let down the color bar and admit to their ranks, socially and otherwise, the half-breed colored people whom they once classified as impossible hybrids, to be despised by both whites and natives. Now they are endeavoring to make common cause with these so-called half-breeds of South Africa, so as to strengthen their position against the threatening ascendency of the demand for a free and redeemed Africa for the blacks of the world.

In an editorial dated March 29, 1923, the Abantu-Batho of Johannesburg states among other things:

"The Cape colored people have been promised absorption by politicians, particularly those of the Dutch race. . . . Indeed we are suspicious that all this talk about absorption is a political trap which has been set to capture the colored vote in the Cape. It is the business of the politician to strengthen his position by getting as many supporters as possible. To do this, he must, of necessity, be diplomatic. That is to say, he must know how to get around the people, and the only way to get around the people is to put before them a beautiful picture of what one intends to do. There can be no doubt that to the Cape colored people the idea of their absorption by the white race presents a beautiful ideal for the attainment of which they are prepared to sacrifice everything. They cannot be blamed for this. As a distinct community they have no past, no traditions, no laws, and no language which things constitute the pride of every race of mankind. These sons of Hagar are in an awkward position. They despise the people of Hagar, because Hagar's people are despised by the people of Abraham. They are suffering because of the gulf that exists between their mothers' people and those of their fathers. . . . The difference between the treatment meted out to the colored people and the Africans does not in any way signify that the whites have more consideration for the colored people. It will be remembered that when Lord Selborne left this country in 1909, he warned the white people of South Africa against putting the Cape colored people in the same category as Africans because that would unite the two sections of the African peoples to fight for their common rights. Since then the policy has been to differentiate in the treatment of the two sections so as to make combined action impossible. Thus it is not saying too much to aver that the real object of the white race is to make the Cape colored people a buffer between the Africans and Europeans. As a buffer, the Cape colored people can never have the same rights as whites. Now the question is: What are they to do? Will they be satisfied with a position of this kind? Or will they follow the lead of our cousins in America and classify themselves as Africans? In our opinion this is the only way to the salvation of the Cape colored people. They are Africans and not Europeans. And the sooner they realize it the better."

White people will seek every opportunity to fraternize with any race in the world, even the one despised yesterday, if by so doing they can strengthen their position, whether it be in Europe, Africa or elsewhere, but it is for 400,000,000 people who have been discriminated against throughout the world to take a decided stand and for once we will agree with the American white man, that one drop of Negro blood makes a man a Negro? So that 100 per cent. Negroes and even 1 per cent. Negroes will stand together as one mighty whole to strike a universal blow for liberty and recognition in Africa.

AN APPEAL TO THE CONSCIENCE OF THE BLACK RACE TO SEE ITSELF

It is said to be a hard and difficult task to organize and keep together large numbers of the Negro race for the common good. Many have tried to congregate us, but have failed, the reason being that our characteristics are such as to keep us more apart than together.

The evil of internal division is wrecking our existence as a people, and if we do not seriously and quickly move in the direction of a readjustment it simply means that our doom becomes imminently conclusive.

For years the Universal Negro Improvement Association has been working for the unification of our race, not on domestic-national lines only, but universally. The success which we have met in the course of our effort is rather encouraging, considering the time consumed and the environment surrounding the object of our concern.

It seems that the whole world of sentiment is against the Negro, and the difficulty of our generation is to extricate ourselves from the prejudice that hides itself beneath, as well as above, the action of an international environment.

Prejudice is conditional on many reasons, and it is apparent that the Negro supplies, consciously or unconsciously, all the reasons by which the world seems to ignore and avoid him. No one cares for a leper, for lepers are infectious persons, and all are afraid of the disease, so, because the Negro keeps himself poor, helpless and undemonstrative, it is natural also that no one wants to be of him or with him.

Progress and Humanity

Progress is the attraction that moves humanity, and to whatever people or race this "modern virtue" attaches itself, there will you find the splendor of pride and self-esteem that never fail to win the respect and admiration of all.

It is the progress of the Anglo-Saxons that singles them out for the respect of all the world. When their race had no progress or achievement to its credit, then, like all other inferior peoples, they paid the price in slavery, bondage, as well as through prejudice. We cannot forget the time when even the ancient Briton was regarded as being too dull to make a good Roman slave, yet today the influence of that race rules the world.

It is the industrial and commercial progress of America that causes Europe and the rest of the world to think appreciatively of the Anglo-American race. It is not because one hundred and ten million people live in the United States that the world is attracted to the republic with so much reverence and respect—a reverence and respect not shown to India with its three hundred millions, or to China with its four hundred millions. Progress of and among any people will advance them in the respect and appreciation of the rest of their fellows. It is such a progress that the Negro must attach to himself if he is to rise above the prejudice of the world.

The reliance of our race upon the progress and achievements of others for a consideration in sympathy, justice and rights is like a dependence upon a broken stick, resting upon which will eventually consign you to the ground.

Self-Reliance and Respect

The Universal Negro Improvement Association teaches our race self-help and self-reliance, not only in one essential, but in all those things that contribute to human happiness and well-being. The disposition of the many to depend upon the other races for a kindly and sympathetic consideration of their needs, without making the effort to do for themselves, has been the race's standing disgrace by which we have been judged and through which we have created the strongest prejudice against ourselves.

There is no force like success, and that is why the individual makes all efforts to surround himself throughout life with the evidence of it. As of the individual, so should it be of the race and nation. The glittering success of Rockefeller makes him a power in the American nation; the success of Henry Ford suggests him as an object of universal respect, but no one knows and cares about the bum or hobo who is Rockefeller's or Ford's neighbor. So, also, is the world attracted by the glittering success of races and nations, and pays absolutely no attention to the bum or hobo race that lingers by the wayside.

The Negro must be up and doing if he will break down the prejudice of the rest of the world. Prayer alone is not going to improve our condition, nor the policy of watchful waiting. We must strike out for ourselves in the course of material achievement, and by our own effort and energy present to the world those forces by which the progress of man is judged.

A Nation and Country

The Negro needs a nation and a country of his own, where he can best show evidence of his own ability in the art of human progress. Scattered as an unmixed and unrecognized part of alien nations and civilizations is but to demonstrate his imbecility, and point him out as an unworthy derelict, fit neither for the society of Greek, Jew nor Gentile.

It is unfortunate that we should so drift apart, as a race, as not to see that we are but perpetuating our own sorrow and disgrace in failing to appreciate the first great requisite of all peoples—organization.

Organization is a great power in directing the affairs of a race or nation toward a given goal. To properly develop the desires that are uppermost, we must first concentrate through some system or method, and there is none better than organization. Hence, the Universal Negro Improvement Association appeals to each and every Negro to throw in his lot with those of us who, through organization, are working for the universal emancipation of our race and the redemption of our common country, Africa.

No Negro, let him be American, European, West Indian or African, shall be truly respected until the race as a whole has emancipated itself, through self-achievement and progress, from universal prejudice. The Negro will have to build his own government, industry, art, science, literature and culture, before the world will stop to consider him. Until then, we are but wards of a superior race and civilization, and the outcasts of a standard social system.

The race needs workers at this time, not plagiarists, copyists and mere imitators; but men and women who are able to create, to originate and improve, and thus make an independent racial contribution to the world and civilization.

Monkey Apings of "Leaders"

The unfortunate thing about us is that we take the monkey apings of our "so-called leading men" for progress. There is no progress in Negroes aping white people and telling us that they represent the best in the race, for in that respect any dressed monkey would represent the best of its species, irrespective of the creative matter of the monkey instinct. The best in a race is not reflected through or by the action of its apes, but by its ability to create of and by itself. It is such a creation that the Universal Negro Improvement Association seeks.

Let us not try to be the best or worst of others, but let us make the effort to be the best of ourselves. Our own racial critics criticise us as dreamers and "fanatics," and call us "benighted" and "ignorant," because they lack racial backbone. They are unable to see themselves creators of their own needs. The slave instinct has not yet departed from them. They still believe that they can only live or exist through the good graces of their "masters." The good slaves have not yet thrown off their shackles; thus, to them, the Universal Negro Improvement Association is an "impossibility."

It is the slave spirit of dependence that causes our "so-called leading men" (apes) to seek the shelter, leadership, protection and patronage of the "master" in their organization and so-called advancement work. It is the spirit of feeling secured as good servants of the master, rather than as independents, why our modern Uncle Toms take pride in laboring under alien leadership and becoming surprised at the audacity of the Universal Negro Improvement Association in proclaiming for racial liberty and independence.

But the world of white and other men, deep down in their hearts, have much more respect for those of us who work for our racial salvation under the banner of the Universal Negro Improvement Association, than they could ever have, in all eternity, for a group of helpless apes and beggars who make a monopoly of undermining their own race and belittling themselves in the eyes of self-respecting people, by being "good boys" rather than able men.

Surely there can be no good will between apes, seasoned beggars and independent minded Negroes who will at least make an effort to do for themselves. Surely, the "dependents" and "wards" (and may I not say racial imbeciles?) will rave against and plan the destruction of movements like the Universal Negro Improvement Association that expose them to the liberal white minds of the world as not being representative of the best in the Negro, but, to the contrary, the worst. The best of a race does not live on the patronage and philanthropy of others, but makes an effort to do for itself. The best of the great white race doesn't fawn before and beg black, brown or yellow men; they go out, create for self and thus demonstrate the fitness of the race to survive; and so the white race of America and the world will be informed that the best in the Negro race is not the class of beggars who send out to other races piteous appeals annually for donations to maintain their coterie, but the groups within us that are honestly striving to do for themselves with the voluntary help and appreciation of that class of other races that is reasonable, just and liberal enough to give to each and every one a fair chance in the promotion of those ideals that tend to greater human progress and human love.

The work of the Universal Negro Improvement Association is clear and clean-cut. It is that of inspiring an unfortunate race

with pride in self and with the determination of going ahead in
the creation of those ideals that will lift them to the unprejudiced
company of races and nations. There is no desire for hate or
malice, but every wish to see all mankind linked into a common
fraternity of progress and achievement that will wipe away the
odor of prejudice, and elevate the human race to the height of
real godly love and satisfaction.

CHRIST THE GREATEST REFORMER
Speech Delivered at Liberty Hall, New York, U. S. A., December 24, 1922.

When man had fallen in sin from his spiritual kinship to his Creator and disgust reigned even in heaven among the angels and the Holy One, who brought out of chaos the great universe, there sprang up divine sympathy, divine love—a sympathy and love within the Trinity caused the Son of God to vouchsafe Himself as the Redeemer of mankind, as the Redeemer of the world. He betook to Himself, with the authority of His Father, the duty, the work, the labor, the sacrifice, to bring man nearer to his Creator, to bring man back to his God.

The angels on that first Christmas morn notified the world that the Christ was to be born. He did not of Himself come down in His spiritual image from the heaven on high, but for the purpose of drawing Himself nearer man He took on the flesh and was born of a virgin woman, and in that stable at .Bethlehem; the whole world, through the message of the angels, was told of the great happening and men journeyed from far and near to see the Christ. To some, His birth was a disappointment, because He was born lowly; He was born amid poor conditions and circumstances; He was not born of the reigning household; He was born only of a carpenter, an humble laborer, and therefore to many His birth was a disappointment. The prophets foretold the birth of Christ; the prophets foretold the birth of the Redeemer, and men were looking for Him everywhere. The race to which he was to be born expected a redeemer in pomp and glory, and when He came in a manger they were disappointed; they were disgusted and they denied Him as the Christ. They said He was not the Christ; He was not the Promised One; He was not the Son of God; He was an imposter; but others who had faith believed that He was the Christ. And the lowly babe that was born to us in the sinful world 1922 years ago grew up amidst the surroundings of prejudice, amidst the surroundings of disgust and dissatisfaction to take on His work, to perform His labor as the Christ, as the redeemer of man, as the redeemer of the world.

Christ As a Living Example to Man

The man who took on flesh, physical as ours, moved among us even as we go about our daily business and occupation today. They could not believe that He was the Son of God, but in Him there was that which no man knew, which no man had; in Him was a spotless soul, was a spotless character never yet known to

the world beyond the Christ in all God's creation. There never
came into the world a character like Jesus, pure, spotless, im-
maculate, divine like unto God, as God would have each of us
to be. When God created man and breathed into his nostrils the
breath of life, when God gave to man a living soul, God expected
that man would live the spiritual life of the Christ, and when
man sinned, when man fell from grace, God became disgusted,
God became dissatisfied. If we could see the sufferings of Christ,
if we could see the patience of Christ, if we could see the very
crucifixion of Christ, then we would see the creature, the being
spiritual that God would have us be; and knowing ourselves as
we do, we could well realize how far we are from God. For man
to see his God, for man to face His judgment and become one of
the elect of the High Divine, of the Holy One, is for man to
live the life of the Christ—the spotless life, the holy life, the life
without sin, and that is a journey that every one in the Christian
world is called upon to make. If we cannot make it, we cannot
expect to see our God. Man has fallen so low, man has fallen
so far from his high estate, as created and given him by God,
that even now man does not know himself except in the physical;
but the physical does not make the man complete. Man is part
physical as well as part spiritual; the physical life we live here
to our satisfaction, the spiritual life we give to God when He
calls us. And how many of us in the world today, if called for the
spiritual life, will give that life as spotless as Jesus by His
example taught? When we look at the world today we think
of sin, we think of injustice, of iniquity, a world where man because of his strength, because of his advantage abuses the rights
of his brother. When we look upon the oceans of injustice that
are placed in the path of the weak, how much must we not realize
the far distance that we are from God and the far distance that
we are from the man Christ, who tried to teach us the life by
which we should see salvation, the life that He came to redeem.

His Doctrine Rejected by the Classes

Christ brought a mission to the world. It was that of love to
all mankind; that which taught man to love his brother, to be
charitable, and when He taught that doctrine after He had
assumed the form of manhood, what did the world do to Him?
The world derided Him; the world scoffed at Him; they called
Him all kinds of names. He was an imposter; He was a disturber of the public peace; He was not fit to be among good
society; He was an outcast; He was a traitor to the king. That
is what they said of Jesus when He went about teaching and
preaching to men the way of salvation, pointing them to the

light by which they would see their Heavenly Father. And even though He was the Son of God, even though He had power from on high, even though He worked miracles to prove that He was not only an ordinary man, they did not believe Him and they did not heed Him. The very people among whom He was born, the very people whom probably He loved most were the people who cried out for the destruction and the death of this man, and even though He was the Christ, the Son of God, He could not save Himself from the dissatisfied rebels of His day and of His time. He went about Jerusalem, He went about the holy places, teaching the multitude; He appealed to the masses of the people to save them from their sins, and when the masses attempted to hear Him, when the masses indicated that they would follow Him, the classes who always rule said that He was a disturber of the peace. "We cannot allow this man to travel at large, disturbing the peace of the community. This man threatens the power of the state, therefore we must imprison Him. We must place Him out of the way so that He will not teach these people this new doctrine, the doctrine of love, the doctrine of human brotherhood and the doctrine of equality."

The Character of Man

Christ was the first great reformer. Christ did not go exclusively to the classes. He devoted His life to all; the classes rejected Him because He was not born of high birth, of high parentage, because He was not born in their immediate circle, He was not born of the physical blood royal, therefore they could not follow such a man—"His doctrine is unsound, and He is receiving the plaudits of the people; He is getting the sympathy of the crowd; can we allow it?" And the answer was no. And even the Son of God—not man only, but the Son of God—was sought by the classes who have always held down the masses, because of His teaching for the spiritual glory (if not the physical) of the people whom He loved.

And so while we commemorate the birth of the Christ today, we must bear in mind the sufferings He underwent, the agony He underwent for the purpose of carrying out completely His mission,—the mission that brought Him down from heaven to earth. Christ came to save a sinful world; the world rejected him, and even at the last hour, after He had preached for years to the people; after He had aroused the suspicion and the curiosity of the masses of His time, when He was about to leave the world, He had not even twelve men who were honest enough to profess the faith; He had not made twelve faithful converts, and He was the Son of God. That proves to you the state of man's mind; that proves to you the character of man, and man has not changed much since Christ was here. If he has changed he has done so for the worse. And that brings me to the thought whether if Christ should come back to the world today in what way would He be received? If Christ were to return to the world today, born in the same lowly state, born of the same humble parentage, and attempted to preach the same redemption, He would be imprisoned, He would be executed, He would be crucified in this twentieth century even as He was crucified nineteen hundred years ago on the Mount of Calvary. Man has not changed much.

Christianity a Moving Force

But there is one lesson we can learn from the teachings of Christ. Even though man in the ages may be hard in heart and hard in soul, that which is righteous, that which is spiritually just, even though the physical man dies, the righteous cause is bound to live. Because the preaching of Jesus, the teaching of Jesus was not something physical; if it was something physical it would have died. The teaching of Jesus, the preaching of Jesus, was something spiritual, and where there is righteousness of spirit there is length of life. Jesus the man was not respected, Jesus the man was not adored, Jesus the man was not even loved by His own people, and for that they crucified Him; but the spiritual doctrines of Jesus were righteous; the doctrines of Jesus were just, and even though He died nearly nineteen hundred years ago, what has happened? After the lapse of nineteen hundred years His religion is the greatest moving force in the world today, morally and spiritually. It shows you, therefore, the power of spiritual force; it shows you, therefore, the power of a righteous cause.

Jesus, who was the first great reformer, taught us the way; after Him followed the other great reformers who shared the same fate. Born, perhaps, in the same lowly station of life, feeling with the masses of people who suffered like them, they have gone out, whether it be Luther or Saint Augustine or some other great reformer, but they have all gone out and they preached their doctrine, to suffer in their time for the doctrine to rise again on the wings of time and to flourish as the green bay tree.

Man's Kinship With His Creator

Christmas symbolizes something other than the amusement that it affords today. Christmas brings us to the realization of the fact that hundreds of years ago, when man was practically lost in his spiritual kinship with his Creator and the world probably was to be wiped away, the Son of God Himself came down from His throne on high for the purpose of saving you and saving me. We rejected Him in the past; our attitude now suggests no better consideration for Him if He should return, but with that patience, but with that love, but with that mercy, with that charity that caused Him to look down, not in revenge, but in the belief, in the hope, that some time man will change his ways—man will get to realize his true kinship with his Creator and be what his God expected him to be.

But before we reach this point we need a better understanding of self, as individuals, and may I not appeal to the strong and mighty races and nations of the world for a better and a closer consideration and understanding of the teachings of the man Christ, who went about this world in His effort to redeem fallen man? May I not say to the strong, may I not say to the powerful, that until you change your ways there will be no salvation, there will be no redemption, there will be no seeing God face to face? God is just, God is love, God is no respecter of persons; God does not uphold advantage and abuse to His own people; God created mankind to the same rights and privileges and the same opportunities, and before man can see his God, man will have to measure up in that love, in that brotherhood that He desired us to realize and know as taught to us by His Son Jesus.

Let us realize that we are our brother's keeper; let us realize that we are of one blood, created of one nation to worship God the common Father. It does not, therefore, suggest a proper understanding of our God or a proper knowledge of ourselves when in our strength we attempt to abuse and oppress the weak—as is done to Negroes today.

The Selfishness of Mankind

The statesmen of the world cry out for peace. They are meeting in many conferences with the hope that they will have peace; but I wonder if they understand the meaning of peace. There can be no peace until that peace reflects the spirit of the message of the angels of nineteen centuries ago. The real peace actuated by love, love as the Christ came to the world to give us; love for the high and mighty, love for the meek and lowly, love for all, is the only peace that will reign, is the only peace that will draw man nearer to his God.

Man is so selfish that he does not seem to realize that there is anyone else in the world but himself. The statesmen who lead America seem to believe that there is no one else in the world but the people who make up America, the statesmen who lead the British Empire (even though they cry for peace and desire peace) seem to believe that no one else lives in the world but men within the British Empire.

Up to now we have not yet got the message of the angels; up to now they have not yet fully interpreted the spirit of Christ. Christ came into the world not to save one set of humanity, otherwise He would not have been the Christ. Christ came into the world to save mankind; therefore, His love must be for all; His love could not be sectional; His love could not be partial; His love was general and universal. Therefore, before we can have peace on earth, before we can welcome the spirit of the high God; before we can get a true understanding of the spirit of the Christ, who came to us born in the lowly stable at Bethlehem, we must get to realize the brotherhood that exists, realize it in truth; realize it in fact, and practise it whether we be white, black or some other hue.

God Not Interested in the Physical Activities of Man

Realizing that Christ came to save all mankind from the fallen state, to restore man to his spiritual kinship with his God, let us practise a spirit of love, a spirit of charity, a spirit of mercy toward mankind; because in so doing we will be bringing God's kingdom down to earth. Let us live that true life, that perfect life in ourselves as spiritual beings, not forgetting that we are physical also; man must not fail to understand his dual personality.

In being charitable and sympathetic like the Christ would have us to be does not mean to say that we must ignore our physical needs. Christ was not so much interested in the physical responsibility of man; neither is God interested in the physical activities of man. That may be something strange to say at this hour when you have heard so much about religion. Christ cared so little for the physical that He offered Himself up and was satisfied to go on the cross and let the physical die. God the Father is interested in the spiritual of man, but man's physical body is for his own protection; is for his own purpose. Whatsoever you want to do with the physical God does not interfere, and I trust at this time when we are going to contemplate Christ that we will get a better understanding of Him and get a better understanding of the religion that He taught, because some of us seem to have some peculiar ideas about the religion of Jesus. Some of us seem to believe that Christ and God the Father are responsible for all our ills—physical ills. They have nothing to do with our physical ills. I repeat, God is not and Jesus is not interested in the bodies of men. If you want to care for your body, that is the privilege and prerogative given to you by God. If you want to destroy it, that is the same privilege and prerogative He has given. If you want to commit suicide, that is your business. If you want to live, that is your business. God has given you the power; He has made you a free agent as far as the physical in life goes. All that God is interested in is the spiritual; that you

cannot kill, because the moment you destroy the physical body God
lays claim to the spiritual with which you are endowed. The spiritual
is never yours.. The spiritual is always God's, but the physical is
your own property. If you want to break your physical life up, that
is all your business. God does not interfere and that should be the
Negro's interpretation in this twentieth century of Christ's religion.
It is no use to blame God and Christ for the things that happen to us
in the physical; they are not responsible; they have absolutely nothing
to do with it. If one man enjoys life and another does not, God
has absolutely nothing to do with the difference between the two
individuals. That is to say, if one man lives in a palace across the
street and enjoys life and the other fellow lives in the gutter, God
has nothing to do with the difference between them. It is purely a
physical regulation left to man himself.

Make your interpretation of Christianity scientific—what it
ought to be, and blame not God, blame not the white man for
physical conditions for which we ourselves are responsible.

THE NEGRO'S PLACE IN WORLD REORGANIZATION
Written March 24, 1923

Gradually we are approaching the time when the Negro peoples of the world will have either to consciously, through their own organization, go forward to the point of destiny as laid out by themselves, or must sit quiescently and see themselves pushed back into the mire of economic serfdom, to be ultimately crushed by the grinding mill of exploitation and be exterminated ultimately by the strong hand of prejudice.

There is no doubt about it that we are living in the age of world reorganization out of which will come a set program for the organized races of mankind that will admit of no sympathy in human affairs, in that we are planning for the great gigantic struggle of the survival of the fittest group. It becomes each and every one engaged in this great race for place and position to use whatsoever influence possible to divert the other fellow's attention from the real object. In our own sphere in America and the western world we find that we are being camouflaged, not so much by those with whom we are competing for our economic, political existence, but by men from within our own race, either as agents of the opposition or as unconscious fools who are endeavoring to flatter us into believing that our future should rest with chance and with Providence, believing that through these agencies will come the solution of the restless problem. Such leadership is but preparing us for the time that is bound to befall us if we do not exert ourselves now toward our own creative purpose. The mission of the Universal Negro Improvement Association is to arouse the sleeping consciousness of Negroes everywhere to the point where we will, as one concerted body, act for our own preservation. By laying the foundation for such we will be able to work toward the glorious realization of an emancipated race and a constructed nation. Nationhood is the strongest security of any people and it is for that the Universal Negro Improvement Association strives at this time. With the clamor of other peoples for a similar purpose, we raise a noise even to high heaven for the admission of the Negro into the plan of autonomy.

Black Africa

On every side we hear the cry of white supremacy—in America, Canada, Australia, Europe, and even South America. There is no white supremacy beyond the power and strength of the white man to hold himself against others. The supremacy of any race is not permanent; it is a thing only of the time in which the race finds itself powerful. The whole world of white men is becoming nervous as touching its own future and that of other races. With the desire of self-preservation, which naturally is the first law of nature, they raise the hue and cry that the white race must be first in government and in control. What must the Negro do in the face of such a universal attitude but to align all his forces in the direction of protecting himself from the threatened disaster of race domination and ultimate extermination?

Without a desire to harm anyone, the Universal Negro Improvement Association feels that the Negro should without compromise or any apology appeal to the same spirit of racial pride and love as the great white race is doing for its own preservation, so that while others are raising the cry of a white America, a white Canada, a white Australia, we also without reservation raise the cry of a "Black Africa." The critic asks, "Is this possible?" and the four hundred million courageous Negroes of the world answer, "Yes."

Out of this very reconstruction of world affairs will come the glorious opportunity for Africa's freedom. Out of the present chaos and European confusion will come an opportunity for the Negro never enjoyed in any other age, for the expansion of himself and the consolidation of his manhood in the direction of building himself a national power in Africa.

The germ of European malice, revenge and antagonism is so deeply rooted among certain of the contending powers that in a short while we feel sure they will present to Negroes the opportunity for which we are organized.

Disablement of Germany Not Permanent

No one believes in the permanent disablement of Germany, but all thoughtful minds realize that France is but laying the foundation through revenge for a greater conflict than has as yet been seen. With such another upheaval, there is absolutely no reason why organized Negro opinion could not be felt and directed in the channel of their own independence in Africa.

To fight for African redemption does not mean that we must give up our domestic fights for political justice and industrial rights. It does not mean that we must become disloyal to any government or to any country wherein we were born. Each and every race outside of its domestic national loyalty has a loyalty to itself; therefore, it is foolish for the Negro to talk about not being interested in his own racial, political, social and industrial destiny. We can be as loyal American citizens or British subjects as the Irishman or the Jew, and yet fight for the redemption of Africa, a complete emancipation of the race.

Fighting for the establishment of Palestine does not make the

American Jew disloyal; fighting for the independence of Ireland does not make the Irish-American a bad citizen. Why should fighting for the freedom of Africa make the Afro-American disloyal or a bad citizen?

The Universal Negro Improvement Association teaches loyalty to all governments outside of Africa; but when it comes to Africa, we feel that the Negro has absolutely no obligation to any one but himself

Out of the unsettled state and condition of the world will come such revolutions that will give each and every race that is oppressed the opportunity to march forward. The last world war brought the opportunity to many heretofore subject races to regain their freedom. The next world war will give Africa the opportunity for which we are preparing. We are going to have wars and rumors of wars. In another twenty or thirty years we will have a changed world, politically, and Africa will not be one of the most backward nations, but Africa shall be, I feel sure, one of the greatest commonwealths that will once more hold up the torchlight of civilization and bestow the blessings of freedom, liberty and democracy upon all mankind.

AIMS AND OBJECTS OF MOVEMENT FOR SOLUTION OF NEGRO PROBLEM

Generally the public is kept misinformed of the truth surrounding new movements of reform. Very seldom, if ever, reformers get the truth told about them and their movements. Because of this natural attitude, the Universal Negro Improvement Association has been greatly handicapped in its work, causing thereby one of the most liberal and helpful human movements of the twentieth century to be held up to ridicule by those who take pride in poking fun at anything not already successfully established.

The white man of America has become the natural leader of the world. He, because of his exalted position, is called upon to help in all human efforts. From nations to individuals the appeal is made to him for aid in all things affecting humanity, so, naturally, there can be no great mass movement or change without first acquainting the leader on whose sympathy and advice the world moves.

It is because of this, and more so because of a desire to be Christian friends with the white race, why I explain the aims and objects of the Universal Negro Improvement Association.

The Universal Negro Improvement Association is an organization among Negroes that is seeking to improve the condition of the race, with the view of establishing a nation in Africa where Negroes will be given the opportunity to develop by themselves, without creating the hatred and animosity that now exist in countries of the white race through Negroes rivaling them for the highest and best positions in government, politics, society and industry. The organization believes in the rights of all men, yellow, white and black. To us, the white race has a right to the peaceful possession and occupation of countries of its own and in like manner the yellow and black races have their rights. It is only by an honest and liberal consideration of such rights can the world be blessed with the peace that is sought by Christian teachers and leaders.

The Spiritual Brotherhood of Man

The following preamble to the constitution of the organization speaks for itself:

"The Universal Negro Improvement Association and African Communities' League is a social, friendly, humanitarian, charitable, educational, institutional, constructive, and expansive society, and is founded by persons, desiring to the utmost to work for the general uplift of the Negro peoples of the world. And the members pledge themselves to do all in their power to conserve the rights of their noble race and to respect the rights of all mankind, believing always in the Brotherhood of Man and the Fatherhood of God. The motto of the organization is: One God! One Aim! One Destiny! Therefore, let justice be done to all mankind, realizing that if the strong oppresses the weak confusion and discontent will ever mark the path of man, but with love, faith and charity toward all the reign of peace and plenty will be heralded into the world and the generation of men shall be called Blessed."

The declared objects of the association are:

"To establish a Universal Confraternity among the race; to promote the spirit of pride and love; to reclaim the fallen; to administer to and assist the needy; to assist in civilizing the backward tribes of Africa; to assist in the development of Independent Negro Nations and Communities; to establish a central nation for the race; to establish Commissaries or Agencies in the principal countries and cities of the world for the representation of all Negroes; to promote a conscientious Spiritual worship among the native tribes of Africa; to establish Universities, Colleges, Academies and Schools for the racial education and culture of the people; to work for better conditions among Negroes everywhere."

Supplying a Long Felt Want

The organization of the Universal Negro Improvement Association has supplied among Negroes a long-felt want. Hitherto the other Negro movements in America, with the exception of the Tuskegee effort of Booker T. Washington, sought to teach the Negro to aspire to social equality with the whites, meaning thereby the right to intermarry and fraternize in every social way. This has been the source of much trouble and still some Negro organizations continue to preach this dangerous "race destroying doctrine" added to a program of political agitation and aggression. The Universal Negro Improvement Association on the other hand believes in and teaches the pride and purity of race. We believe that the white race should uphold its racial pride and perpetuate itself, and that the black race should do likewise. We believe that there is room enough in the world for the various race groups to grow and develop by themselves without seeking to destroy the Creator's plan by the constant introduction of mongrel types.

The unfortunate condition of slavery, as imposed upon the Negro, and which caused the mongrelization of the race, should not be legalized and continued now to the harm and detriment of both races.

The time has really come to give the Negro a chance to develop himself to a moral-standard-man, and it is for such an opportunity that the Universal Negro Improvement Association seeks in the creation of an African nation for Negroes, where the greatest latitude would be given to work out this racial ideal.

There are hundreds of thousands of colored people in America who desire race amalgamation and miscegenation as a solution of the race problem. These people are, therefore, opposed to the race pride ideas of black and white; but the thoughtful of both races will naturally ignore the ravings of such persons and honestly work for the solution of a problem that has been forced upon us.

Liberal white America and race loving Negroes are bound to think at this time and thus evolve a program or plan by which there can be a fair and amicable settlement of the question.

We cannot put off the consideration of the matter, for time is pressing on our hands. The educated Negro is making rightful constitutional demands. The great white majority will never grant them, and thus we march on to danger if we do not now stop and adjust the matter.

The time is opportune to regulate the relationship between both races. Let the Negro have a country of his own. Help him to return to his original home, Africa, and there give him the opportunity to climb from the lowest to the highest positions in a state of his own. If not, then the nation will have to hearken to the demand of the aggressive, "social equality" organization, known as the National Association for the Advancement of Colored People, of which W. E. B. DuBois is leader, which declares vehemently for social and political equality, viz.: Negroes and whites in the same hotels, homes, residential districts, public and private places, a Negro as president, members of the Cabinet, Governors of States, Mayors of cities, and leaders of society in the United States. In this agitation, DuBois is ably supported by the "Chicago Defender," a colored newspaper published in Chicago. This paper advocates Negroes in the Cabinet and Senate. All these, as everybody knows, are the Negroes' constitutional rights, but reason dictates that the masses of the white race will never stand by the ascendency of an opposite minority group to the favored positions in a government, society and industry that exist by the will of the majority, hence the demand of the DuBois group of colored leaders will only lead, ultimately, to further disturbances in riots, lynching and mob rule. The only logical solution therefore, is to supply the Negro with opportunities and environments of his own, and there point him to the fullness of his ambition.

Negroes Who Seek Social Equality

The Negro who seeks the White House in America could find ample play for his ambition in Africa. The Negro who seeks the office of Secretary of State in America would have a fair chance of demonstrating his diplomacy in Africa. The Negro who seeks a seat in the Senate or of being governor of a State in America, would be provided with a glorious chance for statesmanship in Africa.

The Negro has a claim on American white sympathy that cannot be denied. The Negro has labored for 300 years in contributing to America's greatness. White America will not be unmindful, therefore, of this consideration, but will treat him kindly. Yet it is realized that all human beings have a limit to their humanity. The humanity of white America, we realize, will seek self-protection and self-preservation, and that is why the thoughtful and reasonable Negro sees no hope in America for satisfying the aggressive program of the National Association for the Advancement of Colored People, but advances the reasonable plan of the Universal Negro Improvement Association, that of creating in Africa a nation and government for the Negro race.

This plan when properly undertaken and prosecuted will solve the race problem in America in fifty years. Africa affords a wonderful opportunity at the present time for colonization by the Negroes of the Western world. There is Liberia, already established as an independent Negro government. Let white America assist Afro-Americans to go there and help develop the country. Then, there are the late German colonies; let white sentiment force England and France to turn them over to the American and West Indian Negroes who fought for the Allies in the World's War. Then, France, England and Belgium owe America billions of dollars which they claim they cannot afford to repay immediately. Let them compromise by turning over Sierra Leone and the Ivory Coast on the West Coast of Africa and add them to Liberia and help make Libera a state worthy of her history.

The Negroes of Africa and America are one in blood. They have sprung from the same common stock. They can work and live together and thus make their own racial contribution to the world.

Will deep thinking and liberal white America help? It is a considerate duty.

It is true that a large number of self-seeking colored agitators and so-called political leaders, who hanker after social equality and fight for the impossible in politics and governments, will rave, but remember that the slave-holder raved, but the North said, "Let the slaves go free"; the British Parliament raved when the Colonists said, "We want a free and American nation"; the Monarchists of France raved when the people declared for a more liberal form of government.

The masses of Negroes think differently from the self-appointed leaders of the race. The majority of Negro leaders are selfish, self-appointed and not elected by the people. The people desire freedom in a land of their own, while the colored politician desires office and social equality for himself in America, and that is why we are asking white America to help the masses to realize their objective.

Ninety odd years ago a thoughtful, liberty-loving white statesman of America made the following speech in Congress:

CLAIMS OF AFRICA
Extract from a Speech Delivered in Congress by Mr. Burges, of Rhode Island, May 10, 1830.

"1. During the last century, a mighty revolution of mind has been made in the civilized world. Its effects are gradually disclosing themselves, and gradually improving the condition of the human race. The eyes of all nations are turned on these United States, for here that great movement was commenced. Africa, like a bereaved mother, holds out her hands to America, and implores you to send back her exiled children. Does not Africa merit much at the hands of other nations? Almost 4,000 years ago, she, from the then rich store house of her genius and labor, sent out to them science, and arts and letters, laws and civilization.

"2. Wars and revolutions have exhausted this ancient abundance, and spread ignorance and barbarism over her regions; and the cupidity of other nations has multiplied and aggravated these evils. The ways of Providence cannot always be seen by man. When the Almighty comes out of His cloud, light fills the universe. What a mystery, when the youthful patriarch, lost to his father, was sold into slavery. What a display of wisdom and benignity, when we are permitted to see 'all the families of the earth blessed' by the event of their restoration.

"3. Shall we question the great arrangements of divine wisdom; or hold parlance with the Power who has made whole countries the enduring monuments of His avenging justice? Let these people go! They are citizens of another country, send them home. Send them home instructed and civilized, and imbued with the pure principles of Christianity; so may they instruct and civilize their native land, and spread over its wide regions the glad tidings of human redemption. Secure to your country, to your age, to yourselves, the glory of paying back to Africa the mighty arrears of nations. Add another New World to the civilized regions of the globe.

"Do you say your State will be depopulated; your fields left without culture. In countries equal in fertility, and under the same laws, you cannot create a void in population; as well might you make a vacuum in the atmosphere. Better, more efficient labor will come to your aid. Free men, observant of the same laws, cherishing the same union, worshipping the same God with you, will place themselves by your side. This change of moral and physical condition in our population will follow the removal of that pernicious cause, now so productive of alarming difference in political opinions; jealousies, incident to our present state, shall give place to a glorious emulation of patriotism; and, O my country! If God so please, thou shalt be united, and prosperous, and perpetual."

Help the Negro to Return Home

Surely the time has come for the Negro to look homeward. He has won civilization and Christianity at the price of slavery. The Negro who is thoughtful and serviceable, feels that God intended him to give to his brothers still in darkness, the light of his civilization. The very light element of Negroes do not want to go back to Africa. They believe that in time, through miscegenation, the American race will be of their type. This is a fallacy and in that respect the agitation of the mulatto leader, Dr. W. E. B. DuBois and the National Association for the Advancement of Colored People is dangerous to both races.

The off-colored people, being children of the Negro race, should combine to re-establish the purity of their own race, rather than seek to perpetuate the abuse of both races. That is to say, all elements of the Negro race should be encouraged to get together and form themselves into a healthy whole, rather than seeking to lose their identities through miscegenation and social intercourse with the white race. These statements are made because we desire an honest solution of the problem and no flattery or deception will bring that about.

Let the white and Negro people settle down in all seriousness and in true sympathy and solve the problem. When that is done, a new day of peace and good will will be ushered in.

The natural opponents among Negroes to a program of this kind are that lazy element who believe always in following the line of least resistance, being of themselves void of initiative and the pioneering spirit to do for themselves. The professional Negro leader and the class who are agitating for social equality feel that it is too much work for them to settle down and build up a civilization of their own. They feel it is easier to seize on to the civilization of the white man and under the guise of constitutional rights fight for those things that the white man has created. Natural reason suggests that the white man will not yield them, hence such leaders are but fools for their pains. Teach the Negro to do for himself, help him the best way possible in that direction; but to encourage him into the belief that he is going to possess himself of the things that others have fought and died for, is to build up in his mind false hopes never to be realized. As for instance, Dr. W. E. B. DuBois, who has been educated by white charity, is a brilliant scholar, but he is not a hard worker. He prefers to use his higher intellectual abilities to fight for a place among white men in society, industry and in politics, rather than use that ability to work and create for his own race that which the race could be able to take credit for. He would not think of repeating for his race the work of the Pilgrim Fathers or the Colonists who laid the foundation of America, but he prefers to fight and agitate for the privilege of dancing with a white lady at a ball at the Biltmore or at the Astoria hotels in New York. That kind of leadership will destroy the Negro in America and against which the Universal Negro Improvement Association is fighting.

The Universal Negro Improvement Association is composed of all shades of Negroes—blacks, mulattoes and yellows, who are all working honestly for the purification of their race, and for a sympathetic adjustment of the race problem.

WILL NEGROES SUCCUMB TO THE WHITE MAN'S PLAN OF ECONOMIC STARVATION?

(Written March 31, 1923.)

Every day we are discovering new evidence to bear out and support the stand taken by me,—that it is only a question of time when the entire white race will be inflamed against the Negro and all weaker peoples not sufficiently strong and organized to hold their own in the competition of life. I have also contended that the race problem was not absolutely confined to the United States of America, but it was only a question of environment that prevented the other great white nations from treating the Negro as he was being treated in the United States of America. If we were to place the same number of Negroes in any of the European countries as we have in America, that we would have the same problem of hostility, riots, lynchings and burnings.

I have also held and still believe that it is only a question of time when the Negro, economically dependent as he is on the white man, would be forced to the wall, and that the solution of the problem in the future would not be so much by wholesale killing or wiping out of Negro populations by fire or force of arms, but by a well-organized plan of economic starvation.

It is not surprising to us how unreasonable and selfish certain people can make themselves. The English, above everybody else, owe a debt of gratitude to the Negro for nearly all that they possess. Everybody knows that the British have built themselves up on the blood and wealth of the Negroes, especially of Africa and the West Indies. Whilst these "Christian" Britishers are going out to the colonies robbing and exploiting our people, murdering them for their lands and their wealth, we find that in their home, England, they look upon it as an imposition for Negroes to go into their midst, not to exploit, but to seek employment. This convinces us beyond the shadow of a doubt that as far as the economic political interest of the Englishman goes, he has no soul. He believes that he alone is entitled to everything that is worth while, and that others have absolutely no claim upon those things that are necessary to life, except that which he does not want. Following is an article that speaks for itself:—

Nigger Problem Brought to London—Blacks Not Wanted in England

(Daily Graphic, London, England, March 6, 1923.)

The all-black cabaret which, staged at the Empire, is to

be the great attraction of the Darker London season, will be as black as night.

"Indeed, Robert Law, the scenic artist, who is to paint a plantation scene so that niggers can act in front of it, said yesterday that they are even bringing over a black cook. So "Aunt Jemima," of Virginia, the Coal-Black Mammy of all time, will make waffles which, he said, "You could eat forever, and still want more."

Black Cabaret

"I suppose Black and White whisky and black coffee will also be sold at the cabaret—that is, of course, if the black cabaret is ever opened.

I print this proviso because Lord Decies, a prominent member of the London County Council, said yesterday, "When I saw the news that negroes were to act in the cabaret, I thought there must be some mistake. I do not think the L. C. C. will grant the license for a minute.

The license comes up for consideration this afternoon. But, since Sir Percy Simmons, the chairman of the Theatre and Music-Hall Committee, says that, when the license was recommended, he had no idea that black artists were to be employed, there is no doubt that the matter will be referred back."

Protest to the L. C. C.

Protests against black cabarets were heard in all sorts of places in London yesterday. Naturally, the strongest came from Albert Voyce and Monte Bayly, the chairman and organizer of the Variety Artistes' Federation, who were so indignant that they immediately sent the Clerk of the London County Council a protest against the license for a cabaret being granted if negro artistes were to be imported to act in it. A copy of this letter was sent also, to scores of L. C. C. members.

Imported Blacks

"We think it would be a disgrace to both theatrical and music-hall performers if permission were granted to exploit imported black men and women in this way," they said, "while hundreds of talented British artistes are on the verge of want through lack of engagements."

"Over 2,000 variety artistes are unemployed in England," said Mr. Voyce, "and the stories I hear every day of want are heartrending. When employed, these artistes earn anything from £10 to £100 a week; but, so bad is the shortage of money in England, that no fewer than 250 of the smaller music halls which used to employ from four variety acts are now saving money by showing second-class pictures instead.

No Objection to White Americans

"We have no objection to American artistes coming to England. In fact, ninety per cent. of those who come here join our federation and are welcome. There are also in England negro turns that behave themselves and keep their place. But we view with the greatest apprehension a cabaret where black artistes would actually mix with the white folk at the tables."

Spirit of Hate Revealed

The above article reveals the spirit of hate on the part of the Englishman for the Negro in his country. Nevertheless, this same Englishman expects the Negro to exhibit an overabundance of love and obedience to him in his (the Negro's) country. These twentieth century white men are indeed crazy when they believe that self-respecting and ambitious Negroes are going to stand for it without a murmur.

We of the Universal Negro Improvement Association cede to the white man the right of doing as he pleases in his own country, and that is why we believe in not making any trouble when he says that "America is a white man's country," because in the same breath and with the same determination we are going to make Africa a black man's country. The appeal to Christian love is a farce, and the white man, especially the Englishman, preaches it only to suit his own conveniences. In the tropics, when he wants to rob our wealth, mineral and agricultural, he brings us a Bible and a hymn book, and tells us how much he loves us and that we are all children of one common Father, and points us to the hope of a glorious day when all of us will meet around the throne of heaven; but when we meet him on his own soil, he tells us a different tale, even as is being told in the article herein mentioned. After he has robbed our diamond mines and stripped Africa of part of its wealth and taken it all to England, they come to us to tell us that the black man is not wanted there, even as we are being told in America that we are not wanted here. There is but one alternative for ambitious and self-respecting Negroes, and that is to make it warm for all aliens in Africa, so that in the days to come when the line of demarcation between black and white will be more ferociously drawn in countries of whites, we will have a haven of refuge—the land of our fathers.

Whilst the prejudiced whites in England are depriving Negroes of the right to earn a livelihood, in the United States of America, the same methods are employed but on a larger scale, and the plan of economic starvation is more vigorously and rigidly pursued.

The time is coming, as I have often stated, when the Negro will have a hard time finding a place in the economic arrangements of the other races of the world, when not only in Europe, but in America, it will become difficult for him to find even the opportunity to work in the most menial occupations, in that the surplus populations of the other races will seek to perform even the most menial work to the exclusion of any other competitor.

Very few persons would have thought that the white man in America would have sought to compete with Negroes even in the occupation of picking cotton; but the following news article speaks for itself:

Caruthersville, Mo., March 2, 1923.

A carefully organized campaign of intimidation has driven more than 2,000 Negro workers from the cotton fields of Southeastern Missouri within the last thirty days, according to complaints made to local officials here. Negro leaders charge that threats and warnings were sent to the Negroes by white laborers fearful of losing their jobs by the influx of Negroes into the recently reclaimed section. Ambrose Young, Negro, appealed for protection after he had received several warnings. "Nigger, get to hell out of here; this is a white man's country," was one notice delivered by five hooded men. Young says: The next night. I found another note on my front porch weighted down with a cartridge box, which said, "Nigger, if you cannot read, run. If you cannot run, you are as good as dead."

What happened at Caruthersville, Missouri, is what is happening throughout America, as for instance:

South Bend, Indiana, Sept. 12, 1923.

South Bend, once a haven for escaped Negro slaves from the South, is witnessing an exodus of Negroes as the result of a rumor of a threatened race riot. A number of letters addressed to several Negro leaders on the west side of the city caused the flight. Approximately 2,000 Negro men, women and children are said to have fled, some leaving their belongings.

Shortly after this occurrence at South Bend, Indiana, a

similar occurrence took place at Johnstown, Pa., an industrial center, where there has been a great deal of unemployment among the white workers, leaving the town over-run with unemployed whites and Negroes, as well as employed Negroes. The unemployed whites were waiting for an opportunity to run the employed and unemployed Negroes out of town,• so as to brighten their prospects for employment. The opportunity presented itself when two policemen were shot in one of the labor districts of the city. It is apparent that the white labor leaders seized upon the opportunity of getting the Mayor to take immediate action, which he did not fail to do. The result was that thousands of Negroes were driven out of town by the order of Mayor Joseph Cauffiel, with the following declaration as his ultimatum, which cannot be mistaken:—

Johnstown, Pa., Sept. 15, 1923.

"I don't care what authority I have; for their own safety and for the safety of the Johnstown public, the Negroes are going out of this city. Most of them are out, and the rest of them are going fast. If the rest of them don't get out soon, I'll arm the police and send them into the colonies to walk the Negroes out at the point of a gun."

Similar occurrences have taken place in East St. Louis, Tulsa and other industrial centers, accompanied by bloodshed and fire, and will happen in hundreds of instances again; more so as the reaction sets in, in the American labor market. As soon as the country returns to normal, and as soon as employment for the working classes becomes more remote, we will find other mayors all over the United States of America making similar declarations, and in a short while, except where the Negro has created for himself some haven of refuge, he will become the unfortunate man without a country and without a shelter.

What are Negroes going to do? Are we going to live under this farcical impression that one of these days the hearts of the white people will change toward us and give us a square deal? This is preposterous, and that is why we are fighting for the restoration of Africa to the Negro peoples of the world; that is why we are advising American and West Indian Negroes to look forward to the building up of a country of their own, a nation of their own, because all over the world there is an emphatic line of demarcation drawn between the interests of black and white peoples industrially, socially and politically.

The Annoyance of "Misleaders"

It is rather annoying to the conscientious Negro who desires a proper solution of this great race problem to have the so-called "leaders" of the race playing with this great question. Instead of settling down to a sober and practical handling of the situation, we find these "misleaders" of ours trying to point us to every other possible solution than that which is practical.

If some unfriendly acquaintance of yours threatens to burn down your house, there is only one resort for the sensible man, and that is to surround himself and his home with sufficient protection as to make it impossible for the enemy to carry out his threat, instead of hoping that the enemy will have a change of heart and mind and refrain from carrying out the design. In the same way, after being told that this is a white man's country; after being advised time and again that the Negro must "find his place," these so-called "race leaders" insist that the future of the Negro is alongside of the white man in countries where he dominates.

They try to force upon us the belief that later on this good white neighbor and fellow citizen will change his mind and will not carry out his desire of really making America a white man's country. This is foolhardiness of the worst sort, and I trust that Negroes in America and throughout the world where we live as a minority group in a majority white population, will get to realize the fallacy of such a belief.

Political, social and industrial America will never become so converted as to be willing to share up equitably between black and white.

The Solution

It can plainly be seen, that in the question of self-preservation and self-interest the whites nowhere, whether in America, England or France, are going to give way to the Negro to the detriment of their own. We need not look for constitutional protection, or even for philanthropic Christian sympathy, because if that is to be shown it will be to the race that is able to bestow it.

Hence, the Universal Negro Improvement Association has but one solution for this great problem, and that is to work unceasingly for the bringing about of a National Homeland for Negroes in Africa, so that when this wholesale declaration against Negroes takes place we can have a National Home of our own to look to.

Members of the Universal Negro Improvement Association all over the world are pushing forward our program so that the time for its realization and accomplishment will be hastened. We would like to be in a position to start real nation building for the Negro in a short while, but this can only be done when we have succeeded in bringing together sufficient Negroes who are determined to stand behind the idea. If we can get eight or ten million out of the fifteen million Negroes in the United States, and the millions of other Negroes in other parts of the world, to stand behind us, there is absolutely no reason why we cannot get the American Government, along with the governments of Europe, to acquiesce in the demand of creating for the Negro a government in a nation of our own than to have us scattered throughout the universe, driven from pillar to post at the whim and caprice of any mob, governor or official of white governments or communities of the world.

AN ANALYSIS OF WARREN G. HARDING, 29TH PRESIDENT OF THE U. S.

The hand of death has removed from our midst Warren G. Harding, President of the United States, and a voice that was once loud and clear, that resounded around the world, is now silent, to be heard no more.

Notwithstanding opinions to the contrary, Harding was, to my way of thinking, a true friend of the Negro race, as far as we can expect friendship from members of the opposite race who have not yet discovered their souls.

The President's speech at Birmingham in 1921, on the race question, was one that revealed his depth of thought for the Negro and marked him as a careful student of world psychology.

If President Harding did not openly do any good for the Negro, it was because he was but a slave to system and environment which took extraordinary courage to rebuff and surmount, with the intention of doing that which was right and justifiable. Not only Harding, but any President or leader who prefers to please his immediate acquaintances and human circle rather than the voice of God, speaking through the oppressed, is bound to do as he did in all things affecting human rights, liberty and justice, without realizing his mistake.

Mr. Harding was not a Roosevelt, who would do what he thought was morally right, irrespective of what his associates thought. He would not have dined a Booker T. Washington, if he believed it would have hurt him in the opinion of his friends and large numbers of people; but a Roosevelt did that, because he believed it was right, and he said: "Public opinion be hanged, if it flares against the right." President Harding was too physically kind, gentle and considerate to knowingly offend by introducing innovations or changes, and that is why, although he felt for and sympathized with the Negro, he was unable to openly do anything for him, because he was just afraid of hurting public opinion.

To do good, and that which must be permanent, we have to offend public opinion. No better example of the price one has to pay in doing good can be found than that given us by the man Jesus, who, in a life of public activity, taught us that to do good is to offend, and to suffer therefor.

His Soul Humanly Right

President Harding's soul was humanly right. He had a deep sense of human love. He desired to see all men free and happy. He prayed for that. He loved peace and justice, but he was not a Christ; he was not a Reformer. He was but a bold, courageous and sympathetic twentieth century human leader, who dared not break the bounds set by human public opinion. He was bold and courageous, however, to have gone further than anyone else, excepting Wilson, in pointing to us that which we should do. If he had done it himself he would have been a Christ, and who knows if life did not fail Warren Gamaliel Harding because he failed to act the Christ? He failed to do the deed that would justify the righteousness of his own soul and elevate him above the rest of men.

If the world is God's, if the creatures therein are the children of God, and we essay to lead because we know better than the rest of those who sin and suffer, then it becomes our duty and obligation not to only act human, but to act as a Christ in dispensing justice, love and mercy to all those who look to us as leaders and representatives of the ONE who should rule, but who does so through us, his agents.

Service to Humanity and What It Means

For man, elevated to the position of leader, teacher or law giver, having under his control the children of God, not knowing that his act in regulating the affairs of his fellows must be based upon the conscience or soul of a Christ, and not man makes him unfit for the call of service to humanity and misrepresentative of the Divinity of God.

There is nothing in the world as serious as leadership. We can all follow, but we cannot all lead. Christ was a leader, and the greatest of them all. He came to a new and modern age and set the example we should follow, and those who must lead man after Christ cannot but expect to fail, if they act not as He would.

We cannot mix the human and spiritual of life in leadership of humanity. We cannot love and then hate. We cannot be merciful and then revengeful; we cannot take from Paul and give to John. All these irregularities can be, however, if we do not lead; but if we lead, we must do as Christ would do or else we ourselves suffer and not those whom we lead.

Wilson and Harding came nearest to playing the Christ in the leadership of the American people, and in their lessons to the world, than any other human political leader of recent times. Wilson and Harding went up to the Cross, but they were afraid of the crucifixion. One fainted on the wayside; the other, because his life and works were in the immediate hand of God, died, and in his death we mourn, because we know he was only man, and not a Christ. The responsibility of leadership in a modern world after Christ is exceedingly great, and none of us, because of our imperfections, can see the glory of our work. In our sins of omission, caused through the preponderance of our human over our spiritual, we destroy the good of our work, as, no doubt, planned from the most righteous desire of service to humanity. No one will doubt that Harding planned to do good, and all will believe that he did his best as far as the human in him went. No one will dispute that Harding was a successful, illustrious human being, that he attempted great things for humanity as a leader, but his soul failed him as a Christ in being just to all men.

Leadership of the Soul

The leadership of this age must be of the soul and not only of the head, if we are to be just to our fellows and win the love of God. This does not mean to say that our leaders should be bishops and priests, rather than statesmen. The bishop or priest is not a statesman, but the statesman must be bishop, priest and himself. To lead and be spiritual, does not mean that we must be all humility and obliging; we must be ourselves; we must be like Christ; we must resist, yet not resist; we must fight, yet not fight; we must be JUST.

How just Warren Harding was, his God will tell; but those who follow him, and those who must lead, should learn that the responsibility is great, that it is not a mockery; it is a calling, and to each and every one there will come a summons to report the deeds of love, justice and mercy to the greatest of Judges, who pardons not after the judgment.

The World Still in Chaos

Harding has left the world still in chaos, although he humanly tried his best to save it without taking into consideration all the elements that contribute to its undoing. Not only Harding, but Wilson before him, tried to save the world without first realizing that the world holds peoples of different races, whose claim to right and justice is as obligatory and potential as those addressed. Harding addressed himself to white America and Europe, but forgot black Africa, not because the ills of the Negro race were not of the human race, but because he would not offend his associates and human circle. That kind of leadership takes man no further than his grave, but that which is of Christ, that knows not bonds, limits, creeds or races, elevates the soul of the deceased to the realms of glory. Yet, Harding has done more than others. He expressed, if nowhere else, at Birmingham, his sympathy for the Negro, and we must take him at his word and give him credit for being a great and generous man.

Africa has still its lesson to teach the world. We will teach man the way to life and peace, not by ignoring the rights of our brother, but by giving to everyone his due. We glory in Africa's new responsibility, for we know that the Psalmist made no mistake in prophesying that "Ethiopia shall stretch out her hands." The hand of justice, freedom and liberty shall be extended to all mankind, so that in the death of our leaders not only man will mourn, but the angels will rejoice in admitting into the kingdom of everlasting glory the faithful servants of the Son of Righteousness.

Telegraphed Message of Condolence Sent to Mrs. Harding on Death of President Harding

July 31, 1923.

Madam—The world has lost one of its greatest advocates of peace and justice, and America one of her truest and noblest sons. Not only the nation, but the world of grateful, peace-loving humanity mourns the loss of your illustrious husband, and shall never forget the courage, manhood and character of Warren Gamaliel Harding. Four hundred million Negroes of the world and fifteen million of America, in particular, will ever remember your dear husband as a true and sincere friend of our race. His speech and advice to our race at Birmingham, Ala., is a classic in the utterances of American statesmen on the race problem.

We believe he was true and honest in his desire to see the Negro elevated to the standard of man; therefore, how could we do other than mourn with you from our deepest feeling of sorrow and regret in losing a true friend who was your loving and devoted husband, the like of whom the world may never see again.

In the history of our race your beloved husband, as a friend and well-wisher of our progress, shall have a place, and our children shall be taught and they shall remember that amidst all the horrors of prejudice and injustice to the Negro in the civilization of the twentieth century they had one, in the person of your husband, who was always kind and considerate and who never failed to lend a helping hand.

Be assured, dear Madam, that the world of Negroes at this hour mourn with you and pray for the entrance of the President's soul into the realms of Paradise.

AN EXPOSÉ OF THE CASTE SYSTEM AMONG NEGROES

(Written from the Tombs Prison August 31st, 1923)

The policy of the Universal Negro Improvement Association is so clean-cut, and my personal views are so well known, that no one, for even one moment, could reasonably accuse us of having any other desire than that of working for a united Negro race.

The Program of the Universal Negro Improvement Association is that of drawing together, into one universal whole, all the Negro peoples of the world, with prejudice toward none. We desire to have every shade of color, even those with one drop of African blood, in our fold; because we believe that none of us, as we are, is responsible for our birth; in a word, we have no prejudice against ourselves in race. We believe that every Negro racially is just alike, and, therefore, we have no distinction to make, hence wherever you see the Universal Negro Improvement Association you will find us giving every member of the race an equal chance and opportunity to make good.

Unfortunately, there is a disposition on the part of a certain element of our people in America, the West Indies and Africa, to hold themselves up as the "better class" or "privileged" group on the caste of color.

This subject is such a delicate one that no one is honest enough to broach it, yet the evil of it is working great harm to our racial solidarity, and I personally feel it my duty to right now bring it to the attention of all concerned. The Universal Negro Improvement Association is founded on truth, and, therefore, anything that would menace or retard the race must be gotten out of the way, hence our stand in this direction. During the early days of slavery our people were wrested from the bosom of our native land—Africa—and brought into these climes. For centuries, against their will, our mothers were subjected to the most cruel and unfair treatment, the result of which has created among us a diversity of colors and types, to the end that we have become the most mixed race in the world.

The Abuse of Our Race

The abuse of our race was, up to eighty-five years ago in the West Indies and fifty-seven years ago in America, beyond our control, because we were then but chattel slaves of our masters; but since emancipation we have had full control of our own moral-social life and cannot, therefore, complain against anyone other than ourselves, for any social or moral wrongs inflicted upon us.

The Universal Negro Improvement Association realizes that it is now our duty to socially and morally steady ourselves, hence our desire to bring about a united race with one moral code and principle. The types in our race should not be blameable to our generation, but to the abuse and advantage taken of us in the past; but that should not be reason for us to further open ourselves to a continuation of this abuse and thereby wreck our racial pride and self-respect. The Universal Negro Improvement Association believes that the time has come for us to call a halt, and thus steady ourselves on the basis of race and not be allowed to drift along in the world as the outcasts or lepers of society, to be laughed at by every other race beneath their social breath.

Near Whites

Some of us in America, the West Indies and Africa believe that the nearer we approach the white man in color the greater our social standing and privilege and that we should build up an "aristocracy" based upon caste of color and not achievement in race. It is well known, although no one is honest enough to admit it, that we have been, for the past thirty years at least, but more so now than ever, grading ourselves for social honor and distinction on the basis of color. That the average success in the race has been regulated by color and not by ability and merit; that we have been trying to get away from the pride of race into the atmosphere of color worship, to the damaging extent that the whole world has made us its laughing stock.

There is no doubt that a race that doesn't respect itself forfeits the respect of others, and we are in the moral-social position now of losing the respect of the whole world.

There is a subtle and underhand propaganda fostered by a few men of color in America, the West Indies and Africa to destroy the self-respect and pride of the Negro race by building up what is commonly known to us as a "blue vein" aristocracy and to foster same as the social and moral standard of the race. The success of this effort is very much marked in the West Indies, and coming into immediate recognition in South Africa, and is now gaining much headway in America under the skillful leadership of the National Association for the Advancement of "Colored" People and their silent but scattered agents.

The observant members of our race must have noticed within recent years a great hostility between the National Association for the Advancement of "Colored" People and the Universal

"Negro" Improvement Association, and must have wondered why Du Bois writes so bitterly against Garvey and vice versa. Well, the reason is plainly to be seen after the following explanation :

Group That Hates Negro

Du Bois represents a group that hates the Negro blood in its veins, and has been working subtly to build up a caste aristocracy that would socially divide the race into two groups : One the superior because of color caste, and the other the inferior, hence the pretentious work of the National Association for the Advancement of "Colored" People. The program of deception was well arranged and under way for success when Marcus Garvey arrived in America, and he, after understudying the artful doctor and the group he represented, fired a "bomb" into the camp by organizing the Universal "Negro" Improvement Association to cut off the wicked attempt of race deception and distinction, and, in truth, to build up a race united in spirit and ideal, with the honest desire of adjusting itself to its own moral-social pride and national self-respect. When Garvey arrived in America and visited the office of the National Association for the Advancement of "Colored" People to interview Du Bois, who was regarded as a leader of the Negro people, and who had recently visited the West Indies, he was dumfounded on approach to the office to find that but for Mr. Dill, Du Bois, himself and the office boy, he could not tell whether he was in a white office or that of the National Association for the Advancement of "Colored" People. The whole staff was either white or very near white, and thus Garvey got his first shock of the advancement hypocrisy. There was no representation of the race there that anyone could recognize. The advancement meant that you had to be as near white as possible, otherwise there was no place for you as stenographer, clerk or attendant in the office of the National Association for the Advancement of "Colored" People. After a short talk with Du Bois, Garvey became so disgusted with the man and his principles that the thought he never contemplated entered his mind—that of remaining in America to teach Du Bois and his group what real race pride meant.

Garvey at N. A. A. C. P.'s Office

When Garvey left the office of the National Association for the Advancement of "Colored" People, to travel through and study the social life of Negro America, he found that the policy of the Association was well observed in business and professional life, as well as in the drawing room, etc., all over the country. In restaurants, drug stores and offices all over the nation where our people were engaged in business it was discoverable that those employed were the very "lightest" members of the race—as waitresses, clerks and stenographers. Garvey asked, "What's the matter? Why were not black, brown-skin and mulatto girls employed?" And he was told it was "for the good of the trade." That to have trade it was necessary and incumbent to have "light" faces, as near white as possible. But the shock did not stop there. In New York, Boston, Washington and Detroit, Garvey further discovered the activities of the "Blue Vein Society" and the "Colonial Club." The West Indian "lights" formed the "Colonial Club" and the American "lights" the "Blue Vein" Society. The "Colonial Club" would give annual balls besides regular or monthly *soirees* and no one less than a quadroon would be admitted, and gentlemen below that complexion were only admitted if they were lawyers, doctors or very successful business men with plenty of "cash," who were known to uphold the caste aristocracy. At St. Philip's Church, New York, where the Very Rev. Dr. Daniels held sway and dominion, the "society" had things so arranged that even though this man was a brown-skin clergyman, and his rector a very near white gentleman, he had to draw the line and give the best seats in the church and the places of honor to the "Blue Veins" and the others would have a "look in" when they, by fawning before and "humbling" themselves and by giving lavishly to the church, admitted the superiority of caste. (By the way, Dr. Daniels was also an executive officer or director of the National Association for the Advancement of "Colored" People.) In Washington one or two of the churches did the same thing, but in Detroit the Very Rev. "Bob" Bagnall, now director of branches of the National Association for the Advancement of "Colored" people held sway. In his church no dark person could have a seat in the front, and, to test the truthfulness of it after being told, Garvey, incog, one Sunday night attempted to occupy one of the empty seats, not so very near the front, and the effort nearly spoiled the whole service, as Brother Bob, who was then ascending the pulpit, nearly lost his "balance" to see such a face so near the "holy of holies." Brother Bob was also an officer of the National Association for the Advancement of "Colored" People. On Garvey's return to New York he made (incog) a similar test at St. Philip's Church one Sunday, and the Rev. Daniels was nearly ready to fight.

Now, what does all this mean? It is to relate the hidden program and motive of the National Association for the Advancement of "Colored" People and to warn Negro America of not being deceived by a group of men who have as much love for the Negro blood in their veins as the devil has for holy water.

Scheme to Destroy Race

The National Association for the Advancement of "Colored" People is a scheme to destroy the Negro Race, and the leaders of it hate Marcus Garvey, because he has discovered them at their game and because the Universal Negro Improvement Association, without any prejudice to color or caste, is making headway in bringing all the people together for their common good. They hate Garvey because the Universal Negro Improvement Association and the Black Star Line employed every shade of color in the race, according to ability and merit, and put the N. A. A. C. P. to shame for employing only the "lightest" of the race. They hate Garvey because he forced them to fill Shiladay's place with a Negro. They hate Garvey because they had to employ "black" Pickens to cover up their scheme after Garvey had discovered it; they hate Garvey because they have had to employ brown-skin "Bob" Bagnall to make a showing to the people that they were doing the "right" thing by them; they hate Garvey because he has broken up the "Pink Tea Set"; they hate Garvey because they had been forced to recognize mulatto, brown and black talent in the association equally with the lighter element; they hate Garvey because he is teaching the unity of race, without color superiority or prejudice. The gang thought that they would have been able to build up in America a buffer class between whites and Negroes, and thus in another fifty years join with the powerful race and crush the blood of their mothers, as is being done in South Africa and the West Indies.

The imprisonment of Garvey is more than appears on the surface, and the National Association for the Advancement of Colored People knows it. Du Bois and those who lead the Association are skillful enough to be using the old method of getting the "other fellow" to destroy himself, hence the activities of "brown-skin" Bagnall and "black" Pickens. Walter White, whom we can hardly tell from a Southern gentleman who lives with a white family in Brooklyn, is kept in the background, but dark Bagnall, Pickens and Du Bois are pushed to the front to make the attack, so that there would be no suspicion of the motive. They are to drive hard and hot, and then the silent influence would bring up the rear, hence the slogan, "Garvey must go !" and the vicious attacks in the different magazines by Pickens, Du Bois and Bagnall.

Garvey Caught the Tune

Gentlemen, you are very smart, but Garvey has caught your tune. The conspiracy to destroy the Negro race, is so well organized that the moment anything interferes with their program there springs up a simultaneous action on the part of the leaders. It will be observed that in the September issue of the "Crisis" is published on the very last page of its news section what purports to be the opinion of a Jamaica paper about Marcus Garvey and his case. The skillful editor of the "Crisis," Dr. Du Bois, reproduces that part of the article that would tend to show the opinion about Garvey in his own country taken from a paper called the "Gleaner," (edited by one Herbert George de Lisser) and not the property of Negroes.

The article in the original was clipped from the "Gleaner" when it appeared, and was sent by a friend to Garvey, so that he knew all that appeared in it. In it the editor extolled the leadership and virtues of Dr. Du Bois, and said it was the right kind of leadership for the American Negro people, and bitterly denounced Garvey. Du Bois published that part that denounced Garvey, but suppressed the part that gave him the right of leadership ; and he failed to enlighten his readers that the editor of the "Gleaner" is a very light man, who hates the Negro blood of his mother and who is part of the international scheme to foster the Blue Vein Society scheme. Dr. Du Bois failed to further enlighten his readers that he visited Jamaica and was part of the "Colonial Society" scheme ; he also failed to state that in the plan De Lisser is to "hold down" the West Indian end of the "caste scheme" and he and others to "hold down" the American end, while their agents "hold down" the South African section.

Entire Race Must Get Together

But now we have reached the point where the entire race must get together and stop these schemers at their game. Whether we are light, yellow, black or what not, there is but one thing for us to do, and that is to get together and build up a race. God made us in His own image and He had some purpose when He thus created us. Then why should we seek to destroy ourselves? If a few Du Boises and De Lissers do not want their progeny to remain of our race, why not be satisfied to abide their time and take their peaceful exit? But why try in this subtle manner to humiliate and destroy our race?

We as a people, have a great future before us. Ethiopia shall once more see the day of her glory, then why destroy the chance and opportunity simply to be someone else?

Let us work and wait patiently, for our day of racial triumph will come. Let us not divide ourselves into castes, but let us all work together for the common good. Let us remember the sorrow of our mothers. Let us not forget that it is our duty to remedy any wrong that has already been done, and not ourselves perpetuate the evil of race destruction. To change our race is no credit. The Anglo-Saxon doesn't want to be a Japanese; the Japanese doesn't want to be a Negro. Then, in the name of God and all that is holy, why should we want to be somebody else?

Let the National Association for the Advancement of Colored People stop its hypocrisy and settle down to real race uplift

If Dr. Du Bois, Johnson, Pickens and Bagnall do not know, let me tell them that they are only being used to weaken the race, so that in another fifty or a hundred years the race can easily be wiped out as a social, economic and political force or "menace."

The people who are directing the affairs of the National Association for the Advancement of "Colored" People are keen observers, it takes more than ordinary intelligence to penetrate their motive, hence you are now warned.

All the "gas" about anti-lynching and "social equality" will not amount to a row of pins, in fact, it is only a ruse to raise money to capitalize the scheme and hide the real motive. Negroes, "watch your step" and save yourselves from deception and subsequent extermination.

RACE PURITY A DESIDERATUM

It is the duty of the virtuous and morally pure of both the white and black races to thoughtfully and actively protect the future of the two peoples, by vigorously opposing the destructive propaganda and vile efforts of the miscegenationists of the white race, and their associates, the hybrids of the Negro race.

Miscegenation will lead to the moral destruction of both races, and the promotion of a hybrid caste that will have no social standing or moral background in a critical moral judgment of the life and affairs of the human race.

The lower animals, some of even similar but opposite species, do not mate, living voluntarily in keeping with the laws of nature; yet man, the highest type of creation, has to be restrained, in some cases by severe human laws and punishment, from mating with even other species of the lower animals. **Something is wrong.**

The agitation about and for social equality is but a sham, and all self-respecting whites and blacks should frown upon the extraneous arguments adduced by its advocates.

The Black race, like the white, is proud of its own society and will yield nothing in the desire to keep itself pure and ward off a monstrous subjugation of its original and natural type, by which creation is to be judged, as a race responsible for its own acts, and held accountable in the final analysis for the presentation of itself, before the Judgment seat of God. **The Ethiopian cannot change his skin;** and we shall not.

AFRICA'S WEALTH

(Written April 18, 1923.)

Gradually, we, as Negroes, are witnessing an increasing encroachment upon our rights on the continent of Africa by the adventurous European races. Already the great colonizing governments of Europe have established themselves all over Africa by way of political control, and we find that they are calling upon their different nationals to go out and take up their residence on the continent for the purpose of exploiting the country and its natural resources.

The following is a news article which appeared in the New York Tribune under date of April 15, 1923:—

PROSPERITY SWEEPS OVER AFRICA
IN ALL LINES OF INDUSTRY

New Railways and Harbors Are Being Constructed to Empty Mineral and Agricultural Wealth of World

"CAPE TOWN.—Probably at no period in the last twenty-five years has there been such manifold activity in the development of Africa's resources as at present. In the southern sub-continent, the Union of South Africa is constructing many new railway lines and electrifying several important existing routes. Projects for new harbors from Cape Town to Kosi Bay are under consideration, while the Portuguese are spending millions in port and railway equipment at Delagoa Bay and Beira.

Portuguese capitalists are discussing other projects of equal magnitude in the Portuguese colonies in conjunction with American, British and Belgian capital.

In the Belgian Congo, which admittedly is the most progressive part of Africa today, the central spine of the Cape to Cairo route is still broken by the existing breach from the Congo to the Nile, but no less than five railway routes are being surveyed for early construction, while a magnificent system of equatorial roads is materializing to synchronize with the growing motor traffic, connecting thereby the numerous profitable mines and tropical plantations with the river steamers and existing main railroads in this prosperous Belgian colony.

In the Nile Valley, from the Delta to Lake Victoria Nyanza, is to be found Africa's richest Pandora's box, which only awaits opening to surprise the world with its great mineral treasures. To the east, along the coast of the Red Sea, there are rich oil wells and huge phosphate deposits.

In Kenya Province there is a great industrial activity, both by the government and the settler community. In Tanganyika territory there are great fertile plantation areas with immense mineral potentialities, and American capitalists are being urged to come there and develop them.

Indications of coal and metaliferous wealth have been found in the Portuguese colonies of Nyassaland and Zambesi, but there is no country that commands sufficient resources to develop them except the United States. Foreign residents of Africa say there are fortunes to be made here by those who are willing to undertake the work of development."

Africa today is the biggest game in the hunt of nations and races. Africa today is regarded, as I have always said, as the richest spot in the world, to be exploited by those who are keen enough and appreciative enough to invest their money and their interests in the development of that continent.

An open appeal is now being made to the white capitalists of different countries to invest in the exploitation of the oil fields, diamond, gold and iron mines of the "Old Homeland." This means that in a short time Africa will become the centre of the world's commercial activities, at which time the black man will naturally be relegated to his accustomed place of being the "under-dog" of the New African civilization. This is about to happen in the face of a highly-developed Negro civilization in the Western world, wherein men of the Negro race seek the same opportunities in things economic as the other races of the world.

White Capitalists Looking Toward Africa

Can we not realize that we of the Negro race have slept for hundreds of years, allowing during that period of time the great Caucasian race and the other great races to develop their own countries, their own homes and habitats until they have reached the point of exhaustion? They have practically extracted from their own countries all the wealth those countries could produce, whilst we have remained dormant for 300 years, ignoring the possibilities of our own country, ignoring the wealth of our own country. Now these other peoples are leaving their own countries—over-exploited and over-developed—and going into Africa to develop and rob its vast resources. What does that mean? It means that in another fifty or one hundred years, if European and American capital develops and exploits Africa, it will become like Europe and the United States of America—the future home of the white man. Wherein with a small amount of investment, with a small amount of capital, they will have so exploited the country as to cause it to produce an abundance of wealth and make Africa the wealthiest country and continent in the world, with probably the greatest civilization that the world will see in another one hundred or two hundred years, which will be a civilization owned and controlled by white men, where Negroes in that period of time, will fall back into the natural life of that country, (just as we are in the United States of America at the present time) as a secondary part of the civilization when we will have to beg for jobs and beg for a chance, as we are now doing in the United States of America. Because when the white man invests his money for the development of Africa it means that he is going to employ labor in doing this, and the same Negroes who say they have lost nothing in Africa, when men like John D. Rockefeller are ready to develop the oil resources there, they will carry them by the thousands to Africa. They will go as quickly as they went from the West Indian Islands to dig the Panama Canal, and West Indian Negroes know well the treatment they received at the hands of white Americans after the Panama Canal was completed. When men like Gary are ready to develop the coal and iron mines they will carry Negroes by the thousands to Africa, and they will go as readily as they go to Pennsylvania to work in the mines. Yet we say we have lost nothing in Africa; while Africa offers to us its possibilities, its untold opportunities. Why should we not go there and take an interest in its development, not for white men, but for Negroes. The white man is now doing it, not with the intention of building for other races, but with the intention of building for himself—for the white race.

The Value of Minerals

Most of us know, or ought to know, the value of minerals and oil. In Oklahoma, Texas and some of the Western States of America, men wake up over night and find themselves millionaires and rich men because oil happens to be discovered on their property. An acre or two of land with oil represents thousands of dollars, every day, according to the quantity of oil the well produces; because oil is being consumed all over the world in every line of industry. As of oil, so of coal, iron, copper and all the other minerals, which are to be found in Africa in abundance. Lately parsonite, a new radium-bearing mineral, has been found in the Belgium Congo. Radium is the most precious mineral in the world. It is sold at $120,000 per gram and is used extensively in scientific experiments, so we can readily realize the vast amount of wealth lying buried in Mother Africa awaiting development.

Native Africans Exploited by White Men

The native Africans unfortunately have not been schooled in the appreciation of the valuable mineral wealth of Africa. They have not been schooled in the methods of exploiting mineral wealth. For a long time they were unable to appreciate the value of diamonds, until the white man went there with his scientific commercial knowledge and took away the diamond fields of Kimberley, Johannesburg and the entire Union of South Africa, where the greatest quantity of diamonds is found. The native Africans once owned all the wealth of South Africa, but Cecil Rhodes and other white men robbed and exploited them, and today the diamond fields are owned by white men, who have practically reduced the native Africans (who once owned the lands) to slavery, and by the system of forced labor, compelled them to mine the diamonds and other minerals and to live on reservations, herded together like cattle, under conditions wholly unsuited to human beings. The British Empire today owes its present financial existence to the wealth which has been recruited from Africa, the wealth that we Negroes could have controlled fifty years ago, when there was not so much interest in Africa. It is only within this period of time that Italy, France, England, Portugal and Belgium have started a wholesale colonization and exploitation of Africa. As for Belgium's contact with the native African in the Congo Basin, every Negro who knows anything about the "Leopoldian System" shudders at the mention of the word Belgian. This system out-rivals any of the most fiendish wholesale massacres and atrocities ever committed by human beings, and all for rubber and ivory. Villages were compelled to furnish a certain amount of rubber every week as a tax. Natives were not allowed to cultivate the soil, all their time was spent in getting rubber. Men, women and children were utilized in rubber getting, hence they died in large numbers from starvation and over work. When certain areas became non-productive by being over-worked, the inhabitants of these areas were massacred by the soldiers who were sent out to collect the rubber, and instead of returning with rubber, they returned with trophies of hands and other parts of the human body, to prove that they had done their work. This system in its entirety lasted for twenty years, with a loss of life of over twenty million black men, women and children.

In the last world war Negroes from every clime were called out to protect "poor Belgium" from the "brutal Hun." In the coming struggle of the "survival of the fittest," we may be able to repay "poor Belgium" measure for measure for her colonization of over one million square miles of African territory.

All Negroes Should Protect Africa

Europe today is bankrupt and cannot advance much capital for the development of African industries, and therefore they are trying to interest American capitalists in the exploitation of the wealth of the great Continent. There is absolutely no reason why the 400,000,000 Negroes of the world should not make a desperate effort to re-conquer our Motherland from the white man, in that, whether he be English, French, German, Italian or Spanish, his one and only interest is selfish exploitation and domination. If native Africans are unable to appreciate the value of their own country from the standard of Western civilization, then it is for us, their brothers, to take to them the knowledge and information that they need to help to develop the country for the common good.

Why should we allow Belgium, Portugal, Spain, Italy, France and England to build up and rehabilitate their bankrupt nations and civilization out of the wealth and resources of our country? They have no room for us in their countries, and surely we have absolutely no room for them as exploiters in our country. We have allowed cowardice and fear to take possession of us for a long time, but that will never take us anywhere. It is no use being afraid of these nations and peoples. They are human beings like ourselves. We have blood, feelings, passions and ambitions just as they have. Why, therefore, should we allow them to trample down our rights and deprive us of our liberty? Negroes everywhere must get that courage of manhood that will enable them to strike out, irrespective of who the enemy is, and demand those things that are ours by right—moral, legal and divine.

Black Millionaires a Possibility

Let us as Negroes, prepare ourselves throughout the world for the conflict that is bound to ensue between the rivalling forces for the ultimate domination of our country—Africa. For we are not going to give up easily, and allow these European intruders to rob, exploit and dominate the land of our fathers.

If the oil of Africa is good for Rockefeller's interest; if iron ore is good for the Carnegie Trust; then surely these minerals are good for us. Why should we allow Wall Street and the capitalist group of America and other countries to exploit our country when they refuse to give us a fair chance in the countries of our adoption? Why should not Africa give to the world its black Rockefeller, Rothschild and Henry Ford? Now is the opportunity. Now is the chance for every Negro to make every effort toward a commercial, industrial standard that will make us comparable with the successful business men of other races.

Africa invites capital to develop its resources. Let not that capital, whether it be financial or man-power, be supplied by white men, but let us as Negroes make our contribution. All that Africa needs is proper education. The Western Negro has much of that, and it is our duty to so prepare our brothers as to place them on guard against the tricky exploiters of Europe who have been deceiving and robbing them of their possessions.

THE NEGRO, COMMUNISM, TRADE UNIONISM AND HIS (?) FRIEND
"Beware of Greeks Bearing Gifts"

If I must advise the Negro workingman and laborer, I should warn him against the present brand of Communism or Workers' Partizanship as taught in America, and to be careful of the traps and pitfalls of white trade unionism, in affiliation with the American Federation of white workers or laborers.

It seems strange and a paradox, but the only convenient friend the Negro worker or laborer has, in America, at the present time, is the white capitalist. The capitalist being selfish—seeking only the largest profit out of labor—is willing and glad to use Negro labor wherever possible on a scale "reasonably" below the standard white union wage. He will tolerate the Negro in any industry (except those that are necessarily guarded for the protection of the whiteman's material, racial and assumed cultural dominance) if he accepts a lower standard of wage than the white union man; but, if the Negro unionizes himself to the level of the white worker, and, in affiliation with him, the choice and preference of employment is given to the white worker, without any regard or consideration for the Negro.

White Unionism is now trying to rope in the Negro and make him a standard wage worker, then, when it becomes generally known that he demands the same wage as the white worker, an appeal or approach will be made to the white capitalist or employer, to alienate his sympathy or consideration for the Negro, causing him, in the face of all things being equal, to discriminate in favor of the white worker as a race duty and obligation. In this respect the Negro if not careful to play his game well, which must be done through and by his leaders, is between "hell and the powder house."

The danger of Communism to the Negro, in countries where he forms the minority of the population, is seen in the selfish and vicious attempts of that party or group to use the Negro's vote and physical numbers in helping to smash and over-throw, by revolution, a system that is injurious to them as the white under dogs, the success of which would put their majority group or race still in power, not only as communists but as whitemen. To me there is no difference between two roses looking alike, and smelling alike, even if some one calls them by different names. Fundamentally what racial difference is there between a white Communist, Republican or Democrat? On the appeal of

race interest the Communist is as ready as either to show his
racial ascendancy or superiority over the Negro. He will be as
quick and eager as any to show the Negro that he is white, and
by Divine right of assumption has certain duties to perform to
the rest of us mortals, and to defend and protect certain racial
ideals against the barbarian hordes that threaten white supremacy.

I am of the opinion that the group of whites from whom
Communists are made, in America, as well as trade unionists and
members of the Worker's party, is more dangerous to the Negro's welfare than any other group at present. Lynching mobs
and wild time parties are generally made up of 99½ per cent. of
such white people. The Negro should keep shy of Communism
or the Worker's party in America. Since they are so benevolent
let them bring about their own reforms and show us how different they are to others. We have been bitten too many times by
all the other parties,—"Once bitten, twice shy"—Negroes have
no right with white people's fights or quarrels, except, like the
humble, hungry, meagre dog, to run off with the bone when
both contestants drop it, being sure to separate himself from the
big, well fed dogs, by a good distance, otherwise to be over-
taken, and then completely outdone.

If the Negro takes my advice he will organize by himself
and always keep his scale of wage a little lower than the whites
until he is able to become, through proper leadership, his own
employer; by so doing he will keep the good will of the white
employer and live a little longer under the present scheme of
things. If not, between Communism, white trade unionism and
worker's parties he is doomed in the next 25, 50 or 100 years to
complete economic and general extermination.

The Negro needs to be saved from his (?) "Friends," and beware of "Greeks bearing gifts." The greatest enemies of the
Negro are among those who hypocritically profess love and fellowship for him, when, in truth, and deep down in their hearts,
they despise and hate him. Pseudo-philanthropists and their organizations are killing the Negro. White men and women of the
Morefield Storey, Joel Spingarn, Julius Rosenwald, Oswald Garrison Villard, Congressman Dyer and Mary White Ovington type,
in conjunction with the above mentioned agencies, are disarming, dis-visioning, dis-ambitioning and fooling the Negro to
death. They teach the Negro to look to the whites in a false
direction. They, by their practices are endeavoring to hold the
Negroes in check, as a possible dangerous minority group, and
yet point them to the impossible dream of equality that shall

never materialize, as they well know, and never intended; at the same time distracting the Negro from the real solution and objective of securing nationalism. By thus decoying and deceiving the Negro and side-tracking his real objective, they hope to gain time against him in allowing others of their race to perfect the plan by which the blacks are to be completely destroyed as a competitive permanent part of white majority civilization and culture. They have succeeded in enslaving the ignorance of a small group of so-called "Negro intellectuals" whom they use as agents to rope in the unsuspicious colored or Negro people. They have become resentful and bitter toward the Ku Klux Klan, and use the influence of their controlled newspapers (white and colored) to fight them, not because they so much hate the Klan, where the Negro is concerned, but because the Klan, through an honest expression of the whiteman's attitude toward the Negro, prepares him to help himself.

This hypocritical group of whites, like Spingarn and Storey, have succeeded an earlier group that fooled the Negro during the days of Reconstruction. Instead of pointing the Negro to Africa, as Jefferson and Lincoln did, they sought to revenge him, for the new liberty given him, by imprisoning him in the whiteman's civilization; to further rob his labor, and exploit his ignorance, until he is subsequently ground to death by a newly developed superior white civilization. The plot of these Negro baiters is wretched to contemplate, hence their hatred of me and their influence to crush me in my attempt to save the black race.

Between the Ku Klux Klan and the Morefield Storey National Association for the Advancement of "Colored" People group, give me the Klan for their honesty of purpose towards the Negro. They are better friends to my race, for telling us what they are, and what they mean, thereby giving us a chance to stir for ourselves, than all the hypocrites put together with their false gods and religions, notwithstanding. Religions that they preach and will not practise; a God they talk about, whom they abuse every day—away with the farce, hypocrisy and lie. It smells, it stinks to high heaven. I regard the Klan, the Anglo-Saxon Clubs and White America Societies, as far as the Negro is concerned, as better friends of the race than all other groups of hypocritical whites put together. I like honesty and fair play. You may call me a Klansman if you will, but, potentially, every whiteman is a Klansman, as far as the Negro in competition with whites socially, economically and politically is concerned, and there is no use lying about it.

CAPITALISM AND THE STATE

Capitalism is necessary to the progress of the world, and those who unreasonably and wantonly oppose or fight against it are enemies to human advancement; but there should be a limit to the individual or corporate use or control of it.

No individual should be allowed the possession, use or the privilege to invest on his own account, more than a million, and no corporation should be allowed to control more than five millions. Beyond this, all control, use and investment of money, should be the prerogative of the State with the concurrent authority of the people.

With such a method we would prevent the ill-will, hatred and conflicts that now exist between races, peoples and nations.

Modern wars are generally the outgrowth of dissatisfied capitalistic interests either among foreign or strange peoples or nations.

Until a universal adjustment takes place the State or nation should have the power to conscript and use without any obligation to repay, the wealth of such individuals or corporations through whose investments or interests, in foreign countries, or among foreign or strange peoples wars are fomented and made; in which the nation is called upon to use its military or naval power as a protection of the rights or interests of such citizens when the conflict cannot be prevented or settled otherwise.

The innocent citizens of the country should not be called upon to make sacrifices in men, money and other resources, as is generally done in times of war, and those most interested or responsible by their acts of selfishness go free, or only bear but a proportionate part of the burden.

The entire burden of the war should rest upon and be the responsibility of those whose interests brought about the difficulties, and they should be made to pay the full cost of such a war.

Men like Morgan, Rockefeller, Firestone, Doheny, Sinclair and Gary should not be allowed to entangle the nation in foreign disputes, leading to war, for the sake of satisfying their personal, individual or corporate selfishness and greed for more wealth at the expense of the innocent masses of both countries.

Oil "concessions" in Mexico or Persia; rubber "concessions" in Liberia, West Africa; sugar or coffee "concessions" in Haiti, West Indies, to be exploited for the selfish enrichment of individuals, sooner or later, end in disaster; hence ill-feeling, hate, and then war. Let us unite and stop it for the good of the people and the nation.

The trick of the selfish capitalist is to stir up local agitation

among the nations; have them shoot or kill some citizen
of the capitalist's country, then he influences the agencies of his
Government to call upon the home authorities for protection.
A harsh diplomatic note is sent that inspires an insult or further
injury, then an ultimatum is served or a demand made for in-
demnities or war declared with the hope of arresting from the
particular weak, unfortunate country such territories where oil,
rubber or other valuable minerals or resources are to be found.

This kind of dollar diplomacy is a disgrace to our civilization
and for the sake of humanity should be stopped.

GOVERNING THE IDEAL STATE

Our modern systems of Government have partly failed and are wholly failing.

We have tried various forms, but none has measured up to the **Ideal State.** Communism was the last attempt, and its most ardent advocates have acknowledged its limitations, shortcomings and impossibility.

The reason for all this failure is not far to seek. The sum total of Governmental collapse is traceable to the growing spirit of selfishness, graft and greed within the individual. Naturally, the state cannot govern itself: it finds expression and executes its edicts through individuals, hence the State is human. Its animation is but the reflex of our human characters. As a Nero, Caesar, Alexander, Alfred, William, Louis, Charles, Cromwell, Napoleon, Washington, Lincoln, Roosevelt or Wilson thinks, so expresses the majesty of the State.

If we must correct the maladministration of the State and apply the corporate majesty of the people to their own good, then we must reach the source and there reorganize or reform.

Under the pressure of our civilization, with its manifold demands, the individual is tempted, beyond measure, to do evil or harm to others; and, if responsible, to the entire State and people, and if by thus acting he himself profits and those around him, there arises corruption in Government, as well as in other branches of the secular and civil life.

All other methods of Government having been tried and failed, I suggest a reformation that would place a greater responsibility upon the shoulders of the elect and force them either to be the criminals, that some of us believe they are, or the good and true representatives we desire them to be.

Government should be absolute, and the head should be thoroughly responsible for himself and the acts of his subordinates.

When we elect a President of a nation, he should be endowed with absolute authority to appoint all his lieutenants from cabinet ministers, governors of States and Territories, administrators and judges to minor officers. He should swear his life as a guarantee to the State and people, and he should be made to pay the price of such a life if he deceives, grafts, bows to special privilege or interest, or in any way undermines the sacred honor and trust imposed upon him by acts of favoritism, injustice or friendly or self interests. He should be the soul of honor, and when he is legally or properly found to the contrary, he should be publicly disgraced, and put to death as an outcast and an unworthy representative of the righteous will of the people.

A President should, by proper provisions made by the State, be removed from all pecuniary obligations and desires of a material nature. He should be voted a salary and other accommodations so large and sufficient as to make it reasonably impossible for him, or those dependent upon him, to desire more during his administration. He and his family should be permanently and substantially provided for after the close of his administration, and all this and possibly more should be done for **the purpose of removing him from the slightest possible material temptations or want.** He, in turn, should devote his entire time to the sovereign needs and desires of the people. He should, for all the period of his administration, remove himself from obligatory, direct and fraternal contact with any and all special friends. His only friends outside of his immediate family should be the State. He should exact by law from all his responsible and administrative appointees a similar obligation, and he should enforce the law by penalty of death.

His administrators and judges should be held to strict accountability, and on the committing of any act of injustice, unfairness, favoritism or malfeasance, should be taken before the public, disgraced and then stoned to death.

This system would tend to attract to the sacred function of Government and judicial administration, only men and women of the highest and best characters, whom the public would learn to honor and respect with such satisfaction as to obliterate and prevent the factional party fights of Socialism, Communism, Anarchism, etc., for the control of Government, because of the belief that Government is controlled in the interest of classes, and not for the good of all the people. It would also discourage the self-seekers, grafters, demagogues and charlatans from seeking public offices, as the penalty of discovery of crime would be public disgrace and death for them and their families.

The State should hold the wife of a President, and the wives of all administrative officials, solely responsible for their domestic households, and they should be required by law to keep a strict and accurate public account of all receipts and disbursements of their husbands during their administrative terms, and if any revenue comes into the household other than provided by law, should be promptly reported to the responsible officer of the State for immediate action, and should the wife conceal or refuse to make such a disclosure, and that it be discovered afterwards, and it was an act of crime against the dignity and high office of the incumbent, she and her husband should be publicly disgraced and put to death, but any child or member of the family who, before discovery, reports the act, should be spared the disgrace and publicly honored by the populace for performing a duty to the State.

The State should require that the husband and his consort under the severest penalty for non-performance, report the full amount of his entire wealth to the State before taking office, and that all incomes and salaries legally authorized be reported promptly to the wife to enable her to keep a proper public account.

Whenever a President or high official during his term has performed solemnly and truly all his duties to the people and State, and he is about to retire, he should be publicly proclaimed and honored by the populace, and all during his life he and his family should occupy a special place of honor and respect among the people. They should be respected by all with whom they come in contact, and at death they should be granted public funerals and their names added to the niche in the Hall of Fame of the Nation. Their names should be placed on the Honor Roll of the Nation, and their deeds of righteousness should be handed down to the succeeding generations of the race, and their memories sung by the poets of the nation.

For those who have abused their trusts, images of them should be made and placed in a national hall of criminology and ill fame, and their crimes should be recited and a curse pronounced upon them and their generations.

Government left to the free and wanton will and caprice of the individual in an age so corrupt as this, without any vital reprimand or punishment for malfeasance, other than ordinary imprisonment, will continue to produce dissatisfaction, cause counter agitations of a dangerous nature and upheavals destructive to the good of society and baneful to the higher hopes and desires of the human race.

This plan I offer to the race as a means to which we may perfect the establishment of a new system of Government, conducive to the best interest of the people and a blessing to our disorganized society of the twentieth century.

THE "COLORED" OR NEGRO PRESS

The "Colored" or Negro press is the most venal, ignorant and corrupt of our time. This is a broad statement to make against an entire institution, and one so essential to the educational and corporate life of a people; but to be honest and to undeceive the Negro, whom I love above all God's creatures, the truth must be told. I make and again emphasize the statement without any regard for friendship, and with the full knowledge that the said false, vicious and venal press will unmercifully criticise me for telling the truth to the unfortunate of my race.

Unfortunately, the "Colored" or Negro press of today falls into the hands of unprincipled, unscrupulous and characterless individuals whose highest aims are to enrich themselves and to find political berths for themselves and their friends, or, rather, confederates.

The white press of today has its element of venality and corruption, but the higher ethics of the profession are generally observed and maintained, and at no time will you find the influence of white journalism used to debase or humiliate its race, but always to promote the highest ideals and protect the integrity of the white people everywhere.

The Negro press, to the contrary, has no constructive policy nor ideal. You may purchase its policy and destroy or kill any professed ideal if you would make the offer in cash.

Negro newspapers will publish the gravest falsehoods without making any effort to first find out the authenticity; they publish the worst crimes and libels against the race, if it pays in circulation or advertisements. A fair example of the criminality of the Negro press against the race is reflected through its most widely circulated sensational publications, namely, "The Chicago Defender" of Chicago, and "The Afro-American" of Baltimore. These newspapers lead all others in their feature of crime, false news and libels against the race.

The primary motive of Negro newspaper promoters is to make quick and easy money. Several of such promoters are alleged to have made large fortunes through their publications, especially through corrupt politics and bad advertisements that should have been refused in respect for the race.

It is plain to see, and is well known, that the sole and only purpose of these promoters is to make money—with absolutely no race pride or effort to help the race toward a proper moral, cultural and educational growth, that would place the race in the category so much desired by the masses and those honest leaders and reformers who have been laboring for the higher development of the people.

To attempt reform or the higher leadership that would permanently benefit the race, is to court the most vicious and cowardly attack from the promoters of Negro newspapers. If you are not in a "ring" with them to support their newspapers or "split" with them, what they would term the "spoils" then you become marked for their crucifixion. All the Negro leaders or organizations that escape the merciless criticism and condemnation of the Negro press are those who stoop to "feed" their graft or who as fellows of the same fold, "scratch each other's backs." To be honest and upright is to bring down upon your head the heavy hammer of condemnation, as such an attitude would "spoil" the game of the "gang" to enrich itself off the ignorance of the masses who are generally led by these newspapers, their editors and friends.

When I arrived in this country in 1916, I discovered that the Negro press had no constructive policy. The news published were all of the kind that reflected the worst of the race's character in murder, adultery, robbery, etc. These crimes were announced in the papers on front pages by glaring and catchy headlines; other features played up by the papers were dancing and parlor socials of questionable intent, and long columns of what is generally called "social" or "society" news of "Mrs Mary Jones entertained at lunch last evening Mr. So and So" and "Mr. and Mrs. John Brown had the pleasure of entertaining last evening at their elaborate apartment Miss Minnie Baker after which she met a party of friends." Miss Minnie Baker probably was some Octoroon of questionable morals, but made a fuss of because of her "color," and thus runs the kind of material that made up the average Negro newspaper until the Negro World arrived on the scene.

"The Chicago Defender," that has become my arch enemy in the newspaper field, is so, because in 1918-1919 I started the "Negro World" to preserve the term Negro to the race as against the desperate desire of other newspapermen to substitute the term "colored" for the race. Nearly all the newspapers of the race had entered into a conspiracy to taboo the term "Negro" and popularize the term "colored" as the proper race term. To augment this they also fostered the propaganda of bleaching out black skins to light complexions, and straightening out kinky or curly hair to meet the "standard" of the new "society" that was being promoted. I severely criticised "The Chicago Defender" for publishing humiliating and vicious advertisements against the pride and integrity of the race. At that time the "Defender" was publishing full page advertisements about "bleaching the skin" and "straightening the hair." One of these advertisements was from the Plough Manufacturing Company of Tennessee made up as follows:

"There were many degrading exhortations to the race to change its black complexion as an entrant to society. There were pictures of two women, one black and the other very bright and under the picture of the black woman appeared these words: 'Lighten your black skin,' indicating perfection to be reached by bleaching white like the light woman. There were other advertisements such as 'Bleach your dark skin,' 'take the black out of your face,' 'If you want to be in society lighten your black skin,' 'Have a light complexion and be in society,' 'Light skin beauty over night,' 'Amazing bleach works under skin,' 'The only harmless way to bleach the skin white,' 'The most wonderful skin whitener,' 'Straighten your kinky hair,' 'Take the kink out of your hair and be in society,' 'Knock the kink out,' 'Straighten hair in five days,' etc. These advertisements could also be found in any of the Negro papers published all over the country influencing the poor, unthinking masses to be dissatisfied with their race and color, and to 'aspire' to look white so as to be in society. I attacked this vicious propaganda and brought down upon my head the damnation of the 'leaders' who sought to make a new race and a monkey out of the Negro."

"The Negro World" has rendered a wonderful service to Negro journalism in the United States. It has gradually changed the tone and make-up of some of the papers, and where in 1914-15-16 there was no tendency to notice matters of great importance, today several of the papers are publishing international news and writing intelligent editorials on pertinent subjects. It has been a long and costly fight to bring this about.

I do hope that the statements of truth I have made will further help to bring about a reorganization of the Negro press. I fully realize that very little can be achieved by way of improvement for the race when its press is controlled by crafty and unscrupulous persons who have no pride or love of race.

We need crusaders in journalism who will not seek to enrich themselves off the crimes and ignorance of our race, but men and women who will risk everything for the promotion of racial pride, self respect, love and integrity. The mistake the race is making is to accept and believe that our unprincipled newspaper editors and publishers are our leaders, some of them are our biggest crooks and defamers.

Situated as we are, in a civilization of prejudice and contempt, it is not for us to inspire and advertise the vices of our people, but, by proper leadership, to form characters that would reflect the highest credit upon us and win the highest opinion of an observant and critical world.

WHAT WE BELIEVE

The Universal Negro Improvement Association advocates the uniting and blending of all Negroes into one strong, healthy race.   It is against miscegenation and race suicide.

It believes that the Negro race is as good as any other, and therefore should be as proud of itself as others are.

It believes in the purity of the Negro race and the purity of the white race.

It is against rich blacks marrying poor whites.

It is against rich or poor whites taking advantage of Negro women.

It believes in the spiritual Fatherhood of God and the Brotherhood of Man.

It believes in the social and political physical separation of all peoples to the extent that they promote their own ideals and civilization, with the privilege of trading and doing business with each other.   It believes in the promotion of a strong and powerful Negro nation in Africa.

It believes in the rights of all men.

UNIVERSAL NEGRO IMPROVEMENT ASSOCIATION.

MARCUS GARVEY, President-General.

January 1, 1924.

HISTORY AND THE NEGRO

To read the histories of the world, peoples and races, written by white men, would make the Negro feel and believe that he never amounted to anything in the creation.

History is written with prejudices, likes and dislikes; and there has never been a white historian who ever wrote with any true love or feeling for the Negro.

The Negro should expect but very little by way of compliment from the pen of other races. We are satisfied to know, however, that our race gave the first great civilization to the world; and, for centuries Africa, our ancestral home, was the seat of learning; and when blackmen, who were only fit then for the company of the gods, were philosophers, artists, scientists and men of vision and leadership, the people of other races were groping in savagery, darkness and continental barbarism.

White historians and writers have tried to rob the black man of his proud past in history, and when anything new is discovered to support the race's claim and attest the truthfulness of our greatness in other ages, then it is skillfully rearranged and credited to some other unknown race or people.

Negroes, teach your children that they are direct descendants of the greatest and proudest race who ever peopled the earth; and it is because of the fear of our return to power, in a civilization of our own, that may outshine others, why we are hated and kept down by a jealous and prejudiced contemporary world.

The very fact that the other races will not give the Negro a fair chance is indisputable evidence and proof positive that they are afraid of our civilized progression.

Every falsehood that is told by the historian should be unearthed, and the Negro should not fail to take credit for the glorious and wonderful achievements of his fathers in Africa, Europe and Asia.

Black men were so powerful in the earlier days of history that they were able to impress their civilization, culture and racial characteristics and features upon the peoples of Asia and Southern Europe. The dark Spaniards, Italians and Asiatics are the colored offsprings of a powerful black African civilization and nationalism. Any other statement by historians to the contrary is "bunk" and should not be swallowed by the enlightened Negro.

When we speak of 400,000,000 Negroes we mean to include several of the millions of India who are direct offsprings of that ancient African stock that once invaded Asia. The 400,000,000 Negroes of the world have a beautiful history of their own, and no one of any other race can truly write it but themselves. Until it is completely and carefully written, for the guidance of our children and ourselves, let us think it.

The white man's history is his inspiration, and he should be untrue to himself and negligent of the rights of his posterity to subordinate it to others, and so also of the Negro. Our history is as good as that of any other race or people, and nothing on this side of Heaven or Hell will make us deny it, the false treaties, essays, speculations and philosophies of others notwithstanding.

GIVE THE BLACKS A CHANCE

If the Negro is inferior why circumvent him; why suppress his talent and initiative; why rob him of his independent gifts; why fool him out of the rights of country; why imprison his intelligence and exploit his ignorance; why keep him down by the laws of inequality? Why not leave him alone to his own intelligence; why not give him a chance to grow and develop as he sees fit; why not free him from the incubus of a "forced upon" superiority; why not allow him, free and unhampered, to travel toward nationhood? If the whites are good sports, they will give the blacks a chance, and, I predict, that in fifty years, undisturbed or unmolested, I will show you a nation of proud, refined and cultured black men and women, whose comeliness will outshine that of the age of Solomon.

THE INTERNAL PREJUDICES OF NEGROES
Those who want to be white and those who want to remain black.

Very few persons, besides those who are deeply and sincerely interested in the Negro race, understand and fully realize the great internal conflict that is silently being waged for the defeat and ultimate destruction of the real Negro who has given a race, character and history to the world.

The unthinking whites and blacks drift along recklessly, and careless of racial consequences. To them, everything happens by chance, hence no effort to regulate or arrange their own lives and outlook. They give no thought toward the future of their respective races; they drift along with the tide. But there is always a number, even though small, of active minds, ever ready and prepared to lay out the course of salvation; and it is to these we look for direction in all those things that affect the human race.

The black and white races are now facing the crucial time of their existence. The whites are rightfully and properly crying out for a pure white race, and the proud and self-respecting blacks are crying out for a morally pure and healthy Negro race. Between both, we have a new school of thought, advanced by the "near white" or "colored" man, W. E. B. DuBois and his National Association for the "Advancement" of "Colored" people, who advocate racial amalgamation or general miscegenation with the hope of creating a new type of colored race by wiping out both black and white.

Gradually the DuBois School has succeeded·in the West Indies and South America—in such places like Cuba, Jamaica, Trinidad, Barbadoes, British Guiana and some of the Central American countries.

They have defeated the whites in the tropics and brought them to terms, hence, in these places the hybrid may intermarry among the pure whites with all freedom. After a generation or two the descendants boldly classify themselves as white, and, like the Rhinelander case in New York, make it difficult to tell who is white and who is not.

By skillfully engineered efforts the DuBois School is winning out in America. Already they have cornered the best governmental and other positions, in the name of the Negro or "Colored" race; with which positions they are better able to entrench themselves for the silent but determined fight to win out against both races.

The men of the DuBois School have succeeded in getting the ear of the Republican government and the leading Republican

politicians of the country, to the extent that they can get anything done from the White House to the Department of Labor.
They can get one of their group appointed an assistant attorney
general, ambassador extraordinary, or demand and get the dis-
missal of any white government employee, as in the case of the
white official who was recently dismissed in Richmond, Va., or
they can have imprisoned anyone they desire.

This school of "colored" leaders is skillfully using the numer-
ical and voting strength of the darker Negroes to strengthen their
position and to force their claim, at the same time having no
more social or honest fraternal use for them than the most
prejudiced southern white man.

The group that holds to and fosters the term "colored" has
a deeper meaning behind the use of the term than can be
imagined on the surface. "Colored" doesn't mean black or Negro.
It has a literal meaning for the group, in so much so that when
you speak of "colored" in the West Indies where the group has
already succeeded, everyone knows you do not mean a black,
dark or Negro person, but a socially superior person in the class
of the whites.

Du Bois has visited the West Indies and has made a keen
study of this West Indian arrangement, and he and his association are making great efforts to make it the adopted social policy
of America as well as internationally.

All the people who call themselves "colored" are not part of
this scheme or plan. The majority of the people called "colored"
are satisfied to be classified as Negroes or blacks, with the hope
of redeeming the race through the promotion of a modern moral
standard. These people, like the blackest Negro, want to see
the race morally united into one, and for this they are steadily
working, but with the hostile opposition of the skillful "colored"
leaders who have social ambitions, designs and plans of their
own.

According to the arrangement of the "colored" leaders, the
following plan is decided and acted upon; it is made very successful in the West Indies, and is now being successfuly fostered
in America and elsewhere:

In countries where the blacks outnumber the whites, the "colored" build up a buffer society, through the financial assistance
and patronage of the minority whites. They convince the minority
whites that the blacks are dangerous and vicious, and that their
only chance of successfully living among them is to elevate to
positions of trust, superiority and overseership the "colored"
element who will directly deal with the blacks and exploit them

for the general benefit of the whites. The whites being not strong enough to stand alone, accept or acquiesce and thus the "colored" element is elevated to a superior position and naturally becomes attached to the whites. The skillful group, however, by its ability to acquire wealth, through the privileged positions allowed, immediately starts out to socially equip itself educationally and culturally to meet the whites on equal terms. They also skillfully strengthen their positions by stirring up the blacks against the whites, explaining to the former that all their ills are caused by the whites, then they go back to the whites and intimidate them by drawing their attention to the great danger of the dissatisfied blacks, and offer as a solution the uniting of the whites and "colored" in a social and economic union to offset the supposed common danger from the blacks. By this artful method the "colored" elements of the colonies have socially subdued the white man, who now looks on and sees the prosperous "colored" gentleman leading away his sister or daughter in the bonds of marriage without the ability to raise the voice of protest.

The "colored" elements have arranged it so that the blacks are always kept down, so that they can use their dissatisfaction and disaffection as an argument to strengthen and further perpetuate their positions of social equality and economic privilege and preferment with the whites.

Such is the game that is being played over in America by the DuBois, Weldon Johnson group of "colored" persons of the National Association for the "Advancement" of "Colored" people. The Universal Negro Improvement Association stands in opposition to this association on the miscegenation question, because we believe in the racial purity of both the Negro and white races. We feel that the moral disadvantage of slavery should not be perpetuated. That where our slave masters were able to abuse our slave mothers and thereby create a hybrid bastardy, we ourselves, at this time of freedom and culture, should not perpetuate the crime of nature.

We desire to standardize our race morally, hence our advocacy of all elements and shades within the race coming together and by well understood and defined codes build up a strong and healthy Negro race with pride and respect in itself, rather than seeking, as the DuBois group does, to practise an unrestricted intercourse of miscegenation.

All the hate that the leaders of the small "colored" group can find has been levied at me for my interference with and interruption of their plans. My indictment, conviction and imprisonment is but a small effort of theirs to help destroy and ruin me because of my effort to save the Negro race from extinction through miscegenation.

The "colored" group has scientifically arranged their method of propaganda. In America and the colonies, they hold out certain baits and hopes to the educated and financially prosperous men of the darker groups; such as encouraging them to marry the very lightest element of their women, and adopting them into their society. These darker men, for the special privilege and "honor" are used as active propagandists to deceive the great mass of dark people so that they would not suspect the motive or the design of the "colored" element. Generally the darker men who marry the very lightest "colored" women, who sometimes pass off as white, become more hostile to their kind in the mass as well as by individual contact than the very leaders, as the leaders are generally careful not to attract or arouse suspicion of their motive. The majority of the "colored" leaders who seek after white women and the darker men who marry very light "colored" women, are seldom on social terms with their own mothers if they are dark. If they have their mothers in their homes, which is generally never so, they hide them away either in the kitchen or a back room where they do not come in contact with either their light "colored" or white guests. Sometimes a mother is referred to, if seen, as one of the servants.

Such is the great problem that I have sought to solve, and no one will wonder why I have been made a criminal in the struggle to rescue and save the Negro race from itself and from continuous suffering and ultimate extermination.

A RACE PARADOX

The Negro or "Colored" race is developing a class of millionaires or money-hoarders, much more dangerous to the race's life and existence than any similar group of men among any other race.

The rich Negro is not philanthropic to his race. He does not proportionately give to or help his racial institutions as the white people of wealth do. A Rhodes, Rockefeller or Carnegie or any other rich white person will create foundations, schools of research and science, clinics, hospitals or scholarships, but the Negro would prefer subscribing or donating to these white institutions to show off rather than to do for his own race.

When the exceptional in the race happens, then you may positively rest assured that it was done merely for show, and to gain some special personal internal racial advantage.

Not half of one per cent. of the rich or wealthy of the Negro or "colored" race gives away for charity or uplift work among their own people, or help to find employment for them. Most of the charity bestowed upon Negro schools, churches, hospitals and institutions and employment comes from the considerate and philanthropic of the white race. The middle class and poor element of the race, however, are doing everything for the good of the race, and were it not for them, truly the race would have been in a more pitiable condition.

The rich are selfish and foolish, and their primary purpose in life is to ape the whites, and as quickly as possible seek their company with the hope of social absorption, and jumping over the race line.

Any ordinarily rich Negro or "colored" person would prefer to give away ninety-nine and one-half per cent. of his wealth to become white, rather than to remain as he is, and to use such wealth in the promotion of racial ideals or industry that would help the mass of his people.

Any well prepared white person may easily influence the rich Negro or "Colored" person to part with his wealth for social patronage and company, while another worthy Negro seeking help in any racially helpful effort or enterprise would be insulted and treated with suspicion and contempt if he were to approach the.same individual for help that would result to mutual benefit.

The new "intellectuals" of the race are adepts in agitating for the possession of those things promoted and contributed to by members of other races, if there is the slightest argument to in any way support the claim, such as Negroes moving into new communities previously settled wholly by whites. The Negro "intellectuals" argue and agitate to show such a school, college, hospital, library or institution, or the political representation of such a district should be run, manned or represented by a Negro, and generally a very light "colored" person at that, because so many Negroes live in the district or community, not taking into consideration that ninety-five per cent. of the Negroes are squatters or rent payers subjected to be moved at any time according to the economic stress (to which these "intellectuals" pay no attention, and the leaders skillfully ignore), and that the real substantial individuals of the district are the owners of the properties in which the Negroes live and the businesses that the Negroes support are belonging to white people. Sometimes, in sheer disgust, the whites who live in the community give up their rights to quiet the agitators. But how long will this last, is the question the thoughtful and energetic Negroes of the Universal Negro Improvement Association are asking?

A TRIBUTE TO THE LATE SIR ISAIAH MORTER

He bequeathed to the Universal Negro Improvement Association about $100,000 in property, for the work of African Redemption, which bequest is being contested in the courts of Belize, British Honduras. Unscrupulous white lawyers of New York and British Honduras have been trying to deprive the Association of this legacy. A fierce legal battle has been waging since the application for probate of the will. The Association at great expense has had to send barristers and agents from other British colonies to represent them at court. There has been more than five postponements extending over a period of one year. Finally the Association to save the tremendous cost has had to retain a native barrister of British Honduras. The Hon. J. A. G. Smith, member of the Legislative Council of Jamaica, British West Indies, and one of the ablest barristers of the British Empire, represented the Association at the first hearing in Belize and secured the probate of the will, pending another hearing on adjournment. He was unable to return to Belize at the time of the adjournment. Since then many adverse rulings have been made. Failing justice for the Association in Belize, the case will be taken to the Privy Council of England.

(Reprint from Negro World)

April 29, 1924.

Sir Isaiah Morter, Knight Commander of the Distinguished Service Order of Ethiopia, another Prince of Africa, has fallen. He, to us as a race, is physically dead, but, spiritually, to us he lives. It is not every man who cometh into the world who lives forever. The absence of the millions who pass away is generally never observed, because their deeds for the good of humanity, their race and their nation were never registered. And ofttimes no attempt was made to serve any but themselves. But not so with Isaiah Emanuel Morter, of Belize, British Honduras, Central America. He was a Negro of lowly parentage, who grew up fighting the oppositions and difficulties generally surrounding one born to his condition, until he lifted himself to the highest pinnacle of service to his race and to his country. In his mature years, after he had honestly accumulated a fair portion of wealth, which he worked for and thriftily secured, he became identified with movements for the uplift of his race, no-

THE LATE SIR IŞAIAH MORTER

tably among them the Universal Negro Improvement Association, of which he was a staunch member and supporter.

He, unlike the majority of Negroes who accumulate wealth, did not seek to find association socially and otherwise among other races, but he was satisfied to confine his success to his race and give his race credit for everything that he accomplished. Most West Indian and Central American Negroes, whenever they accumulate wealth, generally seek to dissipate it either by marriage into the white race, or by fawning before the social patronage of that race, which generally seeks rather to deprive them of their wealth than to accept them as social equals and members of their fraternity.

Sir Isaiah Morter was true to his race, and has written his name down as the first of that successful type of Negro who did not forget Africa and its relationship to the rest of the Negroes throughout the world. Not very long ago Sir Isaiah Morter came to New York for the benefit of his health, and the writer had the honor of entertaining him at his home, where he remained a guest for several weeks. It was during the period when the Universal Negro Improvement Association was being hunted by its enemies, in the height of the trial of the celebrated "Black Star Line" case. The injustices done to the Association, and the subject of the enemies' design were so marked that Sir Isaiah Morter felt (as all Negroes did who read and followed the case), that it was not a fight against an individual, but a fight against the race. He became even more impressed then with the work and usefulness of the Universal Negro Improvement Association than he was before. Unfortunately, his health continued failing him, even though he experienced a marked improvement during his stay in America. He returned to Belize, his native home, and there he lingered for several months, until the grim reaper Death visited him on the 7th instant. His memory lives among the members of the Universal Negro Improvement Association and the Negro race forever. Prior to his death, nothing in the world was as dear to him as the principles of the Universal Negro Improvement Association, and as a proof of his attachment to the movement and his desire to help it, he has become the first great benefactor of the cause of African Redemption. In his will he bequeathed to the Universal Negro Improvement Association, for African Redemption, nearly two-thirds of his entire fortune, to the extent of between $75,000 and $100,000.

This is the first large bequest that has been given to the

Association. It is a fair indication of the loyalty of the members of this great movement. If other Negroes in America and the West Indies will follow the example of Sir Isaiah Emanuel Morter in assisting to make the Universal Negro Improvement Association what it ought to be, then in a few years not only will Africa be redeemed, but the whole Negro race will be elevated to a position of world recognition. Formerly, Negroes were disposed to die and leave their fortunes for white friends and white institutions, and some died without making wills at all, their fortunes going to the State. Billions of dollars have been lost to the Negro race within the last fifty years through disloyalty on the part of successful Negroes, who have preferred to give away their fortunes to members of other races, than to bequeath them to worthy institutions and movements of their own to help their own people.

Sir Isaiah Morter has set a wonderful example, and Africa shall not forget him. Surely the Universal Negro Improvement Association shall carry his name down the ages. Shall we not build monuments in Africa to the memory of Isaiah Emanuel Morter? Shall we not pay honor and respect to him for lending help and assistance to the Cause when it needed such assistance? Fifty or one hundred thousand dollars given to the Universal Negro Improvement Association at this time will help it to accomplish much, and now that we are about to assist in building up the Republic of Liberia, this money can be usefully applied in helping the colonists to establish themselves.

The Universal Negro Improvement Association calls upon Negroes throughout the world to honor and revere the name of Isaiah Emanuel Morter, for he was not only a friend of the cause of African Redemption, but a patriot of the foremost rank.

THE PRINCIPLES OF THE UNIVERSAL NEGRO IMPROVEMENT ASSOCIATION

Speech Delivered at Liberty Hall, New York City, U. S. A. November 25, 1922.

Over five years ago the Universal Negro Improvement Association placed itself before the world as the movement through which the new and rising Negro would give expression of his feelings. This Association adopts an attitude not of hostility to other races and peoples of the world, but an attitude of self-respect, of manhood rights on behalf of 400,000,000 Negroes of the world.

We represent peace, harmony, love, human sympathy, human rights and human justice, and that is why we fight so much. Wheresoever human rights are denied to any group, wheresoever justice is denied to any group, there the U. N. I. A. finds a cause. And at this time among all the peoples of the world, the group that suffers most from injustice, the group that is denied most of those rights that belong to all humanity, is the black group of 400,000,000. Because of that injustice, because of that denial of our rights, we go forth under the leadership of the One who is always on the side of right to fight the common cause of humanity; to fight as we fought in the Revolutionary War, as we fought in the Civil War, as we fought in the Spanish-American War, and as we fought in the war between 1914-18 on the battle plains of France and Flanders. As we fought up the heights of Mesopotamia; even so under the leadership of the U. N. I. A., we are marshaling the 400,000,000 Negroes of the world to fight for the emancipation of the race and of the redemption of the country of our fathers.

We represent a new line of thought among Negroes. Whether you call it advanced thought or reactionary thought, I do not care. If it is reactionary for people to seek independence in government, then we are reactionary. If it is advanced thought for people to seek liberty and freedom, then we represent the advanced school of thought among the Negroes of this country. We of the U. N. I. A. believe that what is good for the other fellow is good for us. If government is something that is worth while; if government is something that is appreciable and helpful and protective to others, then we also want to experiment in government. We do not mean a government that will make us citizens without rights or subjects without consideration. We mean the kind of government that will place our race in control, even as other races are in control of their own governments.

That does not suggest anything that is unreasonable. It was not unreasonable for George Washington, the great hero and father of the country, to have fought for the freedom of America giving to us this great republic and this great democracy; it was not unreasonable for the Liberals of France to have fought against the Monarchy to give to the world French Democracy and French Republicanism; it was no unrighteous cause that led Tolstoi to sound the call of liberty in Russia, which has ended in giving to the world the social democracy of Russia, an experiment that will probably prove to be a boon and a blessing to mankind. If it was not an unrighteous cause that led Washington to fight for the independence of this country, and led the Liberals of France to establish the Republic, it is therefore not an unrighteous cause for the U. N. I. A. to lead 400,000,000 Negroes all over the world to fight for the liberation of our country.

Therefore the U. N. I. A. is not advocating the cause of church building, because we have a sufficiently large number of churches among us to minister to the spiritual needs of the people, and we are not going to compete with those who are engaged in so splendid a work; we are not engaged in building any new social institutions, and Y. M. C. A.'s or Y. W. C. A.'s because there are enough social workers engaged in those praise-worthy efforts. We are not engaged in politics because we have enough local politicians, Democrats, Socialists, Soviets, etc., and the political situation is well taken care of. We are not engaged in domestic politics, in church building or in social uplift work, but we are engaged in nation building.

Misrepresentations

In advocating the principles of this Association we find we have been very much misunderstood and very much misrepresented by men from within our own race, as well as others from without. Any reform movement that seeks to bring about changes for the benefit of humanity is bound to be misrepresented by those who have always taken it upon themselves to administer to, and lead the unfortunate, and to direct those who may be placed under temporary disadvantages. It has been so in all other movements whether social or political; hence those of us in the Universal Negro Improvement Association who lead, do not feel in any way embarrassed about this misrepresentation, about this misunderstanding as far as the

Aims and Objects of the Universal Negro Improvement Association go. But those who probably would have taken kindly notice of this great movement, have been led to believe that this movement seeks, not to develop the good within the race, but to give expression to that which is most destructive and most harmful to society and to government.

I desire to remove the misunderstanding that has been created in the minds of millions of peoples throughout the world in their relationship to the organization. The Universal Negro Improvement Association stands for the Bigger Brotherhood; the Universal Negro Improvement Association stands for human rights, not only for Negroes, but for all races. The Universal Negro Improvement Association believes in the rights of not only the black race, but the white race, the yellow race and the brown race. The Universal Negro Improvement Association believes that the white man has as much right to be considered, the yellow man has as much right to be considered, the brown man has as much right to be considered as well as the black man of Africa. In view of the fact that the black man of Africa has contributed as much to the world as the white man of Europe, and the brown man and yellow man of Asia, we of the Universal Negro Improvement Association demand that the white, yellow and brown races give to the black man his place in the civilization of the world. We ask for nothing more than the rights of 400,000,000 Negroes. We are not seeking, as I said before, to destroy or disrupt the society or the government of other races, but we are determined that 400,000,000 of us shall unite ourselves to free our motherland from the grasp of the invader. We of the Universal Negro Improvement Association are determined to unite 400,000,000 Negroes for their own industrial, political, social and religious emancipation.

We of the Universal Negro Improvement Association are determined to unite the 400,000,000 Negroes of the world to give expression to their own feeling; we are determined to unite the 400,000,000 Negroes of the world for the purpose of building a civilization of their own. And in that effort we desire to bring together the 15,000,000 of the United States, the 180,000,000 in Asia, the West Indies and Central and South America, and the 200,000,000 in Africa. We are looking toward political freedom on the continent of Africa, the land of our fathers.

Not Seeking a Government Within a Government

The Universal Negro Improvement Association is not seeking to build up another government within the bounds or borders of the United States of America. The Universal Negro Improvement Association is not seeking to disrupt any organized system of government, but the Association is determined to bring Negroes together for the building up of a nation of their own. And why? Because we have been forced to it. We have been forced to it throughout the world; not only in America, not only in Europe, not only in the British Empire, but wheresoever the black man happens to find himself, he has been forced to do for himself.

To talk about Government is a little more than some of our people can appreciate just at this time. The average man does not think that way, just because he finds himself a citizen or a subject of some country. He seems to say, "Why should there be need for any other government?" We are French, English or American. But we of the U. N. I. A. have studied seriously this question of nationality among Negroes—this American nationality, this British nationality, this French, Italian or Spanish nationality, and have discovered that it counts for nought when that nationality comes in conflict with the racial idealism of the group that rules. When our interests clash with those of the ruling faction, then we find that we have absolutely no rights. In times of peace, when everything is all right, Negroes have a hard time, wherever we go, wheresoever we find ourselves, getting those rights that belong to us, in common with others whom we claim as fellow citizens; getting that consideration that should be ours by right of the constitution, by right of the law; but in the time of trouble they make us all partners in the cause, as happened in the last war, when we were partners, whether British, French or American Negroes. And we were told that we must forget everything in an effort to save the nation.

We have saved many nations in this manner, and we have lost our lives doing that before. Hundreds of thousands—nay, millions of black men, lie buried under the ground due to that old-time camouflage of saving the nation. We saved the British empire; we saved the French empire; we saved this glorious country more than once; and all that we have received for our sacrifices, all that we have received for what we have done, even in giving up our lives, is just what you are receiving now, just what I am receiving now.

You and I fare no better in America, in the British empire, or in any other part of the white world; we fare no better than any black man wheresover he shows his head. And why? Because we have been satisfied to allow ourselves to be led, educated, to be

A group of Royal African Guards, and a group of the African Legion in parade in New York City during the convention of 1924.

directed by the other fellow, who has always sought to lead in the world in that direction that would satisfy him and strengthen his position. We have allowed ourselves for the last 500 years to be a race of followers, following every race that has led, in the direction that would make them more secure.

The U. N. I. A. is reversing the old-time order of things. We refuse to be followers any more. We are leading ourselves. That means, if any saving is to be done, later on, whether it is saving this one nation or that one government, we are going to seek a method of saving Africa first. Why? And why Africa? Because Africa has become the grand prize of the nations. Africa has become the big game of the nation hunters. To-day Africa looms as the greatest commercial, industrial and political prize in the world.

The Difference Between the U. N. I. A. and Other Organizations

The difference between the Universal Negro Improvement Association and the other movements of this country, and probably the world, is that the Universal Negro Improvement Association seeks independence of government, while the other organizations seek to make the Negro a secondary part of existing governments. We differ from the organizations in America because they seek to subordinate the Negro as a secondary consideration in a great civilization, knowing that in America the Negro will never reach his highest ambition, knowing that the Negro in America will never get his constitutional rights. All those organizations which are fostering the improvement of Negroes in the British Empire know that the Negro in the British Empire will never reach the height of his constitutional rights. What do I mean by constitutional rights in America? If the black man is to reach the height of his ambition in this country— if the black man is to get all of his constitutional rights in America—then the black man should have the same chance in the nation as any other man to become president of the nation, or a street cleaner in New York. If the black man in the British Empire is to have all his constitutional rights it means that the Negro in the British Empire should have at least the same right to become premier of Great Britain as he has to become street cleaner in the city of London. Are they prepared to give us such political equality? You and I can live in the United States of America for 100 more years, and our generations may live for 200 years or for 5000 more years, and so long as there is a black and white population, when the majority is on the side of the

white race, you and I will never get political justice or get
political equality in this country. Then why should a black man
with rising ambition, after preparing himself in every possible
way to give expression to that highest ambition, allow himself
to be kept down by racial prejudice within a country? If I am
as educated as the next man, if I am as prepared as the next
man, if I have passed through the best schools and colleges and
universities as the other fellow, why should I not have a fair
chance to compete with the other fellow for the biggest position in the nation? I have feelings, I have blood, I have
senses like the other fellow; I have ambition, I have hope.
Why should he, because of some racial prejudice, keep me
down and why should I concede to him the right to rise above
me, and to establish himself as my permanent master? That
is where the U. N. I. A. differs from other organizations. I
refuse to stultify my ambition, and every true Negro refuses
to stultify his ambition to suit any one, and therefore the
U. N. I. A. decides if America is not big enough for two
presidents, if England is not big enough for two kings, then
we are not going to quarrel over the matter; we will leave
one president in America, we will leave one king in England, we
will leave one president in France and we will have one president in Africa. Hence, the Universal Negro Improvement Association does not seek to interfere with the social and political
systems of France, but by the arrangement of things to-day the
U. N. I. A. refuses to recognize any political or social system in
Africa except that which we are about to establish for ourselves.

Not Preaching Hate

We are not preaching a propaganda of hate against anybody.
We love the white man; we love all humanity, because we feel
that we cannot live without the other. The white man is as
necessary to the existence of the Negro as the Negro is necessary
to his existence. There is a common relationship that we cannot
escape. Africa has certain things that Europe wants, and Europe
has certain things that Africa wants, and if a fair and square deal
must bring white and black with each other, it is impossible for
us to escape it. Africa has oil, diamonds, copper, gold and rubber and all the minerals that Europe wants, and there must be
some kind of relationship between Africa and Europe for a fair
exchange, so we cannot afford to hate anybody.

Negroes Ever Ready to Assist Humanity's Cause

The question often asked is what does it require to redeem a
race and free a country? If it takes man power, if it takes

scientific intelligence, if it takes education of any kind, or if it takes blood, then the 400,000,000 Negroes of the world have it.

It took the combined man power of the Allies to put down the mad determination of the Kaiser to impose German will upon the world and upon humanity. Among those who suppressed his mad ambition were two million Negroes who have not yet forgotten how to drive men across the firing line. Surely those of us who faced German shot and shell at the Marne, at Verdun, have not forgotten the order of our Commander-in-Chief. The cry that caused us to leave America in such mad haste, when white fellow citizens of America refused to fight and said, "We do not believe in war and therefore, even though we are American citizens, and even though the nation is in danger, we will not go to war." When many of them cried out and said, "We are German-Americans and we can not fight," when so many white men refused to answer to the call and dodged behind all kinds of excuses, 400,000 black men were ready without a question. It was because we were told it was a war of democracy; it was a war for the liberation of the weaker peoples of the world. We heard the cry of Woodrow Wilson, not because we liked him so, but because the things he said were of such a nature that they appealed to us as men. Wheresoever the cause of humanity stands in need of assistance, there you will find the Negro ever ready to serve.

He has done it from the time of Christ up to now. When the whole world turned its back upon the Christ, the man who was said to be the Son of God; when the world cried out "Crucify Him," when the world spurned Him and spat upon Him, it was a black man, Simon, the Cyrenian, who took up the cross. Why? Because the cause of humanity appealed to him. When the black man saw the suffering Jew, struggling under the heavy cross, he was willing to go to His assistance, and he bore that cross up to the heights of Calvary. In the spirit of Simon, the Cyrenian, 1900 years ago. we answered the call of Woodrow Wilson, the call of a larger humanity, and it was for that that we willingly rushed into the war from America, from the West Indies, over 100,000; it was for that that we rushed into the war from Africa, 2,000,000 of us. We met in France, Flanders and in Mesopotamia. We fought unfalteringly. When the white men faltered and fell back on their battle lines, at the Marne and at Verdun, when they ran away from the charge of the German hordes, the black hell fighters stood before the cannonade, stood before the charge, and again they shouted, "There will be a hot time in the old town to-night."

We made it so hot a few months after our appearance in France and on the various battle fronts, we succeeded in driving the German hordes across the Rhine, and driving the Kaiser out of Germany, and out of Potsdam into Holland. We have not forgotten the prowess of war. If we have been liberal minded enough to give our life's blood in France, in Mesopotamia and elsewhere, fighting for the white man, whom we have always assisted, surely we have not forgotten to fight for ourselves, and when the time comes that the world will again give Africa an opportunity for freedom, surely 400,000,000 black men will march out on the battle plains of Africa, under the colors of the red, the black and the green.

We shall march out, yes, as black American citizens, as black British subjects, as black French citizens, as black Italians or as black Spaniards, but we shall march out with a greater loyalty, the loyalty of race. We shall march out in answer to the cry of our fathers, who cry out to us for the redemption of our own country, our motherland, Africa.

We shall march out, not forgetting the blessings of America. We shall march out, not forgetting the blessings of civilization. We shall march out with a history of peace before and behind us, and surely that history shall be our breastplate, for how can man fight better than knowing that the cause for which he fights is righteous? How can man fight more gloriously than by knowing that behind him is a history of slavery, a history of bloody carnage and massacre inflicted upon a race because of its inability to protect itself and fight? Shall we not fight for the glorious opportunity of protecting and forever more establishing ourselves as a mighty race and nation, never more to be disrespected by men. Glorious shall be the battle when the time comes to fight for our people and our race.

We should say to the millions who are in Africa to hold the fort, for we are coming 400,000,000 strong.

SPEECH DELIVERED AT CARNEGIE HALL, NEW YORK CITY, N. Y., U. S. A.

At Opening of the Fourth International Convention of the Negro Peoples of the World, August 1, 1924.

Delegates to the Fourth International Convention of the Negro Peoples of the World, Ladies and Gentlemen:

The pleasure of addressing you at this hour is great. You have re-assembled yourselves in New York, coming from all parts of the world to this Annual Convention, because you believe that by unity you can alleviate the unfortunate condition in which racially we find ourselves.

We are glad to meet as Negroes, notwithstanding the stigma that is placed upon us by a soulless and conscienceless world because of our backwardness.

As usual, I am not here to flatter you, I am not here to tell you how happy and prosperous we are as a people, because that is all false. The Negro is not happy, but, to the contrary, is extremely miserable. He is miserable because the world is closing fast around him, and if he does not strike out now for his own preservation, it is only a question of a few more decades when he will be completely out-done in a world of strenuous competition for a place among the fittest of God's creation.

Negro Dying Out

The Negro is dying out, and he is going to die faster and more rapidly in the next fifty years than he has in the past three hundred years. There is only one thing to save the Negro, and that is an immediate realization of his own responsibilities. Unfortunately we are the most careless and indifferent people in the world! We are shiftless and irresponsible, and that is why we find ourselves the wards of an inherited materialism that has lost its soul and its conscience. It is strange to hear a Negro leader speak in this strain, as the usual course is flattery, but I would not flatter you to save my own life and that of my own family. There is no value in flattery. Flattery of the Negro for another quarter of a century will mean hell and damnation to the race. How can any Negro leader flatter us about progress and the rest of it, when the world is preparing more than ever to bury the entire race? Must I flatter you when England, France, Italy, Belgium and Spain are all concentrating on robbing every square inch of African territory—the land of our fathers? Must I flatter you when the cry is being loudly raised for a white

America, Canada, Australia and Europe, and a yellow and brown Asia? Must I flatter you when I find all other peoples preparing themselves for the struggle to survive, and you still smiling, eating, dancing, drinking and sleeping away your time, as if yesterday were the beginning of the age of pleasure? I would rather be dead than be a member of your race without thought of the morrow, for it portends evil to him that thinketh not. Because I cannot flatter you I am here to tell, emphatically, that if we do not seriously reorganize ourselves as a people and face the world with a program of African nationalism our days in civilization are numbered, and it will be only a question of time when the Negro will be as completely and complacently dead as the North American Indian, or the Australian Bushman.

Progress on Sand

You talk about the progress we have made in America and elsewhere, among the people of our acquaintance, but what progress is it? A progress than can be snatched away from you in forty-eight hours, because it has been built upon sand.

You must thank God for the last two generations of whites in our western civilization; thank God that they were not made of sterner stuff, and character and a disposition to see all races their rivals and competitors in the struggle to hold and possess the world, otherwise, like the Indian, we would have been nearly all dead.

The progress of the Negro in our civilization was tolerated because of indifference, but that indifference exists no longer. Our whole civilization is becoming intolerant, and because of that the whole world of races has started to think.

Can you blame the white man for thinking, when red and yellow men are knocking at his door? Can you blame the tiger for being on the defensive when the lion approaches? And thus we find that generations ago, when the Negro was not given a thought as a world competitor he is now regarded as an encumbrance in a civilization to which he has materially contributed little. Men do not build for others, they build for themselves. The age and our religion demand it. What are you going to expect, that white men are going to build up America and elsewhere and hand it over to us? If we are expecting that we are crazy, we have lost our reason.

If you were white, you would see the rest in hell before you would deprive your children of bread to give it to others. You would give that which you did not want, but not that which is to be the sustenance of your family, and so the world thinks;

yet a Du Bois and the National Association for the Advancement of Colored People will tell us by flattery that the day is
coming when a white President of the United States of America
will get out of the White House and give the position to a Negro,
that the day is coming when a Mr. Hughes will desert the Sec-
retaryship of State and give it to the Negro, James Weldon
Johnson; that the time is just around the corner of constitutional rights when the next Ambassador to the Court of Saint
James will be a black man from Mississippi or from North Carolina. Do you think that white men who have suffered, bled and
died to make America and the world what it is, are going to
hand over to a parcel of lazy Negroes the things that they prize
most?

Stop flattering yourselves, fellowmen, and let us go to work.
Do you hear me? Go to work! Go to work in the morn of a new
creation and strike, not because of the noonday sun, but plod on
and on, until you have succeeded in climbing the hills of opposition and reached the height of self-progress, and from that pinnacle bestow upon the world a civilization of your own, and
hand down to your children and posterity of your own a worthy
contribution to the age of human materialism.

We of the Universal Negro Improvement Association are fair
and just. We do not expect the white man to rob himself, and
to deprive himself, for our racial benefit. How could you reasonably expect that, in an age like this, when men have divided
themselves into racial and national groups, when the one group
has its own interest to protect as against that of the other?

The laws of self-preservation force every human group to look
after itself and protect its own interest; hence so long as the
American white man or any other white man, for that matter,
realizes his responsibility, he is bound to struggle to protect
that which is his and his own, and I feel that the Negro today
who has been led by the unscrupulous of our race has been
grossly misguided, in the direction of expecting too much from
the civilization of others.

The Carpet-Bagger

Immediately after emancipation, we were improperly led in
the South by this same group and ultimately lost our vote and
voice. The carpet-bagger and the thoughtless, selfish Negro
politician and leader sold the race back into slavery. And the
same attempt is now being made in the North by that original
group, prompted by the dishonest white political boss and the
unscrupulous Negro politician. The time has come for both

races to seriously adjust their differences and settle the future of our respective peoples. The selfish of both races will not stop to think and act, but the responsibility becomes more so ours, who have the vision of the future.

Criminals Out of Jail

Because of my attempt to lead my race into the only solution that I see would benefit both groups, I have been maliciously and wickedly maligned, and by members of our own race. I have been plotted against, framed up, indicted and convicted, the story which you so well know. That was responsible for our not having a Convention last year. I thank you, however, for the tribute you paid me during that period in postponing the Convention through respect to my enforced absence. Last August I spent three months in the Tombs in New York, but I was as happy then as I am now. I was sent there by the evil forces that have always fought and opposed reform movements, but I am as ready now to go back to the Tombs or elsewhere as I was when I was forced to leave you. The jail does not make a criminal, the criminal makes himself. There are more criminals out of jail than in jail, the only difference is that the majority of those who are out, are such skillful criminals that they know how to keep themselves out. They have tried to besmirch my name so as to prevent me doing the good that I desire to do in the interest of the race. It amuses me sometimes to hear the biggest crooks in the Negro Race referring to me as a criminal. As I have said before, Negro race leaders are the biggest crooks in the world. It is because of their crookedness that we have not made more progress. If you think I am not telling the truth in this direction you may quizz any of the white political bosses, and those who will tell the truth will reveal a tale most shocking as far as our Negro leaders are concerned. This is true of the group of fellows of our race that lead universally as well as nationally. They will sell the souls of their mothers and their country into perdition. That is why the Universal Negro Improvement Association has to make such a fight, and that is why the opposition is as hard and marked. You can pay the Negro leader to hang his race and block every effort of self-help. This is not commonly so among other races. We must give credit to the great white race, to the extent that they will fight among themselves,.that they will cheat each other in business, but when it approaches the future and destiny of the race, a halt is immediately called. Not so with the Negro, he does not know when and where to stop in hurting himself.

Reorganizing the Race

I repeat that we must reorganize ourselves as a people, if we are to go forward, and I take this opportunity, as you assemble yourselves here from all parts of the world, to sound the warning note.

To review the work of our Association for the past two years is to recount the exploits of a continuous struggle to reach the top. Our organization has been tested during the past two years beyond that of any other period in the history of Negro movements. I am glad to say, however, that we have survived all the intrigues, barriers, and handicaps placed in the way. Some of our enemies thought that they would have been able to crush our movement when I was convicted and sentenced to prison. They had depended upon that, as the trump card in their effort to crush the new spirit of freedom among Negroes, but like all such efforts, it was doomed to failure. I will bring to your recollection a similar effort made a little over nineteen hundred years ago when on Calvary's Mount, the Jews after inspiring the Romans, attempted to crucify the man, Christ, the leader of the Christian religion. They thought that after the crucifixion, after he was buried, that they would have silenced the principles of Christianity forever, but how successful they were, is made manifest today when we find hundreds of millions of souls the world over professing the principles for which the man died on Calvary's cross. As in the rise of Christianity, so do we have the spiritual rise of the Universal Negro Improvement Association throughout the world. They tried to crucify it in America, and it has arisen in Africa a thousand fold. They tried to crucify it on the American continent, and it is now sweeping the whole world. You cannot crucify a principle; you cannot nail the souls of men to a cross; you cannot imprison it; you cannot bury it. It will rise like the spirit of the Great Redeemer and take its flight down the ages, until men far and near have taken up the cry for which the principle was crucified.

We of the Universal Negro Improvement Association are stronger today than we ever were before. We are strong in spirit, strong in determination; we are unbroken in every direction; we stand firm facing the world, determined to carve out and find a place for the four hundred millions of our suffering people. We call upon humanity everywhere to listen to the cry of the new Negro. We ask the human heart for a response, because Africa's sun cannot be downed. Africa's sun is rising, gradually rising, and soon shall take its place among the brilliant constellations of nations. The Negro wants a nation, nothing less, nothing more; and why shouldn't we be nationally free, nationally independent, nationally unfettered? We want a nationality similar to that of the English, the French, the Italian, the German, to that of the white American, to that of the yellow Japanese; we want nationality and government because we realize that the American nation in a short while will not be large enough to accommodate two competitive rivals, one black and the other white.

Black Man's Aspirations

There is no doubt about it that the black man of America today aspires to the White House, to the Cabinet, and to the Senate, and the House. He aspires to be head of State and municipal governments. What are you going to do with him? He cannot be satisfied in the midst of a majority group that seeks to protect its interest at all hazards; then the only alternative is to give the Negro a place of his own. That is why we appeal to the sober white minds of America, and not the selfish ones. The selfish ones will see nothing more than the immediate present, but the deep thinking white man will see the result of another fifty or one hundred years, when these two peoples will be brought together in closer contact of rivalry. As races we practically represent a similar intelligence today. We have graduated from the same schools, colleges and universities. What can you do with men who are equally and competently fitted in mind, but give them an equal chance, and if there is no chance of equality, there must be dissatisfaction on the one hand. That dissatisfaction we have in our midst now. We have it manifested by W. E. B. Du Bois, by James Weldon Johnson; we have it manifested by the organization known as the National Association for the Advancement of Colored People, that seeks to bring about social equality, political equality, and industrial equality, things that are guaranteed us under the Constitution, but which, in the face of a majority race, we cannot demand, because of the terrible odds against us. In the midst of this, then, what can we do but seek an outlet of our own unless, we intend to fight a losing game. Reason will dictate that there is no benefit to be derived from fighting always a losing game. We will lose until we have completely lost our stand in America.

The Period of Self-Protection

To repeat myself, we talk about progress. What progress have we made when everything we do is done through the good will and grace of the liberal white man of the present day? But can he always afford to be liberal? Do you not realize that in another few decades he will have on his hands a problem of his own—a problem to feed his own children, to take care of his own flesh and blood? In the midst of that crisis, when he finds not even enough to feed himself, what will become of the Negro? The Negro naturally must die to give way, and make room for others who are better prepared to live. That is the danger, men; and that is why we have the Universal Negro Improvement Association. The condition that I have referred to will not only be true of America and of continental Europe; it will be true wherever the great white race lives. There will not be room enough for them, and others who seek to compete with them. That is why we hear the cry of Egypt for the Egyptians, India for the Indians, Asia for the Asiatics, and we raise the cry of Africa for the Africans; those at home and those abroad. That is why we ask England to be fair, to be just and considerate; that is why we ask France, Italy, Spain and Belgium to be fair, just and considerate; that is why we ask them to let the black man restore himself to his own country; and that is why we are determined to see it done. No camouflage, and no promise of good-will, will solve the problem. What guarantee have we, what lease have we on the future that the man who treats us kindly today will perpetuate it through his son or his grandson tomorrow?

Races and peoples are only safeguarded when they are strong enough to protect themselves, and that is why we appeal to the four hundred million Negroes of the world to come together for self-protection and self-preservation. We do not want what belongs to the great white race, or the yellow race. We want only those things that belong to the black race. Africa is ours. To win Africa we will give up America, we will give up our claim in all other parts of the world; but we must have Africa. We will give up the vain desire of having a seat in the White House in America, of having a seat in the House of Lords in England, of being President of France, for the chance and opportunity of filling these positions in a country of our own.

That is how the Universal Negro Improvement Association differs from other organizations. Other organizations, especially in America, are fighting for a political equality which they will never get, and never win, in the face of a majority opposition. We win so much today and lose so much tomorrow. We will lose our political strength in the North in another few years, as we lost it in the South during Reconstruction. We fill one position today, but lose two tomorrow, and so we will drift on and on, until we have been completely obliterated from western civilization.

Changes Among Negroes

You may ask me what good has the Universal Negro Improvement Association done, what has it accomplished within the last six years? We will point to you the great changes that have taken place in Africa, the West Indies and America. In the West Indies, black men have been elevated to high positions by the British Government, so as to off-set and counteract the sweeping influence of the Universal Negro Improvement Association. Several of the Colonies have been given larger constitutional rights. In Africa, the entire West Coast has been benefited. Self-government has been given to several of the African Colonies, and native Africans have been elevated to higher positions, so as to offset the sweeping spirit of the Universal Negro Improvement Association throughout the Continent of Africa. In America, several of our men have been given prominent positions; Negro commissions have been appointed to attend to affairs of state; Negro Consuls have also been appointed. Things that happened in America within the last six years to advance the political status, the social and industrial status of the Negro were never experienced before. All that is traceable to the Universal Negro Improvement Association within the last six years. In the great game of politics you do not see the immediate results at your door, but those who are observant will be able to trace the good that is being done from the many directions whence it comes. If you were to take a survey of the whole world of Negroes you will find that we are more highly thought of in 1922 than we were in 1914. England, France and the European and Colonial powers regard the Universal Negro Improvement Association with a certain amount of suspicion because they believe that we are antagonistic. But we are not. We are not antagonistic to France, to England or Italy, nor any of the white Powers in Europe. We are only demanding a square deal for our race. Did we not fight to help them? Did we not sacrifice our blood, give up our all, to save England, to save France, Italy and America during the last war? Then why shouldn't we expect some consideration for the service rendered? That is all we ask; and we are now pressing that claim to the throne of white justice. We are told that God's throne is white, although we believe it to be black. But if it is white, we are placing our plea before that throne of God, asking Him to so touch the hearts of our fellow-men as to let them yield to us the things that are ours, as it was right to yield to Caesar the things that were Caesar's.

As we deliberate on the many problems confronting us during the month of August, let us not lose control of ourselves; let us not forget that we are the guardians of four hundred millions; let us not forget that it is our duty to so act and legislate as to help humanity everywhere, whether it be black or white. We shall be called upon during this month to take up certain matters that are grave, but dispassionately we shall discuss them; and whenever the interest of the different race groups clash, let it be our duty to take the other fellow's feelings into our consideration. If we must be justly treated, then we ourselves must treat all men similarly. So, let no prejudice cause us to say or do anything against the interest of the white man, or the yellow man; let us realize that the white man has the right to live, the yellow man has the right to live, and all that we desire to do is to impress them with the fact that we also have the right to live.

SOCIETY AND THE SELFISH EXPLOITER AND PLUNDERER

Those who make or accumulate their wealth by robbing, exploiting and plundering the innocent, ignorant and helpless of humanity, are worse than murderers and hardened criminals; they are fiends, and should be outlawed and ostracized from society, caring not how munificent their after gifts and philanthropy to care for those they have already morally destroyed or harmed.

SPEECH ON DISARMAMENT CONFERENCE DELIV-
ERED AT LIBERTY HALL, NEW YORK,
U. S. A., NOVEMBER 6, 1921

Just at this time the world is again preparing for a reorganization. Since the war of 1914 the world became disorganized.
Many conferences have been held, in which statesmen of all the
reputable governments have taken part, for the purpose of settling a world policy, by which humanity and the world could
return to normal. Several of the conferences were held in France,
others in Switzerland and England. On the 11th of this month
will assemble in Washington what is to be known as an Armament Conference. At this conference statesmen from Great
Britain and her self-governing dominions, statesmen from
France, Japan, China, Norway, Holland and several other countries will there assemble and partake in the discussion for regulating the armaments of the world.

Every race will be represented at that conference except the
Negro race. It is a sad confession to make, nevertheless it is true.
The world wants to return to normal and the only people preventing it from returning to normal, apparently, are the white and
yellow peoples, and they only are taken into account. I suppose
after they have met and discussed the issues, the world will
return to normal, but I believe someone has a second thought
coming. I have no faith in the disarmament plan of the nations.
I am a pessimist as far as disarmament goes. I do not believe
that man will disarm until there is universal justice. Any
attempt at disarming when half of the world oppresses the other
half is but a farce, because the oppressed half will make somebody get armed sooner or later, and I hope Negroes will pay no
attention to what is said and what is done at the conference. It
does not concern you one bit. Disarmament may sound good
for heaven and paradise, but not for this world that we live in,
where we have so many robbers and plunderers. You keep a
pistol or a gun in your home because the robber is at large,
and you are afraid while you sleep he will creep
through the window or get through the door and make an
attempt to rob your property; and because you know he is at
large, and may pay you a visit, you sleep with a gun under your
pillow. When all the burglars and all the robbers are put in
jail, and we know they are in jail, then we will throw away our
pistols and our guns. Now everybody knows that the robber—
the thief—is at large; he is not only robbing domestic homes,
he is robbing continents; he is robbing countries, and how do

you expect, in the name of reason, for races and peoples to disarm when the thief is at large trying to get into your country, trying to get into your continent to take away your land—your birthright. The whole thing is a farce, and I trust no sensible Negro will pay any attention to it.

Negroes Must Arm Through Organization

I am not advising you to arm now with the things they have, I am asking you to arm through organization; arm through preparedness. You do not want to have guns and bombs just now; you have no immediate use for them, so they can throw away those things if they want in Washington on Armistice Day. I am saying to the Negro people of the world, get armed with organization; get armed by coming together 400,000,000 strong. That is your weapon. Their weapon in the past has been big guns and explosive shells; your weapon must be universal organization. You are a people most favorably situated today for getting what you want through organization. Why? Because universally Negroes have a common cause; universally Negroes suffer from one common disadvantage. You are not like the other people in that respect. The white people cannot organize as you are organizing. Why? Because their society is disrupted—is in chaos. Why do I say this? They are so disrupted—they are in such chaos that they have to fight against themselves—capital fighting labor, labor fighting capital. There is no common cause between capital and labor, and, therefore, they cannot get together, and will never get together until they realize the virtue of justice—the virtue of equity to all mankind. You have no fight among yourselves as between capital and labor, because all of us are laborers, therefore we need not be Socialists; we have no fight against party, because all of us are belonging to the "Suffering Party." So when it comes to organization we occupy a unique position.

England cannot organize with France, for England will be looking to rob France, and France looking to rob England, and they will be suspicious of each other. The white races will never get together. They have done so many injustices one to the other that between here and heaven they will never get together. Do you think Germany and England will ever get together? Do you think France and Germany will ever get together? They have no cause that is in common; but 400,000,000 Negroes have a cause that is in common, and that is why I pointed out to you that your strongest armament is organization, and not so much big guns and bombshells. Later on we may have to use some of those things, however, because it appears that some people cannot hear a human voice unless something is exploding nearby. Some people sleep too soundly, when it comes to a question of human rights, and you have to touch them up with something more than our ordinary human voice.

Believes Arms Conference Will Be Fiasco

This conference on disarmament, I have said, is all a joke, and every one of them is going there to see what can be gotten. Japan to see what she can get out of America; America to see what she can get out of France; England to see what she can get out of Japan; Italy to see what she can get out of England, and the greatest vagabond will come out with the big stick. Everybody knows that; all sensible statesmen know that. They do not want any conference on disarmament, because you must arm to a certain extent. Swords are in heaven to keep the angels in good order. So since human nature is what it is, the world cannot afford to disarm. But do you know what they are getting together for? Not so much disarmament; they are getting together to form a pact by which they can subdue and further oppress the weaker peoples, who are not as strong as themselves to demand a place in this conference now to be held.

I told you during the war in my speeches throughout the length and breadth of this country and through my writings in The Negro World week by week in 1916 it was planned in England that the Negro should pay the cost of the war. You will remember (some of you) my saying that several years ago it was the determination in Europe that Africa was to be exploited to pay the cost of the war and Negroes everywhere were to be used to supply the source of revenue by which the bankrupt nations would be able to declare themselves once more solvent. Since peace was declared—since the armistice was signed—those of you who have seen the conduct of statesmen in Europe, of governments and of subsidized commercial agents, will recall that great demands have been made and are being made to commercialize the raw, and mineral products of Africa, and by the spoils gained out of exploiting Africa they hope to reimburse themselves of the billions of dollars lost in the war of 1914 to 1918.

The Aim of European Statesmen

It does not take the vision of a seer; it does not take the vision of a prophet, to see what the future will be to us, as a race, through the ambitions of the present-day statesmen of Europe.

Black Star Line Band in Convention Parade, August 1, 1921

They feel that they have a divine right because of the strength of arms; because of their highly developed power to go into any part of the world and occupy it, and hold it; if that part of the world is occupied by weaker peoples. The statesmen of today believe that might makes right, and until they get that feeling out of them, until they destroy that spirit, the world cannot disarm. They fail to take into consideration, they fail to take into account, that there are 400,000,000 black men in the world today and that these 400,000,000 people are not going to allow anybody to infringe upon their rights without asking the question why. They have been playing all kinds of dodges; they have been practicing all kinds of schemes and adopting all kinds of tactics, since the armistice was signed, to keep the Negro in his old-time place, but they have failed; they cannot successfully do it. When they created the emergency, they called the Negro to battle; they placed in the Negro's hands the gun and the sword; they told him to go out and kill—kill so that the side for which you are fighting might be victorious. The Negro killed. The Negro fought his way to victory and returned the standard with honor. After the battle was won, after the victory was declared, the Negro became a puzzle. He became a puzzle to Great Britain; he became a puzzle to France; he became a puzzle to America. The American Negro was no longer wanted in active service by the American Government. What did they do? They disarmed him; they took away his pistol and his gun before he landed, so that he could not do any harm with them, and they sent him back South without any armament. What did the Frenchman do? The Frenchman is puzzled up to now; they cannot send them back yet.

All this noise they have been making about Negro soldiers being on the Rhineland, it is not because the French want the Negro to be on the Rhineland so much, but they do not know where to send him.

And do you know what they are keeping those Negroes there for? Those Negroes may never be returned to Senegal; they may never be returned to Africa. Those Negroes probably will be kept in France until they die. With the knowledge they have gained in the four years of war, they do not want those Senegalese to go back to Africa. That is why they are now on the Rhineland, and these French statesmen come and tell us it is because they love Negroes so much why they are kept in France.

It is because they fear the Negroes so much why they have kept those black Senegalese on the Rhineland and in France.

A Conference of the "Bigger Brotherhood"

They do not know what to do. They are puzzled, and are holding conferences in France, in Switzerland, in England and now in America, and have not decided on anything. Why won't they be honest? Why won't they have a real conference? Why won't they say, "We are going to solve this great human problem; we are going to have peace forever; let us meet, whether it be in Washington, London, or Paris; come on Asia, meet us, too; come on, Africa, let us all sit around the table and let us not call this conference a disarmament conference or any such conference; let us call it a "conference of the bigger brotherhood." That is the conference the world is waiting for, and until that conference is called, it is all a farce talking about disarmament and the rest of it. Until these statesmen get ready to give Asia what is belonging to Asia, to give to Europe what is belonging to Europe, and then, above all, to give to Africa what is belonging to Africa, their conferences will be in vain.

If Great Britain will take my advice she would call a conference tomorrow morning, and say to all Englishmen leave India, leave Africa and go back to England because we want peace. If France takes my advice she will call out her white colonists from her African dominions, because so long as this injustice is perpetrated against weaker peoples there is going to be wars and rumors of wars. It is human nature and the world knows it. If you take my property, and I know it, is a different proposition, to taking my property and my not knowing it. In the past they took our property and we did not know about it, therefore we did not say anything; but they do not seem to count on the change that has come about. We know all about it now. If a man breaks into my house and steals some of my things and I do not know him, I will meet him on the street and shake hands and say, "Brother, how are you?" If he salutes me and says "Hello, how are you?" I will return it. But when I come home and find out that my property is robbed, and that he is the man who robbed my property, I am going to change my attitude. Just give me what is belonging to me. That is the situation between weaker peoples and stronger ones. They have fooled us; they have robbed us, when we did not know any better; but it is a different proposition now.

The new Negro is going to strike back or is going to die; and if David Lloyd George, Briand and the different statesmen believe they can assemble in Washington, in London, in Paris, or anywhere and dispose of black people's property without first consulting them they make a big mistake, because we have reared many Fochs between 1914 and 1918 on the battlefields of France and Flanders. It will be a question later on of Foch meeting Foch.

Now the world of oppressed peoples have got the spirit of liberty and from far-off India we hear the cry of a free and independent India; from far-off Egypt we hear the cry of a free and independent Egypt. The Negro loves peace; the Negro likes to disarm, but the Negro says to the world, "Let us have justice; let us have equity; let us have freedom; let us have democracy indeed"; and I from Liberty Hall, on behalf of 400,000,000 Negroes, send a plea to the statesmen at Washington in their assembly on the question of disarmament, give the Negro the consideration due him; give the Hindoo the consideration due him; give the Egyptian the consideration due him; give the weaker peoples of the world the consideration due them, and let us disarm. But until then, I repeat, there will be wars and rumors of wars.

TEXT OF TELEGRAM SENT TO THE DISARMAMENT CONFERENCE

November 11, 1921.

President and Members of the International Conference on
  Disarmament,
    Care of Secretary of Conference,
      Pan-American Building,
        Washington, D. C.

Honorable Gentlemen:

I salute you in the name of Democracy, and for the cause of Justice on behalf of the four hundred million Negroes of the world. Your Honorable Conference now sitting in Washington has a purpose that has been announced and advertised to the world for several months. You were called together by the President of the Democratic Republic of the United States of America to discuss the problem of armaments, the settlement of which you believe will ensure the perpetual peace of the world. As the elected spokesman of the Negro peoples of the world who desire freedom, politically, industrially, educationally, socially and religiously, as well as a full enjoyment of world democracy and a national independence all our own on the Continent of Africa, it is for me to inform you of a little slight that has been shown to four hundred million Negroes who form a part of this world's population. At the Versailles Peace Conference, the statesmen who gathered there made the awful mistake of legislating for the disposition of other people's lands (especially in Africa) without taking them into consideration, believing that a world peace could have been established after such a conference. The mistake is now apparent. There can be no peace among us mortals so long as the strong of humanity oppresses the weak, for in due process of time and through evolution the weak will one day turn, even like the worm, and then humanity's hope of peace will be shattered. All men have brains; some use their abilities for inventing destructive elements of warfare, such as guns, gun-powder, gas, and other destructive chemicals. The Negro for hundreds of years has attempted nothing destructive to the peace and good-will of humanity; in fact, he has not even made an attempt to make the world know that he is alive; nevertheless, like the worm, the Negro will one day turn. I humbly ask you therefore that your Honorable Conference act, not like the one at Versailles, but that you realize and appreciate the fact that the Negro is a man, and that there can be no settlement of world affairs without proper consideration being given to him with his rights. President Harding of America has but recently sounded the real cry of Democracy. He says to his own country, and I think it should be an advice to the world, "Give the Negro equality in education, in politics, in industry, because he is entitled to human rights." I humbly beg to recommend to your Honorable Conference those quoted words of President Harding. Negroes have blood, they have souls, and for the cause of Liberty they feel that the conduct of men like Alexander, Hannibal, Caesar, Napoleon, Wellington, Lafayette, Garabaldi, Washington, is imitable, and that peace not founded on real human justice will only be a mockery of the divine invocation, "Peace, perfect peace." I trust your Honorable Conference will not fail to take into consideration, therefore, that there are four hundred million Negroes in the world who demand Africa as their rightful heritage, even as the European claims Europe, and the Asiatic Asia. I pray that your Conference will not only be one of disarmament, but that it will be a congregation of the "Bigger Brotherhood," through which Europe will see the rights of Asia, Asia and Europe see the rights of Africa, and Africa and Asia see the rights of Europe and accordingly give every race and nation their due, and let there be peace indeed. On behalf of the four hundred million Negroes of the world not represented at your Honorable Conference.

I have the honor to be

Your obedient servant,

MARCUS GARVEY,

President General of the Universal Negro Improvement Association and First Provisional President of Africa, New York City.

REPLY

November 17, 1921.

Conference of the Limitation of Armament,
Secretariat General.

Sir: I am directed by the Secretary General, the Chairman of the Conference, to acknowledge the receipt of your communication, which has been read with attention.

I am charged to express to you his appreciation of the interest and support which you have been so good to evince.

I am, sir,

Yours very truly,

T. G. W. PAUL,
For the Secretary General.

Mr. Marcus Garvey, President-General Universal Negro Improvement Association, 56 West 135th Street, New York.

THE MORALS OF OUR TIME!

It is remarkable to contemplate the deception of man, as practised upon his brothers. The human race has degenerated into select groups of liars and thieves, who practise their profession and carry out their depredations through the media of high-sounding philosophies. Chief among the deceivers who parade as sanctified moralists and reformers are some of the leading statesmen of the white race. The white man has given us morals from his head, and lies from his heart.

SPEECH DELIVERED AT MADISON SQUARE GARDEN, NEW YORK CITY, N. Y., U. S. A., SUNDAY, MARCH 16, 1924

In Honor of the Return to America of the Delegation Sent to Europe and Africa by the Universal Negro Improvement Association to Negotiate for the Repatriation of Negroes to a Homeland of Their Own in Africa

Fellow Citizens:

The coming together, all over this country, of fully six million people of Negro blood, to work for the creation of a nation of their own in their motherland, Africa, is no joke.

There is now a world revival of thought and action, which is causing peoples everywhere to bestir themselves towards their own security, through which we hear the cry of Ireland for the Irish, Palestine for the Jew, Egypt for the Egyptian, Asia for the Asiatic, and thus we Negroes raise the cry of Africa for the Africans, those at home and those abroad.

Some people are not disposed to give us credit for having feelings, passions, ambitions and desires like other races; they are satisfied to relegate us to the back-heap of human aspirations; but this is a mistake. The Almighty Creator made us men, not unlike others, but in His own image; hence, as a race, we feel that we, too, are entitled to the rights that are common to humanity.

The cry and desire for liberty is justifiable, and is made holy everywhere. It is sacred and holy to the Anglo-Saxon, Teuton and Latin; to the Anglo-American it precedes that of all religions, and now come the Irish, the Jew, the Egyptian, the Hindoo, and, last but not least, the Negro, clamoring for their share as well as their right to be free.

All men should be free—free to work out their own salvation. Free to create their own destinies. Free to nationally build up themselves for the upbringing and rearing of a culture and civilization of their own. Jewish culture is different from Irish culture. Anglo-Saxon culture is unlike Teutonic culture. Asiatic culture differs greatly from European culture; and, in the same way, the world should be liberal enough to allow the Negro latitude to develop a culture of his own. Why should the Negro be lost among the other races and nations of the world and to himself? Did nature not make of him a son of the soil? Did the Creator not fashion him out of the dust of the earth?—out of that rich soil to which he bears such a wonderful resemblance?—a resemblance that changes not, even though the ages have flown? No, the Ethiopian cannot change his skin; and so we appeal to the conscience of the white world to yield us a place of national freedom among the creatures of present-day temporal materialism.

We Negroes are not asking the white man to turn Europe and America over to us. We are not asking the Asiatic to turn Asia over for the accommodation of the blacks. But we are asking a just and righteous world to restore Africa to her scattered and abused children.

We believe in justice and human love. If our rights are to be respected, then, we, too, must respect the rights of all mankind; hence, we are ever ready and willing to yield to the white man the things that are his, and we feel that he, too, when his conscience is touched, will yield to us the things that are ours.

We should like to see a peaceful, prosperous and progressive white race in America and Europe; a peaceful, prosperous and progressive yellow race in Asia, and, in like manner, we want, and we demand, a peaceful, prosperous and progressive black race in Africa. Is that asking too much? Surely not. Humanity, without any immediate human hope of racial oneness, has drifted apart, and is now divided into separate and distinct groups, each with its own ideals and aspirations. Thus, we cannot expect any one race to hold a monopoly of creation and be able to keep the rest satisfied.

Distinct Racial Group Idealism

From our distinct racial group idealism we feel that no black man is good enough to govern the white man, and no white man good enough to rule the black man; and so of all races and peoples. No one feels that the other, alien in race, is good enough to govern or rule to the exclusion of native racial rights. We may as well, therefore, face the question of superior and inferior races. In twentieth century civilization there are no inferior and superior races. There are backward peoples, but that does not make them inferior. As far as humanity goes, all men are equal, and especially where peoples are intelligent enough to know what they want. At this time all peoples know what they want—it is liberty. When a people have sense enough to know that they ought to be free, then they naturally become the equal of all, in the higher calling of man to know and direct himself. It is true that economically and scientifically certain races are more progressive than others; but that does not imply superiority. For the Anglo-Saxon to say that he is superior because he introduced submarines to destroy life, or the Teuton because he compounded liquid gas to outdo in the art of killing, and that the Negro is inferior because he is backward in that direction is to leave one's self open to the retort "Thou shalt not kill," as being the divine law that sets the moral standard of the real man. There is no superiority in the one race economically monopolizing and holding all that would tend to the sustenance of life, and thus cause unhappiness and distress to others; for our highest purpose should be to love and care for each other, and share with each other the things that our Heavenly Father has placed at our common disposal; and even in this, the African is unsurpassed, in that he feeds his brother and shares with him the product of the land. The idea of race superiority is questionable; nevertheless, we must admit that, from the white man's standard, he is far superior to the rest of us, but that kind of superiority is too inhuman and dangerous to be permanently helpful. Such a superiority was shared and indulged in by other races before, and even by our own, when we boasted of a wonderful civilization on the banks of the Nile, when others were still groping in darkness; but because of our unrighteousness it failed, as all such will. Civilization can only last when we have reached the point where we will be our brother's keeper. That is to say, when we feel it righteous to live and let live.

No Exclusive Right to the World

Let no black man feel that he has the exclusive right to the world, and other men none, and let no white man feel that way, either. The world is the property of all mankind, and each and every group is entitled to a portion. The black man now wants his, and in terms uncompromising he is asking for it.

The Universal Negro Improvement Association represents the hopes and aspirations of the awakened Negro. Our desire is for a place in the world; not to disturb the tranquillity of other men, but to lay down our burden and rest our weary backs and feet by the banks of the Niger, and sing our songs and chant our hymns to the God of Ethiopia. Yes, we want rest from the toil of centuries, rest of political freedom, rest of economic and industrial liberty, rest to be socially free and unmolested, rest from lynching and burning, rest from discrimination of all kinds.

Out of slavery we have come with our tears and sorrows, and we now lay them at the feet of American white civilization. We cry to the considerate white people for help, because in their midst we can scarce help ourselves. We are strangers in a strange land. We cannot sing, we cannot play on our harps, for our hearts are sad. We are sad because of the tears of our mothers and the cry of our fathers. Have you not heard the plaintive wail? It is your father and my father burning at stake; but, thank God, there is a larger humanity growing among the good and considerate white people of this country, and they are going to help. They will help us to recover our souls.

As children of captivity we look forward to a new day and a new, yet ever old, land of our fathers, the land of refuge, the land of the Prophets, the land of the Saints, and the land of God's crowning glory. We shall gather together our children, our treasures and our loved ones, and, as the children of Israel, by the command of God, faced the promised land, so in time we shall also stretch forth our hands and bless our country.

Good and dear America that has succored us for three hundred years knows our story. We have watered her vegetation with our tears for two hundred and fifty years. We have built her cities and laid the foundation of her imperialism with the mortar of our blood and bones for three centuries, and now we cry to her for help. Help us, America, as we helped you. We helped you in the Revolutionary War. We helped you in the Civil War, and, although Lincoln helped us, the price is not half paid. We helped you in the Spanish-American War. We died nobly and courageously in Mexico, and did we not leave behind us on the stained battlefields of France and Flanders our rich blood to mark the poppies' bloom, and to bring back to you the glory of the flag that never touched the dust? We have no regrets in service to America for three hundred years, but we pray that America will help us for another fifty years until we have solved the troublesome problem that now confronts us. We know and realize that two ambitious and competitive races cannot live permanently side by side, without friction and trouble, and that is why the white race wants a white America and the black race wants and demands a black Africa.

Let white America help us for fifty years honestly, as we have helped her for three hundred years, and before the expiration of many decades there shall be no more race problem. Help us to gradually go home, America. Help us as you have helped the Jews. Help us as you have helped the Irish. Help us as you have helped the Poles, Russians, Germans and Armenians.

The Universal Negro Improvement Association proposes a friendly co-operation with all honest movements seeking intelligently to solve the race problem. We are not seeking social equality; we do not seek intermarriage, nor do we hanker after the impossible. We want the right to have a country of our own, and there foster and re-establish a culture and civilization exclusively ours. Don't say it can't be done. The Pilgrims and colonists did it for America, and the new Negro, with sympathetic help, can do it for Africa.

Back to Africa

The thoughtful and industrious of our race want to go back to Africa, because we realize it will be our only hope of permanent existence. We cannot all go in a day or year, ten or twenty years. It will take time under the rule of modern economics, to entirely or largely depopulate a country of a people, who have been its residents for centuries, but we feel that, with proper help for fifty years, the problem can be solved. We do not want all the Negroes in Africa. Some are no good here, and naturally will be no good there. The no-good Negro will naturally die in fifty years. The Negro who is wrangling about and fighting for social equality will naturally pass away in fifty years, and yield his place to the progressive Negro who wants a society and country of his own.

Negroes are divided into two groups, the industrious and adventurous, and the lazy and dependent. The industrious and adventurous believe that whatsoever others have done it can do. The Universal Negro Improvement Association belongs to this group, and so you find us working, six million strong, to the goal of an independent nationality. Who will not help? Only the mean and despicable "who never to himself hath said, this is my own, my native land." Africa is the legitimate, moral and righteous home of all Negroes, and now, that the time is coming for all to assemble under their own vine and fig tree, we feel it our duty to arouse every Negro to a consciousness of himself.

White and black will learn to respect each other when they cease to be active competitors in the same countries for the same things in politics and society. Let them have countries of their own, wherein to aspire and climb without rancor. The races can be friendly and helpful to each other, but the laws of nature separate us to the extent of each and every one developing by itself.

We want an atmosphere all our own. We would like to govern and rule ourselves and not be encumbered and restrained. We feel now just as the white race would feel if they were governed and ruled by the Chinese. If we live in our own districts, let us rule and govern those districts. If we have a majority in our communities, let us run those communities. We form a majority in Africa and we should naturally govern ourselves there. No man can govern another's house as well as himself. Let us have fair play. Let us have justice. This is the appeal we make to white America.

THE POLICY OF THE "COLORED" INTELLECTUAL

The present day Negro or "colored" intellectual is no less a liar and a cunning thief than his illustrious teacher. His occidental collegiate training only fits him to be a rogue and vagabond, and a seeker after the easiest and best by following the line of least resistence. He is lazy, dull and un-creative. His purpose is tc deceive the less fortunate of his race, and, by his wiles ride easily into position and wealth at their expense, and thereafter agitate for and seek social equality with the creative and industrious whites. To every rule, however, there is the exception, and in this case it must be applied.

THE NEGRO'S GREATEST ENEMY

This Article, Which Is Largely a Chapter of Autobiography, Appeared in Current History Magazine, September, 1923

I was born in the Island of Jamaica, British West Indies, on August 17, 1887. My parents were black Negroes. My father was a man of brilliant intellect and dashing courage. He was unafraid of consequences. He took human chances in the course of life, as most bold men do, and he failed at the close of his career. He once had a fortune; he died poor. My mother was a sober and conscientious Christian, too soft and good for the time in which she lived. She was the direct opposite of my father. He was severe, firm, determined, bold and strong, refusing to yield even to superior forces if he believed he was right. My mother, on the other hand, was always willing to return a smile for a blow, and ever ready to bestow charity upon her enemy. Of this strange combination I was born thirty-six years ago, and ushered into a world of sin, the flesh and the devil.

I grew up with other black and white boys. I was never whipped by any, but made them all respect the strength of my arms. I got my education from many sources—through private tutors, two public schools, two grammar or high schools and two colleges. My teachers were men and women of varied experiences and abilities; four of them were eminent preachers. They studied me and I studied them. With some I became friendly in after years; others and I drifted apart, because as a boy they wanted to whip me, and I simply refused to be whipped. I was not made to be whipped. It annoys me to be defeated; hence to me, to be once defeated is to find cause for an everlasting struggle to reach the top.

I became a printer's apprentice at an early age, while still attending school. My apprentice master was a highly educated and alert man. In the affairs of business and the world he had no peer. He taught me many things before I reached twelve, and at fourteen I had enough intelligence and experience to manage men. I was strong and manly, and I made them respect me. I developed a strong and forceful character, and have maintained it still.

To me, at home in my early days, there was no difference between white and black. One of my father's properties, the place where I lived most of the time, was adjoining that of a white man. He had three girls and two boys; the Wesleyan minister, another white man, whose church my parents attended, also had property adjoining ours. He had three girls and one boy. All of us were playmates. We romped and were happy children, playmates together. The little white girl whom I liked most knew no better than I did myself. We were two innocent fools who never dreamed of a race feeling and problem. As a child, I went to school with white boys and girls, like all other Negroes. We were not called Negroes then. I never heard the term Negro used once until I was about fourteen.

At fourteen my little white playmate and I parted. Her parents thought the time had come to separate us and draw the color line. They sent her and another sister to Edinburgh, Scotland, and told her that she was never to write or try to get in touch with me, for I was a "nigger." It was then that I found for the first time that there was some difference in humanity, and that there were different races, each having its own separate and distinct social life. I did not care about the separation after I was told about it, because I never thought all during our childhood association that the girl and the rest of the children of her race were better than I was; in fact, they used to look up to me. So I simply had no regrets.

After my first lesson in race distinction, I never thought of playing with white girls any more, even if they might be next-door neighbors. At home my sisters' company was good enough for me, and at school I made friends with the colored girls next to me. White boys and I used to frolic together. We played cricket and baseball, ran races and rode bicycles together, took each other to the river and to the sea beach to learn to swim, and made boyish efforts while out in deep water to drown each other, making a sprint for shore crying out "Shark, shark, shark!" In all our experiences, however, only one black boy was drowned. He went under on a Friday afternoon after school hours, and his parents found him afloat, half eaten by sharks, on the following Sunday afternoon. Since then we boys never went sea bathing.

"You Are Black"

At maturity the black and white boys separated, and took different courses in life. I grew then to see the difference between the races more and more. My schoolmates as young men did not know or remember me any more. Then I realized that I had to make a fight for a place in the world, that it was not so easy to pass on to office and position. Personally, however, I had not much difficulty in finding and holding a place for myself, for I was aggressive. At eighteen I had an excellent position as manager of a large printing establishment, having under my control several men old enough to be my grandfathers.

But I got mixed up with public life. I started to take an interest in the politics of my country, and then I saw the injustice done to my race because it was black, and I became dissatisfied on that account. I went traveling to South and Central America and parts of the West Indies to find out if it was so elsewhere, and I found the same situation. I set sail for Europe to find out if it was different there, and again I found the stumbling block—"You are black." I read of the conditions in America. I read "Up from Slavery," by Booker T. Washington, and then my doom—if I may so call it—of being a race leader dawned upon me in London after I had traveled through almost half of Europe.

I asked: "Where is the black man's Government?" "Where is his King and his kingdom?" "Where is his President, his country, and his ambassador, his army, his navy, his men of big affairs?" I could not find them, and then I declared, "I will help to make them."

Becoming naturally restless for the opportunity of doing something for the advancement of my race, I was determined that the black man would not continue to be kicked about by all the other races and nations of the world, as I saw it in the West Indies, South and Central America and Europe, and as I read of it in America. My young and ambitious mind led me into flights of great imagination. I saw before me then, even as I do now, a new world of black men, not peons, serfs, dogs and slaves, but a nation of sturdy men making their impress upon civilization and causing a new light to dawn upon the human race. I could not remain in London any more. My brain was afire. There was a world of thought to conquer. I had to start ere it became too late and the work be not done. Immediately I boarded a ship at Southampton for Jamaica, where I arrived on July 15, 1914. The Universal Negro Improvement Association and African Communities (Imperial) League was founded and organized five days after my arrival, with the program of uniting all the Negro peoples of the world into one great body to establish a country and Government absolutely their own.

Where did the name of the organization come from? It was while speaking to a West Indian Negro who was a passenger on the ship with me from Southampton, who was returning home to the West Indies from Basutoland with his Basuto wife, that I further learned of the horrors of native life in Africa. He related to me such horrible and pitiable tales that my heart bled within me. Retiring to my cabin, all day and the following night I pondered over the subject matter of that conversation, and at midnight, lying flat on my back, the vision and thought came to me that I should name the organization the Universal Negro Improvement Association and African Communities (Imperial) League. Such a name I thought would embrace the purpose of all black humanity. Thus to the world a name was born, a movement created, and a man became known.

I really never knew there was so much color prejudice in Jamaica, my own native home, until I started the work of the Universal Negro Improvement Association. We started immediately before the war. I had just returned from a successful trip to Europe, which was an exceptional achievement for a black man. The daily papers wrote me up with big headlines and told of my movement. But nobody wanted to be a Negro. "Garvey is crazy; he has lost his head." "Is that the use he is going to make of his experience and intelligence?"—such were the criticisms passed upon me. Men and women as black as I, and even more so, had believed themselves white under the West Indian order of society. I was simply an impossible man to use openly the term "Negro"; yet every one beneath his breath was calling the black man a nigger.

I had to decide whether to please my friends and be one of the "black-whites" of Jamaica, and be reasonably prosperous, or come out openly, and defend and help improve and protect the integrity of the black millions, and suffer. I decided to do the latter, hence my offense against "colored-black-white" society in the colonies and America. I was openly hated and persecuted by some of these colored men of the island who did not want to be classified as Negroes, but as white. They hated me worse than poison. They opposed me at every step, but I had a large number of white friends, who encouraged and helped me. Notable among them were the then Governor of the Colony, the Colonial Secretary and several other prominent men. But they were afraid of offending the "colored gentry" that passed for white. Hence my fight had to be made alone. I spent hundreds of pounds (sterling) helping the organization to gain a footing. I also gave up all my time to the promulgation of its ideals. I became a marked man, but I was determined that the work should be done.

The war helped a great deal in arousing the consciousness of the colored people to the reasonableness of our program, especially after the British at home had rejected a large number of West Indian colored men who wanted to be officers in the British army. When they were told that Negroes could not be officers in the British army they started their own propaganda, which supplemented the program of the Universal Negro Improvement Association. With this and other contributing agencies a few of the stiff-necked colored people began to see the reasonableness of my program, but they were firm in refusing to be known as Negroes. Furthermore, I was a black man and therefore had absolutely no right to lead; in the opinion of the "colored" element, leadership should have been in the hands of a yellow or a very light man. On such flimsy prejudices our race has been retarded. There is more bitterness among us Negroes because of the caste of color than there is between any other peoples, not excluding the people of India.

I succeeded to a great extent in establishing the Association in Jamaica with the assistance of a Catholic Bishop, the Governor, Sir John Pringle, the Rev. William Graham, a Scottish clergyman, and several other white friends. I got in touch with Booker Washington and told him what I wanted to do. He invited me to America and promised to speak with me in the Southern and other States to help my work. Although he died in the Fall of 1915, I made my arrangements and arrived in the United States on March 23, 1916.

Here I found a new and different problem. I immediately visited some of the then so-called Negro leaders, only to discover, after a close study of them, that they had no program, but were mere opportunists who were living off their so-called leadership while the poor people were groping in the dark. I traveled through thirty-eight States and everywhere found the same condition. I visited Tuskegee and paid my respects to the dead hero, Booker Washington, and then returned to New York, where I organized the New York division of the Universal Negro Improvement Association. After instructing the people in the aims and objects of the Association, I intended returning to Jamaica to perfect the Jamaica organization, but when we had enrolled about 800 or 1,000 members in the Harlem district and had elected the officers, a few Negro politicians tried to turn the movement into a political club.

Political Faction Fight

Seeing that these politicians were about to destroy my ideals, I had to fight to get them out of the organization. Then it was that I made my first political enemies in Harlem. They fought me until they smashed the first organization and reduced its membership to about fifty. I started again, and in two months built up a new organization of about 1,500 members. Again the politicians came and divided us into two factions. They took away all the books of the organization, its treasury and all its belongings. At that time I was only an organizer, for it was not then my intention to remain in America, but to return to Jamaica. The organization had its proper officers elected, and 1 was not an officer of the New York division, but President of the Jamaica branch.

On the second split in Harlem thirteen of the members conferred with me and requested me to become President for a time of the New York organization so as to save them from the politicians. I consented and was elected President. There then sprang up two factions, one led by the politicians with the books and the money, and the other led by me. My faction had no money. I placed at their disposal what money I had, opened an office for them, rented a meeting place, employed two women secretaries, went on the street of Harlem at night to speak for the movement. In three weeks more than 2,000 new members joined. By this time I had the Association incorporated so as to prevent the other faction using the name, but in two weeks the politicians had stolen all the people's money and had smashed up their faction.

The organization under my Presidency grew by leaps and bounds. I started The Negro World. Being a journalist, I edited this paper free of cost for the Association, and worked for them without pay until November, 1920. I traveled all over the country for the Association at my own expense and established branches until in 1919 we had about thirty branches in different cities. By my writings and speeches we were able to build up a large organization of over 2,000,000 by June, 1919, at which time we launched the program of the Black Star Line.

To have built up a new organization, which was not purely political, among Negroes in America was a wonderful feat, for the Negro politician does not allow any other kind of organization within his race to thrive. We succeeded, however, in making the Universal Negro Improvement Association so formidable in 1919 that we encountered more trouble from our political brethren. They sought the influence of the District Attorney's office of the County of New York to put us out of business. Edwin P. Kilroe, at that time an Assistant District Attorney, on the complaint of the Negro politicians, started to investigate us and the association. Mr. Kilroe would constantly and continuously call me to his office for investigation on extraneous matters without coming to the point. The result was that after the eighth or ninth time I wrote an article in our newspaper, The Negro World, against him. This was interpreted as a criminal libel, for which I was indicted and arrested, but subsequently dismissed on retracting what I had written.

During my many tilts with Mr. Kilroe, the question of the Black Star Line was discussed. He did not want us to have a line of ships. I told him that even as there was a White Star Line, we would have, irrespective of his wishes, a Black Star Line. On June 27, 1919, we incorporated the Black Star Line of Delaware, and in September we obtained a ship.

The following month (October) a man by the name of Tyler came to my office at 56 West 135th Street, New York City, and told me that Mr. Kilroe had sent him to "get me," and at once fired four shots at me from a .38-calibre revolver. He wounded me in the right leg and the right side of my scalp. I was taken to the Harlem Hospital, and he was arrested. The next day it was reported that he committed suicide in jail just before he was to be taken before a City Magistrate.

Record-Breaking Convention

The first year of our activities for the Black Star Line added prestige to the Universal Negro Improvement Association. Several hundred thousand dollars worth of shares were sold. Our first ship, the steamship Yarmouth, had made three voyages to the West Indies and Central America. The white press had flashed the news all over the world. I, a young Negro, as President of the corporation, had become famous. My name was discussed on five continents. The Universal Negro Improvement Association gained millions of followers all over the world. By August, 1920, over 4,000,000 persons had joined the movement. A convention of all the Negro peoples of the world was called to meet in New York that month. Delegates came from all parts of the known world. Over 25,000 persons packed the Madison Square Garden on August 1 to hear me speak to the first International Convention of Negroes. It was a record-breaking meeting, the first and the biggest of its kind. The name of Garvey had become known as a leader of his race.

Such fame among Negroes was too much for other race leaders and politicians to tolerate. My downfall was planned by my enemies. They laid all kinds of traps for me. They scattered their spies among the employes of the Black Star Line and the Universal Negro Improvement Association. Our office records were stolen. Employes started to be openly dishonest; we could get no convictions against them; even if on complaint they were held by a Magistrate, they were dismissed by the Grand Jury. The ships' officers started to pile up thousands of dollars of debts against the company without the knowledge of the officers of the corporation. Our ships were damaged at sea, and there was a general riot of wreck and ruin. Officers of the Universal Negro Improvement Association also began to steal and be openly dishonest. I had to dismiss them. They joined my enemies, and thus I had an endless fight on my hands to save the ideals of the Association and carry out our program for the race. My Negro enemies, finding that they alone could not destroy me, resorted to misrepresenting me to the leaders of the white race, several of whom, without proper investigation, also opposed me.

With robberies from within and from without, the Black Star Line was forced to suspend active business in December, 1921. While I was on a business trip to the West Indies in the Spring of 1921, the Black Star Line received the blow from which it was unable to recover. A sum of $25,000 was paid by one of the officers of the corporation to a man to purchase a ship, but the ship was never obtained and the money was never returned. The company was defrauded of a further sum of $11,000. Through such actions on the part of dishonest men in the shipping business, the Black Star Line received its first setback. This resulted in my being indicted for using the United States mails to defraud investors in the company. I was subsequently convicted and sentenced to five years in a Federal penitentiary. My trial is a matter of history. I know I was not given a square deal, because my indictment was the result of a "frame-up" among my political and business enemies. I had to conduct my own case in court because of the peculiar position in which I found myself. I had millions of friends and a large number of enemies. I wanted a colored attorney to handle my case, but there was none I could trust. I feel that I have been denied justice because of prejudice. Yet I have an abundance of faith in the courts of America, and I hope yet to obtain justice on my appeal.

Association's 6,000,000 Membership

The temporary ruin of the Black Star Line has in no way affected the larger work of the Universal Negro Improvement Association, which now has 900 branches with an approximate membership of 6,000,000. This organization has succeeded in organizing the Negroes all over the world, and we now look forward to a renaissance that will create a new people and bring about the restoration of Ethiopia's ancient glory.

Being black, I have committed an unpardonable offense against the very light-colored Negroes in America and the West

Indies by making myself famous as a Negro leader of millions. In their view, no black man must rise above them, but I still forge ahead determined to give to the world the truth about the new Negro who is determined to make and hold for himself a place in the affairs of men. The Universal Negro Improvement Association has been misrepresented by my enemies. They have tried to make it appear that we are hostile to other races. This is absolutely false. We love all humanity. We are working for the peace of the world, which we believe can only come about when all races are given their due.

We feel that there is absolutely no reason why there should be any differences between the black and white races, if each stop to adjust and steady itself. We believe in the purity of both races. We do not believe the black man should be encouraged in the idea that his highest purpose in life is to marry a white woman, and we do believe that the white man should be taught to respect the black woman in the same way as he wants the black man to respect the white woman. It is a vicious and dangerous doctrine of social equality to urge, as certain colored leaders do, that black and white should get together, for that would destroy the racial purity of both.

We believe that the black people should have a country of their own, where they should be given the fullest opportunity to develop politically, socially and industrially. The black people should not be encouraged to remain in white people's countries and expect to be Presidents, Governors, Mayors, Senators, Congressmen, Judges and social and industrial leaders. We believe that with the rising ambition of the Negro, if a country is not provided for him in another 50 or 100 years, there will be a terrible clash that will end disastrously to him and disgrace our civilization. We desire to prevent such a clash by pointing the Negro to a home of his own. We feel that all well-disposed and broad-minded white men will aid in this direction. It is because of this belief no doubt that my Negro enemies, so as to prejudice me further in the opinion of the public, wickedly state that I am a member of the Ku Klux Klan, even though I am a black man.

I have been deprived of the opportunity of properly explaining my work to the white people of America, through the prejudice worked up against me by jealous and wicked members of my own race. My success as an organizer was much more than rival Negro leaders could tolerate. They, regardless of consequences, either to me or to the race, had to destroy me by fair means or foul. The thousands of anonymous and other hostile letters written to the editors and publishers of the white press by Negro rivals to prejudice me in the eyes of public opinion are sufficient evidence of the wicked and vicious opposition I have had to meet from among my own people, especially among the very light colored. But they went further than the press in their attempts to discredit me. They organized clubs all over the United States and the West Indies, and wrote both open and anonymous letters to city, State and Federal officials of this and other Governments to induce them to use their influence to hamper and destroy me. No wonder, therefore, that several Judges, District Attorneys and other high officials have been opposing me without knowing me. No wonder, therefore, that the great white population of this country and of the world has a wrong impression of the aims and objects of the Universal Negro Improvement Association and of the work of Marcus Garvey.

The Struggle of the Future

Having had the wrong education as a start in his racial career, the Negro has become his greatest enemy. Most of the troubles I have had in advancing the cause of the race have come from Negroes. Booker Washington aptly described the race in one of his lectures by stating that we were like crabs in a barrel, that none would allow the other to climb over, but on any such attempt all would combine to pull back into the barrel the one crab that would make the effort to climb out. Yet, those of us with vision cannot desert the race, leaving it to suffer and die.

Looking forward a century or two, we can see an economic and political death struggle for the survival of the different race groups. Many of our present-day national centres will have become overcrowded with vast surplus populations. The fight for bread and position will be keen and severe. The weaker and unprepared group is bound to go under. That is why, visionaries as we are in the Universal Negro Improvement Association, we are fighting for the founding of a Negro nation in Africa, so that there will be no clash between black and white and that each race will have a separate existence and civilization all its own without courting suspicion and hatred or eyeing each other with jealousy and rivalry within the borders of the same country.

White men who have struggled for and built up their countries and their own civilizations are not disposed to hand them over to the Negro, or any other race, without let or hindrance. It would be unreasonable to expect this. Hence any vain assumption on the part of the Negro to imagine that he will one day become President of the Nation, Governor of the State, or Mayor of the City in the countries of white men, is like waiting on the devil and his angels to take up their residence in the Realm on high and direct there the affairs of Paradise.

THE CHARACTER OF RACES

Black and white are proportionately bad as well as proportionately good, living under the same conditions and environments of our imperfect civilization.

All beauty, virtue and goodness are the exclusive attributes of no one race. All humanity have their shortcomings; hence no statement of mine, at any time, must be interpreted as a wholesale praise of, or attack upon any race, people or creed.

There are good and bad Catholics, Protestants, Jews and Klansmen. I would not wholesalely condemn any one group of the human race for the selfish good of another. The Negro needs as much moral reformation as anyone else. He lies, he steals, and he breaks the commands of God like any other sinner, and his crimes merit the same punishment as meted out to others. No one can influence me to be against Jews because they are Jews, Catholics because they are Catholics, or Klansmen because they are Klansmen. I condemn evil wheresoever I find it, in friend or foe, but I do not carry prejudice to the innocent because of their friendship for, or association with, the evildoer, for whom they are not responsible.

DECLARATION OF RIGHTS OF THE NEGRO PEOPLES OF THE WORLD

Drafted and adopted at Convention held in New York, 1920, over which Marcus Garvey presided as Chairman, and at which he was elected Provisional President of Africa.

(Preamble)

"Be it Resolved, That the Negro people of the world, through their chosen representatives in convention assembled in Liberty Hall, in the City of New York and United States of America, from August 1 to August 31, in the year of our Lord, one thousand nine hundred and twenty, protest against the wrongs and injustices they are suffering at the hands of their white brethren, and state what they deem their fair and just rights, as well as the treatment they propose to demand of all men in the future."

We complain:

I. "That nowhere in the world, with few exceptions, are black men accorded equal treatment with white men, although in the same situation and circumstances, but, on the contrary, are discriminated against and denied the common rights due to human beings for no other reason than their race and color."

"We are not willingly accepted as guests in the public hotels and inns of the world for no other reason than our race and color."

II. "In certain parts of the United States of America our race is denied the right of public trial accorded to other races when accused of crime, but are lynched and burned by mobs, and such brutal and inhuman treatment is even practised upon our women."

III. "That European nations have parcelled out among themselves and taken possession of nearly all of the continent of Africa, and the natives are compelled to surrender their lands to aliens and are treated in most instances like slaves."

IV. "In the southern portion of the United States of America, although citizens under the Federal Constitution, and in some states almost equal to the whites in population and are qualified land owners and taxpayers, we are, nevertheless, denied all voice in the making and administration of the laws and are taxed without representation by the state governments, and at the same time compelled to do military service in defense of the country."

V. "On the public conveyances and common carriers in the Southern portion of the United States we are jim-crowed and compelled to accept separate and inferior accommodations and made to pay the same fare charged for first-class accommodations, and our families are often humiliated and insulted by drunken white men who habitually pass through the jim-crow cars going to the smoking car."

VI. "The physicians of our race are denied the right to attend their patients while in the public hospitals of the cities and states where they reside in certain parts of the United States."

"Our children are forced to attend inferior separate schools for shorter terms than white children, and the public school funds are unequally divided between the white and colored schools."

VII. "We are discriminated against and denied an equal chance to earn wages for the support of our families, and in many instances are refused admission into labor unions, and nearly everywhere are paid smaller wages than white men."

VIII. "In Civil Service and departmental offices we are everywhere discriminated against and made to feel that to be a black man in Europe, America and the West Indies is equivalent to being an outcast and a leper among the races of men, no matter what the character and attainments of the black man may be."

IX. "In the British and other West Indian Islands and colonies, Negroes are secretly and cunningly discriminated against, and denied those fuller rights in government to which white citizens are appointed, nominated and elected."

X. "That our people in those parts are forced to work for lower wages than the average standard of white men and are kept in conditions repugnant to good civilized tastes and customs."

XI. "That the many acts of injustice against members of our race before the courts of law in the respective islands and colonies are of such nature as to create disgust and disrespect for the white man's sense of justice."

XII. "Against all such inhuman, unchristian and uncivilized treatment we here and now emphatically protest, and invoke the condemnation of all mankind."

"In order to encourage our race all over the world and to stimulate it to a higher and grander destiny, we demand and insist on the following Declaration of Rights:

1. "Be it known to all men that whereas, all men are created equal and entitled to the rights of life, liberty and the pursuit of happiness, and because of this we, the duly elected representatives of the Negro peoples of the world, invoking the aid of the just and Almighty God do declare all men women and children

Group of Juveniles In Convention Parade

of our blood throughout the world free citizens, and do claim them as free citizens of Africa, the Motherland of all Negroes."

2. "That we believe in the supreme authority of our race in all things racial; that all things are created and given to man as a common possession; that there should be an equitable distribution and apportionment of all such things, and in consideration of the fact that as a race we are now deprived of those things that are morally and legally ours, we believe it right that all such things should be acquired and held by whatsoever means possible.

3. "That we believe the Negro, like any other race, should be governed by the ethics of civilization, and, therefore, should not be deprived of any of those rights or privileges common to other human beings."

4. "We declare that Negroes, wheresoever they form a community among themselves, should be given the right to elect their own representatives to represent them in legislatures, courts of law, or such institutions as may exercise control over that particular community."

5. "We assert that the Negro is entitled to even-handed justice before all courts of law and equity in whatever country he may be found, and when this is denied him on account of his race or color such denial is an insult to the race as a whole and should be resented by the entire body of Negroes."

6. "We declare it unfair and prejudicial to the rights of Negroes in communities where they exist in considerable numbers to be tried by a judge and jury composed entirely of an alien race, but in all such cases members of our race are entitled to representation on the jury."

7. "We believe that any law or practice that tends to deprive any African of his land or the privileges of free citizenship within his country is unjust and immoral, and no native should respect any such law or practice."

8. "We declare taxation without representation unjust and tyrannous, and there should be no obligation on the part of the Negro to obey the levy of a tax by any law-making body from which he is excluded and denied representation on account of his race and color."

9. "We believe that any law especially directed against the Negro to his detriment and singling him out because of his race or color is unfair and immoral, and should not be respected."

10. "We believe all men entitled to common human respect,

and that our race should in no way tolerate any insults that may be interpreted to mean disrespect to our color."

11. "We deprecate the use of the term 'nigger' as applied to Negroes, and demand that the word 'Negro' be written with a capital 'N.' "

12. "We believe that the Negro should adopt every means to protect himself against barbarous practices inflicted upon him because of color."

13. "We believe in the freedom of Africa for the Negro people of the world, and by the principle of Europe for the Europeans and Asia for the Asiatics; we also demand Africa for the Africans at home and abroad."

14. "We believe in the inherent right of the Negro to possess himself of Africa, and that his possession of same shall not be regarded as an infringement on any claim or purchase made by any race or nation."

15. "We strongly condemn the cupidity of those nations of the world who, by open aggression or secret schemes, have seized the territories and inexhaustible natural wealth of Africa, and we place on record our most solemn determination to reclaim the treasures and possession of the vast continent of our forefathers."

16. "We believe all men should live in peace one with the other, but when races and nations provoke the ire of other races and nations by attempting to infringe upon their rights, war becomes inevitable, and the attempt in any way to free one's self or protect one's rights or heritage becomes justifiable.

17. "Whereas, the lynching, by burning, hanging or any other means, of human beings is a barbarous practice, and a shame and disgrace to civilization, we therefore declare any country guilty of such atrocities outside the pale of civilization."

18. "We protest against the atrocious crime of whipping, flogging and overworking of the native tribes of Africa and Negroes everywhere. These are methods that should be abolished, and all means should be taken to prevent a continuance of such brutal practices."

19. "We protest against the atrocious practice of shaving the heads of Africans, especially of African women or individuals of Negro blood, when placed in prison as a punishment for crime by an alien race."

20. "We protest against segregated districts, separate public conveyances, industrial discrimination, lynchings and limitations of political privileges of any Negro citizen in any part of the

world on account of race, color or creed, and will exert our full influence and power against all such."

21. "We protest against any punishment inflicted upon a Negro with severity, as against lighter punishment inflicted upon another of an alien race for like offense, as an act of prejudice and injustice, and should be resented by the entire race."

22. "We protest against the system of education in any country where Negroes are denied the same privileges and advantages as other races."

23. "We declare it inhuman and unfair to boycott Negroes from industries and labor in any part of the world."

24. "We believe in the doctrine of the freedom of the press, and we therefore emphatically protest against the suppression of Negro newspapers and periodicals in various parts of the world, and call upon Negroes everywhere to employ all available means to prevent such suppression."

25. "We further demand free speech universally for all men."

26. "We hereby protest against the publication of scandalous and inflammatory articles by an alien press tending to create racial strife and the exhibition of picture films showing the Negro as a cannibal."

27. "We believe in the self-determination of all peoples."

28. "We declare for the freedom of religious worship."

29. "With the help of Almighty God, we declare ourselves the sworn protectors of the honor and virtue of our women and children, and pledge our lives for their protection and defense everywhere, and under all circumstances from wrongs and outrages."

30. "We demand the right of unlimited and unprejudiced education for ourselves and our posterity forever."

31. "We declare that the teaching in any school by alien teachers to our boys and girls, that the alien race is superior to the Negro race, is an insult to the Negro people of the world."

32. "Where Negroes form a part of the citizenry of any country, and pass the civil service examination of such country, we declare them entitled to the same consideration as other citizens as to appointments in such civil service."

33. "We vigorously protest against the increasingly unfair and unjust treatment accorded Negro travelers on land and sea by the agents and employees of railroad and steamship compa-

nies and insist that for equal fare we receive equal privileges with travelers of other races."

34. "We declare it unjust for any country, State or nation to enact laws tending to hinder and obstruct the free immigration of Negroes on account of their race and color."

35. "That the right of the Negro to travel unmolested throughout the world be not abridged by any person or persons, and all Negroes are called upon to give aid to a fellow Negro when thus molested."

36. "We declare that all Negroes are entitled to the same right to travel over the world as other men."

37. "We hereby demand that the governments of the world recognize our leader and his representatives chosen by the race to look after the welfare of our people under such governments."

38. "We demand complete control of our social institutions without interference by any alien race or races."

39. "That the colors, Red, Black and Green, be the colors of the Negro race."

40. "Resolved, That the anthem 'Ethiopia, Thou Land of Our Fathers,' etc., shall be the anthem of the Negro race."

The Universal Ethiopian Anthem
(Poem by Burrell and Ford.)

I

Ethiopia, thou land of our fathers,
Thou land where the gods loved to be,
As storm cloud at night suddenly gathers
Our armies come rushing to thee.
We must in the fight be victorious
When swords are thrust outward to gleam;
For us will the vict'ry be glorious
When led by the red, black and green.

Chorus

Advance, advance to victory,
Let Africa be free;
Advance to meet the foe
With the might
Of the red, the black and the green.

II

Ethiopia, the tyrant's falling,
Who smote thee upon thy knees,
And thy children are lustily calling
From over the distant seas.

Jehovah, the Great One has heard us,
Has noted our sighs and our tears,
With His spirit of Love he has stirred us
To be One through the coming years.
CHORUS—Advance, advance, etc.

III

O Jehovah, thou God of the ages
Grant unto our sons that lead
The wisdom Thou gave to Thy sages
When Israel was sore in need.
Thy voice thro' the dim past has spoken,
Ethiopia shall stretch forth her hand,
By Thee shall all fetters be broken,
And Heav'n bless our dear fatherland.
CHORUS—Advance, advance, etc.

41. "We believe that any limited liberty which deprives one of the complete rights and prerogatives of full citizenship is but a modified form of slavery."

42. "We declare it an injustice to our people and a serious impediment to the health of the race to deny to competent licensed Negro physicians the right to practise in the public hospitals of the communities in which they reside, for no other reason than their race and color."

43. "We call upon the various governments of the world to accept and acknowledge Negro representatives who shall be sent to the said governments to represent the general welfare of the Negro peoples of the world."

44. "We deplore and protest against the practice of confining juvenile prisoners in prisons with adults, and we recommend that such youthful prisoners be taught gainful trades under humane supervision."

45. "Be it further resolved, that we as a race of people declare the League of Nations null and void as far as the Negro is concerned, in that it seeks to deprive Negroes of their liberty."

46. "We demand of all men to do unto us as we would do unto them, in the name of justice; and we cheerfully accord to all men all the rights we claim herein for ourselves."

47. "We declare that no Negro shall engage himself in battle for an alien race without first obtaining the consent of the leader of the Negro people of the world, except in a matter of national self-defense."

48. "We protest against the practice of drafting Negroes and sending them to war with alien forces without proper training,

and demand in all cases that Negro soldiers be given the same training as the aliens."

49. "We demand that instructions given Negro children in schools include the subject of 'Negro History,' to their benefit."

50. "We demand a free and unfettered commercial intercourse with all the Negro people of the world."

51. "We declare for the absolute freedom of the seas for all peoples."

52. "We demand that our duly accredited representatives be given proper recognition in all leagues, conferences, conventions or courts of international arbitration wherever human rights are discussed."

53. "We proclaim the 31st day of August of each year to be an international holiday to be observed by all Negroes."

54. "We want all men to know we shall maintain and contend for the freedom and equality of every man, woman and child of our race, with our lives, our fortunes and our sacred honor."

These rights we believe to be justly ours and proper for the protection of the Negro race at large, and because of this belief we, on behalf of the four hundred million Negroes of the world, do pledge herein the sacred blood of the race in defense, and we hereby subscribe our names as a guarantee of the truthfulness and faithfulness hereof in the presence of Almighty God, on the 13th day of August, in the year of our Lord one thousand nine hundred and twenty.

Marcus Garvey, James D. Brooks, James W. H. Eason, Henrietta Vinton Davis, Lionel Winston Greenidge, Adrion Fitzroy Johnson, Rudolph Ethelbert Brissaac Smith, Charles Augustus Petioni, Thomas H. N. Simon, Richard Hilton Tobitt, George Alexander McGuire, Peter Edward Baston, Reynold R. Felix, Harry Walters Kirby, Sarah Branch, Marie Barrier Houston, George L. O'Brien, F. O. Ogilvie, Arden A. Bryan, Benjamin Dyett, Marie Duchaterlier, John Phillip Hodge, Theophilus H. Saunders, Wilford H. Smith, Gabriel E. Stewart, Arnold Josiah Ford, Lee Crawford, William McCartney, Adina Clem. James, William Musgrave La Motte, John Sydney de Bourg, Arnold S. Cunning, Vernal J. Williams, Frances Wilcome Ellegor, J. Frederick Selkridge, Innis Abel Horsford, Cyril A. Crichlow, Samuel McIntyre, John Thomas Wilkins, Mary Thurston, John G. Befue, William Ware, J. A. Lewis, O. C. Kelly, Venture R. Hamilton, R. H. Hodge, Edward Alfred Taylor, Ellen Wilson, G. W. Wilson, Richard Edward Riley,

Nellie Grant Whiting, G. W. Washington, Maldena Miller, Gertrude Davis, James D. Williams, Emily Christmas Kinch, D. D. Lewis, Nettie Clayton, Partheria Hills, Janie Jenkins, John C. Simons, Alphonso A. Jones, Allen Hobbs, Reynold Fitzgerald Austin, James Benjamin Yearwood, Frank O. Raines, Shedrick Williams, John Edward Ivey, Frederick Augustus Toote, Philip Hemmings, F. F. Smith, E. J. Jones, Joseph Josiah Cranston, Frederick Samuel Ricketts, Dugald Augustus Wade, E. E. Nelom, Florida Jenkins, Napoleon J. Francis, Joseph D. Gibson, J. P. Jasper, J. W. Montgomery, David Benjamin, J. Gordon, Harry E. Ford, Carrie M. Ashford, Andrew N. Willis, Lucy Sands, Louise Woodson, George D. Creese, W. A. Wallace, Thomas E. Bagley, James Young, Prince Alfred McConney, John E. Hudson, William Ines, Harry R. Watkins, C. L. Halton, J. T. Bailey, Ira Joseph Touissant Wright, T. H. Golden, Abraham Benjamin Thomas, Richard C. Noble, Walter Green, C. S. Bourne, G. F. Bennett, B. D. Levy, Mary E. Johnson, Lionel Antonio Francis, Carl Roper, E. R. Donawa, Philip Van Putten, I. Brathwaite, Jesse W. Luck, Oliver Kaye, J. W. Hudspeth, C. B. Lovell, William C. Matthews, A. Williams, Ratford E. M. Jack, H. Vinton Plummer, Randolph Phillips, A. I. Bailey, duly elected representatives of the Negro people of the world.

Sworn before me this 15th day of August, 1920.

[Legal Seal]   JOHN G. BAYNE.

Notary Public, New York County.

New York County Clerk's No. 378; New York County Register's No. 12102. Commission expires March 30, 1922.

PART II

UNITED STATES OF AMERICA

vs.

MARCUS GARVEY

Blessed are they which are persecuted for righteousness' sake; for theirs is the kingdom of heaven.—Matt. v. x.

UNITED STATES OF AMERICA vs. MARCUS GARVEY

Was Justice Defeated?

Some details of the case of the United States of America against Marcus Garvey are herewith submitted in the hope that the reader may be able to form an opinion and reach a conclusion as to whether ERROR TRIUMPHED OVER JUSTICE.

The following excerpt from "The Law's Introspection" written by Attorney H. H. Emmons of Canton, Ohio, defines the Law in its entirety:

"I AM THE LAW. By and through me only is Civilization itself preserved and Anarchy, my arch-enemy, kept in chains. When I am misused or my prerogatives ignored by the courts or my interpreters swayed by Passion, Prejudice or Political Influence—those green-eyed monsters that feed on ignorance and credulity—many and divers crimes are committed in my name and from which the victims, at times, have no appeal.

As I owe my own right to exist to the General Public it must be kept informed as to my principles, actions and inactions—the mistakes I make and the frailties of my being —so that Error cannot triumph over Justice. Discretion, therefore, requires me to invite Publicity to my citadels as the trusted guard against Suspicion, and, as it were, transact my business behind glass doors. Secret Diplomacy must have no admittance to my realm. Honest Criticism, that great genius for Progress, and the twin brother of Publicity, must be well-treated within my Province. Education and Science, those loyal, tried and true friends of Society, shall have every consideration within my power to bestow."

The following facts in connection with the case are worthy of consideration:

1. Marcus Garvey was first indicted alone for using the mails to defraud in the promotion of the Black Star Line and the Universal Negro Improvement Association.

2. Immediately after this indictment all the books, records and documents of the Black Star Line and the Universal Negro Improvement Association were seized by the government and taken from the office of the corporation and association respectively; which books, records and documents were admitted in evidence over the objection and exception of Marcus Garvey, in violation of his constitutional right under Article IV. of the

United States Constitution, in that, by the admission of such books, records and documents Marcus Garvey was, in effect, required to give evidence against himself.

3. After the seizure of the books, the prosecution sent questionnaires to all the stockholders of the Black Star Line, questioning them about Marcus Garvey—a very unusual method.

4. There were about 35,000 stockholders of the Black Star Line, who were also members of the Universal Negro Improvement Association, of which Marcus Garvey was President-General. These stockholders were supremely interested in the development of Africa for the Negro race, which program was advocated by the Universal Negro Improvement Association and for which cause they invested their money.

5. The first indictment, being faulty, in that the Black Star Line was a corporation and not a private enterprise, was withdrawn, and two new indictments returned against Marcus Garvey as President, Orlando Thompson, as Vice-President, Eli Garcia, as Secretary, and George Tobias, as Treasurer, of the Black Star Line, based upon the solicited replies to the questionnaires.

6. These two indictments were referred to at the trial as the first and second indictments. They contained thirteen counts.

7. At the close of the trial the jury, after being out for eleven hours, was called in by the learned judge and given a second series of instructions, without their request, the gist of which is evident when he stated:

"Some men feel that having given their view in the be-
"ginning, it is an indication of their firmness of character,
"their sound judgment, if they stick inalterably to it. . . .
"Now the effect of a disagreement, whether it be as to one
"count, two or three or four of them, as to any particular
"count, means that as to such count or as to such defend-
"ant, or both, as to which you may disagree, the govern-
"ment is put to the expense, the public is put to the loss of
"time, and the Court and the jury, and the witnesses and
"the defendants are put to the expense of having to go
"through the whole thing again."

8. The jury again retired after the second charge and in less than thirty minutes returned with a verdict of guilty against Marcus Garvey alone, under the third count of the second indictment.

9. Marcus Garvey was given the maximum punishment under the law—five years in the Atlanta Federal Penitentiary, One

thousand dollars fine, and ordered to pay the entire cost of the suit.

10. He was denied bail by the Court, and remained in the Tombs Prison, New York City, while his attorneys made several applications for his bail. At the expiration of three months he was granted bail pending his appeal to the Circuit Court of Appeals.

11. The witnesses who testified against Marcus Garvey were for the most part dishonest, dismissed and disgruntled ex-employees of his, who admitted hatred toward him in Court.

12. The contradictory testimony of the mailing clerk, part of which is quoted elsewhere, is worthy of consideration.

13. The attitude of the Assistant United States Prosecutor during the entire conduct of the case toward Marcus Garvey **is** exemplified in the closing remarks of his impassioned address to the jury, when he said:

"GENTLEMEN, WILL YOU LET THE TIGER LOOSE?"

Bear in mind, Dear Reader, that there were FOUR defendants, not ONE.

14. That the Bill of Exceptions filed in Marcus Garvey's behalf after trial contained ninety-four errors alleged to have been committed, and this despite the fact that Garvey, a layman, tried his own case.

The following among other Errors cited by Counsel for Marcus Garvey, should be noted:

(a) The Court erred in not declaring a mistrial after publication in the New York newspapers of articles to the effect that threatening letters were sent to the Judge, Prosecutor and Jury that harm will be done them, if a verdict adverse to the Paintiff-in-Error were returned, said publication having been duly brought to the attention of the Court.

(b) The Court erred in refusing to comply with the request of the Plaintiff-in-Error to restrain persons attached to the Court from giving out to the press, news prejudicial to the Plaintiff-in-Error.

(c) The Court erred in not declaring a mistrial after the Prosecutor referred to the Plaintiff-in-Error as a "liar" in the presence of the Jury, upon the Prosecutor requesting the plaintiff-in-Error to turn over to him certain papers, which papers the Plaintiff-in-Error stated had previously been turned over to the Prosecutor.

15. That the decision of the Honorable Circuit Court of Appeals was given within two weeks after arguments were heard, nothwithstanding the fact that the trial lasted five weeks and the record in connection therewith was voluminous.

16. That the Mandate was handed down within thirty-four hours after the decision was rendered.

17. That Marcus Garvey was in Detroit, Michigan, at the time the Mandate was handed down. His attorneys notified him by telegram to return immediately, and so informed the Assistant United States Prosecutor, who agreed to have him surrender on his arrival. Despite this agreement and the fact that Marcus Garvey came into New York City on the first train leaving Detroit, after receipt of the telegram, he was brutally seized by heavily armed men and dragged from a Pullman car inside 125th Street Station, New York City, to the Tombs Prison.

18. Although the United States Prosecutor had agreed with Garvey's counsel to permit Garvey to remain in the Tombs Prison, New York City, after his surrender for a reasonable time to enable counsel to file a petition for a writ of certiorari, when the application was made in court before Hon. Judge Augustus N. Hand this same Assistant United States Prosecutor vigorously opposed the application.

19. Marcus Garvey was taken to Atlanta Penitentiary the following day without being given an opportunity to arrange the affairs of the Universal Negro Improvement Association, an organization with a membership of six million Negroes all over the world; or to protect their interests in investments made by them in the said organization and its auxiliaries.

20. Marcus Garvey is now serving the prison term in Atlanta Federal Penitentiary, but the fine and costs he has been unable to pay, being without funds. The costs of the trial and appeal on his behalf have been paid by voluntary contributions of stockholders of the Black Star Line and members of the Universal Negro Improvement Association, both of which he was head.

21. The New York Evening Bulletin, a newspaper controlled by white people, under date of February 7, 1925, published a very illuminating editorial on some of the reasons that led up to Marcus Garvey's conviction. The editorial in part states:

Marcus Garvey, handcuffed to U. S. Marshals being taken from Federal Court to the Tombs Prison.

"Garvey is a Negro, but even a Negro is entitled to have
"the truth told about him.

"Garvey has been ridiculed, laughed at and buffooned by
"New York newspapers ever since he came to this city.
"He did many strange things, it is true, but he performed
"many fine acts, too. The Bulletin gains nothing by taking
"up Garvey's cause but truth demands that it be admitted
"that he offered his race an ideal. He proposed a free re-
"public of Negroes in the land which should be owned and
"governed by Negroes—Africa.

"Some day his ideal will be accepted and it will ma-
"terialize. Some day Negro Africa will be free Africa, and
"it will not be divided between France and Great Britain.

"Garvey's troubles began when he stepped on the toes of
"these nations. They saw in him a dangerous agitator who
"would cause trouble and lead the people of his own color
"in Africa to think for themselves. And so hireling
"journalists, acting at the bidding of their foreign masters,
"painted Garvey as a joke and trickster. Had the man been
"given half a fair deal, his financial schemes might have
"been successful and he might have been able to avoid the
"unfortunate disasters which led him into the courts and
"brought punishment upon him."

22. The Buffalo Evening Times, another white newspaper, under
date of February 24, 1925, points out another phase of public opinion bearing on the case when it states:

"It is a very grave question whether justice has been
"done in the case of Marcus Garvey, self-styled President
"of the African Republic and promoter of a plan to facilitate
"the emigration of colored people as colonists for the
"foundation of a republic, populated by them and under
"their control, in the land of their forefathers. . . .

"He had become the idol of the colored race. Other
"leaders were in the discard. White hostility was aroused
"lest he inspire his own people over intensively with race
"consciousness. Without going too deeply into the merits
"or demerits of the case, many elements extraneous to his
"business enterprises seem to have played an atmospheric
"part in his trial and conviction. He was permitted to
"plead his own case, a circumstance that put him at
"tremendous disadvantage as against a trained prosecutor
"in a Federal Court. . . .

"If, for the sake of argument, every contention of the
"authorities be granted, there is still something that is not

"pleasant about this whole business. Intent is the essence
"of a crime. This man's entire proceedings have a certain
"consistency with the possible assumption of great dreams
"and visions for his race. It is conceivable, on the sup-
"position of his entire sincerity, that everybody else might
"regard his plans as chimerical, and it is likewise natural
"to expect that such a man, with even the best of motives,
"might make mistakes—innocently at that—such as would
"bring him within the network of watchful prosecution.
"What we regretfully point out, in the consideration of
"comparative justice, is the fact that this colored man is
"given a sentence of five years when so many greater
"offenders are sentenced to but two years, and still others
"are enjoying complete immunity from any punishment
"whatsoever."

23. Mr. Armin Kohn of the law firm of Kohn and Nagler, attorneys for Marcus Garvey, in a statement to the Associated Press, says:

"In my twenty-three years of practice at the New York
"Bar, I have never handled a case in which the defendant
"has been treated with such manifest unfairness and with
"such a palpable attempt at persecution as this one."

BRIEF FOR PLAINTIFF-IN-ERROR.

UNITED STATES CIRCUIT COURT OF APPEALS
For the Second Circuit

MARCUS GARVEY,
Plaintiff-in-Error
(Defendant below),

against

UNITED STATES OF AMERICA,
Defendant-in-Error
(Plaintiff below).

Marcus Garvey, Ely Garcia, George Tobias and Orlando M.
Thompson were indicted on two indictments, each of which contained counts charging various substantive offenses, of using the
mails to defraud, and each of which contained a count charging
conspiracy to commit the substantive offense.

All of the defendants were acquitted of the charge of conspiracy, and only one defendant, Marcus Garvey, was found
guilty of the substantive offense, and this, under only one count
of the indictment. Upon this single count, Garvey was sentenced to serve five years in the penitentiary at Atlanta and to

pay a fine of $1,000 and the costs of the suit. A trial was had before Judge Julian W. Mack and a jury in the United States District Court for the Southern District of New York and judgment of conviction was rendered on the verdict of the jury on June 22, 1923. The plaintiff-in-error, Marcus Garvey, comes here by writ of error on a bill of exceptions,

The Count of the Indictment Upon Which Garvey Was Convicted

The indictment charged a single scheme to defraud. The various counts which charged the substantive offense of the use of the mails in execution of the scheme to defraud are based upon the separate mailing of letters to different addresses. The conspiracy counts charge a conspiracy to execute this scheme to defraud through the intended use of the mails.

Garvey was acquitted of all the charges in both the indictments, except the charge contained in the third count of the second indictment, that on or about December 13, 1920, "for the purpose of executing said scheme and artifice," Garvey placed in a post office in the Southern District of New York "a certain letter or circular enclosed in a postpaid envelope addressed to 'Benny Dancy, 34 W. 131 St., N. Y. C.'" (p. 11).

There is not a scintilla of evidence that Garvey placed or caused to be placed in the mails the circular or letter described or referred to in this count of the indictment. This is so far beyond any question, that we propose to shorten the labors of the Court in consideration of the lengthy record of the testimony by addressing ourselves at the outset to this proposition. And no other demonstration is required than to refer the Court to the testimony of Dancy and to the exhibits in the record, introduced in evidence to support this count of the indictment.

POINT I

There is not a scintilla of evidence, competent or otherwise, to establish the mailing of the indictment letter, upon which the third count of the second indictment was based. It was upon this count and only this count that Garvey was convicted.

A. The only exhibit offered in support of the mailing of the indictment letter under the Dancy count is the front and back of an envelope, Exhibit 112 (p. 2626).

B. The testimony of Dancy in full is as follows (p. 860):

"Q. What is your business? A. What do you mean, my work?

Q. Yes. A. Pennsylvania station cleaner.

Q. Pennsylvania station? A. Yes, sir.

Q. Was that your business in 1919 and 1920? A. It was, yes, sir.

Q. Did you buy any stock in the Black Star Line? A. Yes, sir.

Q. How much? A. 53 shares.

Q. Was that all your savings or what?

Mr. Johnson: Objected to, absolutely immaterial, if the Court please.

The Court: Sustained.

Q. Did you get any letters? A. Yes, I got a letter.

Q. Did you get a letter from the Post Office Department about it? A. No, sir, I did not.

Q. Let me show you—did you give any papers to anybody in the Government service, to a post office man, to an agent? A. Not that I know of.

Q. Where did the Government get your papers, if you know?

Mr. Johnson: Is this for the purpose of impeaching his witness?

Mr. Mattuck: Not impeaching him at all.

Mr. Garvey: I object to these leading questions.

The Court: That isn't leading.

Q. How did the Government get your mail, do you know? A. They came around to my house, where I live in Brooklyn, and they received my mail over there and I give it to them.

Q. I am going to show you an envelope, Benny, and ask you whether you recognize it? A. Yes, sir.

Q. You do? A. Yes, sir.

Q. Do you remember what came in that envelope? A. No, sir, I do not.

Q. What was it about?

Mr. Johnson: I object.

Q. Let me finish my question, if you please, Mr. Johnson; do you know what the contents of that envelope was, what was it about? A. Some of the envelopes are about—

The Court: This envelope.

Q. I am going to show you the back of it; see if that helps you.

Mr. Garvey: I beg to record my objection and exception to the method of examination and his Honor's ruling in the matter.

The Court: Proceed.

A. I cannot remember what was in the letter.

Q. Did you get a number of letters, Dancy? A. Yes, sir.

Q. Do you remember whether or not any of them were from the Black Star Line? A. Yes, sir, some was from the Black Star Line and from the Universal Negro Improvement Association, and some were from the Negro Factories Corporation.

Q. Now, the letters which you got from the Black Star Line, were about what? A. I got so many letters from them I didn't see them all.

Mr. Johnson: I object. The objection is you cannot go into the contents of letters.

Mr. Mattuck: I offer the envelope in evidence, on the ground it bears on the back of it the stamp "Black Star Line" and it is a reasonable assumption that envelope contained matter from the Black Star Line.

Mr. Johnson: Objected to as immaterial and irrelevant.

The Court: It may go in.

Mr. Garvey: Same objection for Mr. Garvey with an exception.

The Court: Yes.

Received and marked Government's Exhibit 112.

Q. Now, Benny, do you know what these letters which came to you from the Black Star Line were about? A. I cannot remember all of them because I never read all the letters I got and some of them were about one thing and another and a lot of them that I got I just threw it back.

Q. Tell us what these letters were about, Mr. Dancy? A. I couldn't tell you about all of them because I never read them all.

Q. Those that you read? A. Well, some of the letters said invest more money in the Black Star Line for the case of purchasing bigger ships and so forth.

Q. What else that you can think of? A. There is so much I just can't remember it all anyhow.

Q. Give us as much as you can remember; one of the things you said was to buy more ships, bigger ships. Did they say anything about the dividends.

Mr. Johnson: I object.

The Court: No—exhaust his memory first.

Q. Tell us, Dancy, all you can think of?

The Court: I did rule on it; I sustain the objection.

Q. Cannot you think what you were spending your money for, what they said? A. Yes, they said in some of the letters about investing this money to help me and the rest and make bigger progress. I cannot remember the letters unless I see some of them.

Q. Did you read the 'Negro World'? A. Sometimes I read some of it?

Q. Did you hear any of Mr. Garvey's speeches? A. Yes, sir.

Cross examination by Mr. Garvey.

Q. Mr. Dancy, you cannot remember really what you read about the Black Star Line?

Mr. Johnson: He said that.

Mr. Garvey: Please leave me alone.

The Court: He has a perfect right to object.

Q. Can you remember what you read about the Black Star Line? A. Well, a few things, not all.

Q. You wouldn't swear to what you said about the Black Star Line positively? A. What I said about it?

Q. Yes, things you said awhile ago, you wouldn't swear those were the things you saw or read, you wouldn't swear positively, you cannot remember and therefore you cannot swear positively that the things you said awhile ago are what you read? A. Sure, what I said, that is what I read.

Q. You wouldn't swear positively that they were true— yes or no—it is so long a time you could not remember—yes or no—you would not swear positively—just say yes or no, Mr. Dancy, yes or no? A. What do you mean?

Q. That is to say, the things you said, the answers you gave to Mr. Mattuck? A. What answers?

Q. The answers you gave awhile ago? A. Tell me what answer it was.

Q. That you read in a circular about ships and everything and so forth. A. Yes, it was in the circular.

Q. But you wouldn't swear positively those things were in the circular? A. They were in some letters.

Q. Would you swear what letters they were in? A. I don't remember what letters they were in, they were in some Black Star Line, but what letters they were I don't know.

Q. You don't know whether they reached you through the mail or not, you just saw things about the Black Star Line? A. I saw things about it?

Q. Yes. A. I didn't saw things. I saw it in the letter.

Q. Can you remember what you saw in the letter positively? A. I just told you I couldn't remember all—do you understand it?

Q. I am not vexed with you. A. I am not vexed with you; you raised your voice to me; I raised mine to you.

Q. I am not vexed, I just want to hear what you say. A Take your time.

Q. Would you really swear— A. I just told you I couldn't remember all the letter, bring the letter up here.

Q. None of the letters that were shown you were the letters? A. What?

Q. The letters that the District Attorney showed you they weren't the letters? A. They weren't the letters?

Q. Yes. A. Yes, they were the letters.

Q. And you don't remember what was in them? A. I can't remember all of them; I got so many letters I couldn't remember all the letters.

1.

Dancy is not charged in either of the indictments to have been one of the persons whom it was intended to defraud (fols. 8 60). He could not have been included in the description "divers other persons whose names are to the Grand Jurors unknown," for the evident reason that he was known to the Grand Jury, and this appears upon the face of the indictment.

2.

Dancy bought fifty-three shares of stock, but it does not appear when he bought his stock. In order to determine whether any circular or letter addressed to Dancy was in execution of the scheme to defraud, it is essential to know when Dancy became a stockholder.

3.

Dancy did not testify that he received the envelope (Exhibit 112). It does not appear that this envelope was taken from Dancy's possession by the Government's agents. Dancy merely testifies that he recognizes the envelope (fol. 2582).

4.

The envelope was offered in evidence without further testimony than the testimony of Dancy that he recognized it. It was offered by the prosecuting attorney as follows:

"Mr. Mattuck: I offer the envelope in evidence, on the ground it bears on the back a stamp 'Black Star Line' and it is a reasonable assumption that envelope contained matter from the Black Star Line" (fol. 2585).

No letters or circulars received by Dancy were identified in any manner. No letter or circular that is in evidence was shown to Dancy. It is not possible to say, and it was not possible for the jury to determine, whether a single one of the circulars or letters introduced in evidence were ever seen by Dancy.

Dancy says that he cannot remember what was in the letter (fols. 2582, 2584). Here he obviously refers to the letter which may have been enclosed in the envelope. He got a number of letters, not alone from the Black Star Line, but from the Universal Negro Improvement Association and some from the Negro Factories Corporation (fol. 2584).

The jurisdiction of the United States to punish this offense is dependent upon the use of the mails, and the gist of the offense set forth in the count upon which Garvey was convicted, was the specific instance of the mailing of a letter or circular on December 13, 1920. It is true that Dancy testified that some of the letters said "invest more money in the Black Star Line for the case of purchasing bigger ships and so forth" (fol. 2587), and that some of the letters spoke about "investing this money to help me and the rest and make bigger progress" (fol. 2588). But the letters or circulars to which Dancy referred were not identified in any respect. It is a "reasonable assumption" that Dancy was not able to identity any of the letters or circulars which are in evidence as being similar to the letters or circulars that he received, for if this were the fact, it is obvious that the District Attorney would have exhibited the letters or circulars to Dancy for the purpose of identification.

But the fundamental objection to such proof is that it does not support the charge **that the mailing of any of these letters or circulars took place in the Southern District of New York.** It has always been held necessary to prove the mailing of the indictment letter. But if this could under any circumstances be dispensed with, so as to permit the proof of mailing of other letters, certainly the proof must be confined to letters mailed within the jurisdiction, and the essential fact of jurisdiction must be established beyond a reasonable doubt.

Dancy testifies, without any qualification, that he does not know what was in the envelope which was introduced in support of the charge on which Garvey was convicted. He is even unable to say whether it contained any letter or circular that came from the Black Star Line. But it is essential to prove the mailing of the indictment letter. How else can the jury determine whether the mailing which is alleged in the indictment was in execution of the scheme to defraud? The statute never has read, and never has been construed to read, that a person engaged in a scheme to defraud may not use the United States mails. The mails must be used, whether successfully or not, in aid and furtherance of the scheme to defraud, and to effectuate the scheme. When the indictment charges the mailing of a particular letter, then it is the fact of mailing that letter that completes the substantive offense, and gives jurisdiction both to the United States, and to the Court in which the indictment is found.

The general allegations that the defendants planned and devised a scheme to defraud which contemplated the use of the mails is not sufficient to charge the substantive offense. It may be adequate to charge a conspiracy to commit the substantive offense. But the substantive offense has its being and comes into existence only at the moment that the letter is placed in the post-office for the purpose of delivery, and such letter is in execution of the scheme to defraud. The charge is a nullity until it reaches the point where there is alleged the fact of mailing. The mailing of the letter is not an incident; it is of the very essence of the offense. It is therefore proof of the very thing which is the life of the indictment. and cannot be dispensed with, and proof of some other facts, however cogent they may be to establish the offense in another indictment when properly charged cannot be accepted as a substitute.

The indictment letter charged in an indictment for the substantive offense cannot be correlated to the charge of an overt act in the conspiracy indictment. Not alone is the allegation of an overt act required merely by force of the statute, but it is not the essential fact upon which the power of the United States to declare a crime is based. Apart from any overt act, a conspiracy to commit an offense against any law of the United States may be made a crime. And although the overt act may give jurisdiction to the Court of a particular district to try the offense, it has nevertheless been repeatedly held that the overt act is not a part of the offense of conspiracy.

The cases that hold that the proof of the mailing of the indictment letter is essential are many but we refer only to a few authorities.

In Hart v. United States, 240 Fed., 911, the opinion by Hough, J., reads:

"An indictment that did not charge mailing or receiving and in the proper district would be demurrable. The point is jurisdictional, and cannot be slurred over in proof. It is not necessary to descend into particulars, but as to some of these counts there was no proof at all of any mailing of the 'indictment letter.' The defendants requested specifically an instruction that, in order to convict, the jury must believe beyond a reasonable doubt that the particular letter mentioned and described in each count was mailed or received by mail, as the case might be, which request was refused.

Such refusal might be immaterial if the matter had been covered in the general charge, but we find nothing in the charge pointing out in words or substance the absolute necessity of somehow proving, not the mailing or receipt of letters generally, but such action in respect of the particular letter named in each count of the indictment and vital to the jurisdiction of the court."

In Farmer v. United States, 223 Fed., at page 909, the opinion by Lacombe, J., says:

"Devising a scheme to defraud generally anyone whom they might catch in their net would not by itself constitute an offense under Section 215. The actual use of the mails in furtherance of the scheme was a fact essential to be charged and proved. The second indictment charged the mailing of the Preston letter; conviction under that count could not be secured unless the mailing of that letter in furtherance of the scheme were shown. The mailing merely of other letters to other persons would not sustain conviction under this count."

In Olsen v. United States, 287 Fed. at page 89, the opinion by Manton, J., says:

"The mailing of a letter in the execution or attempted execution of a fraudulent scheme is the gist of the offense announced by the statute. It is that act, and that alone, which confers jurisdiction upon the courts of the United States to punish authors of fraudulent schemes."

POINT II

The conviction in this case was based not on facts in evidence, but upon an "assumption" which had absolutely no support in the evidence.

Nosowitz v. United States, 282 Fed. at page 578, opinion by Manton, J.:

"Unless there is substantial evidence of facts which exclude every other hypothesis but that of guilt, it is the duty of the trial judge to instruct the jury to return a verdict for the accused, and where all the substantial evidence is as consistent with innocence as with guilt, it is the duty of this court to reverse a judgment against the plaintiff's in error."

People v. Razezicz, 206 N. Y., 249, at p. 273:

"In a criminal case circumstantial evidence to justify the inference of guilt must exclude to a moral certainty every other reasonable hypothesis. Circumstantial evidence in a criminal case is of no value if the circumstances are consistent with either the hypothesis of innocence, or the hypothesis of guilt; nor is it enough that the hypothesis of guilt will account for all the facts proven."

United States v. Ross, 92 U. S., pp. 283, 284:

"These seem to us to be nothing more than conjectures. They are not legitimate inferences, even to establish a fact; much less are they presumptions of law. They are inferences from inferences; presumptions resting on the basis of another presumption. Such a mode of arriving at a conclusion of fact is generally, if not universally, inadmissible. No inference of fact or of law is reliable drawn from premises which are uncertain. Whenever circumstantial evidence is relied upon to prove a fact, the circumstances must be proved, and not themselves presumed. Starkie on Evid., p. 80, lays down the rule thus: 'In the first place, as the very foundation of indirect evidence is the establishment of one or more facts from which the inference is sought to be made, the law requires that the latter should be established by direct evidence, as if they were the very facts in issue." It is upon this principle that courts are daily called upon to exclude evidence as too remote for the consideration of the jury. The law requires an open, visible connection between the principal and evidentiary facts and the deductions from them, and does not permit a decision to be made on remote inferences. Best on Evid., 95. A presumption which the jury is to make is not a circumstance in proof; and it is not, therefore, a legitimate foundation for a presumption. There is no open and visible connection between the fact out of which the first presumption arises and the fact sought to be established by the dependent presumption. Douglas v. Mitchell, 35 Penn. St., 440."

Roukous v. United States, 195 Fed., 353 at p. 361:

"* * * while it is not necessary that any particular circumstance should of itself be sufficient to prove a criminal case beyond a reasonable doubt, yet it is necessary that each circumstance offered as a part of the combination of proofs should itself be maintained beyond a reasonable doubt, and should have some efficiency, so far as it has efficiency to a greater or less range, beyond a reasonable doubt, and at least be free from the condition of being as consistent with innocence as with guilt * * *."

Vernon v. United States, 146 Fed., 121 at p. 123:

"Circumstantial evidence warrants a conviction in a criminal case, provided it is such as to exclude every reasonable hypothesis but that of guilt of the offense imputed to the defendant; or, in other words, the facts proved must all be consistent with and point to his guilt only and inconsistent with his innocence. The hypothesis of guilt should flow naturally from the facts proved and be consistent with them all. If the evidence can be reconciled either with the theory of innocence or of guilt the law requires that the defendant be given the benefit of the doubt and that the theory of innocence be adopted."

The indictment charges that certain named defendants devised a scheme to defraud. In the substantive count the defendants are specifically named, and do not include "divers other persons unnamed." It is alleged that said defendants "for the purpose of executing said scheme and artifice" did place in the Post Office of the United States "a certain letter or circular enclosed in a postpaid envelope addressed to 'Benny Dancy, 34 W. 131st St., N. Y. C.'" (fol. 32). The only other reference to the use of the mails in the charge of the substantive offense is that the defendants intended as part of the scheme to defraud that certain pretenses and promises should be made "in literature circulated by mail and direct by representatives of said corporation" (fol. 10). The mere intent to use the mails is neither a requisite of the offense under the present statute, nor does it constitute an element of the substantive offense. It is the actual use of the mails that forms the gist of the offense and gives the Court jurisdiction. It must be remembered that all the defendants were acquitted of the conspiracy.

The conviction on the third count of the second indictment does violence to every rule of law applicable to the trial of criminal cases. The proof offered in support of that count of the indictment would not be tolerated in a civil case involving a trivial amount of money. Courts require proof, not "assumptions"; evidence that will support inferences, not vague suggestions that form the basis for mere speculation and conjecture.

However commonplace and elementary these propositions may seem, they have been completely disregarded in this case.

No better confirmation of the foregoing can be found than the statement of the prosecuting attorney:

"I offer the envelope in evidence, on the ground it bears on the back of it the stamp 'Black Star Line' and it is a reasonable assumption that envelope contained matter from the Black Star Line."

With reference to this proposition, and the ground on which the envelope was offered and received, we state the following incontestible propositions:

1. It is assumed that the words appearing on the back of the envelope "Black Star Line" was constituted a stamp or mark, that identified the envelope as coming from the office of the Black Star Line. This basic assumption is without the least support in the evidence. No one anywhere testifies that the stamp or mark, appearing on the back of the envelope, Exhibit 112, was the stamp or mark of the Black Star Line. There was no proof of this fact. The very basis of the "reasonable assumption" was itself an assumption.

2. It is assumed that the envelope contained a circular or letter. It may require very slight evidence to furnish the basis for an inference that an envelope received through the mail contained written or printed matter. But at least some slight evidence there must be. There cannot be a total lack and absence of evidence upon this point. It is not a presumption of law that an envelope necessarily contains matter. It can be only an inference based upon facts. And this inference must be based upon some evidence. Dancy testified as follows:

"Q. Do you remember what came in that envelope? A. No, sir, I do not" (fol. 2582).

3. It is assumed that the contents of the envelope related to the Black Star Line. This assumption is based upon the previous assumption that the envelope contained either a letter or a circular, and upon the further assumption that the stamp on the back necessarily indicated the source of the mailing.

Why was it necessary to produce a witness? Why was it not sufficient for the prosecution to offer a mass of envelopes in evidence, and rely upon these "reasonable assumptions?"

4. It is assumed that the contents of the envelope necessarily were transmitted for the purpose of executing the scheme to defraud. Is the mere use of the mails by one engaged in a scheme to defraud an offense indictable under the statute? Are the words

in the statute "for the purpose of executing such scheme or artifice" of no force whatsoever? If it is possible that the jury could have found that the enclosure in the envelope did not relate to the alleged scheme to defraud, had no connection with the purpose or execution of the scheme, then there must be some evidence as to the contents of the assumed enclosure. Where there is an entire absence of evidence as to the contents, and the jury must find that the contents were in execution of the scheme, they can so find only if there is an irrebuttable, conclusive presumption of that fact. The statute specifies, as an element of the offense, that the matter deposited in the mail must be for the purpose of executing the scheme. Is it sufficient to say that a person engaged in a scheme to defraud has deposited, or caused to be deposited, an envelope, and by this, to cast upon that person the burden of proving that the contents of the envelope did not relate to the scheme, or was not in execution of the scheme? **The presumption that the defendant charged with an offense is innocent protects the defendants not alone as to the ultimate finding, but as to every element of the offense, and as to every material fact, and where there is no basis for an inference, the Court must as a matter of law presume innocence; the jury cannot be permitted as matter of fact to infer guilt.**

5. It is assumed that the envelope was mailed or caused to be mailed by Garvey. There is no evidence whatsoever of the identity, or even possible identity, of the person who mailed this envelope. The indictment does not charge that Garvey, the other named defendants who were acquitted and "divers other persons," devised the scheme to defraud (fol. 8). The persons who are described as defendants are specifically named and limited by the indictment to the defendants on trial. The indictment charges that "Marcus Garvey, Ely Garcia, George Tobias and Orlando M. Thompson, named as defendants herein and hereinafter referred to as the defendants, had theretofore devised a scheme, an artifice to defraud" (fol. 8). While the conspiracy count charges that these defendants conspired with "divers other persons," the substantive count is limited to the named defendants. And the third count of the indictment charges that the named defendants deposited the circular or letter addressed to Dancy in the mail.

While it is true that the act of any person who was acting under the directions, express or implied, of Garvey, might be charged to Garvey as his personal act, there must be some proof that the person who mailed the envelope was such a person. We challenge the prosecution to attempt to specify in the remotest way who it was that deposited this envelope. Was it Garvey himself? Was it Thompson, Garcia, or the other defendants who were acquitted? Is there any evidence as to the person who deposited the envelope? Is there any evidence that he was an employee of the Black Star Line?

Dancy testified that he had purchased fifty-three shares of the stock of the Black Star Line. There is no evidence of the date of this purchase. Dancy testified that he "never read all the letters" (fol. 2586). He also heard some of Mr. Garvey's speeches. There is abundant evidence in the record that at the various meetings held by the different associations in which Mr. Garvey was interested, circulars were passed to the audience. The witness Scott testified that at the meetings he attended in Stamford circulars similar to those that he identified were given out, and he was therefore unable to state what circulars he received through the mail and what circulars were handed directly to him (fol. 2704).

It appears that Dancy delivered certain papers to the Post Office Inspector. If any of these papers, whether letters or circulars, were contained in the envelope, it should have been easily possible for the District Attorney to establish this fact. It is not alone a "reasonable assumption"—it is a necessary and inevitable inference that the District Attorney was unable to establish through the witness that any letter or circular which was produced by the witness was contained, or might have been contained, in the envelope offered in evidence. The District Attorney, recognizing his inability to establish the fact or any possible basis for inference as to the fact, rested upon a "reasonable assumption."

POINT III

The verdict of the jury was induced either by passion or prejudice. It was in entire disregard of the evidence.

It is impossible for anyone to assert that the verdict of the jury can be supported by logic. How is it possible to explain the action of the jury, when it acquitted all the defendants of the charge of conspiracy, and acquitted Garvey of all the substantive counts, except on the single charge contained in the Dancy count. This finding was a vagary. It was clearly based upon an ignorance of the facts shown by the record. It necessarily implies that the jury either misunderstood the charge of the Court or paid not the least attention to it. It necessarily implies that the jury was engaged in administering a lawless justice, uncontrolled by the facts in the record, or the law as charged by the Court.

In a civil case, where the result reached by the jury demonstrates that it indulged in speculation, or in an apparent effort to compromise, the Courts hasten to correct the injustice. It is recognized that the jury has not performed its duty. It is presumed that the jury has been influenced by passion or prejudice, or has yielded to mere conjecture. The reasons for insisting in a criminal case that a jury must render a verdict that is consistent with the record and the law as directed by the Court are far more potent. The sanctity of the jury system, and the maintenance of respect for the jury system are vitally dependent upon the proper performance by the jury of its functions in strict accordance with law. There can be no compromise with this principle, if it is intended to maintain intact the due and effective operation of our jury system as a part of the administration of criminal law. We repeat that the verdict of the jury in this case has not the least possible support in logic, and cannot be defended as in conformity with the facts and the law of the case. It was a leap in the dark.

This case called for the finest discrimination on the part of the jury, and the most scrupulous consideration of the facts. It required the jury to be constantly awake to the danger that it might be influenced by considerations outside of the record. It was a matter in which every juryman had an intimate personal interest. While it is important that the Government should protect a class from the alleged schemes of their accepted leader, it is even more important that the people whose just aspirations Mr. Garvey represents should be left with the feeling that their leader has received a fair trial. It was peculiarly a case where the rights of the defendant should have received the utmost protection.

It is true that we can make no appeal to this Court, based upon the fact that the verdict is contrary to the evidence. It is true, that however slight the amount, and however unconvincing may be the force of the testimony, we are in this respect concluded by the verdict. But when that verdict on its face indicates that it was necessarily arrived at by the jury through a disregard of the facts and of the law, and when the result reached compels the conclusion that the jury speculated upon its verdict, and arrived at a compromise, then it is proper further to test the sincerity of this verdict, its consistency, its honesty, by an understanding of the facts; and if the verdict is so tested, we believe that the Court will not hesitate to conclude that the jury was in fact animated by prejudice and passion, that it acted in ignorance of the record and of the facts, and that it was led by a lawless purpose to produce a result that seemed proper to them, without regard to the issues in the case before them.

In the claim that the jury was actuated not alone by prejudice, but by passion, we do not mean to imply that it was actuated by a purpose to commit an injustice against the individual Garvey. But we do mean to assert that the testimony was such as was calculated to make a most potent appeal to the feelings, the passions, and the prejudices of the jury, and to put them in the position, not of administering justice in the case of an individual, but of dealing with a general situation, represented to them as one fraught with great danger and many evils. It is as if Gandhi were to be tried by a jury of Englishmen for his leadership of the people of India. It is as if De Valera were to be tried by a jury of Ulsterites for his leadership of the Irish people. It is as if a Zionist were to be tried by a jury of Moslems for his plans and activities in the establishment of a homestead for the Jews in Palestine. It may be that the system of laws prevailing in the jurisdiction where such a case might be tried would permit only such a trial. But it does undoubtedly present a situation where the courts must be most careful to scrutinize the result so as to determine whether the jury was guided by law, or was carrying out what it conceived to be a social or political remedy, determined by its own selfish interests.

In all of these movements, money is necessary. In all these movements, great promises are held forth. No one who does not put himself in the place of the stricken and afflicted people to whom the appeal is made can understand or sympathize with the enthusiasm of the leader, and the trust and confidence of the masses. To treat such a situation as this indictment does, as a matter of dollars and cents and monetary fraud, and to judge it as one would judge a criminal transaction, or a speculative mining enterprise, is to warp the facts, and to commit a travesty upon the truth. No movement for the redemption of a people has succeeded in making money. The American Revolution was conducted at a financial loss. During the years that the Revolution was fought, and before the Constitution was adopted, and the finances of the country placed upon a stable basis, any jury would have been justified in convicting the abettors of the Revolution and the Fathers of the country for a money fraud, when they induced peoples to invest in the loans, upon the promise of repayment. It will not do to say that these matters were disposed of by the verdict of the jury. For that verdict is so inconsistent with the acquittal of all the defendants on all the other charges, that it cannot be defended as a verdict in accord with the facts and the law. The only explanation that can be made is that the jury proposed somehow to see that Garvey was stopped. The jury did not believe in Garvey and his movement.

This Court has well said that in a case where defendants charged with a conspiracy are acquitted of that charge, and all or several of them are found guilty of a substantive offense, a heavy burden is laid on the prosecution to uphold the conviction for the substantive offense.

"The verdict of not guilty of conspiracy left for the jury's inevitable consideration a mass of testimony immaterial to the issues passed upon adversely to these plaintiffs-in-error, and their co-defendants, yet extremely prejudicial to them."

Hart v. United States, 240 Fed., 911;
quoted in
Harris v. United States, 273 Fed. at p. 791.

While this was said in connection with the importance to be attached to errors, as affecting the verdict, in this case the principle is equally true, although it has a different application. For it must be remembered that Garvey alone was convicted. There were no fellow-conspirators. There were no others who aided and abetted him in the scheme to defraud. The persons, who, during the many months of Garvey's absence, transacted the business of the Black Star Line, and issued and mailed circulars and letters, were found innocent of any crime. The verdict acquitting the associates must necessarily therefore include a finding that what Garvey did through his associates was innocent and free from wrong. To illustrate our point by an analogy, it is as if, in a suit for negligence, the chauffeur who drove the car was held free from blame, yet damages were assessed against the absent owner, based upon the negligence of the chauffeur.

The theory of the indictment and of the trial was that everything that was done by or in the name of the Black Star Line was chargeable to the defendants; that it was only necessary to show that the matter originated in or emanated from the Black Star Line, in order to receive it in evidence and charge the defendants with responsibility therefor. But the verdict of the jury in acquitting the other defendants necessarily implies that the acts of the other defendants were free from guilt, and were no part, either of the substantive scheme to defraud, or of the conspiracy.

It is alleged in the indictment that the scheme to defraud was made up of three elements.

1. False representations, pretenses and promises;
2. The sale of stock of the Black Star Line;
3. The conversion of part of the proceeds from the sale of the stock to the use of the defendants.

The third element—conversion of part of the proceeds to the use of the defendants—has no support in the record. At the time of the organization of the Black Star Line Garvey received no compensation whatsoever (fol. 6656). He worked for the corporation until September, 1919, when at a directors' meeting, he was voted a salary of $50 a week. He drew this salary until some time in 1920, when it was increased to $100 a week (fol. 6657). Since the latter part of 1920 he received no salary from the Black Star Line. In September or November, 1920, he was voted a salary of $10,000 a year by the Universal Negro Improvement Association (fol. 6659).

The sale of the stock of the Black Star Line was doubtless induced by the representations and promises made by Garvey and his associates. Upon the record, and in view of the verdict of the jury, it is not open to the plaintiff-in-error to contend that the representations and promises made as to the success of the operation of the ships by the Black Star Line did not to some extent form part of the inducing cause. But no one, reading the record, can fail to realize that the ship project was but a small part, an incident, of the large scheme that roused the enthusiasm of Garvey and appealed to the hopes and aspirations of the thousands of his followers. No one can fail to be strongly impressed by the undoubted fact that the persons who contributed were more intent on the ultimate uplifting and salvation that was promised to the Negro race of America, than upon the paltry profits that might be realized from the stock investment.

We do not pretend that a Negro charged with crime is entitled to any special rights or favor. But we do contend that when the crime charged is one that involves the relations between the Negro and white races, the utmost care should be observed to safeguard the actual rights of the defendant. In this connection we present the following considerations:

1. Application was made by Garvey to the trial Judge asking

that the trial Judge declare himself disqualified to try the indictments.

The substantial ground of the application was that the Judge was a member of or a contributor to the Association for the Advancement of Colored People, and it appeared that persons active in that association were opposed to the Universal Negro Improvement Association, of which Garvey was the head. It also appeared that one of the members of the National Association had sought to initiate a criminal prosecution against Garvey. The Judge admitted his connection with the National Association, but denied the fact of bias. The motion was denied on the ground that the affidavit did not comply with the statute.

2.   Testimony was received of acts of Garvey entirely unrelated to the charge in the indictment.

It is true that in many instances this testimony was elicited by cross-examination conducted by Garvey himself. But it is also true that in many instances a plain suggestion of the fact came from the questions of the Assistant District Attorney, and Garvey was provoked to further questioning along these lines. This is particularly true of the matters relating to Garvey's association with certain women.

3.   The Court was unduly severe in its repeated admonition of Garvey.

Time and again the Court appears to have sustained objections that were never made. Time and again the Court suggested to the Assistant District Attorney that an objection would be sustained. Where an examination is being conducted by a defendant on his own behalf, the impression that the Court is taking the part of the prosecution, and assisting the prosecution in the conduct of the case, is bound to be disturbing and hurtful. The cumulative effect of the Court's continued admonitions to the defendant was to give the jury the impression that Garvey was responsible for the undue length of the trial. This may have been the fact, and necessarily so. But it should have been the aim of the Court at all times to divert from the defendant any feeling on the part of the jury by reason of that fact. However annoying the situation was, the defendant was within his rights, and the annoyance should have no possible relation to the question of guilt or innocence.

4.   The attitude of the Assistant District Attorney toward Garvey during the trial was improper.

The Assistant District Attorney had no just right to interrupt Garvey in his examination, except by proper objection to the Court, or to address remarks directly to Garvey.

We do not contend that legally any one of the foregoing matters constitutes in itself legal error. We do contend, however, that the whole situation was one that tended unduly to prejudice the defendant in the conduct of his case, and to suggest an atmosphere of antagonism on the part of the Court and the Assistant District Attorney, that necessarily was reflected in the attitude of the jury. This situation helped to bring about the absurd result, whereby the jury acquitted all the defendants of the charges, except that Garvey through some strange vagary was held on a charge in the indictment that had absolutely no evidence upon which to base that particular charge.

And when we seek to understand how it was that the jury, by some inexplicable, absurd process found that Garvey was guilty of mailing a circular or letter to Dancy, when there was not in the evidence any such circular or letter, and when there was not in the evidence any means by which the circular or letter could be identified, and when the sole exhibit consisted of an envelope, that did not even appear to have been addressed by Garvey, or through his procurement, then we feel fully justified in stating that the verdict was unjust, that it was the result of speculation, if not of passion or prejudice.

POINT IV

The judgment of conviction should be reversed and the indictment dismissed.

Dated, New York, October 18, 1924.

Respectfully submitted,

KOHN & NAGLER,
Attorneys for Defendant Marcus Garvey.

George Gordon Battle,
Isaac H. Levy,
of Counsel.

THE PECULIAR TESTIMONY OF MAILING CLERK

Government Witness, Schuyler Cargill
Cross Examination by Mr. Garvey

Q. What is your name? A. Cargill.
Q. What Cargill? A. Schuyler.
Q. Where were you born?
Mr. Mattuck: I will object to it as being immaterial.
The Court: Sustained.
Mr. Garvey: Exception.

Q. Where do you live? A. Roselle, New Jersey.

Q. You always lived there? A. No.

Q. How long since you have been living in New Jersey?
A. About three or four years; between three and four years.

Q. When were you working for the Black Star Line?.
A. About 1919.

Q. To when? A. From 1919 until 1921.

Q. Speak louder, please. A. From 1919 until 1921.

Q. From 1919 to 1921? A. Yes.

Q. Who employed you? A. Mr. Prentice.

Q. Who paid you? A. Mr. Tobias, the treasurer.

Q. And he paid you from 1919 to 1921? A. Yes, sir.

Q. In whose office did you work? A. Mr. Prentice.

Q. Worked in Mr. Prentice's office? A. The mailing division.

Q. What did you do in Mr. Prentice's office. A. I was office boy, mailing.

Q. What did you do? A. Keep the files together, file letters and run errands and go to the post office.

Q. That is all you did? A. Yes, sir.

Q. You didn't do anything more? A. No.

Q. Now, tell the Court and gentlemen of the jury all you did in Mr. Prentice's office, everything you ever did, going for water, buying stamps, and everything. Tell us what you remember.
A. I mailed the letters, filed all the letters that came in, and once in a while I went to the post office and got stamps.

Q. Yes, anything else? A. That is all.

Q. I show you Government's Exhibit No. 24. Do you remember seeing that a while ago (handing paper to witness)? A. Yes, sir.

Q. Did you mail that for the Black Star Line? A. I did.

Q. How do you know this circular was in the letter of the Black Star Line? A. We kept those in our office.

Q. What? A. We kept those circulars in our office.

Q. Because you kept those circulars in your office makes you know it was in the letters? A. They were sent out separate.

Q. Sent out separate. How do you know that that circular, that particular circular or a circular like that was in the envelopes or letters you took to the post office? A. I had it all to do.

Q. What do you mean, all to do? A. Yes, sir.

Q. What do you mean, all to do? A. That was part of my work.

Q. What do you mean by all to do?

Mr. Mattuck: He has answered the question and I object to it. He says that was part of his work.

Q. Do what? A. Mail those circulars.

Q. I know you said you mailed them, but I want to know how you know that particular circular or circulars of that sort was in the letter or letters you mailed, how do you know? A. We had those to mail them and we mailed them.

Q. That is all the information you had?

The Court: Did you or didn't you say you put the letters inside the envelopes?

The Witness: Yes, sir.

The Court: You did.

Q. What did you say?

The Court: You mean you did, did you say that?

The Witness: Yes, sir, I say that.

Q. Who put them in? A. I did that.

Q. You put them in? A. Yes.

Q. Now, John, or Schuyler, whatever your name is, you know you are not telling the truth, don't you?

Mr. Mattuck: I will object to the question.

The Court: It is cross-examination. He may answer.

Q. Don't you know that Mr. Prentice never came to the Black Star Line during 1920? A. No, sir, I did not; he was there when I was there.

Q. What did you say? A. He was there when I was there; I do not know when he came.

Q. But you testified you worked for Mr. Prentice in 1919. I want to bring out you are not telling the truth, that Mr. Prentice was not there in 1919 and you did not work in the Black Star Line in 1919, or at no time.

Mr. Mattuck: You want to prove he didn't work for the Black Star Line at any time?

Q. Now, don't you know Mr. Prentice was not with the Black Star Line in 1919? A. What is that question again?

Q. You heard me, didn't you? Don't you know Mr. Prentice was not with the Black Star Line in 1919, that is my question. A. He was there when I was there. I do not know when he was there.

Q. You were told to mention certain dates before you came to this court? Isn't it a fact somebody told you to mention certain dates like 1919 and 1920 before you came to this court, isn't it a fact?

The Court: Did anybody tell you to mention certain dates, 1919 or 1920 when you would be on the witness stand, and if so who told you that? Can't you answer the question?

The Witness: Yes, sir.

The Court: Did somebody tell you to mention those dates when you got on the witness stand?

Q. Go on, say yes or no, somebody told you?

The Court: Why don't you answer the question?

The Witness: All right—yes.

The Court: Somebody did tell you to mention those dates?

The Witness: Well, I realize and I know—

The Court: Did somebody tell you to mention those dates, that is the question that is put to you?

The Witness: Yes, sir.

The Court: If so, who told you to mention those dates? Talk up so we can all hear you.

The Witness: Mr. Mattuck.

Q. Mr. Mattuck? A. Yes.

Mr. Mattuck: Mr. Mattuck told you to tell certain dates?

Q. Now, Schuyler, what time you left the Black Stare Line? Come on, you must remember it? A. What time?

Q. Yes, what year, what month and what year?

A. I can't remember what month it was.

Q. What year then? A. 1921.

Q. In whose office did you work in 1921? A. Mr. Prentice.

Q. Can you remember some more people who were working in Mr. Prentice's office and in the general office of the Black Star Line in 1921?

A. In Mr. Prentice's office you mean?

Q. Both in Mr. Prentice's office and in the general office of the Black Star that is in Mr. Garcia's office, that is in Mr. Garvey's office, Mr. Tobias' office and the other offices, you remember some other people who worked there? A. Yes, sir.

Q. In 1921? A. Yes, sir.

Q. Who was the timekeeper during your time, in 1921? A. I can't remember that.

Q. You can't remember the man to whom you went with your card every morning and who punched your card there for you and who took your time in the afternoon? You can't remember that man's name? A. No, sir.

Under Re-Direct Examination

Q. You said you mailed these circulars at what station? A. College Station.

Q. Where is that? A. 149th street around there and 8th avenue.

Q. Don't you know that College station is not at 149th street and 8th avenue? Did anybody speak to you and tell you as to where you should—as to the particular post office you should testify you mailed those circulars? A. Yes, sir.

Q. Who told you that, go ahead, speak up, let us hear. You are here to tell the truth, now we want to know. Who told you that? A. I remember mailing those letters up there.

Q. Answer my question. You have said already, you have just answered somebody told you where you should say you mailed those circulars. I am asking you to tell me that—go on now, you have answered pretty well, I want you to continue? Go on, the jury wants to get at the truth of this thing you know? A. Inspector Shea.

Q. Mr. Shea? A. Yes.

DECISION OF CIRCUIT COURT OF APPEALS
United States Circuit Court of Appeals
For the Second Circuit

Before:

HON. HENRY WADE ROGERS
HON. CHARLES M. HOUGH
HON. LEARNED HAND,

Circuit Judges.

Marcus Garvey

Plaintiff-in-error

vs.

United States of America

Defendant-in-error

Writ of error to judgment of conviction entered in the District Court for the Southern District of New York.

Garvey and others were indicted under Crim. Code 215, for having devised a scheme to defraud and for the purpose of executing the same, or attempting so to do, causing to be placed in and delivered by the Post Office establishment of the United States, certain letters or circulars enclosed in postpaid envelopes.

The nature of the scheme as set forth in the indictment was an endeavor to persuade, especially colored men and women, to purchase stock in the Black Star Line, Inc., a corporation existing under the laws of Delaware and having for its purpose the acquisition and management of steamships, which vessels were ultimately intended to transport to Africa many colored men and much material, there to build up a greater country for the Negro race.

The substance of indictment is that, while there center around Garvey other associations or corporations having for their object the uplift and advancement of the Negro race, the entire scheme of uplift was used to persuade Negroes for the most part to buy shares of stock in the Black Star Line at $5 per share, when the defendants well knew notwithstanding florid representations to the contrary, that said shares were not and in all human probability never could be worth $5 each or any other sum of money.

The voluminous testimony shows at length great efforts on the part of Garvey to constitute himself a "leader of the colored race of the world," and he called himself at times the "provisional President of Africa," his purpose being to promote solidarity among Negroes by and through several organizations of his begetting quite different from the Black Star Line.

The matter may be summarized in the language of Garvey's counsel at this bar, thus:

> "Upon the record it is not open to the plaintiff in error to contend that the representations and promises made as to the success of the operation of the ships by the Black Star Line did not to some extent form part of the inducing cause"

of the sale of stock thereof.

But, adds the brief of counsel,

> "no one reading the record can fail to realize that the ship project was but a small part of the large scheme that roused the enthusiasm of Garvey and appealed to the hopes and aspirations of the thousands of his followers. No one can fail to be strongly impressed by the fact that the persons who contributed were more intent on the ultimate uplifting and salvation that was promised to the Negro race of America than to the paltry profits that might be realized from the stock 'investment.' "

The persons indicted with Garvey were acquitted and Garvey himself convicted on one count. The effect of the conviction is that Garvey is declared to have been guilty of the scheme or artifice to defraud set forth in the indictment, and of having for the purpose of executing the same caused to be sent through the United States Post Office "a certain letter or circular enclosed in a postpaid envelope addressed to Benny Dancy, 31

West 131st street, New York City." Thereupon Garvey took this writ of error.

George Gordon Battle and Isaac H. Levy for Plaintiff-in-error.

Maxwell L. Mattuck, Assistant U. S. Attorney, opposed.

HOUGH, C. J.

Justice to the community and rules of law combine to prevent Courts or juries from looking upon the testimony in this case in the spirit sought to be aroused by the brief for plaintiff-in-error.

It may be true that Garvey fancied himself a Moses, if not a Messiah; that he deemed himself a man with a message to deliver, and believed that he needed ships for the deliverance of his people; but with this assumed, it remains true that if his gospel consisted in part of exhortations to buy worthless stock, accompanied by deceiving false statements as to the worth thereof, he was guilty of a scheme or artifice to defraud, if the jury found the necessary intent about his stock scheme, no matter how uplifting, philanthropic or altruistic his larger outlook may have been. And if such scheme to defraud was accompanied by the use of the mails defined by the statute he was guilty of an offense under Crim. Code 215.

We need not delay to examine in detail the fraud scheme exhibited by practically uncontradicted evidence. Stripped of its appeal to the ambitions, emotions, or race consciousness of men of color, it was a simple and familiar device of which the object (as of so many others) was to ascertain how "it could best unload upon the public its capital stock at the largest possible price." (Horn vs. United States 182 Fed., 721 at 731). At this bar there is no attempt to justify the selling scheme practiced and proven, it was wholly without morality or legality.

This writ rests solely on an asserted failure to prove the "indictment letter" in the single count on which Garvey was convicted.

We pointed out in Hart vs. United States 240 Fed., 911 at 917, that Congress by Sec. 215, has made any fraudulent scheme a crime, if for the purpose of executing the same any letter, etc., be sent or received by post. The corrollary is that in this case it was necessary for the prosecution to prove not only that there was a scheme to defraud, but to show that there was a communication sent through the mail to Dancy within the jurisdiction of the Court for the purpose of executing or attempting to execute the same.

As was said in Lefkowitz vs. United States (273 Fed. 664 Cert. denied 257 U. S., 637), in such a prosecution as this it is competent to show every part of the method of conducting the scheme, that is calculated to shed light on the intent and purpose of its deviser. Some schemes have a relation to the use of the mails so plain that any court or juryman can take notice thereof; and so the general use of the mails may be established by showing that the success of the scheme depended on a wholesale utilization of the post. This is fully set forth in Kellogg vs. United States 126 Fed. 323. And in this case there was proven a widespread and wholesale use of the mails for the purpose of soliciting subscriptions to the worthless stock offered by Garvey to the public. The connection between his scheme and the use of postal facilities was manifest, and this circumstance was proper for the consideration of the jury.

Starting with this, there was abundant proof of the style of "literature" used in falsely puffing the Black Star Line stock. It was directly proven that Dancy received through the mail an envelope addressed as in the indictment averred, that such envelope was like many similarly proven to have been mailed by Garvey's mailing agent, and bearing upon them the legend "Black Star Line, New York City."

It was also directly proven that Dancy received many communications not only from the Black Star Line, but from other organizations with which Garvey was concerned, and that some of the letters thus received advised him to invest "more money in the Black Star Line," and he did purchase some fifty shares. But there was no direct evidence as to what particular circular, letter, or the like came in the envelope identified by Dancy as having been sent to and received by him through the post, and mentioned in the indictment. It was further directly proven that Dancy had received through the post communications distinctly calculated to aid in executing the scheme to defraud; so that the point raised by this writ is that this evidence is insufficient to justify a conviction upon the single count before us, because there was no direct proof of what the envelope had contained.

To this we cannot agree; the circumstantial evidence is sufficient. The rule is elementary that any fact which becomes material in a criminal prosecution may as a rule be established by circumstantial as well as by direct evidence. (16 C. J. 762.) So also is the rule fundamental that in arriving at their verdict, a jury is not confined to considering the palpable facts in evidence, but it may draw reasonable inference and make reasonable deductions therefrom (16 C. J. 760).

Consequently a conviction may well be had upon circumstantial evidence, although to warrant such conviction the proven facts must clearly and satisfactorily exclude every other reasonable hypothesis save that of guilt. (United States vs. Greene 146 Fed., 863 Aff'd 154 Fed., 401; Cert. denied 307 U. S., 596).

The only matter here not proven by direct evidence is that some particular circular or letter was enclosed in the envelope produced by Dancy—a man evidently both emotional and ignorant, whose caliber may be judged by the following excerpts from a cross-examination conducted by Garvey pro se:

"Q. You don't know whether they (letters or circulars) reached you through the mail or not, you just saw things about Black Star Line? A. I saw things about it.

"Q. Yes? I didn't saw things, I saw it in the letters.

"Q. Can you remember what you saw in the letters positively?. A. I just told you I couldn't remember all; do you understand it? . . .

"Q. The letters that the District Attorney showed you, they weren't the letters? A. They weren't the letters.

"Q. Yes? A. Yes, they were the letters.

"Q. And you don't remember what was in them? A. I can't remember all of them, I got so many letters I couldn't remember all the letters."

It is a reasonable inference that men regularly sending out circulars in envelopes do not send out empty envelopes; also that one who received an empty envelope would remember the emptiness, and further and finally that when Dancy identified the envelope and testified to letters and circulars so numerous that he could not remember all of them, the inference was justifiable that some or one of those documents came in the envelope.

Which one was of no importance; the nature of the matter sent by mail is immaterial, it is the purpose inspiring the sending that brings the scheme-deviser under national law, not the language of his communication.

Thus the circumstantial evidence justified the jury in finding that the envelope did not come empty to Dancy. We note that it is the language of the count that required the envelope to have contained a letter or the like; so far as the statute goes it would be quite possible so to use an empty envelope or a postal card blank except for address, as to satisfy the statute.

Judgment affirmed.

STRIPPING THE EFFECT OF ITS CAUSE TO SHOW CRIME

Cessante causâ, cessat effectus.

In the decision of the learned Court of Appeals in my case, the distinguished and honorable Judges were so eager, ready and positive, in face of the apparently unread record of four thousand pages (which, on careful examination, reveal the most glaring contradictions of prosecution testimony, not only by the defense witnesses, but by the prosecution's witnesses themselves on cross-examination, as admitted by the Prosecutor in his rebuttal summation when he admitted to the jury that his witnesses were liars) that they have introduced a new departure in American Jurisprudence by the following statements on record of their opinion; "We need not delay to examine in detail the fraud scheme exhibited by practically uncontradicted evidence." "Stripped of its appeal to the ambitions, emotions or race consciousness of men of color, it was a simple and familiar device of which the object (as of so many others) was to ascertain how it could best unload upon the public its capital stock at the largest possible price."

The stock of the Black Star Line was never offered to the public. It was offered only to Negroes and only those of the Universal Negro Improvement Association who were interested in, and themselves fostering, the idea of an African Nationalism to which the Black Star Line was contributory. No white person could buy stock in the Black Star Line, and none was offered to them anywhere. But in this case of Conviction, the Cause had to be "stripped" of its appeal to the ambition, emotions, or race consciousness to leave it bare as a crime. Let us "strip" Government of its moral community, social appeals and we have despotism, violence and crime; let us strip War of its economic and political appeals, and we have murder and highway robbery; let us strip the great George Washington and his noble compatriots of the appeal, emotions and race consciousness that lead to liberty, and we have treason, murder and crime; let us strip the whites of race consciousness in their idea and practice of white supremacy, and we have wholesale crime against humanity; let us strip the paid elected or appointed official or employee of Government or institutions of the moral, racial, ethical or emotional usefulness of his office and power of enforcement and we have malfeasance—an imposter, vagrant and vagabond who lives off the bounty, earnings and tributes of the hard working people; let us strip the Christian religion of its moral, ethical appeals and emotions and we have robbery, pocket-picking and virtual hold-ups in the name of Christ in our churches every Sunday by way of appeals for financial support, and so we find analogies ad infinitum. This twist of the law is dangerous to the fundamentals of American liberty and justice.

HOW SOCIALISM, SOVIETISM, BOLSHEVISM, ANARCHISM AND OTHER ISMS ARE FORMED

Encouragement of unworthy and unprincipled public officials in office does incalculable harm to good Government, and supplies the cause for unrest among the dissatisfied citizenry that sometimes result in agitations and movements that could have been avoided among large groups, harmful to the good of society and reflective on the character of those who are responsible for Government.

Government being so sacred, should be in the hands of only those who are morally or ethically clean and upright.

Most of the isms that plague the world are the direct result of the crude and unprincipled acts of selfish and unworthy representatives of Government inflicted upon innocent people, who, being conscious of their innocence, and cognizant of the injustice done them, resort to measures of their own for justification that generally result in the formation and promotion of new policies, ideas or means for the proper administration of justice to other mortals, and those who suffer like themselves, never fail to appreciate the benefits to be derived and join in to give strength and character to the new adventure.

LAST SPEECH BEFORE INCARCERATION IN THE TOMBS PRISON, NEW YORK CITY, U. S. A., DELIVERED AT LIBERTY HALL, NEW YORK CITY, JUNE 17, 1923

Among the many names by which I have been called, I was dubbed by another name a couple days ago. The District Attorney, with whom I have been contesting the case for my liberty and for the existence of the Universal Negro Improvement Association, in his fervid appeal, in his passionate appeal, to the gentlemen of the jury last Friday cried out: "Gentlemen, will you let the tiger loose?"

The tiger is already loose, and he has been at large for so long that it is no longer one tiger, but there are many tigers. The spirit of the Universal Negro Improvement Association has, fortunately for us, made a circuit of the world, to the extent that harm or injury done to any one, will in no way affect the great membership of this association or retard its great program. The world is ignorant of the purpose of this association. The world is ignorant of the scope of this great movement, when it thinks that by laying low any one individual it can permanently silence this great spiritual wave, that has taken hold of the souls and the hearts and minds of 400,000,000 Negroes throughout the world. We have only started; we are just on our way; we have just made the first lap in the great race for existence, and for a place in the political and economic sun of men.

Those of you who have been observing events for the last four or five weeks with keen eyes and keen perceptions will come to no other conclusion than this—that through the effort to strangle the Universal Negro Improvement Association—through the effort to silence Marcus Garvey—there is a mad desire, there is a great plan to permanently lay the Negro low in this civilization and in future civilizations. But the world is sadly mistaken. No longer can the Negro be laid low; in laying the Negro low you but bring down the pillars of creation, because 400,000,000 Negroes are determined to a man, to take a place in the world and to hold that place. The world is sadly mistaken and rudely shocked at the same time. They thought that the new Negro would bend; they thought that the new Negro was only bluffing and would exhibit the characteristic of the old Negro when pushed to the corner or pushed to the wall. If you want to see the new Negro fight, force him to the wall, and the nearer he approaches the wall the more he fights, and when he gets to the wall he is even more desperate.

What does the world think—that we are going back to sixty years ago in America—going back to eighty-five years ago in the West Indies—going back to 300 years ago in Africa? The world is crazy if they indulge that thought. We are not going back; we are going forward—forward to the emancipation of 400,000,000 oppressed souls; forward to the redemption of a great country and the re-establishment of a greater government.

Garvey has just started to fight; Garvey has not given his first exhibition of his fighting prowess yet. Men, we want you to understand that this is the age of men, not of pigmies, not of serfs and peons and dogs, but men, and we who make up the membership of the Universal Negro Improvement Association reflect the new manhood of the Negro. No fear, no intimidation, nothing can daunt the courage of the Negro who affiliates himself with the Universal Negro Improvement Association. The Universal Negro Improvement Association is light, and we have entered into light and shall not go back into darkness. We have entered into the light of a new day; we have seen the light of a new creation; we have seen the light of a new civilization, and we shall follow where that light leads.

I was amused when my friend, the district attorney, said that he was more interested in Negroes than Marcus Garvey. They are so accustomed to the old camouflage that they believe they can plead it everywhere to the satisfaction of every Negro, and to everyone who comes in contact with them. That is the old camouflage that made them our missionaries sixty years ago; it is the same camouflage that made them our leaders since emancipation; but it is the camouflage that will not stand today. It is impossible for a Negro to be more interested in a Jew than a Jew is interested in himself. It is impossible for an Englishman to be more interested in an Irishman than that Irishman is in himself. It is a lie for any Jew to say he is more interested in Negroes than Negroes are in themselves. It is an unnatural lie to talk about one race being more interested in another race than that race is interested in itself. But that only shows how desperate they are. Sometimes we have to beware of Greeks bearing gifts. Unfortunately, I did not have the last word and therefore I was silenced after I placed my defense in; but, nevertheless, the world will know tomorrow the outcome of this case wherein Marcus Garvey and the Universal Negro Improvement Association is involved. One way or the other, the world will not be disappointed. There is no verdict that would disappoint me. I tell you this, that there is to be no disappointment; if they were to give any other verdict than guilty, Marcus Garvey will be very much disappointed; Marcus Garvey knows them so well that Marcus Garvey will expect anything from them; so, whether they give a verdict of guilty or not guilty, it is immaterial to Marcus Garvey; the fight will just then be starting.

Not Fighting the Government

Now, understand this is a fight to the finish. We are not fighting this great government, because all Negroes in America—all Negroes all over the world—know that the greatest democracy in the world is the American democracy, the greatest government in the world is the American republic. We are not fighting America; we are fighting hypocrisy and lies, and that we are going to fight to the bitter end. Now, understand me well, Marcus Garvey has entered the fight for the emancipation of a race; Marcus Garvey has entered the fight for the redemption of a country. From the graves of millions of my forebears at this hour I hear the cry, and I am going to answer it even though hell is cut loose before Marcus Garvey. From the silent graves of millions who went down to make me what I am, I shall make for their memory, this fight that shall leave a glaring page in the history of man.

They do not know what they are doing. They brought millions of black men from Africa who never disturbed the peace of the world, and they shall put up a constitutional fight, that shall write a page upon the history of human affairs that shall never be effaced until the day of judgment. I did not bring myself here; they brought me from my silent repose in Africa 300 years ago, and this is only the first Marcus Garvey. They have thought that they could for 300 years brutalize a race. They have thought that they could for 300 years steep the soul of a race in blood and darkness and let it go at that. They make a terrible mistake. Marcus Garvey shall revenge the blood of his sires. So don't be afraid of Marcus Garvey. When Marcus Garvey goes to jail the world of Negroes will know. They have come at the wrong time.

I appreciate the splendid way in which you have behaved and conducted yourselves during the trial. We shall observe to the letter the laws of this great country, but Africa shall tell the tale. Marcus Garvey has no fear about going to jail. Like MacSwiney or like Carson, like Roger Casement, like those who have led the fight for Irish freedom, so Marcus Garvey shall lead the fight for African freedom.

I repeat that if they think they can stamp out the souls of 400,000,000 black men, they make a tremendous and terrible mistake. We are no longer dogs; we are no longer peons; we are no longer serfs—we are men. The spirit that actuated George Washington in founding this great republic—the spirit that actuated the fathers of this great nation, is the spirit that actuates 6,000,000 black men who are at the present time members of the Universal Negro Improvement Association; it is the spirit that will actuate 400,000,000 Negroes in the redemption of their motherland, Africa. Tell us about fear; we were not born with fear. Intimidation does not drive fear into the soul of Marcus Garvey. There is no fear, but the fear of God. Man cannot drive fear into the heart of man, because man is but the equal of man. The world is crazy and foolish if they think that they can destroy the principles, the ideals of the Universal Negro Improvement Association.

MR. GARVEY'S ADDRESS TO JURY AT CLOSE OF TRIAL

May it please Your Honor and Gentlemen of the Jury:

I stand before you indicted by the United States Government for conspiring with others to defraud certain persons of their moneys through the use of the United States mails. You have heard the testimony both on the part of the prosecution and the defense.

I feel sure that you have absolutely no doubt in your minds about the innocence of the defendant who now appears before you. We are charged jointly or separately of conspiring and scheming together to defraud the people mentioned in the indictments. We have Louis Schench of Washington, G. Simon Scott of Stamford, Conn.; Mr. Smith of Indianapolis, Ind.; Annie Still of Philadelphia, Pa., and Dancy to testify. Others did not appear.

The prosecution claims that we connived a scheme and conspired to do certain things. What were the things they said we did? That we bought the Shadyside with the intention of wrecking her. That we bought the Yarmouth for the purpose of laying her in drydock and having her sold for $1,600, as they allege; that we absolutely connived never to have bought the Orion, but to have taken the stockholders' money and given it to someone, whether it be Silvertsone, the Jew, or anyone else. These are the things that they allege that we have done, and years ago, when the Black Star Line was incorporated, that we had in our minds the doing of these things. For what purpose? For the purpose of getting commissions and so on. Gentlemen, no one has testified here on the part of the government that one individual officer of the Black Star Line who started this corporation along with the rest of people who are interested ever collected one nickel for commission or for profit. They talk about salary; every man is worthy of his hire. If a treasurer gives his time to the service of the corporation from eight to twelve hours per day, don't you expect that he must be paid? If the president gives his time, all his time, in that they say I speak all over the country, I travel all over the country, giving all my time day and night, don't you believe that such a servant is worthy of his hire? If the secretary gives his time, do you not believe his service is also worthy to be rewarded in some kind of a way? The very prosecutor of this case, Mr. Mattuck himself, draws a salary from the government for the service he renders to the government, and if he did not get that money he

S. S. Yarmouth, Re-christened S. S. Frederick Douglass, Merchant Flag Ship of the Black Star Line, Purchased for $165,000.00

would probably sue the government or give up his job. If he is worthy of his pay, so also is the treasurer of the Black Star Line, and the secretary, and the president worthy of whatsoever salary they get. And how much did they get? Mr. Merriles, an expert accountant, taking his figures to be correct, said that Marcus Garvey got $5,000 as president of the Black Star Line for the time that the Black Star Line was in existence, from its incorporation, from the 27th of June, 1919, to the present time; and all he got by testimony of their experts was $5,000. And how much did we take in? Nearly $1,000,000. Now, gentlemen, let us reason if anyone wanted to defraud, to take the people's money, and to conspire, as charged by the government, would they have taken only $5,000 salary during that period of time, when they said that about $800,000 or nearly $1,000,000 was taken in? How much the treasurer got has been produced in testimony. Tobias got $50 per week for being treasurer of a big steamship company, and they said we took in nearly one million dollars. Gentlemen, you are business men. I feel confident that you have judged this case; you have watched this case carefully, and that you will allow no prejudice, no sentiment, no machinations on the part of anyone who desires a conviction, to carry out any feeling of his, to swerve you from the course of justice.

Law and Justice

Justice, gentlemen, as I have said before, is greater and above the law; if justice was not included in the law, then the law would be of no use to us as human beings. The law is supposed to be the expression of justice, and caring not how technical the charge may be, if there is no justice, the law counts for naught.

It is true that I am not a lawyer, but I feel sure that His Honor and the district attorney meant no offense when they said that Marcus Garvey was not a lawyer. It does not mean that every man who is brought before the bar of American justice must appear by a lawyer, otherwise we would be living under peculiar circumstances. The Constitution allows every man the privilege to defend himself, to so prove his innocence before an American court of justice, and I decided to do so, irrespective of being a lawyer, because, gentlemen, it is not the law that I am concerned so much about, it is the truth.

If I have committed any offense in truth, and it is a violation of the law, I say your duty is to find me guilty and let me have the fullest extent of the law. I ask no mercy. I ask no sympathy. I ask but for justice based upon the testimony given in this court.

The Law on Fraud

They brought several persons here to testify on these complaints of fraud. I will read you what the highest judgment in law of this country says about fraud as His Honor will direct at the proper time.

The Supreme Court of the United States, in the case of Southern Development Co. vs. Silva, lays down the following rules for the detection of fraud:

1. That the defendant must make a representation in regard to a material fact.

2. That such representation must be false.

3. That such representation must be actually believed by the complainant on reasonable grounds to be true.

4. That it must be made with intent that it should be acted on.

5. That it must be acted on by complainant to his damage, and

6. That in so acting on it, the complainant must be ignorant of its falsity and reasonably believe it to be true.

That is laid down as His Honor will direct, as the interpretation of fraud by the highest tribunal in law in this great country, America.

Gentlemen, did any of the officers of the Black Star Line who were part of the organization of this company make any statement, any material fact that they did not believe to be true? What evidence, if any, have they brought here to prove that Marcus Garvey made any statement that he at any time did not believe was true? The only matter of doubt was the matter of the purchase of the S. S. Orion to be named the Phyllis Wheatley. You have heard the testimony, whose fault was it that the Phyllis Wheatley was not obtained? Everybody believed that there was going to be a Phyllis Wheatley, every officer in the office believed it. Garcia believed that there was going to be a Phyllis Wheatley, all the directors believed it, and all the members of the executive council of the Universal Negro Improvement Association believed that there was going to be a Phyllis Wheatley, according to what they were told by Thompson, as I will bring to you gentlemen.

You have heard the statements of the respective persons. You have watched them, and I feel sure you will have absolutely no difficulty in centering your minds once more on the individual and individuals in the chair. Before I go into details, however, I desire to assure you that in the beginning of the case I had

S. S. Orion, to have been re-christened S. S. Phyllis Wheatly, the mother ship that should have carried colonists to Liberia. Mr. Garvey went to the West Indies and Central America in 1921. Immediately after leaving the United States the vice-president and the treasurer of the Black Star Line paid to one Silverstone, a broker of New York, $25,000 of the corporations money on the pretence of securing a ship for the African trade. Mr. Garvey was informed in the West Indies that the ship had been secured. His trip to the West Indies was to have been for thirty (30) days. After the $25,000 had been extracted from the Black Star Line he was forcibly kept out of the country for five (5) months. By great efforts he was able to regain admittance to America. Upon his return to America he found that the supposed ship named the Phyllis Wheatly had not been turned over to the Black Star Line. He started an investigation and found that only $5,000 had actually been deposited with the United States Shipping Board from May, 1921, to September, 1921. He threatened to go into the whole matter of the purchase of the boat which was being made by the vice-president and he was informed that if he interfered the transaction would not go through. He held up his investigation until November, 1921, to allow time for the consummation of the purchase. In November Mr. Garvey again wrote to the Shipping Board, at which time $22,500 had been deposited with the board, supposedly of the $25,000 taken from the treasury of the Black Star Line after he left for Central America. In December the Massachusetts Bonding Company of New York wrote to the Black Star Line demanding the payment of $11,000 borrowed from them on account of the corporation, and on which the corporation's securities had been pledged. Mr. Garvey found that the $11,000 was part of the money used to make up the $22,500 deposited with the Shipping Board after September, 1921, making a gross payment of $36,000 to the broker or whosoever concerned. In the effort of Mr. Garvey to probe the matter and safeguard the interest of the corporation he was indicted in January of 1922. The deposit of $22,500 is still with the Shipping Board.

absolutely no desire or intention to delay the activities of this court; my one desire was to secure justice, and to so have my case laid before you gentlemen, who are to be my judges, that there would be absolutely no mistake, in that a man's liberty is at stake. Liberty is man's dearest possession, and I feel sure that you appreciate your liberty and would do everything in your power to secure it. You will, therefore, place yourselves in my position.

I will leave no stone unturned to protect my liberty, and life, and see that justice is done.

I have to apologize to His Honor and the Court if, in their opinion, I have committed any breach. It was not my intention, and whatsoever happened otherwise in this court, you will realize that it was done by a man who desired to give himself the fullest opportunity to prove his innocence, and one who was compelled to take the floor, if I might so term it, on his own account. I felt that no one could interpret to you, gentlemen of the jury, the circumstances surrounding the activities of the Black Star Line and its auxiliaries as I could do it, in that it would have taken two or three years to explain to anyone the circumstances surrounding the activities of these organizations.

First of all, the person would have had to enter into the spirit of the movement. It was not purely a professional job for someone to do some work; it was a position that I was placed in where I had to interpret my soul to someone who probably could not appreciate the interpretation of that soul. Hence my appearance on my own behalf as my attorney. So, gentlemen, if anything should be said by the prosecutor touching on my conduct of my own defense, you will understand and appreciate my position in the matter.

The Dignity of the Race

Now, you have heard the indignities hurled at my race by the district attorney when questions were asked of certain witnesses as to whether they were dukes or ladies, which was offensive to me, because the Negro has as much right as any other race to dignify the person or individuals whom they believe worthy of honor, and, therefore, gentlemen, you will not believe that I meant any insult to any race or any one when I made certain retorts.

The Type of Witnesses

Now, whom did the government bring to testify? The government brought in Edgar Gray, and, gentlemen, that was where Garvey and his attorney came to the parting of the ways. Garvey did not know whom the government relied on to support its charges against him, and when Garvey came into the court and saw the scoundrel, Edgar Gray, he wanted the opportunity to produce sufficient evidence of the character of Edgar Gray. Garvey asked his attorney to keep Edgar Gray over until he was able to search for the records. His attorneys rushed three witnesses off the stand in one day, which were Edgar Gray, Richard Warner and Kilroe, the principal offensive characters of this charge, whom Garvey never knew would be here, and whom he desired to place under cross-examination to bring out the truth for the good of this court and for the cause of justice. And when Garvey found that his liberty was at stake, he had to ask the attorney to retire to protect his own liberty.

An Analysis of Gray

Who is Edgar Gray? You saw him on the stand—a reckless, irresponsible man, full of talk, representing nothing, a great politician who has no office, a great know-all who has nothing in all his years, who is still a messenger at probably a meagre $18.00 per week. That is the man with a superabundance of intelligence; that is the man who up to now has not told us his real birthplace, who says he was born in Sierre Leone, West Africa, when he was born in Antigua, as testified to by witness for the defense. Edgar Gray everybody knows came from the West Indies. He was born in Antigua. Can you believe the testimony of such a man as Edgar Gray, who left the Black Star Line, who left the Universal Negro Improvement Association when he was called upon to account for the funds of these organizations, which funds he handled during the absence of Garvey, Davis, Tobias and Ashwood in Virginia? Gray, who disappeared from the office with the funds of the organization, and for whom a warrant was to be sworn out in the Heights Court by Garvey and his attorney, James Watson, which was postponed by the discretion of the judge, no doubt for the convenience of Kilroe, and a few hours after Garvey met Gray and Warner at the office of the District Attorney Kilroe. Gentlemen, can you see the situation?

Warner Described

Who is Warner? A man who testified that he would say anything that the District Attorney told him to say. If the District Attorney said so, it was so. Would you call Warner a man? If Warner is a man, then God save the world of men. The rubber-stamp man without any character, who will be willing to say anything anybody else says, can you vouch for the testimony of such a man? Can you convict another man on the testimony of such a man? Remember, gentlemen, you are to be judged one day; you will therefore appreciate what it is to judge, to take away one's life, one's liberty. There is but one Great Judge, and that Judge will judge all mankind at the right time, the opportune time, and you at this hour are placed in the position of this Great High Judge to dispense justice to another as you would expect Him to dispense justice to you. Would you condemn a man, take away the liberty of a man, of four men, on the testimony of Gray, on the testimony of Warner? Would the great God condemn a Christian soul on the testimony of the devil? Gentlemen, I appeal to your sense of reason, and I appeal to your higher sense of justice. Warner, who said that the Black Star Line's funds were used for the restaurant of the Universal Negro Improvement Association and the African Communities League while he was secretary; Warner, not remembering that he signed a statement showing what he did with some of the funds that he could not account for, not showing that which he could not account for which he received from the Universal Negro Improvement Association. I will show you Warner's statement, which disclosed that he received certain amounts of money and disbursed same for the Universal Negro Improvement Association, and not the Black Star Line's money, as he testified to.

Hon. Marcus Garvey,
    56-58 West 135th Street,
      New York City.

Dear Sir:

Below is an itemized account as to how the $275 credited to House, Grossman and Vorhaus, lawyers for the Black Star Line, Inc., which money, when borrowed from the Universal Negro Improvement Association, was finally disbursed for the Universal.

June 30, salaries to the office employes by checks as follows: W. A. Domingo, $20; Edgar M. Gray, $18; A. G. Coombs, $15; Mrs. Leadett, $11; Mrs. Whittingham, $9; R. E. Warner, $20.

Salaries to restaurant employes by check as follows: Two waiters, $12 each, $24; one cook, $12. June 30, check to printer for paper issued to Mr. Gray, $150. Total, $279. It is believed your check book will verify said amounts, all of which you are well acquainted with. Signed, R. E. Warner,

Thus you will see, gentlemen, that it was the funds of the Universal Negro Improvement Association that were being used, and not the funds of the Black Star Line, as this gentleman Warner tried to make you understand. This Warner, who was such a business man, he had such great business ability he could advise Garvey, and what is he now? As a business man, where is his business? What benefit has he derived out of his great business ability? But for the Government he no doubt would have been a tramp, as we know him in the Harlem District.

And Now for Kilroe

Watch the testimony of Kilroe. I am sorry to speak of an officer of the State government in this manner. I regret it because I may be misinterpreted in this respect, because I have the highest respect for all American institutions.

I revere this great country and its great flag. I look to this country as the greatest democracy in the world, as the greatest government in the world. No other country in the world affords the opportunity for human liberty as this great American government, as this great American republic, but, gentlemen, nothing is at fault with the government. A government cannot commit any wrong, because governments do not administer themselves. It is the individual who administers government that sometimes bring ignominy upon the honor and integrity of the government.

Kilroe Characterized

Kilroe, the man who harbored Warner and Gray after he was told of their characters—had them sitting up in his office as if they were presidents of nations or governors of states, treating them with the greatest courtesy and respect, after he was told of the crimes they had committed against an American corporation. But not only one, but two American corporations. And he evinced no more interest in finding out if it were true, as far as the crime went, than to prosecute Garvey because he had some animus against Garvey, because Garvey could not politically, at that time, assist him, and these men were politicians who no doubt held out great promises as to what they could do for him at the next election. Kilroe, who tormented Garvey; who tormented the Universal Negro Improvement Association on over nine occasions, having nothing to say, nothing to do; up to now Garvey and the Universal Negro Improvement Association would have remained in his grip as an officer of the machinery of the government. Garvey would have been prosecuted to the fullest extent. Garvey probably would have rotted in jail if Kilroe had a case against him; but for nine times, after calling Garvey and having nothing to say, he expected Garvey to be docile! Gentlemen, as business men, busy in attending to your own affairs, how would you feel if someone unfortunately attached to the District Attorney's office, sent for you at your busiest hours, having nothing to say, using your time, humiliating you? How would you feel about it? Would you smile about it? And would you expect that Marcus Garvey, a human being, would smile at the attacks of Kilroe? Kilroe testified that he advised Garvey to do this and to do that. He knew he was not speaking the truth, but Garvey had not the opportunity to question Kilroe. And who is Kilroe? You, gentlemen, must have observed what happened in court—something about Mr. Kilroe that was not very pleasant. I will not go into it because it was not brought to your knowledge, but I will only ask you, gentlemen, to remember what happened for the few minutes when Mr. Johnson got on the floor and interrogated Kilroe about certain things. Imagine what these certain things were, who Kilroe was, and then you will have the character of the man.

Mr. Healey

And now we come to our friend Mr. Leo Healey. I am sorry to have to say anything about Mr. Healey, because I respect him. I had regarded him as a friend. The very morning when he came to testify here I met him on the outside. I shook his hand, and we were good friends then, as we were before. I never knew Healey was to be here as a witness testifying against me, and I was surprised to hear the things Mr. Healey said, but we will not take Mr. Healey seriously. He was only talking, I suppose, in the same character, in the same way Mr. Kilroe made a joke of Garvey being indicted. They come in contact with crime so often, and sending people to jail so often, for short and long terms, that they can smile about it. It is nothing surprising if a man goes to jail for twenty years. They smile over the matter. But, gentlemen, you are the judges. You will not smile over such a matter. Once he said that Garvey was a good gentleman, impressed him as being honest and upright; then later on he said Garvey was a bad man. He called Garvey a bad man because he did not pay him the bills for the Black Star Line. Now Garvey is not the Black Star Line. We were not asking him his opinion of the Black Star Line; we were asking his opinion about Garvey, and because Garvey did not **pay him** what the Black Star Line owed Harris McGill or the

North American Steamship Company, of which he was attorney, then Mr. Garvey became a bad man, and he had a different opinion about Mr. Garvey, and he talked to Mr. Mattuck about it.

He said they talked it over, and he told Mr. Mattuck that Garvey was a bad man. But let us see if Mr. Healey was really serious. Mr. Healey, a member of the bar, and I asked him if he was a member of the Bar Association, and he said yes, and he was qualified as an assistant district attorney in the County of Brooklyn, and Mr. Healey knew about certain laws that went into effect in this country at a certain time, especially the prohibition law, and he testified that he wanted some whisky off the Yarmouth, and he was willing to buy it or get it anyhow, after prohibition had gone into effect. A member of the bar, remember; a district attorney of the County of Brooklyn, wanted to buy or get whisky after the prohibition law went into effect. But not only in that did Mr. Healey joke with us, but Mr. Healey said he wanted this money from the Black Star Line, and if he got the money he would keep it. He was only attorney for the North American Steamship Company. He was not even the treasurer of the North American Steamship Company, but if he received the money, that balance of $35,000, he would keep it. He did not know where the directors were, he did not care to know where Harris, the president, was; and I asked him what he would do with it, and he said he would frame it. Now Mr. Healey was jolly and was not serious; because Mr. Healey, as attorney, an intelligent man, knows that if he was treasurer or attorney of a corporation, and received $35,000 for that corporation, his duty would be to report it to the office of the corporation, especially the president of the corporation, and give a proper account of it, that it would have to pass through the books of that corporation. Did Mr. Healey mean to suggest that he would commit a fraud, and even while he was assistant district attorney in the County of Brooklyn? Surely we could not believe that. We know Mr. Healey was only playing with the court and the gentlemen of the jury, and smiling away the liberty of Marcus Garvey. He told us all about the contracts between Harris McGill. Mr. Harris and the Black Star Line, and Marcus Garvey; did he tell us the truth about them? I feel sure you gentlemen of the jury know that he was not telling the truth, but only joking; he was only trying to carry out his promise to the district attorney.

He told us that contracts were signed. He acted as the attorney for the North American Steamship Company. Mr. Healey knew that there was an oral understanding between the Black

Star Line and Mr. W. Harris of the North American Steamship Company, that whether a bill of sale was actually passed in document or through legal process, that the Black Star Line was to be the owners of the Steamship Yarmouth. Mr. Healey knew that Mr. Harris was retiring from business, and going to Europe; he said he had no further use for the ship, and that he was willing then to sell his ship to the Black Star Line at that time, under any contract. And Mr. Healey drew these contracts, and kept that away from the court. Gentlemen, if you read the contracts, the many contracts, that were subsequently signed, you will find that there must have been some understanding why there were so many contracts, because good business men know that an original contract which involves the forfeit of money must be lived up to by the party of the second part, that they were not going to amend so many contracts for the convenience of the person who failed, they would have seized the ship on the first contract, and let the forfeit go. Did they do that? At no time did they compel the Black Star Line to forfeit the contract. Why, because there was a common understanding. So everybody knows Mr. Healey did not tell the truth. True and keen business men like Mr. Harris, do not do things that way. They wanted to sell us a Canadian boat, they wanted to sell an American corporation a Canadian boat, and they could not immediately give a bill of sale, that is why Healey was sent to Ottawa to see if they could do it, and they made these supplementary contracts, and then advised that we incorporate in Canada, the Black Star Line Steamship of Canada so as to take over the bill of sale in the legal way under these circumstances. They were the geniuses of the whole affar, Healey and Harris were the men who engineered the way how we could get the ship, because we knew nothing, we were innocent men trying to do the best for our people, and did not know all about the intricacies of business, and the ways we could get in and out. Healey knew it, and Harris himself, knew it, and they showed us the way, that is how we have a Canadian Black Star Line. We never dreamt of it. But they told us about the Canadian Black Star Line as the easiest way of getting the legal title, and that there was an oral title passed between us when we signed the first contract.

Healey himself told us that he got insurance for the ship Yarmouth on the first voyage. Admitting that that be true, why should he get insurance on the Yarmouth if they were not interested in the sale of the Yarmouth? Why didn't they make the Black Star Line live up to its contract after they signed the contract? You will find that there is something beneath the whole affair that Healey did not tell in that chair.

Healey said that he is a church brother of mine, that is true. That he is a friend of mine, that is true. But when it comes to justice, you cannot play with people's liberty that way.

He became offended when I asked him if his brother was a colored man, he knew I meant no offence, I was trying out his logic in a previous statement he made, when he said that Mr. Garvey was there with certain gentlemen of his race when he said certain things, and when I asked him again he said his brother only was there. I asked him if his brother was a colored man, in that sense, and he became offended, but I did not mean any offense to Mr. Healey, because when it comes to a matter of race, I have absolutely no feeling about the matter. I think every race should stand on its own bottom, whether it be white race, black race, yellow race, or the brown race, each race should paddle its own canoe. I believe that the white man should look out for the white man, the black man should look out for the black man, and the yellow man should also look out for the yellow man. Mr. Healey said that he was of the belief that I was a member of the Ku Klux Klan. He knows that there is no black man in the Klan. How could I be a member of the Ku Klux Klan? For what reason? He wanted to be nasty to me, I suppose. If I were of his denomination, how could I be a member of the Ku Klux Klan?

So you know, gentlemen, that Mr. Healey is not to be taken seriously in whatever he said on the witness stand.

We next had the real estate man Pilkington, who said that he sold Amy Ashwood some property, in October, 1919. Under cross-examination and under direct examination we asked him if he ever sold Marcus Garvey any property, he said no; we asked him if he ever knew Marcus Garvey, he said no. Why he was brought here I cannot tell. Why Pilkington was brought here to testify I cannot tell. I never saw the man before, never knew the man, never bought any property from the man, it was only a waste of the court's time.

They also brought one Whitfield, who said that he purchased property from one Amy Ashwood, whom I subsequently married as Amy Ashwood Garvey, and divorced six weeks later because of her crookedness. She was supposed to have sold property to this Whitfield. I knew nothing about it. The first time I saw Whitfield was on that witness stand. I could not tell what the man was going to testify about, until I heard the question of property and Amy Ashwood; then I realized that there was something they were trying to connect me with Amy Ashwood before she became Amy Ashwood Garvey. That, gentlemen, I will touch again, but whatsoever explanation I gave I feel sure will stand, and if you believe that I got a penny out of that $500 that Amy Ashwood got, that I would look upon the struggles of a people to rob them of a penny, I should die, and not only before man, but to be sent to the farthest depths of hell by my God.

Captain Cockburn.

We have the testimony of the man Cockburn—Cockburn the swindler—Cockburn, who admitted to the hearing of the president of the Black Star Line in this court for the first time, and before this honorable court and these gentlemen of the jury, that he got $1,600 as his part for selling the Yarmouth to the Black Star Line, and that five others got a like amount of money. The crook Cockburn, taking $1,600 out of the coffers of the Black Star Line, out of the dimes and nickles of the poor people at that time when we were struggling to get a boat, who pretended that he was a member of the race and wanted to help. The very first boat we could not even pay enough money at the first time for, which was only $16,500, and these crooks got $8,000 out of it, and had the nerve to go and sit in the chair as witnesses for the prosecution. That is the character of the witnesses we had from the government, crooks and sharks and men who know how to change up figures and amounts. All of them were not here, because some got scared and kept away. Where was Smith-Green? When I asked Cockburn the District Attorney said: "I can get him for you if you want." Why didn't he produce Smith-Green here? Why didn't he indict Smith-Green on the investigation of the books of the Black Star Line for nearly two years? Did he not know the name of Smith-Green? In the second indictment they produced two letters signed by Edward Smith-Green, and yet they did not produce the author of the letters, although they knew his name and his address and his whereabouts. It did not suit them at that time to bring Smith-Green, but we are going to find Smith-Green. If the District Atorney won't get Smith-Green, after you, gentlemen of the jury, have disposed of this case we will get Smith-Green and we will present him before the bar of American justice.

Cockburn told you how the Yarmouth was no good, after he had told us to buy the Yarmouth as a splendid boat. It is all in the record, gentlemen, what this man Cockburn said, and what he subsequently said under cross-examination. Cockburn the drunkard, when asked about his sober condition, stood before you and said: "It is my business." Because, no doubt, he knew he was a drunkard, a drunkard on the high seas, sailing the ships of the Black Star Line. And didn't you hear the testimony, gentlemen, that on the first trip from New York to Cuba the ship Yarmouth struck a reef? Didn't you hear the man Hercules testify for the defence (he was very talkative)? And another engineer testified that the ship would have been a total wreck under the command of Cockburn the drunkard. If he got $1,600 out of that first payment for himself, God knows how much he got out of the balance of $125,000 that was subsequently paid into the coffers of Harris, McGill & Co., from whom we bought the boat under the instructions of Cockburn.

Did Cockburn return after that first trip when he got the $1,600 for commission?—He returned to make the second trip, and when he came he found it was a cargo of whiskey, and he said, "Now is the time for me to get what is coming to me," and he said the ship could not go to sea, but when he found out he was getting $2,000 to split between himself and Smith-Green, the ship went to sea at quick speed. Nothing was wrong with the ship then. And, gentlemen, was it only $2,000 that was split between himself and Smith-Green, which Mr. Healey knew about, and he did not want to tell the facts. After the ship sailed and they got $2,000, it went only a short way out, a radio was sent, "We are drunk, we are sinking," and immediately 500 cases of Green River Whiskey and champagne were thrown overboard, and tugboats were around. What were these tugboats doing there? Who got the money for the cargo? Didn't Hercules tell you on the witness stand that he was ordered by the captain to put so many cases of whiskey in a lighter? Who got the money for that whiskey?

Cockburn said that he bought property in his wife's name after he came back from his trip to make it appear that it was one bit of property; we were not allowed the privilege to search and bring the testimony here; the search has been made, but the testimony could not be produced.

He tells us now that he is a real estate broker. Do you wonder that Cockburn is a real estate broker after that historic trip of the Yarmouth with that cargo of whiskey? Gentlemen, it is for you to think matters over and see the characters of the men who were placed here to testify against the defence— men who got $25 for a few weeks, men who got $50 a week for about one and a half years, men who got $100 a week for

S. S. Kanawha, of the Black Star Line, re-christened S. S. Antonio Maceo, ex-yacht of H. H. Rogers, the multi-millionaire, purchased for $60.000 and fitted at a cost of over $25.000 as an inter-colonial passen-

just a year, while Cockburn got at one time what the president got for all the time he was president of the corporation. And Cockburn was getting how much? $400 per month, the same amount of money that the president was supposed to get as salary. At times the President was only getting $50 per week; Cockburn was not only getting $100 per week, but $10 a day allowance, according to his own statement that a captain gets daily allowances outside of his salary. How much did Cockburn get? He got all the money of the Black Star Line and the rest. It is no wonder that he became so haughty and demonstrated so much viciousness on the witness stand.

These are the characters of the witnesses who were brought here by the District Attorney to represent this great government, and convict a man. Gentlemen, do you think that is the spirit of this great government, the spirit of justice, of honesty and truth? When that great father of our country, George Washington, brought into existence this great Republic, did he contemplate that the name of America would have been besmirched by such rascals as demonstrated here by these witnesses, who were brought by the District Attorney to convict four men, and take away their liberty.

Gentlemen, as American citizens, I feel sure you will save the name of America from a scandal and from shame that is becoming worldwide, because the case of the Black Star Line is not a local matter, it is a case which 400,000,000 Negroes of the world are watching with an eagle eye to test America's justice, and you gentlemen have in your hands at this hour, the name of America, where black men are concerned, and I feel sure you will not pollute the fair name of this nation, to please anyone, who has vengeance in his heart against someone he desires to get even with, as Kilroe desires to get even with Garvey, Kilroe, who sent Tyler to shoot Garvey, and when Tyler shot four times and Garvey was only wounded and did not die, Tyler was taken to the jail and the next morning was said to commit suicide, was found dead on the first floor, supposed to have dropped from the sixth floor of the jail house.

Gentlemen, I feel sure you understand the situation as presented to you. I have no desire to hide anything. Did I hide anything about the character of Marcus Garvey? Didn't I ask them to tell what they knew of Marcus Garvey, and did not they tell the limit of what they knew, and afterwards when they knew no more, didn't they lie, and say, yes, there is more? the liars that they are.

We will pass from Cockburn, because it pains me to linger so long with a crook and a scoundrel. We come to Adrian Richardson, the master of 1919 and 1920 without a master's license, who so lied on the witness stand that he had a master's ticket when he came to the Black Star Line, and met me in 1919 in Boston. Captain Swift, the man for whom he worked in the latter part of 1920, testified that he it was who tried to get a ticket for the man Richardson as a master. We subpoenaed the records of the Shipping authorities of New York, the records were brought that showed the same thing that Captain Swift testified to, but the defence was not permitted to question on the record, and I excused the shipping master.

Captain Richardson

The shipping master came with certain papers, and I was not allowed to question him in that the matter of Richardson, was then closed, and it was not within the legal procedure. This man Richardson, another crooked captain, said he was not anxious to get into the service of the Black Star Line.

Who would believe a Negro like Richardson sitting there, saying that he was not anxious to get into the service of the Black Star Line? Gentlemen, he said he met me in Boston. Now, I must be some great magician to know that the man is a captain just by way of looking at him. He says he saw me in a public meeting. Now, is it reasonable to expect a man whom you never met before that you could just pick out as a captain and start to talk to him? Does it not suggest that the person would speak to the man he knew was head of a steamship company, and say that he was a captain and tell him something about himself? It is reasonable that Richardson would beg for a job in the Black Star Line, would come to the Black Star Line with the idea of seeing if he could get what Cockburn got.

It is no wonder he advised us not to buy the Kanawha, even though the Kanawha was bought before he came, because he probably wanted to buy another boat to get his $1,600 out of the split of the brokers. Do you wonder, gentlemen, why Captain Richardson and Captain Mulzac were grieved? They were grieved because they did not get the chance like Cockburn had to make theirs, and become real estate brokers afterwards; but Mulzac afterward became president of a steamship company, so he was in search for his, anyhow, but did not get it in buying the Yarmouth, so thought he would be president himself of some other steamship company. Richardson, the man who is supposed to have spent his thousands for the Black Star Line, when you could have seen that that Negro did not have a thousand cents. Thousands of dollars that he paid for crews' wages. Well, we were trying to get the book in evidence, but it was denied, and we could not put it in, so you could see how this Richardson manipulated figures; how he put down his receipts and disbursements, how he made one thousand dollars look like two, and charged the balance up to himself.

As to Silverstone, the Jew, I did not know the man Silverstone any more than I saw him once or twice, and I do not want to see him again unless when he returns the $25,000, we will see that the Black Star Line gets it back to pay its liabilities, also the last $11,000.

This Richardson who was dismissed in Jamaica, this Richardson, the man whom Thompson sent out with that beautiful ship, the Kanawha, because, gentlemen, indeed that ship was beautiful. It was the yacht of that great millionaire Rogers. The Kanawha was the name of some interest he had; it was a palace, but the government took it over one time and used it as an auxilliary cruiser, and when we refitted her she was nearly as perfect as when Rogers had it.

The boat was a twin screw boat, its machinery was intricate and instead of placing a competent crew to manage such a boat, we had a captain without a license, a captain who got a license afterwards either by his fraternal signs or his political pull, a captain who was drunk with his engineers, a captain who gambled on the deck, a captain who had not enough discipline to see that his engineers were in the engine room while the ship was at sea. Think of it, a ship at sea with nobody in the engine room, no engineer. Do you wonder the cylinder covers blew off and piston rods were broken? Do you wonder the Kanawha became a wreck so many times?

I did not tell you about Cockburn and the bills he made, the repair bills for which they got commission. Do you know why the ship balked so many times, because commissions were paid for her repairs. Bills for $11,000 probably meant a commission of 15 or 20 per cent to the master, and no wonder our ships foundered so many times. Because we had made a statement that we were going to show that Negroes could run ships and because we were the responsible officers of the corporation, they took the opportunity of blackmailing us, because they knew that we had to keep our word. We made a mistake in a way, but, gentlemen, who do not make mistakes? Didn't the Pilgrims make mistakes when they found this great country? Did we indict the Pilgrims for making an American Republic through mistakes? Indict us for trying to show the world that black men are capable, but you will not destroy the sentiment of the Negro for business and progress. Send Marcus Garvey to prison for what Silverstone has done. I am satisfied to go to jail even though I say so, for fraud, for money that some white man received. Am satisfied, but I feel sure that the sense of American justice will secure fair play to me.

Now for the circular advertising the sailing of the Phyllis Wheatley. Somebody might have suggested to the District Attorney what the questions and the answers shall be to excuse Garcia and Thompson so the two may get Garvey under indictment. And that was why Hunt the printer was so eager to say Garcia and Thompson gave me this and Garcia gave me that. Gentlemen, you yourselves, heard Hunt admit that any printing one printer does can be duplicated by another printer and that they can slip in words that were not in the original. You can slip in a libelous word and a fraudulent word, and produce it as original, but Garvey denies that he wrote circulars identical to those submitted. Garvey never writes any circu'ars in his own handwriting. Why didn't they produce the handwriting of Garvey instead of the printed circular? You can take it to the printing shop and get the whole Bible printed for that matter. So, gent!emen, you will not convict a man on a printed slip that can be duplicated by any printer?

This Hunt was getting $250 a week and sometimes $400 a week in printing, but when the Universal Negro Improvement Association suddenly acquired a printing plant, he became sore and was willing to do anything to damage Garvey for the loss of business.

The Negro World

I would like to draw to your attention the Negro World of March 13, 1921, placed in evidence. These Negro Worlds, government exhibits, are too long for me to go through all of them, but they are in evidence and you will see them. Garvey admits writing some of the articles in the Negro World. Garvey denies some of those articles in the Negro World. At times Garvey would be away and his articles would not get to New York in time and someone would write the articles and stick Garvey's name to them. I knew the phraseology was not mine, but the district attorney seized upon it as a valuable bit of evidence against Garvey. Garvey does not hold himself responsible. If you gentlemen desire to convict Garvey, Garvey is satisfied. When Garvey's conscience and soul are clear before man and God, he does not care what man does with his body. Man may condemn the body but not the soul and conscience of the man.

In one of these Negro Worlds appears a ship that was supposed to be re-named the Phyllis Wheatley. You will see that when you go to the jury room. Garvey knows about that ship; he knew the time the photograph was got out. He read the words under that ship. The District Attorney did not read all of them. He read only that part which he be'ieved would incriminate me. Why didn't the District Attorney read the entire sentence and all the words beneath the photograph? I would not believe the honorable District Attorney desired to deceive the court and the gentlemen of the jury. Surely, the government would not deceive itself? The government is too honorable for deceit. So, I will not impute any motive to the honorable District Attorney for not reading entirely and completely all the words appearing on that page. What did it say? "If you will subscribe enough money, we will have the ship." You will find that whenever you see anything about any ship. It was always "If you give enough money you will have this," because I knew the people would not be crazy enough to expect us to give them something without money, and they knew that the officers had no money. We were not buying ships for ourselves but for the race. For what? For the industrial and commercial development of the race. That race was paying a price. Garvey, as a member of that race, contributes his part, and with the exception of a few who thought more of salary than of service, those of us who were officers of the Black Star Line, did not remember anything about salary. When there was no salary, Garvey did not squeal; Tobias did not squeal, but Thompson squealed, when there was no salary. He disappeared when he couldn't get that $50 per week, and we never found Thompson until a month ago. Yes, gentlemen, we assumed responsibility, at least, Marcus Garvey assumes the responsibility for the photograph which Thompson gave him and which Thompson advised to be put in the Negro World, because Thompson was negotiating on behalf of the Black Star Line for the purchase of the Tennyson which was to become the Phyllis Wheatley. He brought the photograph and gave it to Garvey and we all decided what to do.

Mr. Mattuck: I object as there was no testimony that Thompson gave him the photograph.

Judge: I do not remember hearing him testify to——

Mr. Garvey: But it was in evidence.

Judge: But not as Thompson gave it to you.

Mr. Garvey: All right, I withdraw it.

Mr. Garvey continues his address:

The photograph that the District Attorney held up to the Court and the gentlemen of the jury with the words underneath, but he didn't read you the entire truth. We were, I testified, negotiating for the Tennyson, in continuation of which Marcus Garvey went to the West Indies, South and Central America to raise money. $30,000 had to be raised in order to get the ship within twenty (20) days after Garvey left as per arrangements explained here in testimony. The others were to raise so much and Garvey was to raise so much. In six (6) weeks Garvey raised $17,000 for the Black Star Line and as Jacques' books proved, Amy Jacques, for the Universal Negro Improvement Association, raised $13,000 or $14,000 in six weeks. We had over $30,000 from Garvey's side alone. Then they had raised over 20,000 odd dollars in America. If Thompson had not sent Richardson down with the dirty crew and Garvey did not have to spend the Black Star Line and Universal Negro Improvement Association's money on the Kanawha repairs all of the $30,000 would have been cabled to New York instead of only a part, and they would have had in New York enough to make the payment on the ship. And, gentlemen, as business men, you know that if you don't use good judgment in business whether the Standard Oil Company, even with its millions of capital, it will go out of business. If you take $30,000 here and so many thousands dollars there, even the Standard Oil Company will go to pieces, and J. D. Rockefeller and Carnegie would look as tramps, as frauds and no good. What could Garvey do with such a crew bent on mischief in the West Indies.

We will go over these exhibits. Now we have the testimony of William Boody, the man from Rogowski's, the printer. The man who knew nothing; who could say nothing, only what he heard. Gentlemen, will you condemn a man on hearsay? He was brought in to testify about the mailing of the Negro World. Did he tell where the Negro World went to? Did he say he posted the Negro World to Washington, to Connecticut, to Indiana? He said he got copies from the foreman. Where did the foreman get them, I believe from the Negro World, was his answer. How do you know? I saw some one from the Negro World handling copies. Did some one from the Negro World hand copies to the foreman? Yes. Can you remember who he was? No.

Gentlemen, can you convict anyone on such a testimony? He never received a mailing list from the Negro World. Yet, he came in to testify. Why didn't the District Attorney bring in the foreman from Rogowski's to tell from whom he received the copies?

Gentlemen, surely, you shall discount the testimony of William Boody.

Cargil, The Little Boy.

Now we come to Cargil, a little boy who spilt the beans on the District Attorney. Cargil, the little fellow of about 20 years, who was placed there and said such beautiful things as the District Attorney arranged with him to say. When we asked him the question, "Who told you to say those things; to identify those circulars." He answered: the District Attorney, and for the first time in the case we had the District Attorney hanging his head down. We had got him then. When we asked where he was born we could not get it out of him, because if we did we would have proved something. Who can tell if there was a Cargil in the employ of the Black Star Line? Let us see the pay roll book of the Black Star Line. The boy testified that he was working with the Black Star Line from 1919 to 1921. We will see how much he got for all that period of time in the cash book.

Gentlemen of the jury, you have heard the little boy, Cargil, if that was his name, testify that he was employed with the Black Star Line from 1919 to 1921. In the books you will not find any record. When you come to look on the treasurer's book (he said he got his pay from George Tobias) you will find there was one Cargil working only from July 2, 1920, to November 5, 1920, so when he testified he posted circulars in 1919 to 1921, Cargil was not telling the truth. Where did that Cargil come from? We have not found out his first name yet. Such a Cargil never worked with the Black Star Line from 1919 to 1921, and the treasurer's book of the Black Star Line will tell the tale.

We have Mr. B. O'Shannon, the mail foreman in the post office, bringing here a mass of figures about the Negro Worlds being sent out. (From where to where?) If these people were supposed to buy stock at certain points, why didn't they testify to what points the mail went, so as to establish the truth in their case and why didn't they show the signature of some representative from the Negro World to prove that such a delivery was made to the postoffice? Oh, we can make up anything we want to suit our convenience when we wish. Gentlemen, will you take away some one's liberty on such things, just a mass of figures, dates, etc., to where?—to anywhere, some probably went to Limbo and Saturn for that matter because aeroplanes carry the mails nowadays.

Other Witnesses

We come to Mrs. Lawson, another one who spilled the beans on our good friend, the District Attorney. When we placed her under cross-examination, we asked her to show her subpoena. She fumbled around and looked at the District Attorney and bowed her head awaiting his approval. Garvey saw it. You must have seen it, too. The lady with the dark glasses, who wore them so that you could not follow the movements of her eyes, and the lines of her stare. Oh, a lot of things are hidden behind some dark glasses. The movement of the eyes tell when we are speaking the truth and when we are not going to speak the truth we hide our vision from the public for deception. She could not help bowing and waiting approval from the District Attorney. Gentlemen, you will surely not pay any attention to Mrs. Lawson. She said she bought stock in 1917 when the Black Star Line never sold stock in 1917, it was not in existence then. A woman who told such an untruth to testify away the liberty of other people. She was sick she said, and wanted money, but you remember how her sickness coincided with the sickness of Mrs. Harrison from Philadelphia, and the other lady, Mrs. Carington? They were all sick. It was the arrangement to be all sick, so as to appeal to the finer sympathy of you gentlemen. Their money was taken by Marcus Garvey, the arch villian, the arch thief. The actions of that woman on the stand showed that she could get $30 in five minutes, the woman was such a bully. She read an advertisement in the Negro World and bought her shares. That is what she said; then she went back and said she heard Garvey speak and bought her shares then. When did she buy her shares? When she read the advertisement in the Negro World or when Garvey spoke—which time? Surely you will not believe a character like that and take away anybody's liberty, not even a dog's liberty on such testimony? She, who said that Garcia told her the company was bankrupt, but she didn't remember the time, but wanted so badly to say that Garvey said the same thing.

I supposed she didn't remember the arrangement so as to hold Mr. Garvey for selling stock in a company after he said it was bankrupt. She placed it on Garcia, not on Garvey, in her testimony, she got confused.

Then we come to Edward Orr, the yellow man from the West Indies, who pretended that there is no prejudice between yellow, brown and black people in his part of the world. He sued Garvey before for $305 for stock bought in the Black Star Line. He didn't buy stock in Garvey. Garvey was not the corporation by himself. He bought stock in the Black Star Line, but sued Garvey to get back $305. Now, didn't that show malice? Why didn't he sue the Black Star Line? He testified that Garvey never sold stock, but the secretary did, and he got his stock from the secretary of the Black Star Line. The malice of the man is enough evidence to satisfy you, gentlemen of the jury, that you could not take away the liberty of any one on the testimony of such a man.

Then we have Mr. Schenck. This Mr. Schenck from Washington. He couldn't remember or identify anything until he reached the point where he had to. The District Attorney made him identify something, and then he said he treated it as trash, threw it away. A man who treated something like trash is really not a man who is defrauded. But he testified he bought his stock at the meeting where Garvey spoke, at a Baptist Church in Washington and not through the mail. From an agent at a meeting at Washington, where Garvey spoke. Where, then, can you establish that the mail was used to defraud in Washington? If he received literature in the mail after he bought his stock, he treated it as trash; therefore, it had absolutely no influence on him. There was no fraud. But he is an employee of the Government Printing Office in Washington, and he thought he was doing a wonderful thing to testify, not knowing the spirit of our great government, which does not support anyone in falsehoods, untruths and lies. Could a government support a man like Warner in his lies? The whole world looks to this country for justice. Can we allow men like Warner to represent the Government? It is a shame, a disgrace, that they should link up these discredited persons for the government. Schenck never bought stock through the mails. Now we will go to Mrs. Annie Still. You remember, she was very still when she came in. She was still because she was sick. She was ever so still. Remember this sick lady from Philadelphia, who was so sick she could hardly talk?

But when she found out she was cornered telling an untruth and we noticed it, she was as loud and as boisterous as any one here, and I believe I am the loudest one here.

So, you won't convict and take away one's liberty on this testimony. Her testimony was so confused we could not understand it. When the District Attorney asked her "Where did you get this letter?" she answered, "In New York." Can you convict anyone on such testimony? The testimony itself was not clear. She said she got some circulars and could not identify them. How flimsy this testimony for this charge for which we are indicted and are to be condemned. She testified that she bought her stock at a meeting when Fred A. Toote was president in Philadelphia, where Garvey spoke. Surely, there is no harm in Garvey speaking to sell stock? So that testimony is not worth the time consumed in giving it. Whether Garvey sold stock in Liberty Hall, New York, a church in Washington or Philadelphia, does not enter into this case, as the judge will charge you at the proper time.

Now we come to Benny Dancy, one of the witnesses of the second count. Mr. Dancy knew nothing. When the District Attorney pounded at him, then he admitted that "He went to my address in Brooklyn." Then he said: "I cannot remember." Then he said: "Did you read anything about a ship in Africa?" Then the man got sore and said: "'Yes." Then I cross-examined him and his next move he said: "Yes. I read something about going to Africa." Can you convict a man on testimony like that? He said no first and yes afterwards. So, gentlemen, these persons that the District Attorney will tell you about, these poor washerwomen, these poor men who have not a dime; now remember their testimony well. If you had an office and a woman came into it in the attitude of Mrs. Lawson, you would throw her out. I didn't do that. I asked her to leave. She went to the District Attorney, who is the collecting agent for people who want to spite and get even with others. When some employees are dissatisfied, when someone believes they are taken advantage of, they go to him. She told the District Attorney who takes away your books and holds you up many days and makes your business go to pieces, because someone wants to get even with Garvey and somebody else, and the only way to do it is to go to the District Attorney, who is representing the government. Surely the government is not a collecting agent for people who want to spite others.

Now we come to Mr. Smith of Indianapolis, Ind. He also could not identify anything about envelopes. Couldn't say what came in them. Could not remember that he signed a questionnaire; that he went to the postoffice and made it out, but after a while Mr. Smith was forced to say that this is the circular and that circular came through the mail. Surely you will not convict anyone on the memory of Smith, which failed to recognize anything but the envelope. And he had to recognize that somehow. The paper had no name when it was shown, and he could not remember until the District Attorney in his masterly manner got him to say "Yes, I think this kind of a circular came," and then he admitted he made out a questionnaire. Will you conacted the same way in my office only two years ago and went out with threats, as she did on the stand, then I suppose she

vict and take away one's liberty on the testimony of such people?
I feel you will not.

Before I close, let's go to De Bourg, the aged man—I respect
him for his years, but for nothing else—the man who has lost
the spirit of truth, the man who has sent his soul to hell.

Now we come to the other man from Stamford, Conn. He
could not remember anything until from mere exhaustion he said,
"I think I remember seeing this circular." So these testimonies
on these counts are the ones on which you are supposed to convict four men, indicted before you for fraud.

Watkis, the white wife kicker, Watkis, the man who talked about
spending 60 per cent of the Black Star Line money in a trip.
Who told him to do that? When Garvey found out, didn't
Garvey get him arrested? Did not Garvey get him indicted and
brought up before the grand jury? And then he talked about
the $300 he spent to get out of trouble. You remember I made
several efforts to put in the letter of the police commissioner
of Youngstown and I was not permitted to do so? Gentlemen,
imagine what is in that letter. Imagine who got that $300.
Watkis got the $300 and split with Brooks. There is absolutely
no testimony to convict. Could the jury convict a man on
Watkis' testimony. This innocent? Watkis, this crooked Watkis,
is another star witness for the District Attorney, and Watkis
was held in the Heights court before the grand jury of the
county of New York, when Kilroe was Assistant District Attorney. Do you wonder that Watkis was not indicted by the grand
jury? That he went free?

Mrs. Foley vs Powell.

We pass from Watkis to Powell. Look at Powell and you
could see that there was something about him that you yourself
would not trust. A man who looked like him convicts himself.
Would you trust him with your cash? A man who said he was
always broke, looking anxious like that for years and a student
of law? Gentlemen, surely you did not pay any attention to what
Powell said to you. Look at the man, the fellow who said
Garvey put the cold hand on him. Yes, I did, because he didn't
look right and would not allow him to handle the cash, and
that is why he has it in for Garvey.

He said he gave Garvey money for stock that Garvey never
turned over. But Garvey came to his office and got Mrs. Foley,
his secretary to make up the stock. He leaves a doubtful impression in your minds. After he said that on the stand Garvey
sent a telegram to Mrs. Foley, at Atlanta, Ga., to be here at the

expense of over $200, and you heard Mrs. Foley on that witness stand, during which time I searched the office of the Black Star Line and found the receipt, which you saw in evidence—the receipt signed by Powell himself in getting the money. Mrs. Foley surely impressed you as an honest woman. She had absolutely no cause to tell a lie, because the very morning she came in is the very morning she testified. This is the receipt, gentlemen, with Powell's name on it.

Then we will go back to Mr. DeBourg. I am sorry to speak of that man, and the things that he told me, and said on the witness stand to the contrary, for the government. I tried to get in certain papers with Mr. DeBourg's handwriting for him to identify, but I could not get them in. If I could have, they would tell a different tale to what he said in that box. But it is too late. I am sorry for the man; I am sorry for his soul, and I need not say more about him. I leave him to his God.

The Defense Witnesses.

And now the witnesses for the defense. I need not say one word about them. You have had your impression. You have seen them, and I feel sure you are impressed with what they said. You heard Miss Davis, the woman who lived at my house for years, the woman who said things that could have been misunderstood in many ways, the woman who was in Jamaica with me and lived in my house for over three years. Her testimony was such that you could not very well understand the situation. I asked her if I had money, if I went to the races. If I had been the kind of man the District Attorney painted me to be, Garvey could have fixed up Miss Davis and she could have given a testimony that would have sent me to heaven, but Garvey never talked to her. Garvey doesn't even talk to his wife about his case, outside of what goes on, as far as his liberty is concerned. Garvey desires the world to hear the truth. I did not fix up any testimony with Henrietta Vinton Davis. She told what she knew.

We have Carrie Leadett, the black girl, who was Garvey's first secretary, who told the truth as she knew it, and believed it to be, and whom the District Attorney tried to trip. Gentlemen, in the name of the government the District Attorney tried to trip her, and when he could not get her to tell lies, he left her in disgust. Surely, it is not the purpose of this great government to charge the jury under lies.

We have Mr. J. M. Certain, the man who testified what he knew, what he could remember. I believe as vice-president he tried to save himself and didn't want to tell all that he knew. I sympathize with him. But he told you what he knew about Garvey. I would not save myself at the expense of anyone else.

We have Jennie Jenkins. You saw that woman was telling the truth. You understood that she was one of the first directors of the Black Star Line. She was assistant treasurer of the Black Star Line.

Next, Alice O'Gara, another woman, a brown-skinned woman, who told the truth.

Gwen Campbell, the girl I asked if she was a friend of Garcia and Thompson. The girl who was my private secretary and desk clerk in my office during my absence in the West Indies, who signed all the orders in my absence and placed my name on them. You saw her. You heard what she had to say, I wanted her to speak the truth. She told some of the things she knew and kept back some things she should have said because, I suppose, she didn't want to hurt her friends Thompson and Garcia. She was a government witness first. I suppose they could not use her in the way they wanted. Nevertheless, she testified for me.

We had Jas. Hercules, the man who sailed with Captain Cockburn. Look at his face, Decide for yourself whether he spoke the truth or not. You have Amy Jacques Garvey as witness. I will not go over the testimony of Amy Jacques Garvey. You formed your own impression of what she said.

You have John Garrett, the engineer who testified twice. The last time he testified that he recommended many ships for the purchase by the Black Star Line to be named the Phyllis Wheatley.

You had Mr. Morton, who carried out the contracts for Briggs in selling the Kanawha to the Black Star Line. He testified he knew no commission was given to Garvey.

We have Balfour Williams, the man from Boston, whom the District Attorney tried to make lie. Enid Lamos, who told all the methods used in Garvey's office and his methods when he went to speak when she was with him. That she received the money, when she was with Garvey, and other secretaries did the same.

Did Garvey, who could speak at these meetings for 50 cents and 75 cents admission, bringing in $300 and $500 a night and turning it all over, have to send a letter through the mail to get $5.00 when he could speak at a meeting and collect $600? Garvey can speak and collect $2,000 or $3,000 and Garvey gets but a meagre salary a year, is that the way men defraud.

You have the testimony of Clifford Bourne, who told of the trouble Garvey had in getting back to this country. He had to cable Secretary Hughes and the President of the United States in order to get back, because of others who tried to throw the Black Star Line into bankruptcy and keep Garvey in the West Indies, and say he stole the money. You see the connection between the Black Star Line of New Jersey and the Black Star Line Inc., of Delaware. You heard the testimony of William Ware, president of one of the large divisions. You have the testimony of all the other presidents from respective parts of this country, representing six million members of the Universal Negro Improvement Association, part of whom are stockholders in the Black Star Line. Will such men lie? Could Garvey live if Garvey had defrauded so many people? Garvey, they testified, spoke at all their meetings. Garvey went to Detroit, they said, Cincinnati, Philadelphia, wherever stockholders are supposed to be. He spoke to 30,000 members of the organization in New York, and Garvey is in his body and his flesh safe, yet Garvey has defrauded the poor people according to the District Attorney.

Wilford Smith

I need not go over the testimony of the fifty-odd witnesses. It would take away from the time allotted to me. I will now touch upon this Orion vessel, but before doing so I want to remind you about this power of attorney of Wilford Smith. You will find that there was never any power of attorney given him. It was only a matter of understanding that Mr. Smith would protect the signature and name of Marcus Garvey wheresoever it was used. That didn't mean that Smith was constituted president of the Black Star Line, or President-General of the Universal Negro Improvement Association, because these were corporate bodies and its officers could only be elected by the Board of Directors, and not by the president, especially when there was a vice-president. I had to protect my name because of the system used in the office, because they used my name and made me the scapegoat. They talk about Thompson being a scapegoat. Garvey is the scapegoat when Garvey is about three or four thousand miles away and his name is being used. He had to try some kind of protection to save himself from things of this kind. Smith was a director. He was the attorney of the company. To whom better could I go than to such a man, an aged man of good reputation in the community, and especially when the vice-president had no financial interest in the company? He was sore, (Thompson) according to what he

said, but suppose Smith had not done that, not only would
$25,000 been gone, but the whole company would have been
stolen.

That is what they are sore about, because Smith had to keep
some kind of a check on the use of Garvey's name. They didn't
want that. They wanted to get the use of Garvey's name, a
free license to use Garvey's name. Then when anything went
wrong they would resign and poor Garvey would be in a fix.

Garvey used the mails to find some folks, and could not get
them. Let's take down that letter of Ware's written by Thompson, which Thompson on the stand, denied that he wrote. Will
you turn to the back of that letter, gentlemen, and do you not
observe the symmetry of impression. On the back of the letter
you have the same impression above and below the man's signature. If one was typed before the other, the impression would
not be the same. That man looked at the letter and denied it.
Now consider the supposed Hong Kaeng. Hong Kong was the
original name they typed in. But when this man Garcia sent
that cablegram about the Hong Kong, which was only a 400-
ton boat, they said no, it is the Hong Kaeng, not the Hong
Kong, and they slipped the "a e" in instead of the "o."

The Black Star Line.

Gentlemen, we come to the point where this Black Star Line
was said to be bankrupt. Bankruptcy papers were never filed
against the Black Star Line. The Black Star Line had times when
it might not have been in the best financial condition, but no one
had filed any papers for bankruptcy. We had liabilities and
assets not only in money, not only in property, but the good
will of the people, which was the greatest asset, and if somebody had not taken the funds and dissatisfied the people about
that boat, we would have been a success.

Where did the Black Star Line get money to buy the Yarmouth? From the same people who would have been willing to
buy the other boats. When we bought the Yarmouth we had
no assets other than the good will of the people, and they subscribed the money to buy the Yarmouth, and the Kanawha and
the Shady Side. If the people did that, then would not they have
done more? They would have given one-half more if they had to
acquire that African ship, but they were told the ship would be
here tomorrow. Tomorrow never came, and the people, who
were the assets, became doubtful and we could have no ships.

When Garvey was in the West Indies over $30,000 was
wasted. If the management had signed a proper contract with

Morse we probably would have had the ship Kanawha in **different** condition. It was not so much the money, but intelligence and brain. We started the organization with only 13 members, and today we have an organization of six million members throughout the world with 900 branches.

We had no monetary considerations or reward before us, but the good we could do for our race, for this and succeeding generations. Those of us who started the work did not think about salary of $50 a week. We thought of giving what we could in body and soul for the emancipation of a race and for our country. I hardly believe you understand the situation. You will say it was bad business. But, gentlemen, there is something spiritual beside business. You will say that we sold $800,000, in stock. They ought to have good ships. Did we get all that money at the same time? And during the time we were gathering this money we had to invest and carry on and show good faith. We had to pay in parts on the Kanawha and Shady Side. If we had all the money at the one time we could have bought one of the best ships in this country.

When we made our purchase the tonnage on ships was high. When we were supposed to have bought the Phyllis Wheatley tonnage had fallen, ships were going practically for nothing. If we were able to get ships during the war, we would have gotten ships then, when shipping had fallen in this country, as low as the price went. The Shipping Board had numbers of ships. The failure of the Black Star Line was only a drop in the bucket. You had numbers of failures among your own race, gentlemen. Your experts failed by the hundreds and during the period the Black Star Line had the difficulties the Shipping Board of the United States lost $300,000,000. Was there fraud on the part of the Shipping Board in the use of the millions? The taxes, your money and my money, were converted into ships and the ships failed. Did we indict our great President for the use of the millions? Sometimes to fail is but stepping stones to greater things.

The Universal Negro Improvement Association and the Black Star Line employs thousands of black girls and black boys Girls who could only be washer women in your homes, we made clerks and stenographers of them in the Black Star Line's office. You will see that from the start we tried to dignify our race. If I am to be condemned for that I am satisfied.

I Am a Negro.

I am a Negro. I make absoutely no apology for being a Negro

because my God created me to be what I am, and as I am so will I return to my God, for He knows just why He created me as He did. So, gentlemen, you will understand that behind the whole business proposition lies the spirit of the movement. I have no time to go into the work of the Universal Negro Improvement Association, but I say this: I know there are certain people who do not like me because I am black; they don't like me because I am not born here, though no fault of mine.

I didn't bring myself into this western world. You know the history of my race. I was brought here; I was sold to some slave master in the island of Jamaica. Some Irish slave master who subsequently gave my great-grandfather his name. Garvey is not an African name; it is an Irish name, as Johnston is not an African name, Garcia is not an African name, Thompson and Tobias are not African names. Where did we get those names from? We inherited them from our own slave masters, English, French, Irish or Scotch. So, if I was born in Jamaica, it was no fault of mine. It was because that slave ship which took me to Jamaica did not come to American ports. That is how some Negroes of America were not born in the West Indies.

We did not come here of our own free will. We were brought here, and so the question of birth does not enter into the question of the Negro. It was a matter of accident. Will you blame me for the accident of being a Jamaican Negro and not an American Negro? Surely you will not. But there is a bigger question involved. It is a question of race. What are you going to do with this question of race. You may sit quietly by, but it is going to be serious later on, and that is why the Universal Negro Improvement Association is endeavoring to assist you in solving the Negro problem by helping the Negro to become enterprising, independent politically, and by having a country of his own. If you follow me down the ages you will see within a hundred years you are going to have a terrible race problem in America, when you will have increased and the country will become over-populated. It will be a fight for existence between two opposite races, The weak will have to go down in defeat before the strong. In the riots of Washington, East St. Louis, Chicago, Tulsa, study the race question and you will find that some serious thinking must be done now to solve this problem; otherwise our children will be confronted with it. Do you know when you want bread and the other fellow wants it, when there is only one loaf—what is going to happen? Enmity and pressure is going to spring up and a fight will ensue. That is why the Universal Negro Improvement Association has started this proposition to redeem Africa and build up a country of our own, so as not to molest you in the country your fathers founded hundreds of years ago.

Some Negroes believe in social equality. They want to intermarry with the white women of this country, and it is going to cause trouble later on. Some Negroes want the same jobs you have. They want to be presidents of the nation. What is going to be the outcome? Study the race question and you will find that the program of the Universal Negro Improvement Association and the Black Star Line is the solution of the problem which confronts us, not only in this country, but throughout the world.

Folks try to misrepresent me and say I don't like white people. That is not true. Some of the best friends I have are white men. The bishop who testified here has been my friend from youth. He said other things that some of us did not understand. I asked him, Do you know Marcus Garvey?— he said yes. What is the opinion of him? He said doubtful. Now probably you didn't understand what he meant. Garvey was a public man. Opinions differ. He was a priest and he had to tell the truth. Surely some men are doubtful of Marcus Garvey, and there are some who are not doubtful. He didn't say that Garvey was doubtful. He gives it as it was, when I asked him about his personal opinion I was not allowed because it was not the proper question, the court ruled. He said, however, Garvey was a worthy man, so I trust you will not have the wrong impression.

A Heart Untainted.

Now, gentlemen, I will not touch on the other witnesses, I leave it all to you. But, gentlemen, remember this, I assure you that you are all at this time to judge a man, to judge me by the testimony, by what has been brought here, by your judgment of what is right and what is wrong. You condemn the body but not the soul. It is not in your power to condemn a soul, it is only the power of God. You can only condemn the body, but God condemns the soul. Yes, judge me and God will judge you for judging Marcus Garvey. You can believe me, it is satisfactory to Marcus Garvey because some writer says, "What greater breastplate than a heart untainted. Thrice is he armed who hath his quarrel just and he but naked—though locked up in steel whose conscience with injustice is corrupted." I stand before you and the honorable court for your judgment and I do not regret what I have done for the Universal Negro

Improvement Association; for the Negro race, because I did it from the fullness of my soul. I did it with the fear of my God, believing that I was doing the right thing. I am still firm in my belief that I served my race, people, conscience and God. I further make no apology for what I have done. I ask for no mercy. If you say I am guilty, I go to my God as I feel, a clear conscience and a clean soul, knowing I have not wronged even a child of my race or any member of my family. I love all mankind. I love Jew, Gentile, I love white and black.

I have respect for every race. I believe the Irish should be free; they should have a country. I believe the Jew should be free and the Egyptian should be free, and the Indian and the Poles. I believe also that the black man should be free. I would fight for the freedom of the Jew, the Irish, the Poles; I would fight and die for the liberation of 400,000,000 Negroes. I expect from the world for Negroes what the world expects from them.

I thank you for your patience, gentlemen, and his Honor for the patience he has exhibited also. There has been some differences, but I have great respect for this court. I respect the constitution of this great country, the most liberal constitution in the world. This great government, the most liberal in the world. Could I go to Washington without paying my homage and respect to that hero, George Washington, and Abraham Lincoln, the emancipator of our million slaves? Then, how dare anyone accuse me of being disrespectful to the United States or the courts—I feel that my rights are infringed upon. If I differed from the judge, it is but human. I know you are business men just as I am. My business has been going to pieces and I know how much yours is going to pieces, but if you were to be tried and I were a juror I would give you the same consideration as you have given me, therefore, I leave myself to you, feeling that you should judge me as your God shall judge you, not for friendship, not for satisfying the whims of someone, but because of truth and justice.

The District Attorney will tell you it is Garvey, Garvey, Garvey, Garvey is the master mind, Garvey is the genius; Garvey is but a man. Garvey is but human. But Garvey must be destroyed, but in destroying the physical in Garvey, you cannot destroy the soul and I feel you, gentlemen, will not do anything except that which is prompted by justice, truth and the law, as you know the law is but an expression of truth, of justice, and of thought. The law demands truth and justice so that justice can be done.

I leave myself to you. I have not denied anything that I know of and have done.

The trial of my case has added to my knowledge new information of the depths to which members of my race will descend to injure each other in the rivalry for place, patronage and position.

However, the masses are ever willing to appreciate and reward services rendered unselfishly to the Cause of African Redemption and an Emancipated Race.

N. B.—It was originally intended to publish in this volume the testimony of Captain Joshua Cockbourne and that of Mr. Leo Healy, government witnesses, as also the Writ of Errors and exceptions taken in the case, so that the reader could even more clearly judge the case, but the insertion of other matter prevented the inclusion.

MESSAGES SENT TO THE NEGRO PEOPLES OF THE WORLD FROM THE TOMBS PRISON, NEW YORK CITY, U. S. A.

June 19, 1923.

"I am satisfied to be a victim of an international "frame-up," a conspiracy, not only engaged in by members of the opposite race, but including selfish and jealous members of my own.

"It has taken my enemies more than ordinary effort to injure my fair name. They have tried to rob me of the precious treasure, but that cannot soil my soul and conscience.

"I am sorry that the name of the United States should be drawn into a "frame-up" and conspiracy to "get me," but the Government is not at fault. We have and must expect misrepresentations in Government, as well as in other human activities, hence I shall not entirely blame the Government for my present position.

"In the trial of the case, I have had occasion to observe the ferocious attacks and unfair methods of Assistant District Attorney Maxwell Mattuck, and his hirelings. If he were a typical representative of our Government, then I should have no hope for America, but I feel sure that we have men of honor in this Government, and this great country who will jealously guard its fair name.

"Mattuck through his agents, used the press to stir up white public opinion against me during the trial. They made a cowardly noise about the African Legion which they know to be untrue. To imagine that Mattuck would be afraid of Negroes in an overwhelming population of a well prepared race. The thing is shameful and a disgrace to white bravery. I will dismiss the evil thought for what it is worth. It shows however how scared some people are. I know I have been sacrificed by the jury to bolster up the reputation of Mattuck. I am no lawyer, but in the face of evidence and the conduct of the case, Mattuck had easily lost to the defense. His handling of the case was a mean job and low down, it lacked dignity even though he was assisted by the shrewd and able jurist, Judge Julian Mack.

"The peculiar and outstanding feature of the whole case is that I am being punished for the crime of the Jew Silverstone, who during my absence in the West Indies took $36,000 of the Black Star money, without being able to account for it, and which has caused the ruin of the company.

"I was prosecuted in this by Maxwell Mattuck, another Jew, and I am to be sentenced by Judge Julian Mack the eminent Jewish Jurist. Truly I may say "I was going down to Jericho and fell among friends.""

"The Jury remained out for eleven hours after being directed twice by a skillful Judge. After the verdict, there was not one member of the Jury who could look me in the face. I am sorry for these twelve men, for the innocence of my soul shall rest with them, and haunt their consciences through the coming years.

"My work is just begun, and as I lay down my life for the cause of my people, so do I feel that succeeding generations shall be inspired by the sacrifice that I made for the rehabilitation of our race. Christ died to make men free, I shall die to give courage and inspiration to my race."

Returning Thanks.

June 20, 1923.

To the Members and Friends of the Universal Negro Improvement Association:

I take this opportunity to return thanks to you for the splendid interest you have manifested in me during the trial of my case.

I bear with me the kindliest feelings toward you, I commend to your care and attention, my wife, who has been my helpmate and inspiration for years. She has suffered with me in the cause of service to my race, and if I have any sorrow, it is only on her account, that I cannot be alongside of her at all times to protect her from the evil designs of the enemy, but I commend her to your care and keeping and feel that you will do for her as much as you have done for me.

Her tale of woe has not been told, but in my belief that truth will triumph over wrong, I feel sure that a day will come when the whole world will know the story of her noble sacrifice for the cause that I love so much.

With very best wishes,
I have the honor to be,
Your obedient Servant,
MARCUS GARVEY
President-General
Universal Negro Improvement Association.

Interest and Sympathy.

June 25, 1923.

To the Members and Friends of the Universal Negro Improvement Association, Liberty Hall, N. Y.

"Ladies and Gentlemen:

"I have been informed by my wife of the keen interest and deep sympathy you have shown in my case and imprisonment. This, as I have always said, was to be expected.

"No one, in a day like this, can successfully lead a movement of reform like ours without making enemies and causing plotters to seek his ruin. Imprisonment or death means nothing to me in my service to our race. I am only expecting that you will hold fast to the glorious faith and work unceasingly for the triumph of our sacred cause.

"You must pray for strong men and women to grow up among you to continue leading the race as your martyrs and heroes fall. Fall they must, as they do appear, but there must be a continuous procession until the goal is reached.

"You must not mistake lip-service and noise for bravery and service. We have been so deceived for too long. True courage, bravery and real manhood cannot fail to show itself when embodied in the individual. It has no time and no place, it is ever evident.

"Men and women who will bow, cringe and hide when the cloud seems dark are those whom we should avoid in choosing leaders. True leadership looks at dreadful odds, and smiles at them for the cause that needs assistance. I say to you, cheer up. A better and brighter day is in store—that day when Ethiopia shall in truth stretch forth her hands unto God.

MARCUS GARVEY
President-General
Universal Negro Improvement Association.

Arousing Public Opinion.

July 1, 1923.

Members and Friends of the Negro Race:

I have been informed of your efforts on my behalf, that of holding a protest meeting to draw the attention of the public of our great country to the injustice that has been done me in the name of our great government.

I appreciate very highly the step you have taken to arouse public opinion. I have an abiding faith in the justice of the people, and believe that when the truth is brought home to them they will not be slow to register their protest against any and all acts of injustice.

I need not repeat that I have been "framed up" and sacrificed because of prejudice and the political and organization designs of my enemies.

I believe that when my case is properly presented to the higher and responsible officials of our government they will see that justice is done, and that they will not hesitate in upholding the sacred principles of the Constitution. America is founded upon truth, liberty and justice, and these, I feel sure, will not be denied the lowest of her citizens.

I desire that you be peaceful and loyal in your assembly and that you be mindful of the fact that I am always willing to suffer for the cause of my race. and the general uplift of humanity.

Be cheerful, be loyal, be firm, be men, is the prayer of your humble and obedient servant.

MARCUS GARVEY
President-General
Universal Negro Improvement Association.

"All Is Well."

July 7, 1923.

Fellow Members of the Universal Negro Improvement Association:

It is indeed a pleasure to me to send you a message of love and cheer at this time, when you are all anxious to learn of my condition.

What more can I say to you than that all is well? I am not peeved nor sad because of my confinement. Surely not. And I hope you are not thinking thus of me.

The road is hard and rocky, and we must make up our minds to travel the whole way. I am only a part of the journey, and the end is still afar.

Our generation is only signaling to the watchman on duty, the sentinel that guards our entry into the realm of a future that shall give to the world a nation and a flag that shall compel the respect of all men.

It is for you to keep up the fight. Be brave soldiers in the cause of African redemption, and never say die!

A group of ladies of the African Motor Corps on parade in New York City during the convention of 1925.

With abundance of good wishes, I have the honor to be, your obedient servant,

MARCUS GARVEY
President-General
Universal Negro Improvement Association

Insistence For Justice

July 16, 1923.

"To the Negro People of Liberty Hall and of the World:

"Your insistence for justice on my behalf is very much appreciated by me.

"Whether your effort is successful or not will not disturb me in the conclusion I have reached.

"Our struggle for right and justice is eternal. So long as man through conceit and selfishness arrogates to himself the authority, because he is strong, to abuse and trample upon the rights of his fellows, we will ever find cause for protest.

"The strong, through their unfair methods and practice of injustice will not always last. Their day and time will be numbered, so let us work and pray for the restoration of Ethiopia's glory, for in that time, and then only, will black men enjoy the full rights of liberty and justice.

"Keep up the spirit of service to Africa and to the race. Fight the good battle of organization to the end, and surely victory will crown our efforts.

"With deepest affection and best wishes,

"I remain,

Your obedient servant,
MARCUS GARVEY
President-General
Universal Negro Improvement Association.

Posterity Will Not Forget.

July 22, 1923.

Members and Friends of the Universal Negro Improvement Association, Liberty Hall:

Again it affords me a great deal of pleasure to salute you with a few words of comfort and cheer.

Your splendid demonstration during my imprisonment for

our cause will, I feel sure, go down in history as the sign by which we conquer.

No other people or organization could have done more than you, under the circumstances, to prove your loyalty to one of your own who was called upon to pay the price, small though it be, for the advancement of African redemption.

Posterity will not forget you, for truly the historian will dip his pen into the ink of truth and record your deeds as they stand out nobly, patriotically and loyally.

Our cause is won because of our confidence; it is lost because of our lack of faith; but by your actions we know that Ethiopia will triumph and Africa will be free.

It is a new experience to be in jail, but life is made up of variety, and I have absolutely no objection in knowing and seeing everything, so that I can, from a fullness of knowledge, better serve the cause of my race.

It is not likely that our African jails of the future will be as massive as the one in which I now have my residence, but there will be improvements I hope, for the accommodation of those who will be in for good and those who will be awaiting their "TURN OF JUSTICE."

If you can imagine what is in my mind, then you ought to be truly cheerful and happy.

With love and best wishes,

Your obedient servant,
MARCUS GARVEY
President-General
Universal Negro Improvement Association.

The Cost of Service.

July 29, 1923.

"Members and Friends of the Universal Negro Improvement Association:

"I trust you are not over-worried and disturbed over my continued confinement without bail, other than to realize that all those who make efforts to serve humanity are bound by the same law of suffering and injustice.

"I fully calculated the cost of service to my race, and know that what is being done to me is only a part of the price I must pay for daring to arouse the consciousness of four hundred million Negroes to the hope of Empire.

"But a few days ago my attention was drawn to the new slogan for Africa on the part of the Europeans 'Keep Africa for the White Man'. In this slogan lies the doom of our race. Because I attempted to combat the sinister effort with the retort of 'Africa for the Africans', I find myself where I am.

"You have enough intelligence to know that I am not here because I committed any crime against society or defrauded anyone, but because I have led the way to Africa's redemption.

"Keep your spirits high and yield nothing in the fight we are making to emancipate our race and free our Motherland.

"With God's choicest blessings, I remain your obedient servant,

MARCUS GARVEY
President-General
Universal Negro Improvement Association.

Anniversary of Convention

Aug. 1, 1923.

"Officers, Members and Friends of The Universal Negro Improvement Association, Liberty Hall, New York City.

"To-day marks the anniversary day of our annual international convention, which is being celebrated all over the world. For reasons, we do not assemble ourselves in international conclave this year, but the divisions are holding local conventions. I trust, as you gather in your local conventions, that you will be mindful of the fact that our greatest work is still ahead. The best you can do to-day is to re-dedicate yourselves to the grand and noble cause of Africa's redemption.

"Personally and physically I am prevented from being with you, but in the spirit I am one of your assembly, and your joy shall be my joy, and your sorrow shall be my sorrow.

"We shall look forward to many more anniversaries of our convention, and wait and watch until the anniversary of our REAL emancipation and Africa's redemption comes around.

"Be of good cheer and remember that I am with you always.

"I pray God's blessing on your meeting, and hope for a speedy realization of our dreams.

"With my best wishes, I have the honor to be,
Your obedient servant,
MARCUS GARVEY
President-General
Universal Negro Improvement Association.

Holding the Fort.

Aug. 2, 1923.

To the Members and Friends of the Universal Negro Improvement Association:

Gratefully do I thank you for the wonderful spirit you have shown in continuing and promulgating the work and ideals of the Universal Negro Improvement Association.

Nothing in the world affords me greater pleasure than to learn of the spiritual earnestness of those of you who pledge yourselves to "hold the fort" for our ideals until our generations rise in their consciousness to the salvation of their own souls, and the redemption of their own country.

The wait seems long, and the distance is far, but nothing worth while is achieved in a day. Have patience, be strong and firm, and as surely as the night changes into day, so also shall our condition of oppression and wrong change into liberty and justice.

Real members and co-workers of the Association as you are, make me feel that our time, energy and sacrifice are not in vain, but a meagre contribution to a noble cause that shall live when all human opposition will have crumbled and the ashes of our enemies mingled with the dust.

Time is eternal and the Everlasting Watchman, who stands at the Gate of Eternity, beckons to us; and we, in humble obedience, stretch out our hands as our "Princes rise from the dust of past ages."

Why be sad? Have you not heard the news? It is not to-day, it is not to-morrow, but God knows when, and the time shall come when Ethiopia will be free and our race redeemed.

Carry on the work of love! Hold high the banner of the red, black and green and stumble not until the Cape's silvery waters roll back the echo: "Ethiopia, thou Land of our Fathers." Carry on! Carry on! Is the wish and prayer of

Your obedient servant,
MARCUS GARVEY
President-General
Universal Negro Improvement Association.

Sending Representative to League of Nations.

August 14, 1923.

Members and Friends, Universal Negro Improvement Association:

That you have assembled to bid farewell to our delegate who is to attend the forthcoming sessions of the Assembly of the League of Nations at Geneva, Switzerland, is encouraging and befitting.

As you are aware, our work at the League is still unfinished. Last year we petitioned the League, in the name of the Negro peoples of the world, for the turning over to us of the former German-African colonies for the purpose of enabling our race to demonstrate our fitness to govern. The petition is still being considered, hence we feel it our duty to return our delegate to the League until the matter has been fully disposed of.

Our delegate will not only attend the sessions of the League, but all International Conferences in Europe as the representative of our race. He has been named and appointed the First Provisional Ambassador of the Negro peoples of the world to France, and he shall take up his residence in Paris as our representative.

Let us work and pray for the hastening of the day when "Ethiopia shall stretch forth her hands unto God" and our race be lifted from the mire of prejudice and injustice to the realm of freedom and true liberty.

With very best wishes, I have the honor to be,

Your obedient servant
MARCUS GARVEY
President-General
Universal Negro Improvement Association.

The Battle of Human Opposition"

Aug. 19, 1923.

"Members and Friends, Universal Negro Improvement Association,

"Dear Comrades:—

"More and more we become convinced of the hard and difficult task that confronts our race in the struggle upward. At every turn within and without our own group we find treachery, disloyalty and deception as to make us feel that the climb to the top of racial glory is never ending, but, withal, there is a courage manifested by you, that is bound to win out and thus save posterity and ourselves from the pit of destruction, planned by the evildoers of human society.

"To face the battle of human opposition is the duty of the courageous oppressed, and as four hundred million of us who suffer from the grinding heels of prejudice and injustice prepare ourselves the world over, the world may laugh, but surely by the character of our make-up we shall surprise them all, and lead our children into the light of freedom, that for which the noblest men of all ages have suffered.

"You need no compliment from me to further encourage you, because by your works you are known and seen. Your loyalty, courage and determination, constitute the talk of the entire world.

"People there are of little faith, who thought you would have fallen by the wayside and given up. They are now more than surprised at your boldness, yet from your courage we know that the best in us has not been made manifest.

"With our treacherous and disloyal elements ostracized, and our enemies confounded, we shall in the days ahead create a new situation out of which will come that wholesome appreciation once enjoyed and maintained by our fathers.

"You are doing well. Keep it up, and thus bestow upon our children the realization of the new born day.

"With best wishes and thanks for your efforts,
"I beg to remain
"Your obedient servant,
MARCUS GARVEY
President-General
Universal Negro Improvement Association.

Unmasking Deceptions.

August 26, 1923.

"'Members and Friends, Universal Negro Improvement Association, Liberty Hall:

"In another few days our convention month will have come to a close and another year of determined activity started for the furtherance of the work of our organization. It is for me to remind you that we have just touched the fringe of the great work that must be done for Africa's redemption .

"Steadily we are moving ahead, and I have absolutely no doubt that in a short while, if we keep up the glorious spirit, we will of ourselves observe a healthy and helpful change for the good of our cause.

"We must now prepare to unmask deception within our race. Our greatest ills to-day come not from without, but from within our own race, and caused through that blatant hypocrisy that seems to be akin to so many of the so called men, who have been our professed leaders for so long.

"Our organization, and the race, have reached the point where we need no flattery, to succeed and move ahead, but must expose the truth for its own sake.

"The school of 'intellectual deception' of which so many of our leaders are graduates, may as well close its doors, for we of the Universal Negro Improvement Association shall surely expose the hypocrisy and scheme of its leadership without mercy.   There is a great work for us to do, and I do hope that as our convention period draws to a close we will re-dedicate ourselves to duty and service to the great cause.

"With my best wishes for your success, I have the honor to be,

Your obedient servant,
MARCUS GARVEY
President-General
Universal Negro Improvement Association.

STATEMENT TO PRESS ON RELEASE ON BAIL PENDING APPEAL.

Sept. 10, 1923.

My detention in jail pending the appeal of my case has in no way affected my vision of justice. To those who are conscious of themselves there can be no incrimination from without, it must be from within. When a man's conscience convicts him then there is no appeal: Thank Goodness I am not convicted.

I am not peeved at what has been done to me; it is natural and to be expected, that in an effort like mine to serve humanity, —and black humanity at that,—that powerful enemies will be encountered. The enemies I have are chiefly of my own race. and they have worked hard and long to discredit and destroy me.

They have only succeeded however in arousing the fighting spirit of millions of black men all over the world. There is nothing to fire a people to action like injustice, and I feel sure that time will tell the good that has been done to my cause, by the injustice meted out to me within the last three months.

The experience I have had, will help me greatly in the determination and conduct of the work that is ahead of me. A large number of people only looked at and enjoyed what to them seemed the humorous side of my program. There is no more humor in it than we find in all the other serious reform movements started for the uplift of humanity. The newspapers will, however make the people laugh as a recreation, and a break in the monotony of a life of economic drudgery and social discord. If I afforded some amusement, I hope that the public will not blame me for it, for I am the direct opposite of the clown. I am serious, I have but one purpose, and that is the uplift and betterment of my race.

My detention in jail after my application for bail pending appeal, was but a reflex of the state of mind of Mr. Maxwell S. Mattuck, the Assistant District Attorney who tried my case for the Government.

I am not blaming the Government for my conviction and detention in jail. The Government cannot represent itself. If at times we meet disappointments in the representation of Government. we must reason that all men do not think and act alike. Some persons are worthy of, and dignify any position that they hold, others on the other hand, at their best are but libels to decency and propriety.

The methods that have been used to prejudice the court and the public against me, are of such as to make we shiver in fear that probably hundreds of thousands of innocent persons have lingered and died in prisons from the practise of such a system by unfair and unworthy representatives of Governments.

I shall make a fight to bring to the attention of the people and government of this great country the evil methods used to railroad me to prison, to rob me of my name, to destroy my work for the pleasure of rival organizations, and the attempt to prevent me from speaking to the great American conscience by a suppression of free speech, and a muzzling of the press.

I am glad, and feel proud, we have worthy representatives in Government to out-balance any singular attempt at misrepresentation and injustice. Our institutions and country shall live forever, so long as the people have such worthy men as representatives to whom we can always appeal from the doings and machinations of the unjust.

I love America for her laws, constitution and her higher sense of fairplay and justice. One can always find justice in America.

I have to thank my white friends and the members of my organization, as also the large number of liberal minded colored citizens who raised their voice in protest, and who helped generally in my being admitted to bail. I have to thank the Judge and all those who had to do with my being liberated.

The few unfair white persons who have acted against us were misinformed, therefore I have no blame for them. They, like the great majority, do not understand the Negro, but I hope they will now make a closer study of the tale-bearers of our race who fabricate against their own for special favors.

My imprisonment of nearly three months, has but steeled me for greater service to the people I love so much and who love me. I had no money before I was indicted. I had none when I was tried, and none when I was convicted and sentenced, because I gave all to the movement, but the people whom I served, and who know me, did not desert me. They stuck by me and paid for my defense, and subscribed for my bail. These are the people whom my enemies accuse me of defrauding. 'Tis hounded me haven't lost a penny in the ventures of our organization. They never placed a penny in it, yet they are so aggrieved. I feel sure that white America will, when properly informed, agree with us that the only solution of the **Negro** problem is to give the Negro a country of his own in Africa and for this I am working without any apologies.

I was kindly treated by the Warden and prison officials. I shall ever remember the kindly and sympathetic attitude of those worthy representatives of our Government. I am also glad to state that not one of my white fellow prisoners believed me guilty of the crime charged against me. It is amazing, but the prisoners seem to keep a tab on all that is going on in the courts. My case was well known to them, so that when I arrived at the jail, they were all surprised and disgusted at the results. They had a kind word of sympathy for me.

Some of the prisoners I met were honest enough to admit their guilt for whatever crimes they were charged, but I believe that there are others who are also innocent victims of circumstances.

Several liberal minded white friends visited me in jail, and did their best for me in the cause of justice. I am not asking for mercy or sympathy, I am asking for justice, and I have confidence in our constitution to know that it will not be denied me.

CRIME AND CRIMINALS

It should be the duty of those empowered to deal with crime to seek measures and methods to prevent commission, than to inspire and manufacture it. Most of those who are responsible for the correction of crime boast more of how many unfortunates they have convicted as a means for a reputation, than how many they have helped to go straight and lead useful and helpful lives to themselves and society. Seek more to prevent crime rather than to punish it. If the method of making criminals of 95 per cent. of those charged with crime is continued, it will be only a short time when everybody in the nation will have in him, potentially, the blood of criminals.

FIRST SPEECH AFTER RELEASE FROM TOMBS PRISON DELIVERED AT LIBERTY HALL, NEW YORK CITY, SEPTEMBER, 13, 1923.

"Ladies and Gentlemen:

"It is needless for me to say that the pleasure of meeting you in Liberty Hall, the shrine of Negro inspiration, after an enforced absence of three months, is beyond my ability to express.

"The news of the trial of the celebrated case of fraud, and my so-called conviction, have made the circuit of the world, and black humanity everywhere, even to the remotest parts of our homeland, Africa, have formed their opinion of Western twentieth century civilization and justice, as controlled and administered by the white man.

"My absence from you did not leave me despondent, nor desolate, for in the daily silence of the passing hours in my cell I thought of you, the warriors of true liberty, who were working for the consummation of our ideal——a free and redeemed Africa, and my meditations led me into greater flights of hope that shall strengthen me for the nobler work of self-sacrifice for the cause that we represent.

"The amusing part of my trial is that I was indicted along with others for conspiracy to use the United States mails to defraud in the promotion of the Black Star Line Steamship Company, yet my conviction was void of conspiracy, in that I alone was convicted, and, if I understand my conviction clearly, I was convicted for selling stock in the Black Star Line after I knew it to be insolvent. The difference between us and the trial court is that they wanted a conviction, caring not how it came about, and they had it to suit themselves, to the extent that all the others, who had more to do with the actual selling of stock than I, went free, because they were not wanted, while I received the fullest penalty that the law could impose—five years in the penitentiary, the maximum fine of one thousand dollars as provided by law, and the entire cost of the case, a condition not generally imposed but, maybe, once in twenty-five years.

"Our point of view is that we cannot defraud ourselves in the sense of promoting the Black Star Line, for the idea of a line of steamships operated by Negroes for the promotion of their industrial, commercial, fraternal and material well-being can never be insolvent or bankrupt; for, as long as the race lasts, and as long as humanity indulges in the pursuit of progress and achievements, the new Negro will be found doing his part to hold a place in the affairs of the world. It is true that we have been defrauded, but it was done, not by those of us who love our work and our race, but by disloyal and dishonest ones, whom we thought had the same feelings as we do, and by crooked white men, who were not even ashamed of hiding their crookedness. One white man said in court that he sold us a ship when he knew it was not worth the money paid for it. Another took $25,000. and an additional $11,000. to buy the Phyllis Wheatley to go to Africa, which never materialized, and which money was never returned, the reason of which supplied the legal cause for my indictmemnt. And yet it is said in the law of those who tried me that there was fraud and I should pay the penalty.

"The Black Star Line, as we all know, was but a small attempt, or experiment, of the race to fit and prepare ourselves for the bigger effort in the direction of racial self-reliance and self-determination. To say that we have failed, beause a few black and white unscrupulous persons deceived and robbed us, is to admit that the colonization scheme of America failed because a few Pilgrim Fathers died at Plymouth, and that the fight of the Allies to save the world for a new civilization failed, because the Crown Prince met with early success at Verdun. The Black Star Line was only part of an honest effort on the part of real Negroes to re-establish themselves as a worthy people among the other races and nations of the earth, and but a small contribution in the plan of a free and redeemed African nation for the Negro peoples of the world. The idea of a Black Steamship Line, therefore, can only fail when the Negro race has completely passed away, and that means eternity.

"I was convicted, not because any one was defrauded in the temporary failure of the Black Star Line brought about by others, but because I represented, even as I do now, a movement for the real emancipation of my race. I was convicted because I talked about Africa and about its redemption for Negroes. I was convicted because an atmosphere of hostility was created around me. I was convicted because wicked enemies, malicious and jealous members of my own race, misrepresented me to those in authority for the purpose of discrediting and destroying me.

"I would not blame the few white persons who contributed to my conviction, neither would I blame the Government and the illiberal of the white race who had prejudices against me. They knew no better than the information they received from treacherous, malicious and jealous Negroes who, for the sake of position and privilege, will sell their own mothers.

"I feel, however, that these white persons and the Government have now the opportunity of learning the truth, not only about my case and my conviction, but about the differences in the Negro race, that set one against the other.

Appealing the Case.

"I have no fear of the ultimate outcome of my case. I shall take it to the highest courts in the land, and from there to the bar of international public opinion, and even though I go to jail because of prejudice, I will have left behind for our generations a record of injustice that will be our guide in the future rise of Ethiopia's glory. Nevertheless, I believe that the higher courts of this country will not mingle prejudice with justice and condemn a man simply because he is black and attempts to do good for his race and his fellow men.

"Whatsoever happens, the world may know that the jail or penitentiary has no terrors for me. Guilty men are afraid of jail, but I am as much at home in jail for the cause of human rights as I am in my drawing room, the only difference being that I have not my good wife's company even as I know how glad she would have been to share my lot, but hers must be a life of sacrifice also, painful though it be. When my life is fully given for the cause, and she is left behind, I trust that you will give her the consideration that is due a faithful and devoted wife, who gave up her husband for the cause of human service. During my trial cowards tried to blemish her character, but it is an accepted truth that character is not blemished from without; it is from within, and the noblest souls that ever peopled this world were those maligned and outraged by the vile and wicked.

"Service to my race is an undying passion with me, so the greater the persecution, the greater my determination to serve.

"As leader of the Universal Negro Improvement Association, of which the Black Star Line was an auxiliary, I must state that the millions of our members in this country and abroad look to America as a national friend, and, citizens and residents as we are, we are jealous of her fair name among the other nations of the world and zealous in the effort to be to her loyal and true.

"The Universal Negro Improvement Association seeks to do for Africa similarly what the Pilgrims and, later George Washington sought to do for America. We Negroes want a government of our own in Africa, so that we can be nationally, if not industrially and commercially, removed from competition in race, a condition that will make both races better friends, with malice toward none, but respect and appreciation for each.

"Our greatest trouble, however, is with our own people. There are some in the race who are not in sympathy with an independent Negro nation. To them 'they have lost nothing in Africa.' They believe in the amalgamation of races for the production of new racial and national types; hence their doctrine of social equality and the creating of a new American race Feeling as they do, divides us into two separate and distinct schools of thought, and, apparently, we are now at war with each other, and they have gained the first victory in having me (through their misrepresentation) indicted and convicted for the purpose of rendering me *hors de combat*.

"We who believe in race purity are going to fight the issue out for the salvation of both races, and this can only be satisfactorily done when we have established for the Negro a nation of his own. We believe that the white race should protect itself against racial contamination, and the Negro should do the same. Nature intended us morally (and may I not say socially?) apart, otherwise there never would have been this difference. Our sins will not make the world better; hence, to us of the Universal Negro Improvement Association the time has come to rebuild our ancient and proud race.

"My personal suffering for the program of the Universal Negro Improvement Association is but a drop in the bucket of sacrifice. To correct the evils surrounding our racial existence is to undertake a task as pretentious and difficult as dividing the sea or uprooting the Rock of Gibraltar; but, with the grace of God, all things are possible, for in truth there is prophecy that 'Ethiopia shall stretch forth her hand, and Princes shall come out of Egypt.'

"We are expecting the co-operation and support of liberal White America in the promulgation of the ideal of race purity, and the founding of a nation for Negroes in Africa, so that those who, after proper industrial and other adjustments, desire to return to their original native homeland can do so in peace and security.

"Now that the world is readjusting itself and political changes and distributions are being made of the earth's surface, there is absolutely no reason why certain parts of Africa should not be set aside absolutely for the Negro race as our claim and heritage. If this is not done, then we may as well look forward to eternal confusion among the races.

Superstate for Negroes.

"Negro men will never always feel satisfied with being ruled, governed and dictated to by other races. As in my case, I would never feel absolutely satisfied with being tried and judged by a white judge, district attorney and jury, for it is impossible for them to correctly interpret the real feelings of my race and appreciate my effort in their behalf; hence, the prejudice from which I suffer. A white man before a black district attorney, judge and jury would feel the same way, and thus we have the great problem that can only be solved by giving the Negro a government of his own. The Black Star Line was an effort in this direction and bore a relationship to the Universal Negro Improvement Association as the Shipping Board does to the Government. My effort was not correctly understood, and that is why some people have become prejudiced toward me. Yet in the final presentation of truth the fair-minded is bound to come to the conclusion that the program of the Universal Negro Improvement Association is reasonable and proper for the solution of the vexed question of races.

THE AMERICAN NEGRO LEADER

The Value of Life

The average American Negro Leader is a fool to expect everything and give nothing in dealing with the whites, and I say American, because in the Western Hemisphere, America is the only place where Negroes have any kind of a leadership, the other groups of Negroes are leaderless. I am criticized and called a member of the K. K. K., in alliance with the Anglo-Saxon Clubs, the White America Societies, etc., but how could any reasonable person expect the white man to be such a fool, in an age so aggressive, as to give the Negro voluntarily and without resistance all he wants and asks for in America and Africa, too, with the grave problem of the future before him.

The Negro must learn first the laws of sociology, economics, then equity, reason and diplomacy. We must learn to give and take. If we want Africa, as we surely do, we must reasonably make up our minds to yield some things and make concessions in America and other white countries by sane and proper arrangements. You must not expect to grab the two birds and run off. The other fellow is not such a fool, neither is he paralized, he will bring you down with the same shot that killed the birds. Now, say, what does the Negro want? Africa, for those at home and those abroad, for it is our only hope and salvation; other than this, the race is lost, and it will only be a question of time, and the thoughtful white statesman knows it, and is working for it, and because I love my race to the point of objecting to his secret and cunning policy of destruction and extermination, he claims that I am a "Bad Nigger"' I would rather die than be good, if being good in this respect means that I must acquiesce to the extermination of my race, like the American Indian and other native peoples. Life to me is not so sweet, as to be enjoyed at the price of racial treachery and disloyalty.

FIRST MESSAGE TO THE NEGROES OF THE WORLD FROM ATLANTA PRISON.

February 10, 1925.

Fellow Men of the Negro Race, Greeting:

I am delighted to inform you, that your humble servant is as happy in suffering for you and our cause as is possible under the circumstances of being viciously outraged by a group of plotters who have connived to do their worst to humiliate you through me, in the fight for real emancipation and African Redemption.

I do trust that you have given no credence to the vicious lies of white and enemy newspapers and those who have spoken in reference to my surrender. The liars plotted in every way to make it appear that I was not willing to surrender to the court. My attorney advised me that no mandate would have been handed down for ten or fourteen days, as is the custom of the courts, and that would have given me time to keep speaking engagements I had in Detroit, Cincinnati and Cleveland. I hadn't left the city for ten hours when the liars flashed the news that I was a fugitive. That was good news to circulate all over the world to demoralize the millions of Negroes in America, Africa, Asia, the West Indies and Central America, but the idiots ought to know by now that they can't fool all the Negroes at the same time.

I do not want at this time to write anything that would make it difficult for you to meet the opposition of the enemy without my assistance. Suffice it to say that the history of the outrage shall form a splendid chapter in the history of Africa redeemed, when black men will no longer be under the heels of others, but have a civilization and country of their own.

The whole affair is a disgrace, and the whole black world knows it. We shall not forget. Our day may be fifty, a hundred or two hundred years ahead, but let us watch, work and pray, for the civilization of injustice is bound to crumble and bring destruction down upon the heads of the unjust.

The idiots thought that they could humilate me personally, but in that they are mistaken. The minutes of suffering are counted, and when God and Africa come back and measure out retribution these minutes may multiply by thousands for the sinners. Our Arab and Riffian friends will be ever vigilant, as the rest of Africa and ourselves shall be. Be assured that I planted well the seed of Negro or black nationalism which cannot be destroyed even by the foul play that has been meted out to me.

Continue to pray for me and I shall ever be true to my trust. I want you, the black peoples of the world, to know that W. E. B. DuBois and that vicious Negro-hating organization known as the Association for the Advancement of "Colored" People are the greatest enemies the black people have in the world. I have so much to do in the few minutes at my disposal that I cannot write exhaustively on this or any other matter, but be warned against these two enemies. Don't allow them to fool you with fine sounding press releases, speeches and books; they are the vipers who have planned with others the extinction of the "black" race.

My work is just begun, and when the history of my suffering is complete, then future generations of Negroes will have in their hands the guide by which they shall know the "sins" of the twentieth century. I, and I know you, too, believe in time, and we shall wait patiently for two hundred years, if need be, to face our enemies through our posterity.

You will cheer me much if you will now do even more for the organization than when I was among you. Hold up the hands of those who are carrying on. Help them to make good, so that the work may continue to spread from pole to pole.

I am also making a last minute appeal for support to the Black Cross Navigation and Trading Company. Please send in and make your loans so as to enable the directors to successfully carry on the work.

All I have I have given to you. I have sacrificed my home and my loving wife for you. I entrust her to your charge, to protect and defend her in my absence. She is the bravest little woman I know. She has suffered and sacrificed with me for you; therefore, please do not desert her at this dismal hour, when she stands alone. I have left her penniless and helpless to face the world, because I gave you all, but her courage is great, and I know she will hold up for you and me.

After my enemies are satisfied, in life or death I shall come back to you to serve even as I have served before. In life I shall be the same; in death I shall be a terror to the foes of Negro liberty. If death has power, then count on me in death to be the real Marcus Garvey I would like to be. If I may come in an earthquake, or a cyclone, or plague, or pestilence, or as God would have me, then be assured that I shall never desert you and make your enemies triumph over you. Would I not go to hell a million times for you? Would I not like Macbeth's ghost, walk the earth forever for you? Would I not lose the whole world and eternity for you? Would I not cry forever before the footstool of the Lord Omnipotent for you? Would I not die a million deaths for you? Then, why be sad? Cheer up, and be assured that if it takes a million years the sins of our enemies shall visit the millionth generation of those that hinder and oppress us.

Remember that I have sworn by you and my God to serve to the end of all time, the wreck of matter and the crash of worlds. The enemies think that I am defeated. Did the Germans defeat the French in 1870? Did Napolean really conquer Europe? If so, then I am defeated, but I tell you the world shall hear from my principles even two thousand years hence. I am willing to wait on time for my satisfaction and the retribution of my enemies. Observe my enemies and their children and posterity, and one day you shall see retribution settling around them.

If I die in Atlanta my work shall then only begin, but I shall live, in the physical or spiritual to see the day of Africa's glory. When I am dead wrap the mantle of the Red, Black and Green around me, for in the new life I shall rise with God's grace and blessing to lead the millions up the heights of triumph with the colors that you well know. Look for me in the whirlwind or the storm, look for me all around you, for, with God's grace, I shall come and bring with me countless millions of black slaves who have died in America and the West Indies and the millions in Africa to aid you in the fight for Liberty, Freedom and Life.

The civilization of today is gone drunk and crazy with its power and by such it seeks through injustice, fraud and lies to crush the unfortunate. But if I am apparently crushed by the system of influence and misdirected power, my cause shall rise again to plague the conscience of the corrupt. For this I am satisfied, and for you, I repeat, I am glad to suffer and even die. Again, I say, cheer up, for better days are ahead. I shall write the history that will inspire the millions that are coming and leave the posterity of our enemies to reckon with the hosts for the deeds of their fathers.

With God's dearest blessings, I leave you for awhile.

USING THE GOVERNMENT AND PUBLIC OPINION TO DEFEAT THE ENDS OF JUSTICE

For the public to understand the cause and nature of the opposition to me from certain quarters, I beg to submit the names of individuals and newspapers whose animi are prompted by self-interest, and the desire to escape punishment for criminal and other libels against me, suits for which have been pending in the courts of the country, and the trials of which they hope to prevent through my deportation.

Before my trial and imprisonment suits for libel were brought by me against the following persons and newspapers:

The New York Times: White capitalist paper.

The New York Call: White Socialist paper.

The New York News and George Harris: Miscegenationist Light Colored Weekly Paper.

The Crusader and Cyril Briggs: Miscegenationist Light Colored Communist Monthly Magazine.

The Emancipator and W. A. Domingo: Miscegenationist Communist Weekly Paper.

The Messenger and Chandler Owen and Asa P. Randolph: Miscegenationist Red Socialist Monthly Magazine.

The Chicago Defender and Robert S. Abbott: Miscegenationist Weekly Paper, Chicago.

The Afro-American and Murphy Bros.: Miscegenationist Weekly Paper, Baltimore.

The Pittsburg Courier and Robert Vann: Miscegenationist Weekly Paper, Pittsburg.

William Pickens, Field Secretary of the National Association for the Advancement of Colored People (Miscegenationist organization).

Robert W. Bagnall, Director of Branches of the National Association for the Advancement of Colored People (Miscegenationist organization).

APPLICATION FOR PARDON

United States Federal Prison
Atlanta, Georgia, June 5th, 1925.
The President of the United States:

Your petitioner, **Marcus Garvey,** a Federal prisoner confined in the **Federal Penitentiary** at **Atlanta, Georgia,** hereby respectfully prays your Excellency to grant him a **Pardon** for reasons herein set forth.

Petitioner states that he is a resident of **New York City, State of New York,** his correct address at the time of conviction being **133 West 129th Street, New York City;** that he is a citizen **First Paper U. S., Subject of Great Britain,** a **Negro** man. and was **35** years of age at the time the crime was committed; that he had **never** before been convicted of crime or indicted therefor, and his prior record respecting crime is as follows: **None.**

Petitioner states that he was convicted upon a plea of **Not** guilty in the U. S. **District** Court for the **Southern** district of **New York City,** at **New York,** of the crime of **Using the Mails to Defraud,** and was sentenced 21st of June, 1923, to imprisonment for **Five Years** in the **Federal Penitentiary** at **Atlanta, Georgia,** and to pay a fine of **One Thousand Dollars and Cost of Court (Cost of Court about Five Thousand Dollars);** that the case was taken on **Appeal with Writ of Errors,** to the U. S. Circuit Court of Appeals for the **Second N. Y.** Circuit, where the judgment was **Affirmed, February, 1925,** after which it was taken to the Supreme Court of the United States on **Petition for Writ of Certiorari,** where the petition was **Denied, March, 1925.**

Petitioner states that he began the service of his sentence on **8th February, 1925,** in the **Federal Prison** at **Atlanta, Georgia,** where he is now confined; that he **will be** eligible for parole **October, 1926.** His term, with the allowances for good conduct, will expire 1928.

Petitioner states that the facts in his case are as follows:

It is alleged that I mailed "on or about December 13, 1920," a certain letter to one Benny Dancy, addressed to 34 West 131st St., New York City, Borough of Manhattan, who was residing at an address in the Borough of Brooklyn, New York, with the intent to defraud. I never knew of or about Dancy at any time until I saw him in Court. I never knew such a man lived. I knew nothing of any letter mailed to Dancy. I never authorized the mailing of any such letters or letter. With the many

N. B. **The form of this page is the regulation form used by all prisoners for clemency.**

enemies, political and otherwise, operating against me, because of my views of creating in Africa a nation for the black race, and because of the many organizations of which I was head, employing several hundred persons at the headquarters in New York, such envelope if posted could have been prepared and purposely posted, to establish the case for my conviction, as subsequent happenings justify.

The only Government witness, Schuyler Cargill, who testified as to the mailing of the letters for the Black Star Line, Inc., of which I was President, was unable, on cross-examination, to properly identify himself as an employee of the Corporation during the period of years he claimed on examination to have worked with the company. His testimony under cross-examination was nothing short of perjury, when he admitted that he was "told" to say the things he did under examination, by the Prosecutor himself, Mr. Maxwell S. Mattuck, and that he was further told by Mr. Shea, one of the Post Office Inspectors who "worked up" the case, to make the statement about posting letters at the College Station—he was unable to identify the location of College Station—and yet claimed to have been in the employ of the Corporation and mailed its letters for years. College Station being the principal mailing center for Negroes in the Borough of Manhattan, yet the witness had to be "told." A review of Cargill's testimony under cross-examination would support the above statement.

Having had to conduct my own defense, because of discovered conspiracy to have me convicted of crime without proper defence, so as to discredit me in the leadership of the Negro race, and not being a lawyer, certain points of law that should have been raised in my defense at trial were unconsciously allowed to pass by, in that even the attorneys who appeared for the other defendants were made to feel by movements, signs and expressions in Court, by the Prosecutor and his aides, Amos and Davis, of the Department of Justice, that it was unwise to raise any point in my behalf. On one occasion Amos shouted to Attorney Lincoln Johnson, "So you are defending Garvey, eh!" As to suggest that any attempt to give me legal protection would be regarded with disfavor by the Government.

I learned after the trial that Cargill could have been indicted for perjury, but I received no impartial help from the learned Judge, who, on the contrary, all through the trial helped the Prosecutor, who was versed in the law, while I was only a layman. In the case of Cargill, the Court did question him to prove his falsity, but that was after he had already made manifest that he was giving false testimony and had stopped answering the cross-questions, so I had to appeal to the Court to make the witness answer.

That a Juror on several occasions during the trial had conversations with the learned Judge in Court, by approaching the bench, the conversations ending in laughter, with the Juror staring at me, etc., and during the trial a Juror was heard to say "he was going to do what the Judge tells him to." The verdict of the Jury was arrived at after a second charge by the learned Judge, who himself called for the Jury. I was not aware during the trial that this was improper conduct on the part of the Juror.

That the learned trial Judge, being a member and active supporter of an antagonistically rival Negro organization, known as The National Association for the Advancement of Colored People, was petitioned by me not to preside at the trial of the case, but he ruled to the contrary and did sit during the trial, and during the trial agents and officers of the said organization were busy promulgating sentiment against me, and immediately at the close of the Prosecutor's summation, one of the chief agents of the organization, and one who had signed on their behalf a wicked and vicious letter appeal to the Attorney General to "hurry up" my conviction and deportation, in the person of William Pickens, rushed into the Court in glee, shook the hands of the Prosecutor, Amos, and with amorous salutation grasped the hand of Davis and shook him cordially and clapped him on the shoulder.

That the chief director of this association, W. E. B. DuBois, wrote in the official organ of the society that one of its greatest achievements for the year was my conviction, and he subsequently wrote in the same organ that I was convicted for my "monkey shines" in Court.

That immediately after my conviction, on the return of the learned Judge from Europe, he was a special guest at a reception given in honor of the said W. E. B. DuBois, who had just returned from a mission, during which time he took the opportunity to do incalculable harm in Liberia and elsewhere to my plans of colonizing that country with Negroes from America as a solution of the race problem, of which plans the organizing of the Black Star Line by Negroes was contributory.

That one Amos, a colored man of the Department of Justice, who brags he can have anything done because he was bodyguard to the honored and deceased President Theodore Roose-

velt, unconstitutionally and wickedly went from home to home
and place to place among colored people—and he is still doing
so—stirring up hatred and adverse feeling against me, and inspiring individuals to so act as to bring about my conviction and
downfall. Witnesses were even promised a return of their investments if they would testify against me. On the opening
day of trial this man was heard to state to a U. S. Marshal,
stationed at the entrance of the Court door, immediately after
the Prosecutor had delivered his opening address to the Jury,
"See, I have started my fireworks." (See record of Court in this
particular.)

That before and during the trial the said Amos and one
Adolphus Domingo, a red communist arch enemy and plotter
against my liberty, who was dismissed from my employ as
editor of one of my newspapers because of his dangerous com-
munistic principles, were constantly together, plotting my downfall; Domingo being a draft evader, having renounced his application for citizenship during the pendency of the war, so as to
be in non-draftable status, and that the allegation of anonymous
letters of a damaging nature sent to the learned Judge, Prosecutor and Jury, threatening their lives, were to my belief promulgated by and the contrivance and concoction of the said
Domingo, who is an arch plotter, Amos and others, to creat unredeemable prejudice against me during the trial and to prevent
my getting justice, and the fact that these inspired reports were
"timed" and given to the press for publication during the final
days of the trial by the said Amos and Mr. Davis, which conduct was called to the attention of the Court by me without any
effective action, is further proof of the accuracy of my belief.

That on several occasions since my conviction Domingo has
published statements that he—along with one Cyril Briggs, another communist of red radicalism, who wickedly attacked and
attempted to persecute me through the same Government
agencies as Domingo, because in August of 1921 I refused to
endorse and support communism, through the appeal to a convention over which I presided, by Mrs. Rose Pastor Stokes, and
which party was represented by Briggs and Domingo among
Negroes in New York and elsewhere—was instrumental in having me convicted. (See publications of articles in "Survey
Graphic," "Boston Chronicle" and "Jamaica Gleaner.") And
that on the final decision of the Supreme Court and on my
apprehension, the said Domingo sent a telegram to the Prosecutor, Mr. Maxwell S. Mattuck, with whom he collaborated

directly and through Amos, complimenting him on "Bagging the Tiger."

That long before decisions were reached in my trial, appeal to Circuit Court and appeal to Supreme Court, Domingo, Amos and agents of the rival Negro organization and other socialist enemies, who also signed the petition to the Attorney General, working in conjunction with the Prosecutor's office, could tell by bravado what the decisions would be and just what time I would be "sent up the river," etc.

That Amos on several occasions was heard to brag of what he was "going to do to me," etc., and that the last pertinent statement of evil intent he made in this particular was to the effect that he was "going to get my neck."

That the said Amos had falsely sworn to an affidavit that I never applied for and secured my first paper of citizenship, the intent being to further prejudice and defeat the cause of justice.

That the said Amos has improperly and unconstitutionally, as a representative of the Department of Justice, busied himself in inspiring civil litigations to recover large sums of money against the organizations with which I am identified, for the purpose of causing failure and to justify prosecution in which he is interested. That he has personally attended the trial of some of these cases and has been seen coming out of chambers talking to Judges and Court attendants at the immediate trial of these cases.

That I was convicted on the third count of the second indictment, an indictment of January, 1923, yet I was prevented from introducing testimony in my behalf on the said indictment, the Court ruling that the testimony, a letter to the Shipping Board, re; the negotiation for the purchase of the ship Orion, on which $22,500.00 had been paid, and which money is still in the hands of the Shipping Board (see Mr. Philbyn), was a self-serving declaration, because it was written after the indictment. The fact is that it was written after the first indictment, but eleven months before the second indictment, on which I was convicted. The fact that I was convicted of only one of the counts of the indictment and that the learned Judge imposed the severest penalty, with the addition of the cost of the Court, not provided for as a penalty in the particular law supposed to have been violated, is respectfully submitted for consideration.

That my rivals and enemies tried to use the honorable Court and all prospective Jurors of Jewish and Catholic origin and faith in prejudice against me, by circulating before and during the trial thousands of printed circulars and letters wickedly and viciously stating that I was a member of the Ku Klux Klan and against all Jews and Catholics; hence they should send me to prison because Catholics and Jews were Judges, District Attorneys, Jurors and policemen.

That during the trial a witness for the Government, an Assistant District Attorney, Mr. Leo Healy, who was, before he became a District Attorney, attorney at one and the same time for Harris, McGill & Co., the sellers of the first ship, the S. S. Yarmouth, to the Black Star Line, Inc., for $165,000.00, and the purchasers, the Black Star Line, Inc., whose testimony showed that he confesses to the fact that he turned against me because he did not get a certain balance of money from me on the purchase, which was a gift to him by the principal of the firm of Harris, McGill & Co., after more than $135,000.00 had been paid, and after he himself on the stand admitted that when he was selling us that ship he knew it was not worth $100,000.00. (See testimony of Healy examination and cross.) He also told the Court under cross-examination that he was against me because he was told that I was a member of the Ku Klux Klan and that immediately before he testified he had just had lunch with his friend the Prosecutor, Mr. Maxwell S. Mattuck.

That any conduct of mine during the trial that might have appeared and interpreted as unseemly was prompted with no intention of disrespect for the dignity of the Court, which I hold in the highest regard, but because of the feeling of apparent persecution, which was aggravated by the many attempts of ridicule, sarcasm and unkindly reprimands and remarks from the Prosecutor and the learned Judge, who at times would prejudice my case by referring to the fact that he was not conducting a law school, when at the same time he would be most painstaking with the mistakes and efforts to deceive the Court of the Prosecutor, which all tended to place me in an unfavorable position and further create prejudice.

That the Court room all during the trial was "packed" with "canvassed enemies" and "demonstrators" by Amos, who had the directing of the entrants to the Court in charge or under his orders. He purposely refused admission to all those whom he recognized as friendly toward me, or in sympathy with me, but crowded in all those whom he recognized as of the group to demonstrate against me for the effect upon the Jury and the Court.

That the select group would pass remarks for the hearing of

the Jury on their way through the corridors with the intent of creating prejudice.

That my deportation, of which I was officially notified in less than twenty-four hours after the Supreme Court had handed down its decision, was a matter of common determination and knowledge before my trial as per the satements made by Domingo, Amos and others. The primary circumstance of the desire for my deportation is explained as follows:

That at a political meeting held in Liberty Hall, New York City, during the mayoralty campaign of the Fall of 1920, the unsuccessful Republican candidate, who subsequently became Commissioner of Immigration for the Port, who spoke there—the consent for the holding of which meeting was given by me as President of the organization that owned the hall—was not well received by a few persons who heckled him during a certain part of his speech by crying out approvingly for his opponent, Mayor John F. Hylan, who had spoken in the hall the night before, and who carried the election by a large majority, and that the defeated candidate was heard to have avowed on leaving the hall that he would "fix that fellow Garvey." In fact, I had nothing to do with the demonstration on the night he spoke, as I was not present, but spoke in support of the other candidate the night before, but never mentioned the name of the opposing candidate, but gave the hall to his organization in fairness that he should be heard and the people of themselves decide for the better man in the exercise of the franchise which was their constitutional right. His defeat at the polls reflected against the leadership of the Negro politicians of the district, and it is common knowledge, that they then and there raised the cry of "Garvey must go," which has become notorious because of my subsequent indictment, trial and conviction in New York, under the circumstances that have become historic in the effort of the Negro to assert his manhood.

It is further common knowledge that these Negro politicians and others used every effort to incriminate and discredit me, and that my deportation is but part of a scheme to deprive me of service to my race in the fostering and promoting of the idea of Negro independence of thought and leadership so admirably advocated by the late President Warren G. Harding in his speech at Birmingham, Alabama. My indictment and conviction in New York by a Republican prosecutor was a means to an end, which I feel sure will not be endorsed and supported by the great Republican Government in the name of Justice.

That I am cognizant of the fact that I do not fall under the deportable statute, yet for the purpose of satisfying my enemies who are politically powerful enough to frame, indict and convict me without ordinary hope of redress, and for showing my willingness to obey the laws as interpreted by those in authority, I have waived my rights to contest, beyond the allotting of a reasonable time for me to straighten out all of my many business affairs in the interest of my race in America, by signifying my willingness to leave the country—the land of the Pilgrims and of Liberty, the land that has been inhabited by the fathers who came here from other lands to become good, useful and helpful citizens, as I did seek to become, but as shall be determined by my contemporaries on whose shoulders it falls to administer the law and mete out Justice.

That the Prosecutor, for the purpose of creating general prejudice against me, and to further prevent me from receiving justice, influenced, along with Amos, one Ramus of several aliases, who during my trial was serving a sentence of three years for burglary at Sing Sing, New York, to falsely swear that I instructed him and supplied him with money to buy arms and ammunition from one Remington Arms Co. or a company of such similar name, and at the time of my trial this wicked and vicious news was broadcast for the purpose of irreparably injuring me and holding me up as a desperate character. The canard stated that said arms and ammunition were kept and stored at Liberty Hall and the headquarters of the organization of which I was head in New York. The day after my conviction and apprehension, Amos led a contingent of Secret Service men, marshals and policemen to the office and Liberty Hall, and discovered not even a wooden pistol or even a grain of ammunition, so much for his wicked contrivance to have me convicted; and for the myth that the man Ramus was influenced to swear to along with other wicked, malicious and manufactured statements for which he was promised clemency and protection in criminal charges against him, if he would implicate me in crime of murder, etc., to show me an undesirable character and a menace to society.

That while four of us were indicted and tried in the case of the Black Star Line, on not one occasion did the Prosecutor make any effort to convict anyone else but me; he even defended the co-defendant, Thompson, who was the active manager of the Black Star Line, Inc., and Vice-President, and his appeal to the Jury was colorfully passionate and personal, as manifest through

Office Buildings of the Black Star Line, New York City

his impassioned climax, "Gentlemen, will you let the Tiger loose?"

That my conviction was also made the means of creating reputation for the Prosecutor, who referred to the case in a newspaper report of January, 1925, as his most successful case.

That these statements of fact are not made with malice of feeling, but only with a desire to explain the truth so that the ends of Justice might not be defeated by influence, power and authority.

That the Prosecutor's briefs and motions of opposition, if closely studied, will reveal embellished statements of prejudice and exaggerations and distortions of facts on trial, as to make them fixed features of prejudice and disgust and to court an adverse judgment for me even though the issues were not pertinently fair in law.

That the attitude of unfairness and prejudice is made manifest on every motion for consideration. The learned Judge and Prosecutor opposed and denied every plea, and that where motions were made before other Judges, whispered approach to the bench or after chamber interviews prevented favorable action in my behalf, or resulted in again referring the cause to the trial Judge, making it an appeal from Caesar to Caesar. Motions for bail were denied for three months, during the sojourn of the learned Judge in Europe, necessitating my remaining in jail all during that period, pending my appeal to the Circuit Court of Appeal; bail was finally granted by a third Judge on the second appeal to him.

That up to now the learned Judge and Prosecutor have withheld on their order the cash bail bond of $15,000.00 loaned by my several friends and well wishers to see me have justice—even though they have made repeated requests for the return of this money before the Court and otherwise through their agent in whose name the said bail was posted; and that when their request was made before another Judge to order the refund of their money, the Prosecutor whispered to him and the matter was again referred to the learned trial Judge.

That the suave manner and apparent impersonal attitude of the Prosecutor when he appears before strange Judges in the case, is only superficial and done with the motive of getting favorable rulings from such Judges so as to enable him to further wreak his vengeance upon me with the concurrent authority and sanction of the Court, and at the same time make it appear that he is performing his duty and safeguarding the rights of society. A careful study and investigation of the history of the case will reveal the positive truthfulness of this statement.

That the Prosecutor takes a deep interest in and uses his powerful office to bring about financial and general embarrassment and failure to all of my efforts to do good for the Negro race, and that my last arrest, which Domingo was able to foretell with accuracy by circulated reports in the Negro neighborhood of Harlem, New York, was timed to occur at the time when the association of which I was head had proposed sailing from New York a large ship, the S. S. General Goethals, purchased and equipped at a cost of $140,000.00, and when the success of the venture depended largely upon my presence and direction.

That the money for the purchase of this ship was subscribed by the very people I was accused of defrauding and in just a couple of months, and after I was convicted of defrauding them.

That the Prosecutor uses the influence of his office to scatter adverse propaganda against me, and that a strange relationship exists between him and enemy rival Negro newspapers and their editors; chief among them "The Chicago Defender" and "Afro-American," which papers are always in a position to print and circulate before decisions are given just what my status would be.

That a peculiar relationship seems to exist between the Prosecutor, Amos and one Tussig, an attorney of the firm of Avery, Tussig & Fisk of New York, who prosecutes fictitious and other civil cases against all the organizations with which I am identified, to collect large judgments of alleged salary and other claims of enemy ex-employees and officers, and that influence and power have operated against said association receiving fair consideration before the Courts, and that these judgments, that aggregate over $60,000.00, were secured with the purpose of inflicting injury upon the organizations causing their failure and further holding me up as a fraud, and that the plaintiffs in these actions never received the full amounts of these judgments, but only a minor part, the other portions being paid for legal expenses.

That the said Tussig has been seen on many occasions coming from the office of the Prosecutor. That I am ready, with the proper facility afforded me, to supply the facts and data supporting these statements of mitigating and other circumstances, surrounding, conducive and pertinent to my trial, conviction and subsequent imprisonment.

That the testimony of Benny Dancy, on whose count I was convicted, was insufficient to warrant conviction, and that I was convicted on the allegation that I posted an empty envelope. Dancy's testimony reveals the fact that he was approached, that he was asked to surrender his mail and was brought into Court, not on his complaint, but on the engineered and manufactured indictment to incriminate me.

That the Post Office Inspector, Mr. Williamson, was heard to remark that "they (meaning the Prosecution) could not get Negroes to testify against me," hence the Wholesale release by the Prosecution of several thousand questionnaires all over the United States, addressed to the stockholders of the Black Star Line, Inc., after the books of the company had been seized, asking them to send in to the Post Office authorities all letters received from the Black Star Line, Inc., and from me, and canvassing their opinion if they were satisfied with their investment, and these queries were made after I had been arrested, and the news published in every paper throughout the United States.

That Dancy's testimony was of the nature that made it doubtful, and I was therefore entitled to the benefit of the doubt.

That the opinion of the learned Judges Charles M. Hough, Henry Wade Rogers and Learned Hand stating the following is to my favor, and in view of the fact that I was convicted on the Dancy count, should have been given the benefit of any misunderstanding through the alleged ignorance of Dancy. The opinion of the Judges:

"The only matter here not proven by direct evidence is that some particular circular or letter was enclosed in the envelope produced by Dancy, a man evidently both emotional and ignorant, whose caliber may be judged by the following excerpts from the cross-examination conducted by Garvey pro se."

That the opinion of the learned Judges of the Circuit Court of Appeals was prejudiced and not based upon the facts of the entire record. The opinion stated that the record "shows at great length efforts on the part of Garvey to constitute himself leader of the colored race of the world, and he called himself Provisional President of Africa, his purpose being to promote solidarity among the Negroes and through several organizations of his begetting quite different to the Black Star Line." The record shows that the positions I held were all by popular election and not self-appointed. I was elected by thousands of delegates at a regularly and properly called convention of the Negro race as President General of the Universal Negro Improvement Association, and subsequently as Provisional President of Africa. Nowhere in the record does it show that I personally assumed such leadership or title. If it is a crime for me to accept office after election, then I am not singular in the committing of such crime, as millions of persons all over the world, in democratic countries, hold offices and titles by election.

That it is no crime for one to make an honest effort to promote his own ideas, otherwise Mohammed, Luther, Peter, St. Augustine, Washington, Lincoln, O'Connell, Emmett, Voltaire, Tolstoy, Gandhi, Mrs. Pankhurst and others were criminals for promulgating their ideas and winning converts to the same.

That the following statement of the learned Judges of the Court of Appeals show an unreasonable prejudice toward me in their opinion: "It may be true that Garvey fancied himself a Moses, if not a Messiah." There is no evidence in the record to show that I at any time ever asserted the belief of being a Messiah; the records will show, to the contrary, that I have always been a Christian and was confirmed by the Catholic Bishop who testified in my behalf.

That the reference to my being a Moses is based upon colorful and prejudiced newspaper exaggeration, and the undercurrent of whispered and propagated enemy movements.

That I was convicted in an atmosphere of "prepared prejudice," skillfully arranged by whisperings, undercurrents, secret approaches, harmfully "timed" newspaper reports, suggestions of delaying the Jury and Court, who without my knowledge or consent had been promised a hurried trial of but a couple weeks, allowing the prosecution the major time, and to facilitate the learned Judge going immediately on his vacation to Europe, and to accommodate the gentlemen of the Jury going on vacation and back to their businesses—the trial lasting five weeks in a case as important, for the cause of justice, as other cases of a similar nature that have taken six weeks, two and three months to be tried.

That the learned Judge was so "pleased" with the verdict that, viewed through a physiognomical and psychological study, he was moved to excuse the Jury from any further jury service for a long number of years. That a physiognomical and psychological study of the entire proceedings revealed the greatest travesty upon American justice and a direct drive at the fundamentals of the Constitution of this country, the practice of which Constitution and for whose protection the noble fathers of the Republic have bled and died.

That the conviction was an effort to revenge a hated adversary of a rival organization and other enemies, and that the Court erred in allowing itself to be so used, consciously or unconsciously.

That because of my universal appeal to the Negroes, as the elected leader of the masses, for uniting them to found and develop a nation for the race in Africa—the land of our forefathers, from which they were stolen centuries ago and brought here, and into these climes, as slaves, for us to become their descendants—the nations and individuals interested in the selfish domination and exploitation of the continent have used their influence to incriminate me so as to hold me up to the attention of said African peoples as a criminal and thus deprive me of the force of honest and responsible leadership, and because I have sought to repatriate large numbers of Negroes from America to Liberia, West Africa (a country founded by the American Colonization Society years ago), as a solution of the race problem in America, I have been plotted against by said nations and individuals.

I have been undermined and misrepresented to the Government as a dangerous person by a group of "colored men" who neither want to be black nor Negroes, and a combination of these agencies, with the powerful influences behind them, brought about the circumstances of my indictment, trial, conviction and imprisonment.

That for the purpose of undermining, embarrassing, humiliating and adding to the scheme of persecution, a divorced wife, one Amy Ashwood, who sometimes uses the name of Amy Ashwood Garvey, an alien, was brought back into this country without proper immigration procedure and that she was allowed to land from Ellis Island without complying with the statutes, and that the said Negro newspapers with which the Prosecutor is friendly associated have featured pronouncements of this woman, one of which is that she knows the "papers" are "ready" and have been signed for my deportation even though I am still at the Atlanta Prison.

That only a thorough, painstaking and impartial investigation of the Department of Justice or by a Congressional or Senatorial Committee or Grand Jury can fathom the positive truthfulness of each and all of these statements of mitigating circumstances, facts and errors that I have most respectfully stated, and for such investigation and all other relief I do pray.

That the late President Harding had been petitioned for the consideration of an investigation, but as he was about to act he was removed by the untimely hand of death.

That the very rivals and enemies mentioned and referred to were instrumental in influencing the Government in 1921, while I was on a business trip to the West Indies and Central America, to deny me the vise of my passport to return to the country in the thirty days that I had planned and announced publicly, and that I was kept out against my will for five months, during which time it was that the said enemies and rivals and others made the premier effort and did their best to bring about the embarrassment of the Black Star Line, Inc., in its immediate effort to secure a particular ship for going to Africa, and that they so used propaganda as to defeat every effort that would lead to the successful accomplishment of the undertaking. It was only on a final appeal to the head of the Department of Labor, the Secretary of State, Mr. Hughes, and President Harding, by cables, telegrams, etc., that I was allowed to re-enter the country.

That I am the largest stockholder in the Black Star Line, and did subscribe my money at all and every time, when other Negroes were asked to do so for the good of the cause of African development, and that it is illogical to believe that I would have committed a fraud against myself, even though an unsympathetic white Prosecutor and Jury may have thought so. The record shows that I had no financial advantage to gain; because at the time I was indicted and convicted I was not receiving any salary from the corporation, but my time was given "free, gratis and for nothing," with the one desire of honestly helping my race. The salary I received during the short period that I accepted it was less than five thousand dollars, while other officers were paid continuously and consistently, and they were in no way censured by the Court.

That the assets of the company would have been generally intact but for the espionage, plots, disloyalty and corruption practised against the corporation and my efforts to help my race by "inspired" employees who were egged on by enemies, rivals and influential power and authority to so act as to bring about the failure of the enterprises and my downfall.

That the Prosecutor unreasonably and unfairly at the trial and in briefs stressed, that at the time of trial the assets of the corporation were nil, and that the ships were no good, when in fact $22,500.00 was then, and is still, on deposit with the United State Shipping Board, as the record will show.

That the boat "Shadyside," for which $35,000.00 was paid and which he referred to as being a wreck, was covered by insurance and at the time of the trial a civil suit for the recovery was pending, and that since the trial judgment has been returned in favor of the Corporation.

That the ship "Yarmouth," on which the company could have realized a substantial amount of money, was allowed to be disposed of by connivance without my knowledge or consent, and the third vessel of the corporation was made a wreck by the connivance and plot of my enemies and rivals, a condition over which I had no control, and was almost powerless to prevent in the face of the strong influence used against me in the West Indies by those in authority, who should have aided me when I sought to protect the interests of the corporation. I was not recognized as President of the corporation by the American Consul in Jamaica, who obstructed me at every turn, and at which place the ship was at anchor and where he gave the captain and crew the fullest latitude to work evil and harm against the corporation and against me. The said captain was used by the Government as one of its principal witnesses against me, and I was denied the right in Court to prove that the man never had a captain's license at the time when he undertook to master the boat.

That although refused recognition as President of the Corporation during the period above referred to, I was indicted, tried and convicted for alleged crime committed during said period.

That before my trial and before the disposition of my case, one Mr. Crimm, of New York politics, and of the Department of Justice of Washington, was heard to state in words most hateful and uncomplimentary that they are going to lock me away in Atlanta for five years or some such period, the exact language of which I am unable to recall just at this time.

That it is common knowledge as by the propagation of Amos, Domingo and others, that I was indicted on an income tax charge, which is now pending, so that if I was not convicted on the mail fraud I could be convicted on the latter, and if that failed, on a "framed up" charge of white slavery or some other charge that would carry with it the order of deportation.

That I was indicted on the income tax charge for not paying enough tax on an imaginary income of salary in excess of what I really earned and received and for a period when I was forcibly kept out of this country and forced to live in foreign ports; the data that supplied the imaginary cause for indictment were taken from multitudinous books and checks of the Black Star Line and Universal Negro Improvement Association, seized at the time of my arrest on the mail fraud charge, without an explanation, and that the major number of checks charged by the Prosecutor to me were for expenses of the corporations, etc.

That I was arrested a second time on the one and same charge and just at a time when I was presiding over the International Convention of Negro Peoples of the World at New York and receiving favorable press notice, and it was stated by Amos and Domingo in bravado that it was done by the Prosecutor at that particular time with the intent of further discrediting me before the Convention and to break up the Assembly during my absence; and at the time the said Prosecutor made a big display of the pending arrest by statements to the press for effect.

That the persons and organizations that signed the letter to the Attorney General asking for my speedy prosecution, and other enemies who busied themselves in my prosecution and aided and abetted the Prosecutor, were persons and newspapers against whom were pending in the Courts civil and criminal suits and charges for libeling and injuring me, and that they resorted by combination to have me prosecuted and subsequently deported as the means of getting rid of me and preventing the ends of justice being reached.

That the chief enemies and rivals among the Negro race are actuated in hatred and opposition to me by jealousy and prejudice because I was not born in America, but a British subject, and, in my brief sojourn here, I was able to snatch from them the real leadership of the Negro masses of the country by organizing several million Negroes into several hundred branches of the Universal Negro Improvement Association all over the United States as well as in foreign lands where Negroes reside.

That the people had lost confidence in such leaders who had dickered with their interests for fully sixty years without giving them a program of hope.

That I am not responsible, neither is any other Negro, for the accident of birth in the Western World, for we are all relics of slavery, an institution that was forced upon our fathers and made justified in the name of Christianity, without the right or chance to state whereat their progeny shall be born.

S. S. Shadyside, River Boat of the Black Star Line, Purchased for $35,000

That with the endless network of espionage, plot, "inspired disloyalty of employees," prejudice and sabotage it was impossible for me to escape the traps for prosecution, conviction as a criminal and deportation.

That the fact that millions of Negroes still believe in and follow me is proof that those interested in my work and on whose account I was supposed to be indicted, convicted and imprisoned, do not believe that I have defrauded them and have more confidence in me than the Prosecutor and those allied with him to injure me. The Prosecutor's reference to such a large number of people as being ignorant is a gross reflection against the race, and an illogical assumption, for in experience, if the world has found it so hard to lead intelligence, how much more difficult would it not be to lead large numbers of ignorant people, and to have those people believe in a single leadership, when around him is organized all the power and authority of destruction to discredit him, and court failure for all his efforts in which the said people have invested their money and with the individual arrested by the law, convicted and imprisoned?

That after I secured my first paper for naturalization and the information became known, my political enemies hurried up and forced my indictment so as to prevent me from acquiring the full rights of citizenship to further lend force to my leadership, which they feared for selfish personal reasons, and that my trial and conviction was made returnable just immediately prior to the time when I would have become eligible for the full rights of citizenship.

That the Prosecutor during and after the trial threatened to suppress the newspapers of my connection, "The Daily Negro Times" and the "Weekly Negro World," and frightened and scared the editors so as to prevent their reporting his conduct during the trial for public information, and that he actually seized without further process of law and retained the subscribers mailing list of the "Negro World," and that immediately after the trial subscribers started to receive copies of enemy Negro newspapers with which the Prosecutor is on friendly terms and relationship. That Amos has threatened on each and every occasion of my many appeals for justice that if I were to receive favorable decisions from either of the Courts, that he would have me indicted on other charges, and that his last statement in this direction is that if the President should **pardon** me, he would again have me indicted and convicted.

That the Prosecutor has used undue ex-parte chamber approaches and influence on Judges to create prejudice against me and influence actions and decisions.

That it is my firm belief that Amos is either under the influence or pay of the rival organization, "The National Association for the Advancement of Colored People," of which he is a member, or its officers or its agents, for the purpose of using his connection with the Department of Justice to hound and ruin me by persecution.

That for the purpose of humiliating me and gloating over my condition and predicament, Amos has unwarrantedly, improperly and unnecessarily busied himself in being vindictively and maliciously active at my arrests, by posing and demonstrating grimaces, actions, demeanor, passing remarks and staring me in the face with bravado and glee, and that on the very last occasion of my being arrested and dragged off a Pullman train at 125th St. Station in New York City, on my way in from Detroit by the first train to surrender to the office of the Prosecutor (and even by the arrangement between my attorney and the Prosecutor), and on the act of assisting my wife off the train, being on the train's alighting platform, was crudely and viciously pounced upon under the direction of Amos, handcuffed and marched off with a large number of armed guards, and that the said Amos subsequently accompanied the lone Marshal who finally took me to the Tombs Prison that night, and that the following morning the New York newspapers carried glaring news that I was arrested by the said colored man Amos of the Department of Justice, described as once being the bodyguard of the late President Theodore Roosevelt. That all this demonstration was staged even though this man and the Prosecutor knew I was on my way from Detroit to surrender, in that they had such official information, that on arrival at Albany or some nearby station, the train was boarded by two secret service men, who fully recognized and spoke to me, and they did inform the Prosecutor's office that I was on that particular train bound for New York City with Grand Central connections.

That they, the Prosecutor and Amos, knew that I was in Detroit on business and available (and my presence in Detroit was most public and well known, in that I was advertised all over the city to speak there, and I did speak) and that I am cognizant that my presence there was known to the Department of Justice, in that I recognized several agents whom I knew were observing me. They had several groups of armed men haunting the colored neighborhood of Harlem and watching and parading before the places of my residence, business and Liberty Hall and the offices of my lawyers, etc., to create undue and unnecessary excitement and to show off the importance of the said Amos and the vested power of the Prosecutor in the name of the United States and its people.

That Amos had been heard to state that the greatest pleasure of his life would have been to be granted the privilege of taking me to the Atlanta Penitentiary.

That it is my belief that the Prosecutor objected to and refused the immediate release and return of the cash bond to facilitate one of his informants and collaborators, one Lexington Woodley, represented at bar by Tussig, to attach the said account and collect therefrom, in anticipation of a judgment in his favor, for an imaginary salary claimed against the committee that sponsored my defense and in whose names the cash bond money was borrowed from my friends and sympathizers, but that the judgment so anticipated did not materialize, as an unfavorable decision was given by the Court of the City of New York against the said Woodley, thereby preventing the said attachment, and that the Prosecutor willfully directed the non-return of the said bond, so as to establish doubt in the minds of the lenders about the honesty of intention on my part to see that their money was refunded, so as to divorce from me their further friendship and sympathy, and at the same time to hold the amount as a bait to the aforesaid Tussig, who may manufacture causes whereby the said amount should be attached for judgments against the Universal Negro Improvement Association.

That the Prosecutor had the argument of motion for the release of the cash bond referred from Mr. Justice Hand to the learned trial Judge, so as to give him easier influence over the Court.

That it is my belief that the request of the Prosecutor and learned trial Judge for supplying them with the names and addresses of the lenders of the money of the cash bond was done for the purpose of conducting propaganda among said persons inimical to my interest and with the further intent to do harm and injury to my good name, directly or through collaborators or agents.

That the learned Judge and Prosecutor being of the same race and religion, and in view of the fact that my enemies maliciously impressed them that I hated and was opposed to Jews because of my alleged membership in or connection with the Ku Klux Klan, were prejudiced and that my persecution before and by them was the result of such set prejudice.

That the Prosecutor did summon to New York from Atlanta, Ga., for questioning about me Mr. Edward Young Clark, acting Imperial Wizard of the Ku Klux Klan, who himself at that time was under federal indictment, and that such a conference and such questionings about me and my alleged membership in and relationship to the Klan were irrelevant to my prosecution for using the mails to defraud, and could have had no other intent and result than to increase the prejudice of the Jewish prosecutor against me, and that it is reasonable to infer that the learned Judge also shared a similar prejudice, and that their attitude toward me during the trial and after was actuated by such prejudice.

The fact that I was accused in Court by the wild, evasive, frivolous and irresponsible testimony of the Government witness, Leo Healy, of being a member of the Ku Klux Klan, and at the same time wickedly and maliciously stating for effect on the jury that I did not want any American citizens as officers of the corporation of the Black Star Line, but Liberians, a statement proved false by the fact that the majority of Directors, Officers and Associates were American citizens, and that the said Healy had admitted that he had had special luncheon with the Prosecutor (who used every subterfuge and artifice to create prejudice against me for conviction) before testifying, and the fact that several Jewish gentlemen were members of the Jury, created a prejudice against me that it was hard to overcome, and that said prejudice militated against my receiving justice in the trial Court.

That in the year of 1921, I did, by appointment, visit the headquarters of the Ku Klux Klan at Atlanta, Ga., and conversed for about two hours with Mr. Edward Young Clark, then acting Imperial Wizard of the Klan, at which time there was present another person representing the Klan, as also my private secretary. My reason for the visit and interview was to authoritatively and correctly find out the corporate and objective attitude of the newly organized Klan toward the members of my race. Being the head and leader of a large Negro organization that embraced millions of members scattered all over the country and the world, it was my duty to find out and be thoroughly and competently informed and to advise my race about all and every movement, society or organizations that may tend to impede or jeopardize their interest, and in view of the fact that I was being goaded by sections of the irresponsible, venal Negro press and hot-headed and unthinking Negro agitators and professionally agitating Negro organizations to call upon Negroes to attack the Klan in the wave of attacks that was then levied at them, which I refused to do, because of a desire to prevent further hard feelings between the races, riots and civil strife, and because I had no positive proof except exaggerated newspaper reports that the Ku Klux Klan had any other desire than to preserve their race from suicide through miscegenation and to keep it pure, which to me is not a crime but a commendable desire and did not supply the reason why Negroes should attack them, and because I believed in the purity, honor, pride and integrity of each and every race. Other than this I had no motive in visiting and conversing with the officers of the Klan.

That I am not concerned about, and it is no business of mine, what attitude the Klan adopts toward any other group, as I firmly believe that other groups are better organized and better able to take care of themselves than the Negro, and if there were anything unseemly about the Klan, it was the duty of the Government and not individuals and organizations to incite to bad feeling and riot. I do not see why I should be penalized for using my efforts and better judgment in preventing friction and clashes between the races that would tend to disturb the peace of the community and disgrace our democracy, and that it is unfair and un-American for the Prosecutor to use this as a further prejudice against me, and it is on this account, and because I have not led vicious attacks upon the Ku Klux Klan as a leader of large numbers of Negroes, why I am accused of being a member of the organization.

That a powerful banana and citrus fruit trust engaged in tropical trade, with a large fleet of ships (and on whose plantations in whose services large numbers of Negroes are employed who were stockholders in and supporters of the Black Star Line, with the hope of turning their labor and produce to assisting the corporation to develop so as to further help the cause of African redemption, and to which trust it is believed the President of the rival Negro organization, The National Association for the Advancement of Colored People, is attached as an attorney or stockholder), contributed by its power and influence to bring about my indictment, trial, conviction and imprisonment.

That the woman Amy Ashwood, who sometimes uses the cognomen Amy Ashwood Garvey, and at times that of Mrs. Marcus Garvey, of tender and questionable virtue, who was improperly admitted into this country recently, and who is a colaborator of the Prosecutor in recent movements against me, has been heard to boast of the power behind her to do harm and injury to my reputation and person, without prosecution, and that on the morning, at the very same hour I was being rushed from the Tombs Prison in New York City to the Pennsylvania Station to be taken to Atlanta, with my wife attending at the Tombs with the hope of seeing me and accompanying me on the said train if she could find out the time of departure, as it was proclaimed and announced by the Prosecutor that he would rush me to prison, the said Amy Ashwood, with precision and composure, was attempting to remove and wreck from my home address the furniture and household effects, and that it is my belief that the Prosecutor, directly or through Amos or Domingo, advised and inspired her to do so. That an investigation into the movements, mode of living and associates of this woman would prove the truthfulness of the statements.

Not one in a thousand of the Negro persons who placed their money in the Black Star Line had made complaints. The principal persons who originally complained against me were my rivals, enemies and persons who are afraid of my influence of leadership among the Negro people, and that those who testified against me were people canvassed by questionnaires and agents. The persons who were supposed to have been defrauded were in fact not defrauded; they have not yet actually received money's worth for their investment, but they understood that because of the tremendous difficulties that confronted the operation of a steamship line patronized only by Negroes the risk would be unusually great, and they were willing to take the risk to promote the future good and well being of the principal hope of an African nationality. The people who invested their money understood the risk of this venture as truly as myself or anyone associated with me.

That provisions have been made to in the future redeem with interest the stock held by the investors and that my prolonged stay in prison tends to defeat the hope and possibility of so doing. The difficulties that were actually encountered were beyond the possibilities of foresight, although it was expected that it would be difficult to launch and to make immediately successful, from a financial point of view, a steamship line managed by and patronized only by Negroes; the difficulties encountered far exceeded expectations. This was due to the fact that the persons with whom we had to deal, the persons from whom we purchased the ships, the firms that made repairs and sold supplies only saw an opportunity to defraud the enterprise, even as the testimony of District Attorney Leo Healy, who at the time was connected with Harris, McGill & Company, so amply proved. I personally did not profit by the transactions of the corporation and there was not a single dollar that I received that was not fully known to all who were associated with me, and properly accounted for.

That I, personally, never handled the funds of the corporation, but that was always done by secretaries and treasurers accordingly. This takes this case in a most signal way out of the category and class of the past cases, which have been ordinarily condemned as fraud. It is a complete demonstration of the fact that I was honest and sincere in my actions and motives, however visionary the Court might have imagined the enterprise, but viewed from the standpoint of the larger aims and purposes, the enterprise in the Black Star Line cannot be regarded as visionary. The Black Star Line was merely an incident, whose failure or success as a commercial venture would have little to do with the genuineness and aspirations of the larger movement, to which it contributed and in which all the stockholders were interested. There can be no possible question that the practical solution of the Negro problem as advocated by me would be universally approved. To those who make no effort to solve this question and to those whose minds are only trained to see crime and to profit by the imprisonment of criminals, and those they believe to be criminals, the success along the lines proposed by me seem unattainable. I was and am unwilling to rest in a mere hopeless despair and, knowing what was the right solution, joined in with other Negroes by organization, education and repeated efforts to make as far towards success as possible. It is not surprising that certain of the initial efforts may have suffered of their purpose. No movement of any magnitude has ever succeeded at the first bound.

The Black Star Line was but one of the efforts toward carrying out a general plan that was joined in and endorsed by all the stockholders. As a commercial venture it may have suffered, but the end is not yet reached, and therefore it is not fair to assume permanent failure. As a demonstration to the Negro people that it was possible to attempt and to carry out an organized, concerted plan to overcome certain of their difficulties, it was unquestionably a success, as an investigation among business activities of the Negro race will show, that since the promotion of the Black Star Line and its earlier successes, thousands of new enterprises among Negroes sprang up all over the country and the world, tending to the economic and industrial development of the race, and the proof of this is further evidenced that even now the same organization is attempting success along the same line and has purchased the S. S. General G. W. Goethals from the Panama Railroad Company, a subsidiary of the Government, the success of which the Prosecutor is trying to defeat, and which ship was named after the genius who constructed the Panama Canal with the aid and assistance of Negro labor and skill.   My ultimate hope was to see organized the Negro people into a concerted effort to remedy their condition and to solve their problems.

Experience in such organizations has a great value apart from the mere value of dollars and cents, and from this point of view as well as from others, the Black Star Line was not a failure.   Mere failure commercially to make a success is not evidence of fraud.   The movement to secure the freedom of Ireland, to establish a homeland in Palestine, to mention only recent instances, are not to be condemned because they have met with failure.   The dominant question should be as a test of honesty and sincerity, how much of the large amount subscribed for stock did I receive for salary, at what time did I receive a salary for services?   Did I not accept only a small salary and for only a short period of time, and was I not the largest stockholder in the corporation?   Is it not a fact that the people with whom I dealt and whose money was invested in the Black Star Line still have faith and believe in me and have of themselves subscribed for my defense and protection?   Who can possibly suggest a better test of the honesty and sincerity of one, than to appeal to the people whose money was invested in the Black Star Line, for they are in the best possible situation to understand and sympathize with the plan, and to realize that the Black Star Line was only a part of a program, that the feature of financial profits was unimportant?

The enterprise was at best handicapped, due to the obstacles that the unreasonable, unthinking and prejudiced of the white race would naturally place in the way of the operation of such a steamship line and to the advantages that would be taken of those of the race of frail character and manhood who had to represent the company before skillful and experienced white men who prey upon the unwary and unsuspicious.   By the support and approval of me, by the people, they demonstrated that they were not victims, that they were not defrauded, but were themselves active and willing participants in a plan which had for its object the good of the race and the good of country,

S. S. General G. W. Goethals of the Black Cross Navigation and Trading Co. re-christened S. S. Booker T. Washington, purchased from the Panama Railroad Co. in 1924 for $100,000, equipped at a cost of over $60,000, to convey colonists to Liberia.

then, notwithstanding the verdict of the jury, it is impossible to charge me as engaged in a scheme to defraud.

Unfortunately the trial of the case proceeded solely and entirely upon the line of a commercial fraud as was the wont of the prosecutor. The jury were not permitted to take into account the larger aspects of the plan, and to give me such credit as I was entitled to for sincerity and honesty in carrying out the larger plan. The case was tried exactly as would be a bucket shop case or a fraudulent mining or oil stock case as was the wont of the Prosecutor to impress the jury. The things that were entitled to most account, were permitted no consideration whatsoever.

That the effort of the friendly Negro newspapers to the Prosecutor (but my venal rivals and enemies who were not stockholders or honestly interested in the program I represented), to stir up hatred among stockholders and members of the organization of which I was head, to make them dissatisfied, was with the purpose of justifying the conviction by an imaginary wave of public feeling against me, that would act as further argument against me for consideration before higher tribunals of justice and to bolster up their fictitious profession of leadership, a leadership that has no proof in fact, but only assumed because of the promoters' ability to publish such papers which are generally short lived and universally media of graft and unprincipled policies.

That the Prosecutor designedly and skillfully deferred, postponed and set back on several occasions, the trial of my case before other disinterested Judges, so as to insure having the learned trial Judge, member and supporter of the rival enemy Negro organization, hear the case.

Very respectfully,

MARCUS GARVEY.

P. S.—I am cognizant of the fact that the learned trial Judge and Prosecutor must pass favorably on my application for the formal and routine consideration asked for, but knowing the feeling of the honorable gentlemen toward me, not made manifest on the surface with their dealing with other officials of authority, but suffered by their acts of absolute authority, prompts me to seriously bring the matter most respectfully to your attention for consideration and any such relief as may not continue to leave and expose me to the mercies of these gentlemen and their powerful influence. The statements I have made regarding these gentlemen and the requests are made purely on facts and absolutely on no desire to insult or to be rude in referring to the honorable gentlemen. That I have absolutely no feeling against them and that my only desire is to secure equity and to assist in upholding the American tradition of freedom and justice, that for such Patrick Henry and others declared in the formation of this great nation.

Since the declaration of these facts and mitigating causes, I have been reliably informed that the cash bail above referred to was refunded on Monday, 8th June, four months after my imprisonment and four months and three days after my surrender and in spite of the heretofore related repeated requests.

MARCUS GARVEY.

Petitioner respectfully prays that he be granted a Pardon for the following reasons:

Because I am not guilty, and one can only be truly convicted by his own conscience and Christian soul.

Because I have been "framed up" for the indictment and conviction.

Because I have been convicted on prejudice.

Because my constitutional rights were sought to be abridged in preventing me from enjoying the benefits of citizenship, so as to lend force to my work of leading the American Negro in the quest of homeland in Africa in common with other Negroes with whom they are related by ties of blood and common history of suffering.

Because the conviction on the record has no foundation in law. Because the case has been hastily reviewed by the Circuit Court of Appeals and an exceedingly hasty opinion given, not in keeping with the facts of law and evidence established by a careful examination of the record, and that the said opinion breathes prejudice of a preconceived nature.

Because there was no reliable and honestly disinterested or interested evidence to justify the conviction in law.

Because the Honorable Courts erred in not reviewing the case on law, Constitutional rights and facts, but on skillfully arranged statements of prejudice and insinuations, not borne out by the facts on record.

Because it is my belief that the President who represents the highest spirit and sense of American justice, as the Chief Executive of the Nation, will give such careful and impartial consideration to the plea for justice in America's name, as not to allow the sacred traditions of the nation for justice and liberty to be violated, by even the greatest influence; that justice may be given

to one who is consciously innocent of the committal of crime
and whose desire always has been that of being obedient to the
laws of the country and respectful of the rights of society.

Because it is my belief that the President will, by clemency,
remedy a wrong inflicted upon one because of his color and
place of birth and effort to help his race in the desire for freedom and liberty in their ancestral home, a land originally theirs,
and in keeping with the splendid efforts and example of Washington, Jefferson and Lincoln.

Because the act of Pardon will tend to convince millions that
a Black man aspiring for the highest and best for his race can
get justice under a Republican form of Government presided over
by a Republican President.

Because the millions of blacks in America affiliated with the
organizations of which I am the elected head, and the millions
of like affiliations in Central America, South America, the West
Indies, Africa, Europe and Asia, may have no other feeling nor
desire than to continue to support the professions of established
Christian appeal and Government and to feel that justice is not
only for white men and a privileged class, but for one and all,
irrespective of race or creed.

To prevent enemies of established order making capital out of
the act of injustice, persecution and prejudice to inflame in the
future, and at the time of need, the minds of millions of blacks
throughout the world, against "bureaucracy, oligarchy, imperialism and capitalism," which may have a strong appeal, in the
light of history, for the unfortunate and oppressed whom I am
endeavoring to lead by a peaceful and friendly agitation for the
reasonable return of their African heritage.   To uphold the
sacred principles of American Justice for which the noble fathers
of the Republic have bled and died.   To uphold the undying
and sacred words and declarations of Lincoln.   That this nation
armed with the grand and marvelous achievements for human
liberty and justice in the last couple centuries will not allow
itself to be inveigled into doing a grave wrong to one whose only
crime is an honest effort to liberate his race by the creation of
a new nationalism, and because of his attempt to lead the members of his oppressed race in this direction.

That the Declaration of Independence may not be regarded in
the future, by Negroes, as a selfish expression of a clannish
group, but that its sentiment was intended to bless all humanity,
including the future hope of the black race.

That the effort of Lincoln to free and help the Negro in this
direction will not be in vain.   That the following declaration of

Thomas Jefferson might not be worthless: "When the measure of their tears shall be full—when their groans shall have involved Heaven itself in darkness—doubtless a God of Justice will awaken to their distress and by diffusing light and liberality among their oppressors, or at length by his exterminating thunder, manifest his attention to the things of this world, and that they are not left to the guidance of a blind fatality."

Because the Negro is not happy and will never be until he is restored to his own nationality, and my ability to continue my work in this behalf will bless the nation, for as Thomas Paine says, "No man can be happy surrounded by those whose happiness he has destroyed."

That I may be able to continue to serve the people of my race who believe in me (the efforts of my persecution notwithstanding), and who are watching with eyes of eagerness and keenness, and minds of eternal record, the white man's sense of justice, as practised upon an unfortunate Negro who happens to be born and reared in an environment of American Continental civilization, being the relic of a slavery imposed upon his forebears, without any argument of choice of location on their part, but by the sole desire of their masters to profit from their labor.

That my being born on the American Continent as a descendant of British Colonial slaves, does not bar me from the right of working for the release of my people in America and elsewhere to nation-hood, but entitles me to a respectful hearing with equal force of right—as any Negro, who was only by accident born in the United States and not in the other colonies as my fathers were.

Because I am chronically sick, suffering from bronchial asthma and that continuous confinement from acclimatized atmosphere is undermining my health, which is conducive to premature death.

Because I am willing to leave the country if a reasonable time is given me to properly arrange my many business affairs in the interest of the organizations of which I am the head, and to properly arrange how the investments of the people of my race in the Black Star Line can be easily and reasonably returned to them, and this, further, because of the unreasonable attitude and opposition of the few who do not desire to see a friendly and peaceful settlement of the race problem that plagues America, by helping morally to have the Negro found a nation of his own in Africa, and further because of my desire not to be considered in opposition to the wish of the Government in having me leave the country, and because of my belief that I can materially help my race by pleading their cause before the tribunals and places of Legislature of such Governments that may be friendly inclined to restore the Negro to his heritage in Africa by mutual arrangement and peaceful settlements as did such Governments and peoples in the plea for our first emancipation and the abolition of the slave trade.

Because I do not desire to feel and really believe that the chivalry and conscience of this great nation is dead, and that in the Twentieth Century the voice for human justice and liberty, even though it be a black man's, will go unanswered. Because of my hope that America may continue to lead the World in those things that tend to human justice and liberty, even though it be a question of the Negro. That the recent war principles of American justice enunciated by Woodrow Wilson before and during the war might not perish.

That my race's faith in you as a fair dispenser of justice, might be justified, and I further request this pardon on all those grounds that may be just, proper and legal, which are not known to my layman mind.

Because it would be a national crime to allow the Honorable Courts of the United States and the law officers of the Government to be used by one group of enemies to wreak vengeance upon another, as in my case, and further because when we sing the beautiful National Hymn of S. F. Smith, we want to feel in truth, deed and reality:

"My Country, 'tis of Thee,
Sweet land of Liberty,
    Of Thee I sing;
Land where my Fathers died,
Land of the Pilgrim's pride;
From every Mountainside,
    Let Freedom ring."

That if it pleases Your Excellency to see the fact, that millions of Negroes have consistently and continuously, through their local organizations, contributed and donated to the promulgation of the ideals for which I stand (really on which I am persecuted), and this has been done in the face of forced and extra effort to hold me up to said people, as a criminal, and in every way to discredit me by the disadvantages of arrests, prosecutions and malicious newspaper propaganda and organized undercurrents. This determination and wonderful and exceptional loyalty to a Negro leader reveals beyond the shadow of a doubt that there is some longing in the souls, hearts and breasts of these people, for the realization of the ideals of their repatriation to Africa and the founding and establishing for them there of a nation of their own.

That there must be a sincere desire and longing on the part of these people to be returned to their fatherland, and if a plebiscite of or a referendum to the masses of people were to be taken it would show an overwhelming majority in favor of the plan of returning the race to Africa by careful and proper arrangements and methods, whereby the somewhat settled national equilibrium industrially and generally, would not be disturbed, but by a gradual system of release, and replacement, at the same time, by assimilable duplicates, continue the migration until in the course of probably a half century the problem adjusts itself by the friendly and peaceful removal and by the return to the race of its native home, and the assimilating into the body politic of America those members of the majority race who would have replaced the Negro industrially and generally in the South and other sections of the Country that now depend on Negro labor, and only on which latter account, hostility and opposition from that source would be forthcoming.

That with the commandeering of hundreds of unused ships now owned by the Shipping Board, and which are a source of worry to the Government, the race could be easily and conveniently repatriated.

That the fact of the principal colonizing powers in Africa owing this Government large sums of money, which they cannot immediately repay, and in some cases do not want to repay, amicable arrangements could be reached, by which these countries would turn over to the United States such places in Africa as Sierra Leone, the French Ivory Coast, etc., for the forming of the nucleus of such a nation as would satisfy the Negro Race. The several billion dollars due this Country by Great Britain, France, Belgium and Italy, but principally Great Britain and France, could be partly underwritten by their turning over to America for the purpose of the Negroes who desire to return to Africa, such territories in Africa, where the returned Negroes could easily assimilate with the natives and co-operate as one race for the promotion of national ideals. And when it is considered that the slave trade and slavery in the Western World were made profitable for centuries to Great Britain, France and America, and that our generations are the relic of such a slavery, the force of justice remains indisputable and leaves no other alternative than a righteous and Christian consideration of the poor Negro for his rights. That my efforts

THE REPLY

OFFICE OF THE
ATTORNEY IN CHARGE OF PARDONS

Department of Justice
Washington, D. C.

Marcus Garvey,
United States Penitentiary,
Atlanta, Ga.

Sir:

The reports upon the application for Executive clemency of *—— yourself ——* are adverse or of such a nature as not to entitle the case, under the rules governing applications for pardon, to submission to the President for consideration. This disposes of the case, and the papers have accordingly been filed.

Rule 8 reads as follows:

"When none of the persons so consulted advises clemency, the papers are not sent to the President except by his special request, or by special order of the Attorney General; but when any one of the officers consulted advises clemency the papers are submitted to the President."

By direction of the Attorney General.

Respectfully,

James A. Finch

Attorney in Charge of Pardons.

GOVERNMENT PRINTING OFFICE

Received Aug, 10, 1925

in this direction were with the purpose of blessing the American Nation and removing from its body politic an irritating problem that may otherwise end disastrously to both races. That a strong, decisive, determined attitude and action of any President of the United States, in this direction, would herald to the World another Lincoln, Washington and Jefferson—the fathers and benefactors not only of their Country, but the true advocates and dispensers of human justice and liberty.

And for all such considerations as Your Excellency may grant by way of pardon, I do humbly pray,

Your obedient servant,

MARCUS GARVEY.

We, the undersigned, respectfully indorse the application for Executive Clemency of **Marcus Garvey.** Our approval is based upon the following grounds:

Our complete belief in the honesty and integrity of the applicant, and our desire to see justice done to one who has honestly and faithfully labored in the interest of his race.

..................., Philadelphia, Pa., editor and banker.

..................., Pittsburgh, Pa., president of bank.

..................., New York City, lawyer.

..................., New York City, judge.

..................., Cleveland, Ohio, physician.

..................., Los Angeles, Cal., real estate broker.

I am reliably informed that signatures, petitions, cables, telegrams, etc., representing the sentiment and wishes of countless millions of people in my behalf are filed either with the President's office at the White House, the Attorney-General's office or the Pardon Clerk's office of the Department of Justice. I respectfully ask that the entire file become a part of this document.

GARVEY SENTENCED BY JUDGE ON ALLEGED CONVICTION OF ONE COUNT FOR FIVE YEARS AND FINED OVER SIX THOUSAND DOLLARS

Real White Swindlers Convicted on Seven Counts for Really Defrauding, Get Short Terms for the Seven Separate and Distinct Counts

Several cases of mail fraud among whitemen have been tried within recent months since my imprisonment, as well as hundreds before. In not one instance was a sentence imposed upon any of these white persons to be compared, in severity with mine. My case was not one of commercial fraud, it was an honest effort to help my race, with the many oppositions to be encountered.

I never even knew that there was such a law as using the mails to defraud. I was not thinking of fraud, I was thinking of serving humanity. These other men planned fraud to enrich themselves. They confessed their purpose of swindling the public, yet they received the lightest sentences on their many counts, while I received the severest and maximum on the alleged conviction of one count only. The Montgomery case in New York, where he was convicted and sentenced on all counts, receiving light sentences on all, and the following two cases are fair examples:

(New York Times, June 20, 1925)

8 GET PRISON TERMS FOR TRADING FRAUDS

Five Ordered Goods on Name of Newmarket Co. and Speedily Sold Them Below Cost
OPERATED IN MANY STATES

Three Others Sentenced for Concealing Assets of Aldo Shirt Co.—Five More on Trial

"The work of the Commercial Frauds Bureau, established by United States Attorney Emory R. Buckner last March to prosecute promptly those who prey upon merchants, resulted yesterday in prison sentences for eight defendants. Four others are to be sentenced Monday and five more are on trial.

"Five of the eight sentenced yesterday were convicted on Wednesday of using the mails to defraud and for violating the Interstate Commerce law in connection with the operation of the Newmarket Trading Company, Inc. Federal Judge John C. Knox sentenced Jacob Lerner, President of the concern, to four years' imprisonment in the Atlanta Penitentiary. Isidor Horowitz, Lerner's brother-in-law, was sentenced to the same prison for eighteen months, while Alfred Moscow, alias Mr. Harris, and Joseph Greenberg, alias Joseph Green, alias Mr. Fine, were each sentenced to the Essex County (N. J.) Penitentiary for one year. Walter Fox, alias Walter Brown, was sentenced to the Westchester County Penitentiary for eight months.

"Another count, charging the defendants with having sent through the mails a false statement of the company's assets, carried no prison sentence, but the Court directed the defendants to report once a month for five years to a probation officer after the expiration of their prison terms so that it could be learned whether the defendants were behaving properly. Four other defendants, Max Yucht and Samuel Shapiro, who were also convicted, and Morris Rachmil and Irving Silverman, who pleaded guilty and assisted the Government in the prosecution, will be sentenced on Monday.

Operated Throughout the Country

"Evidence during the trial disclosed that the defendants had obtained control of the Newmarket Trading Company, Inc., which had had a good reputation, and had used it to defraud merchants throughout the country of merchandise valued at many thousands of dollars. It was the purpose of the defendants, the prosecutors showed, to use the good character built up by the former owners of the Newmarket Company to order large quantities of all sorts of goods and sell them speedily at less than cost, this was accomplished by establishing in various States subsidiary companies and then having these smaller concerns pass into bankruptcy.

"After Postal Inspectors Allen and Boyle had begun an investigation into the matter Frederick R. A. Stiefel, the receiver of the Newmarket concern, discovered that large shipments of goods were on their way to the office of the company in this city and that orders for large quantities of additional goods had been placed. It was shown that the group operated in this State, California, New Jersey, Ohio, Michigan, Delaware, Connecticut, Massachusetts, Pennsylvania, Maryland, Illinois, and elsewhere.

"In sentencing the defendants Judge Knox said that it had been shown that Lerner had amassed a large fortune by lending money at usurious rates of interest to persons in dire need and that Horowitz had a reputation for philanthropy. These conflicting traits explained the difference in the sentences of the two men. While the sentences were said to be heavy, Judge Knox explained: "I sometimes think I am entirely too soft hearted to be a Judge, because a Judge is very frequently confronted with a situation where he has got to harden himself."

Three Others Sentenced

"Later in the day Judge Knox sentenced Aaron Davis and Nathan Lachoff to six months each in the Essex County (N. J.) Penitentiary and Samuel Rabinowitz to three months, after they had pleaded guilty to concealing assets from a trustee in bankruptcy. The three operated the Aldo Shirt Company at 593 Broadway, and were petitioned into bankruptcy in December, 1923. Liabilities were said to amount to $70,000 and assets to less than $8,000. The bankruptcy proceedings were instituted about five months after the defendants had issued a statement to the effect that they had assets amounting to $95,000.

"The three were arrested in Brooklyn and sent to the Raymond Street Jail last January for failing to obey an order directing them to turn over $12,000 in their possession. They came from the jail to court, and after they were sentenced they were returned to the jail to await final action on the contempt charge. They will begin to serve their prison sentences after the contempt charge is taken up."

A STRANGE COMPARISON

Year and a day, for outright commercial Fraud of millions, imposed by one Judge upon a white man. Another gave Garvey (Negro) five years, cost six thousand dollars and deportation for alleged conviction on one count in effort to help his race in the promotion of African Nationalism as a solution of race problem. ———

(From New York Times, July 14, 1925)

GUILTY PLEAS END BUCKETERS' TRIAL

George W. Field and George W. Morse Sentenced to One Year in Atlanta Penitentiary

LEON A. FIELD WINS PAROLE

All Involved in Mail Fraud Earn Leniency by Aiding Buckner to Keep Trial Calendar Unclogged

"Trial of the four defendants of the bankrupt brokerage concerns of George W. Field & Co., and George W. Morse & Co., on an indictment charging use of the mails to defraud investors before Federal Judge Trieber and a jury, came to a sudden end yesterday when three of the four pleaded guilty.

"They were George W. Field and George W. Morse, who were sentenced to the Atlanta Penitentiary for a year and a day each, and Leon A. Field, who was paroled for five years. The fourth defendant, Ralph W. Morse, was discharged when United States Attorney Buckner announced that there was not sufficient evidence against him to warrant conviction.

"Two others named in the indictment, Charles J. Anastasia and Louis T. Hall, who had pleaded guilty and were aiding the Government in the prosecution, escaped prison sentences. They were placed on parole for five years.

"The defendants, who operated an interlocking system of bucket shops, where one set of men ruled and business was done under separate names, were indicted in November, 1923, after they had failed with liabilities amounting to about $3,000,-000. Most of their patrons were members of the professional classes in New England States, such as school teachers, professors and the like.

After the indictment was filed it was contended by the Federal authorities that it would be easier to convict them for bucketing than for mail fraud and that the matter should be attended to by District Attorney Banton.

There were long delays until counsel for the creditors raised such repeated clamors that it was decided to undertake the trial without further delay. Besides those named the indictment contained the names of Wilfred A. Creighton, who was separated in the trial, and who is not likely to be tried at all.

The prosecution was conducted by Assistant United States Attorneys David P. Siegel and George S. Leisure. When the trial was resumed yesterday morning the Government had a large number of witnesses ready. The case was going so heavily against the defendants that it was deemed better for them to plead guilty and thus lessen their punishment, Mr. Buckner said:

"After listening to the Government's case for two days Field and Morse became convinced that they were guilty. By promptly pleading guilty they have saved the time necessary to continue the trial and naturally received much lighter sentences than they would have received if the case had been submitted to the jury and a verdict of guilty returned. The recommendation of the District Attorney's office in this respect is in line with the policy of clearing the congested calendars by advocating extreme leniency to those who promptly plead guilty and severity to those who are clearly guilty and who clog the courts by standing trial."

THE SINS OF THE FATHERS

There is no sense in hate; it comes back to you; therefore, make your history so laudable, magnificent and untarnished, that another generation will not seek to repay your seed for the sins inflicted upon their fathers. The bones of injustice have a peculiar way of rising from the tombs to plague and mock the iniquitous.

SALARIES TO OFFICERS OF THE UNIVERSAL NEGRO IMPROVEMENT ASSOCIATION
The Conflict of Ideals

The first "International Convention of the Negro Peoples of the World," under the auspices of the Universal Negro Improvement Association, was called and held in New York City, in August, 1920, from the 1st to the 31st.

Representative delegates, duly elected by the people, from all parts of the world, attended the conclave. Every country where Negroes lived was represented.

It was at this convention that the constitution and by-laws of the Universal Negro Improvement Association was discussed and adopted, and its executive officers elected by popular suffrage. The delegates, who were afterwards named deputies, were so enthusiastic and their hopes for the movement so buoyant that they did things that had to be amended at the following convention in August, 1921.

Among the things they did, unforseeingly, that had to be amended, was the voting of large salaries to the newly elected officers of the movement, without having sufficient capital in the treasury to meet the expenses. The explanation is that every Negro who attended that convention spoke and acted in such a way as to suggest that a new era of love, brotherhood and fraternity had dawned for the race. There was nothing else but absolute confidence in each other. We all believed that there was not a Negro among us who would betray the confidence or the race. We were glad to cut away from the old venal and corrupt leadership. At the convention, where every delegate was given five to ten minutes to speak and explain conditions in his particular part of the world, and where time did not permit each delegate had the privilege to submit his report in writing, the consensus of reports showed that the race universally was suffering from dishonesty among the leaders who would sell out the rights of the people and accept bribes to ignore their interests. With this in mind, and the desire to remove the new leaders from theft, graft and alien influence, a sufficient salary was voted to each to make him independent and true to his trust. The financial condition of the Association was properly brought before the convention in the reading of the Chancellor's report, which showed a balance of $3,000 in hand after the convention had assembled, and which convention lasted for 31 days and nights. Every elected officer knew of the financial condition, but there was such a disposition to do good, and to universally start this new movement, that everybody promised to work hard and sacrifice to build the organization. It was felt that as soon as the delegates returned to their respective homes and explained to the people the new era, the financial support would be forthcoming to capitalize and carry on the movement. Little did I believe that the majority of my associates were still of the old crowd and steeped in selfishness. There was one old man from Trinidad, over sixty years of age, who came to the convention with tears in his eyes. He made a pitiful plea to the convention for help. He stated that he was once a man of means in the Island of Trinidad, but that he fought the battles of the poor blacks and was hounded by the British, who impoverished him and drove him out of the country. His story was plausible. He appeared poorly attired and suggested that he was really in need of help. I, myself, suggested this man for the position of leader of one of the Provinces of the West Indies at a salary of $6,000 per annum. I personally did everything to help the old man, yet he was the principal enemy witness against me for the Government in 1923; who swore vengeance against me because I demanded of him to measure up to the requirements of his office and to make his office sufficiently remunerative as to make it an asset to the organization instead of a tremendous liability. He was the first official of the Association to sue for twelve thousand dollars after he had worked for the Association unsatisfactorily for but one year, during which time he was handsomely paid and enjoyed extraordinary privileges.

The convention voted large salaries, having in mind that proper organization and earnest and hard work on the part of the leaders would have made the venture successful. With this in view they elected 21 executive officers, who were designated the High Executive Council of the Universal Negro Improvement Association and leaders of the Negro peoples of the World. Subsequent experience proved that all the majority of these men wanted were the offices with the titles and the privilege to draw large salaries.

Following are the positions created, with the salaries attached, at the first convention:

Annually

His Highness, The Potentate........................ $12,000

His Excellency, The Provisional President of Africa...⎤
His Excellency, The President General and Adminis- ⎬ 10,000
trator of the U. N. I. A........................ ⎦

His Excellency, The Leader of American Negroes.... 10,000
His Highness, The Supreme Deputy Potentate........ 6,000
Hon. Assistant President General................... 6,000
Hon. Secretary General 6,000
Hon. High Chancellor 6,000
Hon. International Organizer 6,000
Hon. The Surgeon General......................... 7,000
His Excellency, The Leader of the Eastern Province of
    the West Indies, South and Central America...... 6,000
His Excellency, The Leader of the Western Province of
    the West Indies 6,000
His Grace, the Chaplain General.................... 5,000
Hon. The Auditor General.......................... 5,000
Hon. The Counsel General.......................... 7,000
Hon. The Assistant Counsel General................ 6,000
Hon. The High Commissioner General............... 4,000
Hon. The Assistant Secretary General.............. 4,000
Hon. The Minister of Labor and Industry........... 4,000
Hon. The Minister of the Legion................... 3,000
Hon. The Speaker-in-Convention 3,000

As explained, it was the consensus of the convention that its officers would, by their fitness and extraordinary ability, earn their salaries by active remunerative service. They were to go out to the people, working hard, carrying to them the program of the organization. I found that, with the exception of Bishop George Alexander McGuire, who was elected Chaplain General, and Lady Henrietta Vinton Davis, who has remained faithful to her oath and the organization, not one of the elected officers was worth more than $1,200 a year as an office boy or lackey. The men were lazy, incompetent, treacherous and visionless, as after results so amply proved. I called the joint council together after the adjournment of the convention and I wholeheartedly explained to the men the financial state of the organization with its tremendous program. I pointed out that with every man throwing in his whole heart in the work and being honest with the people it would be very easy for us to measure up to every expectation. I tried to inspire the men from my own subconscious feeling, in that I alone, with the help of the people, had built up the tremendous organization, prior to the convention, with property in several parts of the world and the United States. In New York alone the Association controlled property valued at over $100,000.00.

In view of the fact that the Council had no immediate capital to start with in proportion to the tremendous liabilities, we unanimously decided to float a loan of about $200,000 from the membership for periods of one, two, three, four, five and ten years. Every man was drafted to do his part in raising the money and carrying on the work. In the first six months over one hundred and twenty thousand dollars was raised, 95 per cent of which was raised by me through my speeches and writings in the Negro World. After the first six months' period I found out that I was encumbered with a group of lazy men, most of them old enough to be my father. I raved and pleaded with the men. I tried by precept and example to inspire them.

Prior to the convention I worked twenty hours every day from 1918 to build up the Association. When in New York I worked in the office all day, going home at seven o'clock each evening, and at eight o'clock each night I would be at Liberty Hall to take charge of the meeting held there each night of the week and three times on Sunday. After I had built up a following of 35,000 in New York City and by my writings in the Negro World and other literature organized the whole world, I took the field, speaking every night of the week and sometimes twice a day, carrying with me a staff of secretaries, who did my usual office work on the road. The only time on the road I had eight hours' sleep was when I was making a long-distance run at night on the train, and even then I did not have eight hours' rest, for I generally boarded the train at 11.30, after the night meeting, so as to be at the next stop early next morning to keep up with my day's work. It was through such continuous work from 1918 to 1925 that I was able to build up a world-wide organization. Wherever I spoke in America there was an admission of fifty cents, and thousands came out to hear me at every place. The money taken in would be divided as follows: Two-thirds to the parent body organization and one-third to the local organization. I received nothing for speaking at these meetings. All I received was that part of salary that the Chancellor in New York cared to pay, two-thirds of which was again invested in the Association to carry on the work. Sometimes I would be on the road for four to six weeks and sometimes two and three months, running back to New York for a few days and out again. By so doing I was unable to keep up with the other officers, who did things their own way. I spent an average of nine months per year away from New York, building up the other divisions of the organization, after having made New York.

To return, and explain further the attitude of the executive officers, I must state that 60 per cent of the money that was borrowed from the members was on short notes of one year. This

Group of High Officials of U. N. I. A. reviewing parade of units and delegates attending 1922 Convention of the Negro Peoples of the World. Left to right: (1) In white plumes, Rudolph Smith, Leader of the Negroes of the Eastern Provinces of the West Indies. (2) John Sydney DeBourg, Leader of the Negroes of the Western Provinces of the West Indies and South and Central America. (3) W. H. Eason, Leader of the Negroes of the United States. (4) G. O. Mark, Supreme Deputy Potentate and Leader of the Negroes of West Africa. (5) Gabriel Johnson, Mayor of Monrovia, Liberia, Potentate of the Universal Negro Improvement Association and Leader of the Negro Peoples of the World. (6) Marcus Garvey, President General U. N. I. A. and Provisional President of Africa. The reviewing stand is at the Publishing House of the Association. On the second floor are the offices of A. Philip Randolph and Chandler Owen, the socialist enemies of Marcus Garvey, who are also reviewing the parade at a position immediately behind the group of officials.

was known to all the officers. That meant that we had to double up in effort, energy and service to repay the people's money at the end of the year, which could have been done easily. I influenced each of the officers to make a loan to the organization, and I found out that not one of them advanced a penny, but that they agreed to make the loan out of their salaries. I tried to get them to make a loan of a thousand dollars each to show their good faith; some protested, but finally we arranged at from $500 to $1,000. This money was to be deducted from their salaries and at the completion of payment the notes were to be given for a period of five years. Being on the road most of the time, a group conspired to issue their notes for one year so that they could collect from the Association more quickly. I had no suspicion that this was done, in that they made my many notes for five and ten years. I discovered this only when they started to sue the Association before the courts of New York. The money that I had raised and sent to headquarters they used in paying, regularly for the first year, their salaries every 1st and 15th of the month. Yet, unknowingly, they were rendering me very little assistance to build up the movement. Legal work that should have been done by the legal department that was fully staffed was neglected for private practice. Other departments were neglected in the same way. We had a very large staff of employees that ran into hundreds. Some of the heads of the departments were more interested in taking out the young ladies that worked in their departments than giving proper attention to the organization's business.

In February, 1921, I arranged a trip to visit the West Indian and Central American divisions of the organization with an eye to submitting reforms, amendments, etc., at the next convention in August, 1921, to stimulate the work in these parts and raise funds for the Black Star Line and the organization. It was arranged for me to be away thirty days. I sailed from Key West for Cuba on the 23rd of February. I was not out of the country twenty-four hours before my enemies, some of my own executive officers and associates, especially of the Black Star Line, started to plot for my exclusion from the United States. Instead of being out of the country for thirty days, I was kept out for five months. Through great effort I was readmitted to the country just in time to attend the convention in August. During my absence the Council had absolute power. They paid themselves regularly, as usual, doing very little, if anything, constructive to enhance the work of the organization.

They gave me no information during all the months of my

absence. The girl whom I had left as my private secretary, to
supply me with private information, was now head over heels in
love with the principal person who wanted to keep all information away from me.   Out in the West Indies I was informed by
a circular they sent to one of the members that they had acquired
the ship for Africa.   That made me happy and I thought that
they were doing good work at last.   Upon my return to America
I found that it was untrue, and when I started to fathom the
whole affair, they got me indicted.   At the Council meeting I
held immediately after the first convention I was the only officer
who reduced his salary by half, realizing how high the salaries
were.   This was done in spite of the fact that through my
speeches alone I brought in over a hundred thousand dollars net
to the Association each year, to say nothing of my writings and
other financial efforts for the Association and its auxiliaries that
ran into hundreds of thousands annually.   The others held on to
their full salaries as valid.   At the 1921 convention I suggested
to the assembly, in my annual message and report, the reduction
of the salaries by half, as expressed in the following resolution
that passed the house, much to the displeasure of a large number of officials:

"All officials and high officers of the Universal Negro Improvement Association shall be paid their salaries at the minimum,
which shall be half of the maximum, and each shall be allowed
to earn the maximum by ability and fitness, which maximum
shall be paid at the end of each month according to the record
of such official."

The Secretary, whose duty it was to edit the resolutions and
insert them in the constitution, omitted this most important law
from the constitution for two consecutive prints.   I never knew
that the law was not in the constitution until the dismissed or
resigned officials started to sue.   I felt sure that the law was
there to protect the Association, but, lo and behold, it was nowhere to be found.   I requested the official minutes of the convention for submission to the lawyer, and no one knew where
they were.   They were wickedly destroyed in anticipation of the
legal fights to extract money from the Association.

After the adjournment of the 1921 convention some of the
executive officers realized that their maximum salaries would not
be easily forthcoming and resigned, irrespective of the fact that
they had, during the previous year, borrowed over one hundred
thousand dollars from the members, which was used to pay their
salaries, and that they were morally obligated to raise the funds

to repay those members whose notes were becoming due. The more artful group remained as long as possible, then went out and sued for maximum salaries.

Among those who have sued the Association and received judgments in full are:

Rev. G. E. Stewart, ex-Chancellor.

Sydney De Bourg, ex-Leader of the West Indies.

Rev. J. D. Gordon, ex-Assistant President General.

Rev. J. D. Brooks, ex-Secretary General.

Rev. J. W. Eason, ex-American Leader.

Rev. Wm. Ferris, M. A., ex-Assistant President General.

Eli Garcia, ex-Auditor General.

U. S. Poston, ex-Minister of Labor.

E. L. Gaines, ex-Minister of Legion.

Thomas W. Anderson, ex-Minister of Industry.

W. Fowler, ex-Minister of Labor.

J. D. Gibson, ex-Surgeon General.

James O'Meally, ex-High Commissioner General.

Rudolph Smith, ex-Leader of the West Indies and Central America.

Adrian Johnson, ex-Speaker-in-Convention.

The only members of the original Council who have seen continuous service and are still working for the organization are Lady Henrietta Vinton Davis, now Fourth Assistant President General, and myself.

The Rt. Rev. Bishop George Alexander McGuire, who was called to the Primacy of the African Orthodox Church, has still remained with the Association, officiating on all occasions when necessary as Honorary Chaplain General. My salary of five thousand dollars I have received in no one year. As the amounts accumulate I have continued to reduce same by making the Association a present of the balance. When I was first imprisoned I left my wife with a bank balance of only thirty-five dollars. On this, my last imprisonment, I was informed that my balance was eight dollars. The money collected for my defense in 1923 and before that, which ran into thousands of dollars, was mainly used by the Association to carry on its work. What was left was used to pay the attorneys, cost of records, briefs, etc. Since my imprisonment my wife has conducted my defense with the help that the members and friends have given her. I have received no financial support from the executive organization, although I have already spent for them, through money sent me by my wife and friends of other divisions, several hundred dollars. I fully realize that honesty of purpose in public life is not appreciated, and that to do what is right is to "buck" the machinery of corruption and graft, for in so doing one constitutes himself a bad fellow and the cry is raised "he must go." My years of ceaseless toil brought me face to face with a celebrated trial in which my liberty was involved. When I entered the court on the morning of the trial I had hardly given the matter a serious thought. As far as I was concerned, I had given all my time to the Assocition up to the time of trial and spared none for myself. On the second day of the trial I found out that I was to be convicted by arrangement, and that the ideals of the Association were to be destroyed. I immediately decided to save the ideals of the Association and let the conviction take its course. If I had not tried that case they would have convicted me on the thirteen counts, with five years attached to each, and my attorney would have humiliated me by asking for mercy, and they would have then and there destroyed the Universal Negro Improvement Association, the object which they sought. I have asked for no mercy; I still ask for justice, accepting all the formalities to which one so situated is entitled. During the trial of my case I had to attend to the exacting work of the world-wide Association during the mornings up to 9 o'clock, rushing to court, ten miles away, to be there by 10, and in the evenings I had no time to give even my own personal defense the attention necessary. At the time of the trial I had worked my frame to exhaustive nervousness, and the six weeks of extra mental and physical strain in court left me a wreck. If I had been acquitted I would have had to go out on the road again for still more aggressive campaigning. My three months in the New York Tombs quieted my overstrained nerves a little, but immediately on release I was in harness again and continued to the last minute when I was arrested and sent to Atlanta. During my appeal, except for the time at the Tombs, I was unable to find time to consult with the lawyers who prepared the briefs. Up to then I did not have the time to read the record of the case. I gave all my time to the people.

HIS GRACE, ARCHBISHOP GEO. ALEXANDER McGUIRE

Primate of the African Orthodox Church, Honorary Chaplain General of the Universal Negro Improvement Association.

OATH TAKEN BY EXECUTIVE OFFICERS AT CONVENTION, 1920 AND 1921

I, ..., DO SOLEMNLY AND SINCERELY DECLARE:

That I shall be obedient to the Constitution and By-laws of THE UNIVERSAL NEGRO IMPROVEMENT ASSOCIATION and to the commands of the EXECUTIVE COUNCIL.

I shall obey those in authority over me and perform all those duties assigned me to the best of my ability.

I shall uphold and support the Declaration of Rights.

I shall not encourage the enemies of the cause of African redemption, and shall refuse to associate with all those who may be proven enemies of the cause of this Organization.

I shall uphold its principles everywhere and at all times.

The cause of this Organization shall come first to me in all my deliberations.

Should I FAIL this CAUSE, may the Almighty Architect fail me in the purpose of life.

To this CAUSE do I pledge my Life and my Fortune for a free and redeemed Africa. Being now, therefore, in possession of all my senses, I subscribe my name and swear myself in the presence of all those assembled and Almighty God to serve the UNIVERSAL NEGRO IMPROVEMENT ASSOCIATION FAITHFULLY.

SO HELP ME GOD.

OATH TAKEN BY OFFICIALS AT THE THIRD INTERNATIONAL CONVENTION ON NIGHT OF AUGUST 31, 1922

I, ..., solemnly swear and pledge before Almighty God and this Convention here assembled that I will to the best of my ability and with true devotion serve the UNIVERSAL NEGRO IMPROVEMENT ASSOCIATION AND THE NEGRO PEOPLES OF THE WORLD.

The interests of this Association shall in all my public duties come first to me, and, should I fail this cause, may the Almighty Architect fail me in the cause of life. Being in full possession of my senses and knowing full well the penalty of treachery, disloyalty and deceit, I sign my name to this, my oath. And may the Lord have mercy on my soul

THE PASSING NEGRO "INTELLECTUAL"

Scrapping the "Barnacles" of a Race

It is astonishing how disloyal and selfish is the average Negro "intellectual" of the passing generation to his race.

The Negro who has had the benefit of an education of forty, thirty and twenty years ago, is the greatest fraud and stumbling block to the real progress of the race. He was educated with the wrong psychology and perspective. He indulged the belief, and carried out the practice, that to be a man, and be great, is to exploit the less fortunate members of his race, barter their rights economically and politically, and then with the attendant personal success, seek to escape the race through an underground current of miscegenation. Their late effort to protest their desire for "social equality," meaning intermingling with the whites as their highest ambition, is a lie, and they know it. They may deceive a few unthinking whites, and a large number of Negroes, whom they continue to lead, but they cannot fool the wide-awake of our race. Their every day deeds are the greatest evidence against them. They hate their black blood and God and man know it. This old school of Negro "intellectuals" is crafty, unpatriotic and vicious. They cannot be trusted. I would rather give a dime to a dead hog, than to save the skins of all of them. They are barnacles around the necks of a struggling virile people. They lie, steal and misrepresent.

The hope of the Black race lies in our new blood—the New Negro—who is already rising to the heights of nationhood. He is the man of the future. By science, art, history, politics, industry and religion, he will rise above his environments and in another hundred years shall have laid the pillars of the greatest civilization the world ever saw.

It is good for the honest, considerate, humanitarian and progressive elements and blood of the other races to join in with and be friends of this new school for by reasonableness, equity and reciprocal sympathy we can all work together, but racially and nationally separate, for the proper adjustment of our human ills, and thus save future generations the miseries attendant upon a history of injustice, advantage and corruption.

The old schools of all races are obsolete. They should be scrapped for their selfishness, and our youth movements of all races should seize the lever of humanity and pilot the good ships to the haven of peace, human love, fraternity and justice.

A RACE THAT STEALS FROM AND DOUBLE-CROSSES ITSELF IN THE MAKING

How Some Negroes Get Rich at the Expense of Their Race

To steal, exploit, trick or double-cross is no special trait of the Negro; it is common to all peoples within our civilization; but the Negro, being a race in the making, is the only race that performs or practices the evils without method intended not to wholesalely harm itself.

The Jew steals from the Jew, but not to the extent of doing wholesale harm to the rest of the Jewish community. The white man steals from his brother, but not with the intent or to the extent of harming or destroying his race as a community, group, or as a whole. The Negro, on the contrary, steals from his own without the slightest thought of consequences or any regard to what extent the entire race is affected. It is through such disposition and reckless practice that the bigger and idealistic part of my world program, in the interest of the race, has been damaged by the unscrupulous who have affiliated themselves with the organization.

My references to dishonesty among Negroes is confined to themselves as a race; they seldom extend that dishonesty in their dealings with other races. In fact, there is no race as honest in its dealings with the white race as the Negro. Dishonesty within the race must not be interpreted to mean only among the Universal Negro Improvement Association, but includes, in a larger degree, our churches, clubs, lodges, fraternities and all other organizations, not to mention our corrupt political groups. Why there has been so much ado about the Universal Negro Improvement Association is that we have always tried to expose, drive out and disgrace the culprits as we discover them in our organization, in that we are engaged in the work of reform. That is why, in criticising us in one of his brutal articles, Dr. Du Bois, of the National Association for the Advancement of "Colored" People, charged that I cannot get along with my associates, in that my entourage have always changed. The policy of the Universal Negro Improvement Association, under my direction, has always been that of honesty and a square deal. My friend today, became my enemy tomorrow, on the discovery of any act of dishonesty. There was no "confidence game" with me in the Association, and this accounts largely for the disloyalty that has operated against me. In other movements the entourage are held together and never change because of the "confidence game." I refuse to hold office under such conditions. We of the Universal Negro Improvement Association expose, dismiss and get rid of all our dishonest associates as we come across them; hence there is always a fight either of revenge or to break up, as is so customary to human nature. If I had compromised or conspired with the men to cheat the organization or the people, then my entourage would have always remained, and no one would have possibly heard a hard word said against me from within the race, while the poor masses would have paid. I was brought up under a system of private and public life where we knew nothing of graft and the "confidence trick." Until I started my activities in the interests of my people in America I never heard the question, "How much is in it for me?" I thank God that I have not fallen for the system, and may my hands wither away and my tongue be silenced, before I allow myself to be brought under the influence of such a system. I would rather stand alone and be framed for the prison a thousand times than deny the (black) religion of my mother—mark you, not the (white) religion—the religion that taught me to be honest and fair to all my fellow-men.

In our churches and all other organizations our entourage always remain the same because there is always an "understanding." Only when a trustee, deacon or pastor attempts to do what is right by the congregation or people is there a cry for him to go, and a split when he is kicked out of office by the strong confidence group. Other organizations, to preserve the ruling group and prevent them from being put out of office, manoeuvre to appoint and elect from among themselves, to the exclusion of a popular election among the people. If I had clubbed with other Negroes to exploit or fleece the people, these confederate Negroes would have protected me by political power and influence, because in protecting me they would have been protecting themselves. Although I have had dozens of close associates in the administration of the affairs of the Association, I have not had one friend, in that friendship in public life seems to imply that you must steal or concoct to be a good fellow and allow the other fellow to do the same and protect him in doing so in return for a similar exchange. Let such friendship be damned and let me die, instead, a thousand times. It is not a part of my religion. If I have friends, they must be honest and clean and not expect me to do them favors on dishonesty or by betraying others. Because I did not fall a prey to the methods of "graft" I was regarded as a "bad fellow," with the cry around me of "Garvey must go," and left to suffer from a general frame-up that shall have its place in Negro history.

On the average, the Negro loses more than 50 per cent annually in real estate holdings, investments, stocks, bonds, part-time payments on furniture, etc., than any other race group in the United States as well as elsewhere. A general confidence game is carried on in this direction by real estate brokers, crooked lawyers and certain Negro leaders and agents. In this, unscrupulous white men and their Negro associates indulge. For instance, a Negro preacher would start a new church congregation, gathering together as many religious suckers as possible, to worship in a sufficiently accommodating building, or he would be called to the pastorate of an already established church. After being there for a comparatively short time, and without his congregation increasing to any appreciable extent, he would be approached by some Negro real estate broker or agent of some white broker. He would be told of how wonderful a man he is and talked into building or buying a new church more becoming to him as a "leader" of the community. Already the broker has found out that the present congregation holds the major or all the equity in the present church property. By the appeal to the preacher's vanity he is induced to take up the proposition of the new building, although nothing in the world is wrong with the building now occupied. The question of how much is in it for me comes up, and, being the very question the broker subconsciously suggested, he readily offers the preacher a substantial bonus or commission on the deal. He falls for the big offer and immediately he starts out by the preaching of a "powerful" sermon, backed up by some passages from the Bible, to show why there should be a new house of worship. In cases where the pastor is too honest or upright to fall for the bait, a deacon or trustee who has a "pull" with the congregation is influenced to "put it over." In such an event things are made warm for the pastor and he is forced to resign or put out by a "trick." To build the new church or purchase the other, big drives and "rallies" are instituted among the people to raise the amount of money needed for the first payment, out of which bonuses, commissions, etc., are paid. Women and young girls are generally used in these rallies to collect the money from Negro men and white families. When the deal is put through you will find that all the equity the people had in their original building and the monies raised in the rallies are gobbled up in the first payment on the new property, and a first and sometimes a second mortgage are taken out on the new property that tax to the limit its full value, thereby wiping out all equity for the people, as the plan is to charge as much for the new building as will dispose of the equity of the first payment, leaving the property taxed at its full value by the mortgagees. Then the said people are called upon year after year to rally to pay the interest and reduce the payments on the mortgages, and when sufficient of the mortgages is reduced or the property paid for a new scheme is hatched that practically repeats the old performances.

In some cases, such as in the purchase of fraternal buildings and some churches too, another scheme is used by the real estate broker and his confederates. In such cases bonds are sold to the members or people, and it has been a terrible fight for me to keep sundry branches of the Universal Negro Improvement Association from falling into the traps of these sharks, a combination of whom, allied with politicians, are trying to crucify me as being in the way. The following legal opinion on one of their methods is recited for general enlightenment:

"You submitted to me a proposed contract between the U. N. I. A. and the John Doe Company. After reading carefully the said proposed contract, my opinion is not to sign it for the following reasons:

"The U. N. I. A. will bind itself under the proposed agreement with no assurances that the John Doe Company will carry out the intention; that is, to put up the building in the proposed contract. If this proposed contract would be signed by the U. N. I. A. they would be obliged to give a deed in trust for $4,000, which money would go to the John Doe Company. You would further be obliged to pay all the bills that the John Doe Company may incur; that is, for printing, legal fees, architect fees, engraving, trustees' fees, etc., which may amount to a considerable amount of money, and under this proposed contract you are obliged to pay this first before anything else is done. The John Doe Company also will be entitled to 15 per cent of all the bonds sold, as well as 10 per cent for the supervision of the building, and also another 2 per cent on the total bond issue. If you study carefully this proposed contract, it is my opinion that the expense will run above 40 per cent that will go to the John Doe Company.

"There is also another provision in the proposed contract that the U. N. I. A. is to assist them in disposing of the said bond certificates.

"My conclusion is that the John Doe Company is not to invest a five-cent piece in this enterprise, but at all times they will derive benefits by reason of the clause that they are to get their fees first. They intend to create a campaign to sell the bond

certificates among the colored people, and they will insist upon
you to give them all the assistance you can, and if the colored
people will not take up sufficient certificates to go through with
the enterprise, they will drop it under the pretence that if the
colored people are not buying the bond certificates, why should
the white people do so.

"The net result will be that of whatever certificates will be
sold, they will get all the money to cover their expenses and you
will lose the property.

"I also wish to add that this proposed contract does not state
just exactly the nature of the building, what income may be
derived by way of rents, etc., and also actual cost of putting up
such building. Those are necessary elements before a contract
is signed."

In the purchase of private houses the real estate brokers and
agents are even more merciless in their exploitation of the race.
By finding out the individuals in the community who might have
a thousand dollars or two saved, the brokers, directly or through
their agents, would influence such persons to invest in a home,
either by purchasing waste lands in some adjoining State or out-
of-the-way places or a house in their immediate neighborhood.
They influence the purchasers to pay up nearly all the money
they have in hand, and six months, a year or two after they
conspire to foreclose on the property or by well-devised tricks
get the purchasers so disgusted that they themselves give up
the properties, that generally fall back into the hands of the
brokers or their clique. The race is similarly robbed in the part-
time payment on expensive furniture they are induced to buy
through confidence men. A careful study of the situation from
1914 to the present time would reveal an alarming state of affairs.
I have only stated these facts to open the eyes of the people and
to show you from what source my enemies within the race come.
These tricks are common, and no organization, church or community is free from them. I make no exception of the great
Universal Negro Improvement Association. To work reform in
such an atmosphere challenges the divinity of a Christ and not
the frail and weak patience of a mortal. I have made my little
sacrifice in creating the sentiment for reform; let others now
take up the work and carry on while I remain confined.

Since writing the above, information has been telegraphed me
by my Secretary that a group of men within the Organization
in New York City has mortgaged the Liberty Hall there for the

sum of $32,000.00, and used the money to pay their friends—ex-officials of the Association, whom they allowed to secure judgments against the New York Association during my imprisonment without making any defense in the courts.

This Liberty Hall is the most valuable of the many single bits of property owned by the Association the world over. I was able to purchase same at great labor and sacrifice, and now, after nine months of imprisonment, the people have lost nearly all their equity in the property by deception.

I have also learnt that other property that I also worked hard to acquire for the people has been mortgaged or encumbered to the loss of the members.

THE APTITUDE OF THE NEGRO TO DISOBEY ORDERS COMING FROM HIMSELF

The Negro in Western civilization, because of his environments that force upon him a complex inferiority, is the most stubborn individual to discipline within the race. He has but little, if any, respect for internal racial authority. He cannot be depended upon to carry out an order given by a superior of his own race. If the superior attempts, in his presence, to enforce the order he is undermined and accused of "putting on airs." If the order is entrusted to a lieutenant, he, in turn, changes the order to suit himself and endeavors to constitute himself the superior individual.

In my experience, as head of the largest serious Negro organization in the world, I have found that to every hundred orders given to be executed for the absolute good of the organization and the race, not 2 per cent of them have been carried out in their entirety. This lack of obedience to orders and discipline checkmates the real, worthwhile progress of the race. This accounts for the Negro's lack of racial nationalistic ideal. The only cure for him is his removal to an atmosphere entirely his own, where he would be forced under rigid civil and other discipline to respect himself and his own racial authority.

EIGHT NEGROES

WRITE LETTER TO ATTORNEY GENERAL AND WHITE PRESS MISREPRESENTING GARVEY AND MOVEMENT

Tried to Make Out That There Is Hatred Taught by Garvey and U. N. I. A.

U. N. I. A. AND GARVEY STAND FOR LOVE AND HUMAN BROTHERHOOD—WHITE PEOPLE WELL KNOW THAT THE NEGRO IS HIS OWN ENEMY—ACTION OF EIGHT TRAITORS PROVE SAME TO BE TRUE

All Broad-Minded White People Are in Sympathy With U. N. I. A. to Help Race Improve Itself

---

Reprint from "The Negro World."

IN DEFENSE OF SELF.

Eight Negroes vs. Marcus Garvey

I have to bring to your attention the greatest bit of treachery and wickedness that any group of Negroes could be capable of. This thing is so shocking, so vicious and murderous as to make it impossible for any self-respecting person to imagine that any one, other than a culprit of the meanest kind, could be responsible for its authorship.

Honor Among Thieves.

It is said that there is honor even among thieves, but it is apparent that there is no honor and self-respect among certain Negroes, in that they would resort to the meanest and lowest methods possible, not only to pilfer the pockets of their brothers but to rob one of his fair name. Stealing a man's money is, as Shakespeare says, trash, but to injure a man's reputation, to tarnish his character, is a crime of the lowest kind which not even ordinary thieves would indulge in. To further imagine that a group of colored men could be responsible for writing to the Attorney General of the United States of America and to the white people at large in endeavoring to prejudice them against fellow Negroes whose only crime has been that of making an effort to improve the condition of the race is beyond the conception of the most fertile imagination; nevertheless, the thing has been done by a group of New York Negroes who have written their names down everlastingly as enemies of their own race by maliciously, wickedly and treacherously endeavoring to so misrepresent their race which represents the minority group in a majority civilization as to cause that majority to unwillingly, and not of its own accord, impose such punishment upon the race as to make it harder for us to survive in the country of our common adoption.

Writing to U. S. Attorney General

The following vicious and wicked letter was written by a group of men whose names are appended hereto and directed to the Honorable Attorney General of the United States of America. My comment will continue at the end of the communication.

The letter to the Attorney General:

2305 Seventh Avenue,
New York City, Jan. 15, 1923.

Hon. Harry M. Daugherty, United States Attorney-General, Department of Justice, Washington, D. C.

Dear Sir:

(1) As the chief law enforcement officer of the nation, we wish to call your attention to a heretofore unconsidered menace to harmonious race relationships. There are in our midst certain Negro criminals and potential murderers, both foreign and American born, who are moved and actuated by intense hatred against the white race. These undesirables continually proclaim that all white people are enemies to the Negro. They have become so fanatical that they have threatened and attempted the death of their opponents, actually assassinating in one instance.

(2) The movement known as the Universal Negro Improvement Association has done much to stimulate the violent temper of this dangerous element. Its president and moving spirit is one Marcus Garvey, an unscrupulous demagogue, who has ceaselessly and assiduously sought to spread among Negroes distrust and hatred of all white people.

(3) The official organ of the U. N. I. A., The Negro World, of which Marcus Garvey is managing editor, sedulously and continually seeks to arouse ill-feeling between the races. Evidence has also been presented of an apparent alliance of Garvey with the Ku Klux Klan.

(4) An erroneous conception held by many is that Negroes try to cloak and hide criminals. The truth is that the great majority of Negroes are bitterly opposed to all criminals, and especially to those of their own race, because they know that such criminals will cause increased discrimination against themselves.

(5) The U. N. I. A. is composed chiefly of the most primitive and ignorant element of West Indian and American Negroes. The so-called respectable element of the movement are largely ministers without churches, physicians without patients, lawyers without clients and publishers without readers, who are usually in search of "easy money." In short, this organization is composed in the main of Negro sharks and ignorant Negro fanatics.

(6) This organization and its fundamental laws encourage violence. In its Constitution there is an article prohibiting office holding by a convicted criminal, EXCEPT SUCH CRIME IS COMMITTED IN THE INTEREST OF THE U. N. I. A. Marcus Garvey is intolerant of free speech when it is exercised in criticism of him and his movement, his followers seeking to prevent such by threats and violence. Strik-

ing proof of the truth of this assertion is found in the following cases:

(7)   In 1920 Garvey's supporters rushed into a tent where a religious meeting was being conducted by Rev. A. Clayton Powell in New York City and sought to do bodily violence to Dr. Charles S. Morris, the speaker of the evening—who they had heard was to make an address against Garveyism—and were prevented only by action of the police. Shortly afterward members of the Baltimore branch of the U. N. I. A. attempted bodily injury to W. Asbhbie Hawkins, one of the most distinguished colored attorneys in America, when he criticized Garvey in a speech. During the same period an anti-Garvey meeting held by Cyril Briggs, then editor of a monthly magazine—The Crusader—in Rush Memorial Church, New York City, on a Sunday evening, was broken up by Garveyites turning out the lights.

(8) Several weeks ago the Garvey division in Philadelphia caused such a disturbance in the Salem Baptist Church, where Attorney J. Austin Norris, a graduate of Yale University, and the Rev. J. W. Eason were speaking against Garvey, that the police disbanded the meeting to prevent a riot of bloodshed. Reports state the street in front of the church was blocked by Garveyites, who insulted and knocked down pedestrians who were on their way to the meeting.

(9) In Los Angeles, Cal., Mr. Noah D. Thompson, a distinguished colored citizen of that city, employed in the editorial department of the Los Angeles Daily Express, reporting adversely on the Garvey movement as a result of his visit to the annual convention, was attacked by members of Garvey's Los Angeles division, who, it is alleged, had been incited to violence by Garvey himself, and only through the help of a large number of police officers was Thompson saved from bodily harm.

(10) A few months ago, when some persons in the Cleveland, Ohio. Division of the U. N. I. A. asked Dr. LeRoy Bundy, Garvey's chief assistant, for an accounting of funds a veritable riot took place, led, according to the Pittsburgh American, by Bundy himself.

(11) In Pittsburgh, Pa., on October 23 last, after seeking to disturb a meeting conducted by Chandler Owen, editor of the Messenger Magazine, Garveyites who had lurked around the corner in a body rushed on the street car after the meeting, seeking to assault him, but were prevented by the intervention of the police.

(12) When William Pickens, who had co-operated in the ex-

pose of the Garvey frauds, was to deliver an address in Toronto, Canada, Garveyites met him on the steps of the church, with hands threateningly in their hip pockets, trying to intimidate him, lest he should further expose the movement.

(13) In Chicago, after seeking to break up an anti-Garvey meeting, a Garvey supporter shot a policeman who sought to prevent him from attacking the speaker as he left the building.

(14) In New York last August during a series of meetings conducted by the Friends of Negro Freedom to expose Garvey's schemes and methods, the speakers were threatened with death. Scores of Garveyites came into the meetings with the avowed intention of breaking them up. This they were prevented from doing by the stern determination on the part of the leaders, the activities of the New York police and the great mass of West Indians and Americans, who clearly showed that they would not permit any cowardly ruffians to break up their meetings.

(15) In fact, Marcus Garvey has created an organization which in its fundamental law condemns and invites to crime. This is evidenced by section 3 of Article V of the Constitution of the U. N. I. A., under the caption, "Court Reception at Home." It reads: "No one shall be received by the Potentate and his Consort who has been convicted of felony, EXCEPT SUCH CRIME OR FELONY WAS COMMITTED IN THE INTEREST OF THE UNIVERSAL NEGRO IMPROVEMENT ASSOCIATION AND THE AFRICAN COMMUNITIES LEAGUE."

(16) Further proof of this is found in the public utterances of William Sherrill one of the chief officials in the organization and Garvey's envoy to the League of Nations Assembly at Geneva. Speaking at the Goldfield Theatre in Baltimore, Md., on August 18, 1922, he is quoted as saying: "BLACK FOLK AS WELL AS WHITE WHO TAMPER WITH THE U. N. I. A. ARE GOING TO DIE.'"

(17) What appears to be an attempt to carry out this threat is seen in the assault and slashing with a razor of one S. T. Saxon by Garveyites in Cincinnati, Ohio, when he spoke against the movement there last October.

(18) On January 1, this year, just after having made an address in New Orleans, the Rev. J. W. Eason, former "American Leader" of the Garvey movement, who had fallen out with Garvey and was to be the chief witness against him in the Federal Government's case, was waylaid and assassinated, it is reported in the press, by the Garveyites. Rev. Eason identified

two of the men as Frederick Dyer, 42, a longshoreman, and William Shakespeare, 29, a painter. Both of them are prominent members of the U. N. I. A. in New Orleans, one wearing a badge as chief of police and the other as chief of the Fire Department of the "African Republic." Dr. Eason's dying words, identifying the men whom he knew from long acquaintance in the movement, were:

(19) "I had been speaking at Bethany and was on my way home when three men rushed out at me from an alley. I saw their faces and (pointing at Dyer and Shakespeare) I am positive that these two men here are two of the three."

(20) The vicious inclination of these Garvey members is seen in their comments in an interview:

(20) (The N. Y. Amsterdam News reports): "Both Dyer and Shakespeare have denied the attack, but declared they were glad of it, as they said Eason richly deserved what he got. 'Eason', said one of them, 'was a sorehead. The association made him what he was. When he was expelled because of misconduct he went up and down the country preaching against Marcus Garvey, who is doing great good for our race. Someone who evidently thought it was time to stop his lies took a crack at him. I don't blame the one that did it. Eason richly deserved what he got.' "

(22) Eason says he knew the men who shot him were directed to do so. In so much, however, as the assassination of Mr. Eason removes a Federal witness, we suggest that the Federal Government probe into the facts and ascertain whether Eason was assassinated as the result of an interstate conspiracy emanating from New York. It is signficant that the U. N. I. A. has advertised in its organ, The Negro World, the raising of a defense fund for those indicted for the murder, seemingly in accordance with its constitution.

(23) Not only has this movement created friction between Negroes and whites, but it has also increased the hostility between American and West Indian Negroes.

(24) Further, Garvey has built up an organization which has victimized hords of ignorant and unsuspecting Negroes, the nature of which is clearly stated by Judge Jacob Panken of the New York Municipal Court, before whom Garvey's civil suit for fraud was tried: Judge Panken says: "It seems to me that you have been preying upon the guillibility of your own people, having kept no proper accounts of the money received for investments, being an organization of high finance in which the officers received outrageously high salaries and were per-

mitted to have exorbitant expense accounts for pleasure jaunts throughout the country. I advise those dupes who have contributed to these organizations to go into court and ask for the appointment of a receiver."

(25) For the above reasons we advocate that the Attorney-General use his full influence completely to disband and extirpate this vicious movement, and that he vigorously and speedily push the government's case against Marcus Garvey for using the mails to defraud. This should be done in the interest of justice; even as a matter of practical expediency.

(26) The government should note that the Garvey followers are for the most part voteless—being either largely unnaturalized or refraining from voting because Garvey teaches that they are citizens of an African republic. He has greatly exaggerated the actual membership of his organization, which is conservatively estimated to be much less than 20,000 in all countries, including the United States and Africa, the West Indies, Central and South America. (The analysis of Garvey's membership has been made by W. A. Domingo, a highly intelligent West Indian from Jamaica, Garvey's home, in "The Crusader" magazine, New York City; also by Dr. W. E. DuBois, a well known social statistician, in "The Century Magazine," February, 1922, New York City). On the other hand, hosts of citizen voters, native born and naturalized, both white and colored, earnestly desire the vigorous prosecution of this case.

(27) Again the notorious Ku Klux Klan, an organization of white racial and religious bigots, has aroused much adverse sentiment—many people demanding its dissolution as the Reconstruction Klan was dissolved. The Garvey organization, known as the U. N. I. A., is just as objectionable and even more dangerous, inasmuch as it naturally attracts an even lower type of cranks, crooks and racial bigots, among whom suggestibility to violent crime is much greater.

(28) Moreover, since its basic law—the very constitution of the U. N. I. A.—the organization condones and encourages crime, its future meetings should be carefully watched by officers of the law and infractions promptly and severely punished.

(29) We desire the Department of Justice to understand that those who draft this document, as well as the tens of thousands who will indorse it in all parts of the country, are by no means impressed by the widely circulated reports which allege certain colored politicans have been trying to use their influence to get the indictment against Garvey quashed. The signers of this appeal represent no particular political, religious or nationalistic

faction. They have no personal ends or partisan interests to serve. Nor are they moved by any personal bias against Marcus Garvey. They sound this tocsin only because they forsee the gathering storm of race prejudice and sense the imminent menace of this insidious movement, which cancerlike, is gnawing at the very vitals of peace and safety—of civic harmony and inter-racial concord.

The signers of this letter are:

HARRY H. PACE, 2289 Seventh avenue, New York City.

ROBERT S. ABBOTT, 3435 Indiana avenue, Chicago, Ill.

JOHN E. NAIL, 145 West 135th Street, New York City.

DR. JULIA P. COLEMAN, 118 West 130th Street, New York City.

WILLIAM PICKENS, 70 Fifth avenue, New York City.

CHANDLER OWEN, 2305 Seventh avenue, New York City.

ROBERT W. BAGNALL, 70 Fifth avenue, New York City.

GEORGE W. HARRIS, 135 West 135th Street, New York City.

Harry H. Pace is president of the Pace Phonograph Corporation.

Robert S. Abbott is editor and publisher of the "Chicago Defender."

John E. Nail is president of Nail and Parker, Inc., real estate.

Julia P. Coleman is president of the Hair-Vim Chemical Co., Inc.

William Pickens is field secretary of the National Association for the Advancement of Colored People.

Chandler Owen is co-editor of "The Messenger" and co-executive secretary of the Friends of Negro Freedom.

Robert W. Bagnall is director of branches of the National Association for the Advancement of Colored People.

George W. Harris is a member of the Board of Aldermen of New York City and editor of the "New York News."

Address reply to Chandler Owen, secretary of committee, 2305 Seventh avenue, New York City.

Considering The Letter

Let us consider the above letter as written by these wicked Negroes and sent to the Attorney-General of the United States of America and to the white press of the nation.

In the first paragraph of the above communication the writers, being Negroes, made use of the following statement, speaking to the Attorney-General. They say:

"As chief law enforcement officer of the nation, we wish to call your attention to A HERETOFORE UNCONSIDERED

MENACE TO HARMONIOUS RACE RELATIONSHIP.
THERE ARE IN OUR MIDST CERTAIN NEGRO CRIM-
INALS AND POTENTIAL MURDERERS, BOTH FOR-
EIGN AND AMERICAN BORN, WHO ARE MOVED AND
ACTUATED BY INTENSE HATRED AGAINST THE
WHITE RACE. THESE UNDESIRABLES CONTINUAL-
LY PROCLAIM THAT ALL WHITE PEOPLE ARE
ENEMIES TO THE NEGRO."

Good Old Darkies

To imagine that any group of Negroes could be so base as to
attempt to impress upon not only the Attorney General of the
United States of America but the white people at large that
members of their own race, although this is untrue, are desirous
of murdering members of the white race and of maintaining a
hatred against them, knowing well the position of the Negro
in America and his relationship to his white brother, is more
than any one would expect at this time in the struggle for race
uplift. Everyone knows that the statement is false and only
manufactured by these wicked and malicious individuals for the
purpose of directing the hatred of the Attorney General and
the white people of America against the Universal Negro Improvement Association and Marcus Garvey; nevertheless, the
statement reveals in these Negro men the lowest possible trait.
Like the good old darkey, they believe they have some news
to tell and they are telling it for all it is worth—the liars and
fabricators that they are, for everyone who knows the Universal
Negro Improvement Association and Marcus Garvey, white or
black, knows well that there is absolutely no desire on their
part to murder anybody, and that as far as criminals are concerned, more are to be found probably among those who signed
the letter than could be found in the extensive membership of
the Universal Negro Improvement Association.

No Hatred for White People

In paragraph 2 they stated that "the President-General of the
Universal Negro Improvement Association is Marcus Garvey,
an unscrupulous demagogue who has ceaselessly and assiduously sought to spread among Negroes distrust and hatred among
all white people."

About being unscrupulous and a demagogue, we need pay no
attention because the very villians who wrote such a letter are
better able to interpret unscrupulousness and demagogy than
anyone else, in that they seem to know more about it, but when
it comes to the point of "Marcus Garvey assiduously seeking to

spread among Negroes distrust and hatred for all white people,"
it is time for the white and black races to realize the truth
about the Universal Negro Improvement Association and its
President. At no time has the President of the Universal
Negro Improvement Association preached hatred of the white
people. That in itself is a violation of the constitution of the
organization, which teaches all its members to love and respect
the rights of all races, believing that by so doing, others will in
turn love and respect our rights.

No Ill Feeling Between Races

In paragraph 3 they try to make out that The Negro World,
sedulously and continually, seeks to arouse ill-feeling between
the races, yet in the same breath they further try to make out
that there is an alliance between Garvey and the Ku Klux Klan.
If these men were in the possession of their senses, and were
actuated by truth rather than by a desire to do harm and injury, they would have realized that the Ku Klux Klan is a
white organization and stands for white supremacy, so that
Garvey would be illogical and foolish if on the one hand he
preached ill feeling and hatred between the two races and then
went back upon all this and allied himself with the Ku Klux
Klan.

Wicked Maligners

These wicked maligners, above the protest of Marcus Garvey
and the Universal Negro Improvement Association for over one
hundred times, are still endeavoring to make it appear as if
there is some understanding between the President of this organization and the Ku Klux Klan.

"Bunch" of Selfish Grafters

In paragraph 4 these men state that: "An erroneous conception held by many is that Negroes try to cloak and hide their
criminals; the truth is that the great majority of Negroes are
bitterly opposed to all criminals and especially to those of their
own race because they know that such criminals will cause increased discrimination against themselves." And here we have
the high and lofty (?) purposes of these so-called race leaders
and race reformers. Other races try to reform and improve
their criminals whilst these splendid (?) Negro leaders of ours
avow that they are bitterly opposed to them simply because
they know that such criminals will cause increased discrimination against them. The selfish dogs that they are! It is not a
question of improving the condition of the race; it is a question
of how much they will benefit by being members of the race,

and if there is a criminal in the Negro race it is preferable that
he die rather than he should even exist to be improved, because
in so doing he may cause a discrimination against these selfish
individuals. We will prove that these men are just what they
state themselves to be in these paragraphs—a "bunch" of selfish grafters who have been living off the blood of the race and
who feel that the Universal Negro Improvement Association
has come upon the scene to so change and improve conditions
as to make it impossible for them to continue to suck the last
drop of blood out of our people under the guise of race business
men and race leaders.

Primitive Negroes

In paragraph 5 they further state that "the Universal Negro
Improvement Association is composed chiefly of the most primitive and ignorant element of West Indian and American Negroes."

Now we come to the crux of the matter. These fellows
represent a small group of men led by DuBois, who believe that
the race problem is to be solved by assimilation, and that the
best program for the Negro is to make himself the best imita-
tion of the white man and approach him as near as possible with
the hope of jumping over the fence into the white race and be
completely lost in another one hundred years; therefore they
hate everything Negro and they haven't sense enough to hide
it. Now, what do they mean by "the most primitive and ignorant element of West Indian and American Negroes?"

We will all remember that in the slave days the Negroes of
America and the West Indies were taken from Africa, and that
they then represented their tribal primitiveness. The emancipation, both in America and the West Indies, has brought us up
to the present state, with the majority of our people still bearing the resemblance of this tribal primitiveness, whilst a few
have endeavored to make themselves Caucasianized. These
men regard it as a crime to be as nature made us, and for us
to be as nature made us is to be ignorant; this shows how much
love these would-be Negroes have for the motherhood of our
race. The paragraph stating that "The respectable element
identified with the movement are largely professional men without calling," and that "the organization is composed of Negro
sharks and ignorant Negro fanatics," again reveal to us the
prejudice of these so-called business and professional scoun-
drels in that they endeavor to make it appear that only professional men are respectable, and that the organization has no

white sharks or ignorant fanatics in it. Were it not for the ignorant element of Negroes, these very fellows would have starved long ago, because all of them earn their living either by selling out the race under the guise of leadership or by exploiting the race in business. We only hope that the so-called ignorant Negroes of America will get to know these fellows as they are and let them pay the price through their pocketbooks for insulting so large a number of people who are proud of their race and color.

Forced Companionship Between Races

These nonentities show us in paragraph 5 that they do not believe in or cannot tolerate any organization that is not made up of either respectable white people or white sharks and ignorant fanatics. These are the fellows who foment lynching by always endeavoring to encourage forced companionship between the two races.

In paragraph 6 they depict Marcus Garvey as being intolerant of free speech, when, in fact, he has always advocated freedom of a universal kind. Again, in that paragraph they state that "The laws of the Universal Negro Improvement Association encourage violence." That is a lie. In many of the succeeding paragraphs they further endeavor to make out that the Garveyites or members of the Universal Negro Improvement Association have on several occasions disturbed the peace of public meetings and individuals organized to speak against Garvey and the movement.

The persons cited in the paragraphs who were alleged to be disturbed at the respective meetings are, with one exception, all members of the gang who have produced the letter now under criticism. They were all organized for the purpose of injuring the Universal Negro Improvement Association and Marcus Garvey. Nevertheless, at no time has the association or Mr. Garvey ever made any effort to check or embarrass them. Their own unworthiness created in their meetings, no doubt, the displeasure of the people who attended them, and now they try to label the Association and Garvey for it.

Colored Caste Prejudice

It is strange that whenever anything is referred to derogatory to the race, the gentlemen use the term "Negro," but whenever they want to impress either the Attorney-General or the white people of the standing of any member of the race they refer to him as "colored," such as paragraph 7, where reference was made to W. Ashbie Hawkins as one of the most distinguished colored attorneys in America, and to Noah D. Thompson as a distinguished colored citizen of Los Angeles, being employed, as he is in the editorial department of the white Los Angeles Daily Express. This reveals again the hidden motive or intention of these plotters who are endeavoring to set up social caste as distinct from Negro, which they claim to be primitive and ignorant.

Socialist Judge as Propagandist

In paragraph 25 the writers state that Judge Jacob Panken of the New York Municipal Court made certain derogatory remarks against Marcus Garvey and the Universal Negro. Improvement Association in a case brought before him. They hadn't the honesty to tell the public and the Attorney-General in their letter that Judge Jacob Panken is a Socialist and that at the time the case was being tried the Socialist group of Negroes in Harlem, New York, looked upon it as a splendid opportunity to get back at Marcus Garvey and the Universal Negro Improvement Association, who had been against Socialism, to have the Socialist judge take advantage of the situation while hearing a case of Garvey by making use of such remarks as would be used by the Socialist group as propaganda against Marcus Garvey and the Universal Negro Improvement Association.

Now they are making use of the Statement of Panken, as they had hoped he would use certain remarks for propaganda purposes, and they still believe that all Negroes are foolish enough to follow the advice of a Socialist judge against whom, as a Socialist, Marcus Garvey and the Universal Negro Improvement Association stand out. Hundreds of other cases have been heard before other judges of New York, and no one has ever used the remarks of Panken's, hence everyone knows they were made for propaganda purposes. Negro voters will take keen notice of it.

U. N. I. A. Controls Thousands of Votes

In paragraphs 27 they infer that "the Garvey followers are for the most part voteless." This is another lie, because the Universal Negro Improvement Association can marshal twenty times as many voters in the United States of America as all other Negro organizations put together, and that will be proved in a short while for the good of the race. About the "exaggerated membership" of the organization, any reader of the letter has but to take for granted that some of the things said about the organization in different parts of the country were true; but even if they were only partly true they would at least reveal a membership in three or four sections larger than they claim it to be all over the world. No one will ever know accurately the membership of the Universal Negro Improvement Association, because every second Negro you meet, if not an actual member, is one in spirit.

A Barber Shop Philosopher

In reference to W. A. Domingo as an "intelligent" West Indian Negro of Jamaica, who made an analysis of the Garvey membership, all those acquainted with the Universal Negro Improvement Association know that Domingo was a dismissed employee of the association and that he represents no one but himself. He is what is commonly called a "barber shop rat," who talks the kind of philosophy indulged in by frequenters of the tonsorial artist. He also is a Socialist who has a desperate grudge against work and who has the dreamer's vision that one day all the rich people of the world will divide up their wealth with the loafer, thereby bringing into existence the true reign of Socialism.

Crusader Magazine Out of Business

The magazine (Crusader) referred to also will be remembered as the mouthpiece of Cyril Briggs, who collected donations from colored and white people to support the paper some years ago, and who up to nine months ago published that he had received $5,000 for the purpose of starting another weekly paper called the Liberator, and that colored people were to subscribe $5,000 more. It is for me to state that the Crusader has long been out of business and the Liberator has never appeared. What has become of the $5,000 acknowledged and the subscriptions taken for the publication of the Crusader no one knows.

W. E. B. DuBois is a colored man who hates the drop of Negro blood in his veins, and he is as much against the Universal Negro Improvement Association from a prejudiced viewpoint as the Devil is against Holy Water.

The demolition of the Universal Negro Improvement Association is asked for by the writers of the letter. In paragraph 27 they state that the organization is as objectionable and even more dangerous than the Ku Klux Klan. Take it for granted that the Ku Klux Klan sought white supremacy and the Universal Negro Improvement Association sought black supremacy. If there was any such program these Negros would prefer the existence of the Ku Klux Klan to the Universal Negro Improvement Association, because to have the Universal Negro Improvement Association is more dangerous. This shows they are illogical, foolish, wicked and malicious. They seek to destroy the Universal Negro Improvement Association as a Negro organization, not knowing that a precedent will be set for the destruction of all Negro organizations that seek in any way to improve the condition of the Negro race. These bigots believe they own the United States of America. They have no more right in America than other colored men, so that they will be very much disappointed if they believe that the Department of Justice and the Attorney-General would, for the purpose of pleasing eight Negroes, defeat the ends of the Constitution of the United States of America. But who are these Negroes? They themselves have told us what they are in their relationship to business.

Group of Unknown Persons

Take them as they are, one is a business exploiter who endeavors to appeal to the patriotism of the race by selling us commodities at a higher rate than are charged in the ordinary and open markets. Another is a race defamer of Chicago who publishes in his newspaper week after week the grossest scandals against the race, showing up the crimes and vices of our people. He was the man who published in his newspaper for over one year a full page advertisement showing the pictures of two women, a black woman and a very light woman, with the advice under the photograph of the black woman to "lighten your black skin." The other is a real estate shark who delights, under the guise of race patriotism, to raise the rent of poor colored people even beyond that of white landlords, who are generally more considerate, knowing the economic condition of the colored race. Another is a hair straightener and face bleacher, whose loyalty to race is to get the race to be dissatisfied with itself. Still we have another as a turn coat and lackey who has not enough manhood to stand up and defend his own cause in his relationship to others, but who was so mean and low down as to have approached Marcus Garvey for a job about nine months ago, representing to him that he was unfairly dealt with because of his color, and after he was offered a berth he took that as an opportunity of going back to his old employers to get them to raise his salary, which he never would have gotten raised, but for the fact that he had secured new employment in a rival organization. Then we have the grafter Socialist who started so many enterprises among colored people, such as the Elevator Men's Union, and has not been able to account for the funds. We have still another who maintained a Blue Vein Society Church in Detroit, Mich., and who was subsequently relieved of his charge because of alleged immorality; and another unscrupulous politician whom everyone knows to be a man who has lost the respect of the ordinary members of the community. These are the angels and "respectable" citizens who have written this infamous letter to the Attorney-General of the United States of America against Marcus Garvey and the Universal Negro Improvement Association.

Sinners to Purge Their Souls

It is hoped that these sinners will purge their souls of the crime they have committed against their race, for surely in the accusation of their own consciences they shall not see salvation.

Let me implore all members, divisions and friends of the Universal Negro Improvement Association to now make every effort to push forth the cause of our great movement. Now is the time for every man and woman to stand loyally by this organization. Whatsoever might have been the difference of opinions in local divisions or your dissatisfaction, you must stand unitedly as millions of members throughout the world, for the enemy within our race is now knocking at the door. It is for us unitedly to stand together and meet the foe. The greatest weapon we can use at this time is stronger organization.

Let all members come together more than ever everywhere and prove to the world that not by misrepresentation, but by fair play and justice shall the great problem of race be settled.

It is hoped that the white people of America and of the world will take no cognizance of the vicious lies and misrepresentations of these wicked Negroes. Everyone will realize that the Universal Negro Improvement Association preaches the doctrine of human brotherhood and the love of all mankind.

MARCUS GARVEY, President-General,
Universal Negro Improvement Association.

New York, Tuesday, February 6, 1923.

P. S.—The signers of the letter to the Attorney-General are nearly all Octoroons and Quadroons. Two are black Negroes, who have married Octoroons. One is a Mulatto and Socialist, a self-styled Negro leader, who had expressed his intention of marrying a white woman but was subsequently prevented from doing so by the criticism of the U. N. I. A. With this lone exception all of the others are married to Octoroons.—M. G.

N. B. Since the signing of the letter to the Attorney General, George Harris has been twice defeated for election as Alderman.

KEEPING THE NEGRO DOWN

My enemies, and those opposed to the liberation of the Negro to nationhood are so incompetent and incapable of meeting argument with argument and tolerance with tolerance that they have cowardly sought the power of Government to combat and destroy me; and, even there they have failed, because Government has no power to destroy the spiritual urge of men, but can only succeed through persecution to expose its acts of injustice in seeking to serve the interest of one class of its citizenry against that of another. The cowards have forced their friends and associates who happen to be a part of Government to use the majesty of such a Government against me. That shows their weakness and inability to stand up under the onward march of African redemption and real Negro freedom. They are all afraid of the black man. They try to hold him down and yet claim his inferiority. A large number will have to stay down with him if the show goes on. The white man preserves himself by a foul, he cannot, or will not, play a straight game.

W. E. BURGHARDT DU BOIS AS A HATER OF DARK PEOPLE

Calls His Own Race "Black and Ugly," Judging From the White Man's Standard of Beauty

---

Trick of National Association for the Advancement of Colored People to Solve Problem by Assimilation and Color Distinction

(Reprint from Negro World, February 13, 1923.)

W. E. Burghardt DuBois, the Negro "misleader," who is editor of the "Crisis," the official organ of the National Association for the Advancement of "certain" Colored People, situated at 70 Fifth Avenue, New York City, has again appeared in print. This time he appears as author of an article in the February issue of the "Century" Magazine under the caption, "Back to Africa," in which he makes the effort to criticize Marcus Garvey, the Universal Negro Improvement Association and the Black Star Line. This "unfortunate mulatto," who bewails every day the drop of Negro blood in his veins, being sorry that he is not Dutch or French, has taken upon himself the responsibility of criticizing and condemning other people while holding himself up as the social "unapproachable" and the great "I AM" of the Negro race. But we will see who Mr. DuBois is, in that he invites his own characterization. So we will, therefore, let him see himself as others see him.

"Fat, Black, Ugly Man"

In describing Marcus Garvey in the article before mentioned, he referred to him as a "little, fat, black man; ugly, but with intelligent eyes and a big head." Now, what does DuBois mean by ugly? This so-called professor of Harvard and Berlin ought to know by now that the standard of beauty within a race is not arrived at by comparison with another race; as, for instance, if we were to desire to find out the standard of beauty among the Japanese people we would not judge them from the Anglo-Saxon viewpoint, but from the Japenese. How he arrives at his conclusion that Marcus Garvey is ugly, being a Negro, is impossible to determine, in that if there is any ugliness in the Negro race it would be reflected more through DuBois than Marcus Garvey, in that he himself tells us that he is a little Dutch, a little French, and a little Negro. Why, in fact, the man is a monstrosity. So, if there is any ugliness it is on the part of DuBois and not on the part of the "little fat, black man with the big head," because all this description is typical of the African. But this only goes to show how much hate DuBois has for the black blood in his veins. Anything that is black, to him, is ugly, is hideous, is monstrous, and this is why in 1917 he had but the lightest of colored people in his office, when one could hardly tell whether it was a white show or a colored vaudeville he was running at Fifth avenue. It was only after the Universal Negro Improvement Association started to pounce upon him and his National Association for the Advancement of Colored People that they admitted that colored element into the association that could be distinguished as Negro, and it was during that period of time that Weldon Johnson and Pickens got a look-in. But even Pickens must have been "ugly" for DuBois, for they made it so warm for him up to a few months ago that he had to go a-hunting for another job, the time when Marcus Garvey was willing to welcome him into the Universal Negro Improvement Association.

DuBois and White Company

It is no wonder that DuBois seeks the company of white people, because he hates black as being ugly. That is why he likes to dance with white people, and dine with them, and sometimes sleep with them, because from his way of seeing things all that is black is ugly, and all that is white is beautiful. Yet this professor, who sees ugliness in being black, essays to be a leader of the Negro people and has been trying for over fourteen years to deceive them through his connection with the National Association for the Advancement of Colored People. Now what does he mean by advancing colored people if he hates black so much? In what direction must we expect his advancement? We can conclude in no other way than that it is in the direction of losing our black identity and becoming, as nearly as possible, the lowest whites by assimilation and miscegenation.

This probably is accountable for the bleaching processes and the hair straightening escapades of some of the people who are identified with the National Association for the Advancement of Colored People in their mad desire of approach to the white race, in which they see beauty as advocated by the professor from Harvard and Berlin. It is no wonder some of these individuals use the lip stick, and it is no wonder that the erudite Doctor keeps a French Beard. Surely that is not typical of Africa, it is typical of that blood which he loves so well and which he bewails in not having more in his veins—French.

Lazy and Dependent

In referring to the effort of Marcus Garvey and the Universal Negro Improvement Association to establish a building in Harlem, he says in the article: "There was a long, low, unfinished church basement roofed over. It was designed as the beginning of a church long ago, but abandoned. Marcus Garvey roofed it over, and out of this squat and dirty old Liberty Hall he screams his propaganda. As compared with the homes, the business and church, Garvey's basement represents nothing in accomplishment and only waste in attempt."

Here we have this "lazy dependent mulatto" condemning the honest effort of his race to create out of nothing something which could be attributed to their ownership, in that the "dirty old Liberty Hall" he speaks of is the property of Negroes, while in another section of his article he praises the "beautiful and luxurious buildings" he claims to be occupied by other black folk, making it appear that these buildings were really the property of these people referred to, such as, according to his own description, "a brick block on Seventh avenue stretching low and beautiful from the Y. W. C. A. with a moving picture house of the better class and a colored 5 and 10 cent store, built and owned by black folks." DuBois knows he lies when he says that the premises herein referred to were built and are owned by black folks. They are the property of industrious Jews who have sought an outlet for their surplus cash in the colored district. The Y. W. C. A. is a donation from the good white people; but he continues by saying "down beyond on One Hundred and Thirty-eighth street the sun burns the rising spire of an Abyssinian Church, a fine structure built by Negroes who for one hundred years have supported the organization, and are now moving to their luxurious home of soft carpets, stained windows and swelling organ." He also knows that this building has been subscribed to by the Church Extension Society, which is white, and therefore the building is not entirely owned by the members of the Abyssinian Church. Finally, he says "the dying rays hit a low, rambling basement of brick and rough stone." This in reference to Liberty Hall.

Independent Negro Effort

Liberty Hall represents the only independent Negro structure referred to in the classification of DuBois about buildings up in Harlem, but he calls this independent effort "dirty and old," but that which has been contributed by white people he refers to in the highest terms. This shows the character of the man—he

A group of Black Cross Nurses of the Universal Negro Improvement Association on parade in New York City during the convention of 1922.

has absolutely no respect and regard for independent Negro effort but that which is supported by white charity and philanthropy, and why so? Because he himself was educated by charity and kept by philanthropy. He got his education by charity, and now he is occupying a position in the National Association for the Advancement of Colored People, and it is felt that his salary is also paid by the funds that are gathered in from the charity and philanthropy of white people. This "soft carpet" idea is going to be the undoing of W. E. B. DuBois. He likes too much the luxurious home and soft carpets, and that is why he is naturally attracted to white folks, because they have a lot of this; but if he were in Georgia or Alabama he would now be stepping on the carpets of Paradise; but that is not all of the man, as far as this is concerned. He ridicules the idea that the Universal Negro Improvement Association should hold a social function in Liberty Hall on the 10th of August, 1922, at which certain social honors were bestowed upon a number of colored gentlemen, such as Knighthood and the creation of the Peerage.

Social Honors for Negroes

In referring to the matter, he says in the article: "Many American Negroes and some others were scandalized by something which they could but regard as a simple child's play. It seemed to them sinister. This enthronement of a demagogue, a blatant boaster, who with monkey-shines was deluding the people, and taking their hard-earned dollars; and in high Harlem there arose an insistent cry, "Garvey must go!'" Indeed DuBois was scandalized by the creation of a Peerage and Knighthood by Negroes, and in truth the person who is responsible for the creation of such a thing should go, because DuBois and those who think like him can see and regard honor conferred only by their white masters. If DuBois was created a Knight Commander of the Bath by the British King, or awarded a similar honor by some white Potentate, he would have advertised it from cover to cover of the "Crisis," and he would have written a book and told us how he was recognized above his fellows by such a Potentate, but it was not done that way. This was an enthronement of Negroes, in which DuBois could see nothing worth while. He was behind the "Garvey must go!" program started in Harlem immediately after the enthronement, because he realized that Garvey and the Universal Negro Improvement Association were usurping the right he had arrogated to himself as being the highest social dignitary, not only in Harlem but throughout the country.

Marcus Garvey and His Birth and DuBois

In the seventh paragraph of his article DuBois has the following to say: "Let us note the facts. Marcus Garvey was born on the northern coast of Jamaica in 1887. He was a poor black boy, his father dying in the almshouse. He received a little training in the Church of England Grammar School, and then learned the trade of printing, working for years as foreman of a printing plant. Then he went to Europe and wandered about England and France working and observing until he finally returned to Jamaica. He found himself facing a stone wall. He was poor, he was black, he had no chance for a university education, he had no likely chance for preferment in any line, but could work as an artisan at small wage for the rest of his life."

Now let us consider Marcus Garvey in comparison with DuBois. W. E. B. DuBois was born in Great Barrington, Mass., in 1868. Some wealthy white people became interested in him and assisted in his education. They sent him to Fisk University, from Fisk to Harvard, where he graduated as a commencement orator. He raised part of the money for his later education by giving recitals in white summer hotels. Where he was born—that is, in Great Barrington, Mass.—he had early association with white surroundings. He was brought up with white boys and girls of the better type and more aristocratic class as found in rural towns. He had no love for the poor, even the poor whites in his neighborhood, although he was but a poor, penniless and humble Negro. As proof of that he wrote the following on the tenth page of his book known as "Dark Water:" "I greatly despised the poor Irish and South Germans who slaved in the mills (that is, the mills of the town in which he was born), and I annexed myself with the rich and well-to-do as my natural companions." Marcus Garvey's father, who was also named Marcus Garvey, was one of the best known men in the parish in which he was born, St Ann, Jamaica. For a number of years he held prominent positions in the parish and was regarded as one of the most independent black men on the island, owning property that ran into thousands of pounds. Through his own recklessness he lost his property and became poor. His poverty did not in any way affect Marcus Garvey, Jr., in that the mother of the latter assumed the responsibility that the father failed to assume, and he therefore got an early education, not through charity, as did DuBois, but through the support of a loving mother. Marcus Garvey, Jr., never knew the consideration of a father, because at the time when he was born his father had already lost all he had, and had shifted his obligation to his children on to the shoulders of their mother. With the assistance Marcus Garvey got from his mother he educated himself, not only in Jamaica but traveled throughout South and Central America, the West Indies and Europe, where for several years he studied in completing the education that he had already laid the foundation for in his native home. All that was not done by the charity of any one, but by Marcus Garvey himself, and the support he got from his mother. While, on the other hand, DuBois, starting even from the elementary stage of his education up to his graduation from Harvard and his passing through Berlin, got all that through the charity and philanthropy of good white people. Admitting that Marcus Garvey was born poor, he never encouraged a hatred for the people of his kind or class, but to the contrary devoted his life to the improvement and higher development of that class within the race which has been struggling under the disadvantage that DuBois himself portrays in his article.

Comparison Between Two Men

Marcus Garvey was born in 1887; DuBois was born in 1868; That shows that DuBois is old enough to be Marcus Garvey's father. But what has happened? Within the fifty-five years of DuBois' life we find him still living on the patronage of good white people, and with the thirty-six years of Marcus Garvey's (Who was born poor and whose father, according to DuBois, died in a poor house) he is able to at least pass over the charity of white people and develop an independent program originally financed by himself to the extent of thousands of dollars, now taken up by the Negro peoples themselves. Now which of the two is poorer in character and in manhood? The older man, who had all these opportunities and still elects to be a parasite, living off the good will of another race, or the younger man, who had sufficient self-respect to make an effort to do for himself, even though in his effort he constructs a "dirty brick building" from which he can send out his propaganda on race self-reliance and self-respect.

Motive of DuBois

To go back to the motive of DuBois in the advocacy of the National Association for the Advancement of Colored People is to expose him for what he is. The National Association for the Advancement of Colored People executives have not been honest enough to explain to the people of the Negro race their real solution for the Negro problem, because they are afraid that they would be turned down in their intention. They would make it appear that they are interested in the advancement of the Negro people of America, when, in truth, they are but interested in the subjugation of certain types of the Negro race and the assimilation of as many of the race as possible into the white race.

The Negro Problem

As proof of the intention underlying the National Association for the Advancement of Colored People we will quote from DuBois himself. He states in his article:

"We think of our problem here as THE Negro problem, but we know more or less clearly that the problem of the American Negro is very different from the problem of the South African Negro or the problem of the Nigerian Negro or the problem of the South American Negro. We have not hitherto been so clear as to the way in which the problem of the Negro in the United States differs from the problem of the Negro in the West Indies.

"For a long time we have been told, and we have believed, that the race problem in the West Indies, and particularly in Jamaica, has virtually been settled."

Now DuBois speaks of this settlement of the problem of the race in the West Indies and Jamaica with a great deal of satisfaction. What kind of a settlement is it? DuBois knows well, but he is not honest enough to admit it, because he himself visited Jamaica and saw the situation there, wherein an arrangement has been effected whereby the white man is elevated to the highest social and economic heights, and between him is socially and economically elevated the mulatto type of DuBois, and beneath them both is the black man, who is crushed to the very bottom socially and economically.

Settlement of the Problem

DuBois regards this as a settlement of the problem in the West Indies and Jamaica. Now this is the kind of a settlement that he and the National Association for the Advancement of Colored People want in America, and they have not been honest enough to come out and tell us so, that we might act accordingly. This is why DuBois bewails the black blood in his veins. This is why he regards Marcus Garvey and the Universal Negro Improvement Association as impossible. This is why he calls Marcus Garvey "black and ugly." But while this settlement in Jamaica and the West Indies satisfies DuBois, and probably would satisfy him in America, he must realize that the fifteen million Negroes in the United States of America do not

Scene at a court reception of the Universal Negro Improvement Association in New York at which Prince Kojo Tavalou, of Dahomey, the Potentate of the Universal Negro Improvement Association, and Mr. Garvey, as Provisional President of Africa, received the delegates and guests of the International Convention of the Negro Peoples of the World in 1924.

desire such a settlement; that outside of himself and a half-dozen men of his school of thought, who make up the Executive of the National Association for the Advancement of Colored People, the majority of Negroes are not studying him and his solution of the problem, but all of us colored people of whatsoever hue, are going to fight together for the general upbuilding of the Negro race, so that in the days to come we may be able to look back upon our effort with great pride, even as others worse positioned than ourselves have struggled upward to their present social, economic and political standing among races and nations.

Deception and Hypocrisy

To show the deception and hypocrisy of DuBois, he pretends, (in the above-quoted paragraph from his article) as if he were not thoroughly acquainted with the problem in the West Indies, when, in another paragraph, he states the following:

"This is the West Indian solution of the Negro problem:

"The mulattoes are virtually regarded and treated as whites, with the assumption that they will, by continued white inter-marriage, bleach out their color as soon as possible. There survive, therefore, few white Colonials save newcomers, who are not of Negro descent in some more or less remote ancestor. Mulattoes intermarry, then, largely with the whites, and the so-called disappearance of the color line is the disappearance of the line between the whites and mulattoes and not between the whites and the blacks or even between the mulattoes and the blacks.

"Thus the privileged and exploiting group in the West Indies is composed of whites and mulattoes, while the poorly paid and ignorant proletariats are the blacks, forming a peasantry vastly in the majority, but socially, politically and economically helpless and nearly voiceless. This peasantry, moreover, has been systematically deprived of its natural leadership, because the black boy who showed initiative or who accidentally gained wealth or education soon gained the recognition of the white-mulatto group and might be incorporated with them, particularly if he married one of them. Thus his interest and efforts were identified with the mulatto-white group."

This is the kind of settlement that DuBois speaks of; and this is the kind of settlement that he wants in the United States of America. DuBois, you shall not have it!

Garvey Challenges DuBois

DuBois says that "Garvey had no thorough education and a very hazy idea of the technique of civilization." DuBois forgets that Garvey has challenged him over a dozen times to intellectual combat, and he has for as many times failed to appear. Garvey will back his education against that of DuBois at any time in the day from early morning to midnight, and whether it be in the classroom or on the public platform, will make him look like a dead duck on a frozen lake.

Is DuBois Educated

DuBois seems to believe that the monopoly of education is acquired by being a graduate of Fisk, Harvard and Berlin. Education is not so much the school that one has passed through, but the use one makes of that which he has learned.

If DuBois' education fits him for no better service than being a lackey for good white people, then it were better that Negroes were not educated. DuBois forgets that the reason so much noise was made over him and his education was because he was among the first "experiments" made by white people on colored men along the lines of higher education. No one experimented with Marcus Garvey, so no one has to look upon him with surprise that he was able to master the classics and graduate from a university.

DuBois is a surprise and wonder to the good white people who experimented with him, but to us moderns he is just an ordinarily intelligent Negro, one of those who does not know what he wants.

The Man Who Lies

DuBois is such a liar when it comes to anything relating to the Universal Negro Improvement Association, the Black Star Line and Marcus Garvey that we will not consider his attacks on the Black Star Line seriously. He lied before in reference to this corporation and had to swallow his vomit. He has lied again, and we think a statement is quite enough to dispose of him in this matter.

This envious, narrow-minded man has tried in every way to surround the Universal Negro Improvement Association and Marcus Garvey with suspicion. He has been for a long time harping on the membership of the Universal Negro Improvement Association as to whether we have millions of members or thousands. He is interested because he wants to know whether these members are all paying dues or not, in that he will become very interested in the financial end of it, as there would be a lot of money available. DuBois does not know that whether the Universal Negro Improvement Association had money or not he wouldn't have the chance of laying his hands on it, in that there are very few "leaders" that we can trust with a dollar and get the proper change. This is the kind of leadership that the Universal Negro Improvement Association is about to destroy for the building up of that which is self-sacrificing; the kind of leadership that will not hate poor people because they are poor, as DuBois himself tells us he does, but a kind of leadership that will make itself poor and keep itself poor so as to be better able to interpret the poor in their desire for general uplift. He hates the poor. Now, what kind of a leader is he? Negroes are all poor black folk. They are not rich. They are not white; hence they are despised by the great professor. What do you think about this logic, this reasoning, professor? You have been to Berlin, Harvard and Fisk; you are educated and you have the "technique of civilization."

The Failure of a Critic

DuBois harps upon the failure of other Negroes, but he fails to inform the public of his own failures. In his fifty-five years DuBois personally has made success of nothing. In all his journalistic, personal and other business efforts he has failed, and were it not for Mary White Ovington, Moorefield Storey, Oswald Garrison Villard and Spingharn, DuBois, no doubt, would be eating his pork chops from the counter of the cheapest restaurant in Harlem like many other Negro graduates of Harvard and Fisk.

Test of Education and Ability

When it comes to education and ability, Garvey would like to be fair to DuBois in every respect.

Suppose for the proof of the better education and ability Garvey and DuBois were to dismantle and put aside all they possess and were placed in the same environment to start life over afresh for the test of the better man? What would you say about this, doctor? Marcus Garvey is willing now because he is conceited enough to believe that in the space of two years he would make you look like a tramp in the competitive rivalry for a higher place in the social, economic world.

Let not our hearts be further troubled over DuBois, but let fifteen million Negroes of the United States of America and the millions of the West Indies, South and Central America and Africa work toward the glorious end of an emancipated race and a redeemed motherland.

Ignoring Freedom

DuBois cares not for an Empire for Negroes, but contents himself with being a secondary part of white civilization. We of the Universal Negro Improvement Association feel that the

greatest service the Negro can render to the world and himself
at this time is to make his independent contribution to civilization. For this the millions of members of the Universal Negro
Improvement Association are working, and it is only a question
of time when colored men and women everywhere will harken
to the voice in the wilderness, even though a DuBois impugns
the idea of Negro liberation.

THE BLACKS IMPRISONED

A Strange Comparison

The number of Blacks in jails, prisons, and reform-
atories of the United States, the British West Indian
and other colonies and countries, the protectorates
and dominions of Great Britain and France in Africa,
is shamefully in excess, proportionately, of all other
race groups to the populations; and between the
blacks and other shades of Negroes, not including the
sambo or brown skins and dark mullatoes—the percentage is almost 99% against the Black and other
dark ones. Something is wrong.

There is a conspiracy somewhere. I can't stand for
it. I would rather hang than be quiet about it. It is
a sin, crime and shame. It is a blot upon and against
the white man's system of justice meted out to the
blacks, with the history of slavery considered. The
white race cannot escape the blame, and fail to honestly admit that there is a collusion between them and
the near whites against the interests of the blacks,
which in turn is sure to destroy the racial purity of
the white race and inflict grave injury upon the blacks.

WHY I HAVE NOT SPOKEN IN CHICAGO SINCE 1919

1n 1919 the "Chicago Defender," published by Robert S. Abbott, libeled the Black Star Line Corporation and me. Abbott has always, through rivalry and jealousy, been opposed to me, and especially through my not being born in America and my criticism of his dangerous newspaper policy of always advising the race to lighten its black skin and straighten out its kinky hair. I am also hated by him because of my determination to dignify the term Negro as against his policy of referring to the race only as "race men" or "race women" without defining what race, whether Caucasian, Mongolian, African or Negro.

Action was brought against Abbott in New York and subsequently on other charges in Chicago. The libel suit of the Black Star Line was tried in New York in the Fall of 1920 and judgment was returned in favor of the company. My suit in New York was deferred on the calendar for 1921 and the cases in Chicago against Abbott were listed for the Fall of 1921.

In the Fall of 1919 I visited Chicago to address a series of meetings in the interests of the Universal Negro Improvement Association. During my stay in the city the following incidents happened: When the Black Star Line was incorporated in June, 1919, I was told by its colored attorney in New York that among the States the corporation was permitted to sell stock was Illinois. On my preparing to visit Chicago in the Fall he again assured me that it was legal for the company to sell stock in Chicago. On my going to the city the corporation sent one of its stock salesmen along with my party, consisting of five persons, my private secretary, my stenographer, the American leader of the Association and the International organizer and myself. At the meetings where I spoke it was customary for the company, through its salesman, to sell stock to the members of the organization. Not knowing the laws of Illinois and believing the advice of the attorney for the company, I allowed the salesman to sell stock for the corporation at the first meeting I addressed in the series. My name as President of the corporation, along with that of the Treasurer or Secretary, had already been signed to stock certificates in the New York office, and one of the books containing these stock certificates was given to the stock salesman by the New York office. He sold about $90.00 worth of stock at the meeting by filling in the people's names above the signatures and made his own entries on the counterfoil. The "Chicago Defender," I was informed, employed a colored man, connected with a detective agency, to approach me at my lodgings the following morning after I had addressed a large assembly the night previous at the public school where the meetings were being held, to request me to sell him two shares of stock ($5.00 per share) in the Black Star Line. I told him that I did not sell stock, but that there was a stock salesman somewhere about the city who represented the company and who would attend to him. He said his wife attended the meeting I addressed the previous night and she was so impressed with the speeches and had become so interested to join in and help the race and the organization that she sent him right off as he came home from work to get the stock, and that he must take it home, for, "you know," he said, "when a woman wants a thing, she must have it." He implored me to try and find the address where he could locate the salesman. I hadn't the address, so I advised him to be at the meeting that night, when the salesman would be there. He said he would be at the meeting, but he wanted to give his wife the stock before for her satisfaction. My secretary, who had the telephone number of the local division of the Universal Negro Improvement Association, was out, and I advised the man, if he was in such a hurry, to wait in the parlor for the arrival of the secretary, who might give him the telephone number or address of the office. I left the man waiting. About five minutes later my secretary returned, and she informed me that she had given a man on the main floor the address of the local office, as he informed her that I stated he might find the stock salesman there. I dismissed the matter from my mind and never gave it another thought until at eight o'clock that night, five minutes before I was scheduled to speak to a large audience of thousands that had assembled, when I was suddenly called from the platform by two white men in company with the colored man and, informed that I was under arrest for violating the Blue Sky law or something to that effect. I never knew, at that time, that there was such a law as a "blue sky law" or "grey sky law." I had been in the country just over a couple of years and all my time and attention were given to organization work, depending on others to inform me about the law. I was more interested in the good of humanity than the law. When I arrived at the police station, dressed in my evening clothes, I found out what it was all about. My secretary had me released under bond of $2,000 to appear in court the next morning. My release was at ten o'clock that night, which was too late to address the meeting from which I was taken. The plan was to spoil my meetings and humiliate me—the colored man's way of revenging his adversary.

The next morning, when I arrived in court with a lawyer,

who was attorney to a banker friend of mine in Chicago, who arranged the bail, I found the court room crowded with representatives of the "Chicago Defender." The lawyer explained the situation of my not knowing that there was such a law to be violated. The Court sensed the plot, and with the consent of the representative of the State Attorney's office, the amount paid for stock was refunded by the stock salesman, and I believe I was fined $100.00 or the case dismissed. It was all done by the attorney in consultation with the Judge, and I made no further inquiries. Three days after this incident, on preparing to leave Chicago for Pittsburgh, where I had an appointment, I was served with notice of suit filed against me for libel by Robert S. Abbott, editor and proprietor of the "Chicago Defender." I was at a loss to know whereat or how I libeled the man. I took the notice to an attorney (colored) whom I met on my first visit to Chicago in 1917, and whose wife had spoken in New York on special invitation before the members of the Universal Negro Improvement Association. The notice or summons did not state in detail the nature of the offense. He was paid a retainer of $100 and instructed to register his appearance on my behalf immediately. He stated to me that no particulars were filed and that it was just an attempt to scare me. However, he would attend to the matter and keep me informed at my home in New York. I wrote to this attorney several times in 1920, and he informed me that nothing had been filed against me. The two cases I had against Abbott in Chicago were also deferred on the calendar and I was told by the attorney that I would be informed of the time of trial. I planned a thirty-day trip to the West Indies and Central America in the Spring of 1921. A month before I wrote to the attorneys in Chicago about the cases, and I was informed that they would not be called in my absence. I also had the assurance of the New York colored attorney that the New York case against Abbott would not be called. As I have explained many times before, I was forcibly kept out of the United States for five months, during which time the two cases against Abbott in Chicago and the one in New York were allowed to go by default, without any information or notice to me about them, and the Abbott case against me in Chicago was allowed to go to trial and a default judgment taken for $5,000. A month after Abbott took out a body execution warrant against me. On my learning of the matter, I sought to open the case, and I was advised that a reopening would not be allowed. This accounts for my non-appearance in Chicago since 1919.

MESSAGE OF MARCUS GARVEY TO MEMBERSHIP OF UNIVERSAL NEGRO IMPROVEMENT ASSOCIATION FROM ATLANTA PRISON

August 1, 1925.

Fellow members of the Universal Negro Improvement Association and co-workers in the cause of African Redemption:

It is with feeling of deep love and thoughts of a great future for the Negro race that I address you.

My months of forcible removal from among you, being imprisoned as a punishment for advocating the cause of our real emancipation, have not left me hopeless or despondent; but to the contrary, I see a great ray of light and the bursting of a mighty international political cloud which will bring you complete freedom.

We have gradually won our way back into the confidence of the God of Africa, and He shall speak with the voice of thunder, that shall shake the pillars of a corrupt and unjust world, and once more restore Ethiopia to her ancient glory.

Our enemies have seemingly triumphed for a while, but the final battle when staged will bring us complete success and satisfaction.

The wicked and obstructive elements of our own race who have tried to defeat us shall meet their Waterloo, and when they fall we feel sure they shall not rise again. For many years since our general emancipation, certain elements composed chiefly of a few octoroons and quadroons who hate the blood of our race (although part of us) with greater venom, scorn and contempt than the most prejudiced of other races, have tried to undermine and sell us out to the mighty powers of oppression, and within recent years, they have succeeded in getting the ear of the leading statesmen of the world, and have influenced them to treat the bulk of us Negroes as dogs, reserving for themselves, their kind and class, all the privileges and considerations that, as a race, would have been otherwise granted us and merited.

The National Association for the Advancement of Colored People, although pretending to be interested in and working for the race, is really and truly the active representative of   this class. I trust you will not believe that my opposition to the National Association for the Advancement of Colored People is based upon any other motive than that of preventing them from destroying the Negro race that they so much despise and hate.

I am always glad and ever willing to co-operate with all

Negro organizations that mean good by the race, but I am perfectly convinced and satisfied that the present executive personnel of the National Association for the Advancement of Colored People is not serious nor honest in intent toward the black race.

When they shall have removed their white and colored officers who believe in the racial extermination of the Negro type, and honestly promote a program for race uplift, then we can cooperate with them for the general good, until then we regard them as among the greatest enemies of our race. They teach race amalgamation and inter-marriage as the means of destroying the moral purity of the Negro race and our absorption within the white race which is nothing less than race suicide.

You must not forget that we have enemies also within our own organization—men whose motives are selfish and who are only seeking the "loaves and fishes" and not honest in heart in serving the people. Yet we have to make the "wheat and tare" grow together till the day of harvest. It is impossible to know all our enemies at one and the same time. Some are our enemies because they do not want to see the Negro rise; some because the organization supplies the opportunity for exploitation; others because they are unable to resist the temptation of the evil one who would have them betray us in our most righteous effort of racial love and freedom.

I feel that my imprisonment has helped to open the eyes of the world to your true position, and has made friends to your cause. Men and women of other races who were mis-informed and deceived by our enemies, are now seeing the light. The graves that the enemies of race pride and purity dug for us may yet entomb them.

Hold fast to the ideal of a dignified Negro race. Let us work together as one people, whether we are octoroons, quadroons, mulattoes or blacks for the making of a nation of our own, for in that alone lies our racial salvation.

The few who do not want to be with us will find out their mistake sooner or later, but as for us, let us all unite as one people. It is no fault of ours that we are what we are—if we are black, brown, yellow or near white, the responsibility for the accident is not ours, but the time has now come for us to get together and make of ourselves a strong and healthy race.

The National Association for the Advancement of Colored People wants us all to become white by amalgamation, but they are not honest enough to come out with the truth. To be a

Negro is no disgrace, but an honor, and we of the Universal
Negro Improvement Association do not want to become white.
We do not seek for the whiteman's company more than he
would seek after ours. We are proud and honorable. We love
our race and respect and adore our mothers. We are as proud
as our fathers were in the days of old, and even though we
have passed through slavery in the western world, we shall not
hang down our heads for Ethiopia shall again return to her
Glory.

The Universal Negro Improvement Association is a union of
all groups within the race. We love each other with pride of
race and great devotion and nothing in the world shall come
between us.

The truth has to be told so that we may know from whence
our troubles cometh. Yet we must never, even under the
severest pressure, hate or dislike ourselves. Even though we
oppose the present leaders of the National Association for the
Advancement of Colored People, we must remember that we
are all members of one race, rent asunder by circumstances.
Let us help them by advice and conversion. Men like DuBois
need our sympathy. We should teach them to love themselves,
at least, have respect for the blood of their mothers—our mothers, who have suffered so much to make us what we are. We
should take the truth to the innocent members of the National
Association and save them from the mis-leadership of the white
and colored persons who seek to destroy our race by miscegenation and use them as a pawn towards that end, and to foster
their own class interest. Let us reach out and convert these unfortunate people and thus save them from a grave error. They
should not be left to the tender mercies of their vile leaders, for
they are good people and of our race, they mean good, but are
mis-directed.

I have to return many thanks to you, the members of the Universal Negro Improvement Association, for the loyal support
you have given me during my trials and troubles, suffered for
you. I can realize that you have at all times done your best for
me, even as I have done the best for you, as God has directed
me to see. If it were not for you I would have been left helpless and comfortless. I shall never forget you. If it were not
for you the members and some of the officers of local divisions, I
would have been left penniless and helpless to fight my enemies
and the great powers against me, and to even in the slightest
way give protection to my wife whom I neglected and cheated
for the cause that I so much love.

It is surprising how those we serve and help most can be ungrateful and unkind in our absence, and generally seek to take advantage of the one who cannot help himself. My name I leave with you the people. For you I have built up an organization of international standing. Every sacrifice has been made. My youth, money and ability were freely given for the cause. The cause you now see. It was not made in a day, but it took years of steady work and sacrifice. Others will now try to take advantage of my predicament to rob and exploit you in my name and blame the absent and helpless, but ever remember that from nothing, I raised up an organization through which you may see the light; let others, if they may, show the ability to carry on that which they have found, and not seek to exploit, to ruin and then blame the absent one as is so easy to do. It was during my absence in the West Indies when I was helpless to act, that the traitors within and enemies without did the deeds of dishonor that placed me for the Black Star Line where I am. Let not the same characters succeed to enrich themselves at the cost of the name of one who cannot protect himself or protect you. You must protect yourselves—the time has come. My full tale of warning is not to be told here, but suffice it to say that on you I rely for the ultimate success of our great effort, and but for you I would have been hopelessly defeated in the great struggle to "keep the fire burning." Probably I should not have expected better for even our Blessed Master feared worse when his chief disciples failed him. I am not complaining, but I warn you against treachery, deceit, self-seeking, dishonesty and racial disloyalty. Personally, as I have so often stated, I counted the cost years ago, but the responsibility is not all mine, but equally that of the one whom I love with great devotion and fondness. You, I feel sure, have done your duty by her and will continue to shield and protect her, while, because of my imprisonment for you, I find it impossible to do my duty.

The God of our Fathers will raise up friends for the cause of Africa, and we who have struggled in the wilderness for all this time shall surely see the promised land.

Hold fast to the Faith. Desert not the ranks, but as brave soldiers march on to victory. I am happy, and shall remain so, as long as you keep the flag flying.

I hope to be with you again with greater energy and force to put the program over. I have yet to let my real voice and soul be heard in Europe, Asia and continental America in plea for the Negro's rights and for a free and redeemed Africa. Yet, I have not spoken. I await the summons of my God for the greater work that must be done. In the meanwhile pray for success and pray for me.

A STRANGE PARADOX—WHO IS THE NEGRO NEWSPAPER DECEIVING?

Negro newspapers in one breath will publish and make big display of lynchings, mob-violences, riots, injustices perpetrated and heaped upon the race, and denounce them with the most heated ferocity and point out the hopelessness of the race in the midst of its environments, yet in the same issues in another breath denounce most vehemently the plan of nationalism for the race in Africa and attempt to crucify me for advocating it as a solution of the problem. Who are these newspapermen fooling?

LETTER ADDRESSED TO ATTORNEY GENERAL AND MARKED PERSONAL

Atlanta, Ga., Sept. 16, 1925.

Hon. John Sargent,
    U. S. Attorney General,
      Washington, D. C.

Honorable and Dear Sir:

I write to explain a peculiar situation of affairs affecting the financial and other interests of a large number of American citizens in which I am involved, and to ask your consideration in helping me to so adjust the matters concerning them that may lead to the prevention of great loss to the said people.

I am head of the organization known as the Universal Negro Improvement Association, having a membership of several million the world over. I was also head of the Black Star Line, Inc., through which I was convicted on the charge of using the mails to defraud. I was President and one of the managing directors of the Black Cross Navigation and Trading Company. The first and last mentioned of these organizations have assets coveted by a group of conspirators who have been trying to swindle the people out of them. Recently, since the publication of the information that I will be deported, these conspirators have become more active to immediately dispose of these assets for their own good.

Fake judgments have been allowed to pile up against the organizations to increase the liabilities, and now a wholesale effort is being made to gobble up every available penny of the people's investments.

I am powerless to protect the organizations and the people from my confinement. Papers of record left in my office that should have been used in protecting the rights of the people are either being wickedly withheld, stolen or concealed. I was unable, on my arrest, to visit my office or consult with any of my then associates and to properly pass over to them information and directions that could have been used to advantage immediately, in that I was rushed to the city jail and from there to Atlanta, cutting off all communication.

Much is involved. At the present time it is most likely that an investment of over $150,000 in the steamship General G. W. Goethals will be lost without my immediate help on the spot.. Investments in properties (real estate) in New York City involving nearly $100,000 will be lost, as well as other investments in other parts of the country.

I earnestly desire to save these people this great loss, and for that reason I am respectfully and earnestly asking you to permit me, under the proper departmental method, to go to New York City, to there straighten out all of these matters, as well as others involving the investments and interests of the people, so that if I am deported or held in prison, no harm will come to the said interests.

The longer I stay away from properly straightening out these affairs the greater becomes the loss to the people.

The conspirators are acting daily and they have nearly reached the end where they hope everything will be lost to the people, and the only salvation is immediate action.

I am also asking that a Special Agent of the Department be appointed to go over the facts with me in New York for the uncovering of the conspiracy to steal the assets herein referred to. I do not ask this as a personal privilege, but in the name of more than a million black American citizens.

Trusting that you will give this matter your favorable and prompt consideration and attention.

I beg to remain,

Most respectfully,
MARCUS GARVEY.

Box 1733
19359

THE REPLY

DEPARTMENT OF JUSTICE
WASHINGTON, D. C.

DRM-dok

42-793-Garvey

September 18, 1925.

Marcus Garvey,
     United States Penitentiary,
        Atlanta, Ga.

Sir:

    Referring to your letter of September 16, 1925, addressed to the Attorney General, I have to state that your application for Executive clemency has received previous consideration. In view of the facts reported, together with the adverse recommendations received, the case is not entitled to submission to the President for his consideration. The facts you submit would not warrant the Department in reopening your case.

          Respectfully yours,

           James A. Finch
           Pardon Attorney.

N. B. The envelope in which this letter arrived on the 23rd, bears Washington post mark Sept. 21, 11 P. M. and not 18th, as per dictation of letter in reply to communication of the 16th, which left Atlanta on the 17th. The facts and recommendation referred to were those supplied by the Trial Judge and Prosecutor, from whom I have been appealing.   M. G.

STATEMENT OF CONVICTION.

"Let Fate do her worst; there are relics of joy
Bright dreams of the past, which she cannot destroy;
Which come in the night—time of sorrow and care,
And bring back the features that joy used to wear.
Long, long be my heart with such memories filled,
Like the vase in which roses have once been distilled—
You may break, you may shatter the vase if you will,
But the scent of the roses will hang round it still."

———

Justice, in modern jurisprudence, is doubtful, and much more so than that of other ages, with all things considered proportionately.

It is sad to make this confession, and, after so many improvements have been added to our boasted civilization. Justice, however, is left more to the feeling, like or dislike of the individual or group of individuals charged with the responsibility of administering it, rather than to its ethical interpretation or the corporate demands of the community or society, hence, if the individuals are wrong, we suffer from the result, and not because our civilization, in that respect, is all together imperfect.

If you have friends and influence; if you are powerfully allied with the party in control of Government; if you are potently rich or if you are born to the silver spoon and among the elect of society, you may have "justice" your way, whether you are guilty or not. Sometimes it is invoked by the "call" on the telephone, the chat around the dinner table, over the "glass" at the club or by the "written" letter. If the request is made by the friend of the particular individual in power, then with a "clap" on the shoulder, a "shake" of the hand, or a "kick off" of the feet with the hands in the pockets the promise is made, "well, I will see," I will "fix it all right," and there goes a fair sample of "modern justice." It was so with the Greeks and Romans, it is so now, and may be yet for a long while.

The poor wretch who has no such affiliation or means of approach "gets it in the neck," and for him "justice" is clear and positive without the hope of appeal. For his petty or minor crime, he is made "an example" of, and the able jurist admonishes with high-sounding morals, and by the heaviest of sentences imposed "purges" the atmosphere surrounding a privileged society, by locking away in some prison or penitentiary the unfortunate creature, who is looked upon as a menace to established order, an evil-doer and breaker of the solemn and sacred laws of the land.

In such an atmosphere, being a Negro who sought the higher liberities and rights of his people, was I charged, convicted and sentenced to a long term of imprisonment. The facts surrounding my case constitute a moral public scandal for which any people, and even those of despised Russia or Turkey, ought to hang their heads in shame, judged by the professed standards of civilization.

Like the Jews· who "framed" the Man Christ because he sought to do good, other Negroes, jealous of my success and power among the masses as a leader, "framed" me for the convenience and satisfaction of those who sought my elimination and desired to be rid of me because of their fear of my personality in the body politic and international.

During the summation of the Prosecutor before the Jury at my trial, he was bold enough to acknowledge that the witnesses who testified against me were liars and some of them thieves; but that was immaterial as the desire was to convict me. After such a brazen statement and confession, a jury—not of my race, but of the race from which I desired to free the Negro so as to save him from extermination as threatened through the hidden plans of a superior intelligence that now materially rules the world—convicted me of using the mails in a "scheme" to defraud a person I never met, did not know, had nothing to do nor corresponded with, even though he testified that he could not remember what was sent to him, by some one, surely not me, in an empty envelope bearing the rubber stamp imprint of the Black Star Line. To be convicted for using the mails to defraud on the evidence of a rubber stamped, empty envelope that could have been stamped and posted by any enemy or hired agent with the intent that prompted the prosecution, is a departure in our system that may lead to the incrimination and conviction of any man in our civilization who trespasses within the bounds or province where there is such a law. In modern jurisprudence, controlled as it is, by politics, wealth and power, the "marked" person falls a prey to the hunter who sets the "legal" trap that never fails to "catch" the individual when badly "wanted." It is only a question of time when every individual "sought" or "wanted" is "caught" by the legal entanglements prepared for the purpose of rendering harmless and permanently silent those not desired or who may constitute themselves a stumbling block in the way of privileged and hereditary power. Somebody says (but if it were not said, then I say it now), that "the laws of our civilization have but one interpretation for the poor and ignorant, and for those of wealth and power, there are many interpretations, hence the poor are generally convicted on the one meaning, while the rich are freed on the many interpretations."

I am satisfied of having won a glorious victory over all my enemies, in that they found it beyond their own power and ability to defeat me, hence the resort to and use of the sovereign power of Government to destroy me. It took the power of the Roman State to destroy the physical person and influence of Christ who sought to save the souls of men. His enemies failed of themselves, and because He was Christ after three days he demonstrated his power over all. In my case, and that of other reformers, blessed with only physical power, we take satisfaction in seeing the thing we suffer for survive and become of benefit to our fellowmen.

I sought to emancipate the millions of Negroes all over the world from political and industrial thraldom, which was too big an effort for rivals within my own race to stand; and those of other races who profit by their exploitation and servitude regarded me as a dangerous menace to be rid of by all means, hence the combined effort to use the great power of the State to silence and destroy me. How well they have succeeded the future will tell; but I am of the firm belief that "truth one day will get a hearing" and then the shame and disgrace, if any, will be rightly placed.

Ideals of liberty, freedom and righteousness do not prosper in the 20th century except they coincide with oil, rubber, gold, diamond, coal, iron, sugar, coffee and such other minerals and products desired by the privileged, captialists and leaders who control the systems of Government.

Righteousness and justice in the 20th century are interpreted to mean class interest whether it be of the abused "bourgeoise," "plutocrats" or "communists."

The fiery communists are fighting against one class interest for the enthronement of theirs—a group of lazy men and women who desire to level all initiative and intelligence and set a premium on stagnation,—and so our world goes wrong.

I am against the brand of communism that is taught in America, because it is even more vicious than all the other ism's put together. In America it constitutes a group of liars, plotters and artful deceivers who twist—a one third truth to a whole big lie, and give it out to the unthinking clientele for consumption. Communism among Negroes in 1920-21 was

represented in New York by such Negroes as Cyril Briggs and
W. A. Domingo, and my contact with, and experience of them,
and their methods are enough to keep me shy of that kind of
communism for the balance of my natural life.   A group of men
of any ism or party who would seek to kill or illegally or improperly dispose of a political adversary because he doesn't agree
with their particular brand of politics, are no associates for
those who seek the perfection of Government.   Because I sought
to build up in Africa a democratic Negro State and not a Com-
mune the Negro Communists preferred me dead. than alive.
Such class interest is dangerous, and it is foolish for the masses,
as they are now situated, to jump from the frying pan into the
fire.   The American Negro is warned to keep away from communism, as it is taught in this country; he should work, watch
and wait for his own opportunity, which is largely to his own
making.   Such a doctrine as this makes me unpopular to both
extremes, with some of my own race thrown in, hence my predicament.

I pray the day will never come for the Negro and America
when the Government falls into the hands of such representatives of Communism.   I would rather be dead than live under
Government administered by such characters.

To be convicted, as I was, does not mean anything.   Any one
could have been thus incriminated.   No one is responsible for
the lies of others and for the vengeance of his enemies.   To
be "framed" up and convicted in an atmosphere over which you
have no control, or even a fair chance to make yourself clear by
having the truth told doesn't make one a criminal.

For a man who never plays cards and doesn't know the difference between poker and any other game, to be ruthlessly
lied upon by even an Assistant District Attorney, as being a
player of such a game, and to be convicted by a Jury on such
testimony is to leave the subject of conviction surprised, but
amused, at the way things are done, or rather, crimes committed
in the name of Justice.   In addition to being called a poker
player, a game I knew nothing about, I was also accused of
"playing the races," "a white slaver," "a character before whom
Jessie James pales into insignificance," all such lies and non-
sense were paraded before the Jury to arouse prejudice, and
added to all these I was supposed to be a cold blooded murderer
who killed one man, or caused him to be killed and had planned
the killing of the Judge, District Attorney and the entire Jury.
All these lies were manufactured to ensure the conviction of
one man whose only crime is the love of his race.   But didn't

the Prosecutor himself claim in open court in his address to
the Jury and by statement before the Court that he loved
Negroes more than Marcus Garvey did, and it was because of
his love for them why he wanted him convicted, because he
was their greatest enemy? Now don't laugh, it is serious, for
when a child I was told the story of the spider and the fly, and
it seems so applicable in this case of love, that I would not
have you lose the moral for anything in the world. For witnesses to look you in the face and lie on you about things
that never happened, and then to be convicted on such testimony
and to hear a Judge moralize upon your behavior because of
that, is to make you frown upon modern Justice and regard it
as a farce. Imagine that all these things happened to you and
then you will become better appreciative of the strain I underwent during the eventful days of my trial and confinement.

My head is as high as Olympus. My character is as firm as
Gibraltar's rock, and no Judge, Jury or Prosecutor in the
world, shall make me a criminal when I am not. In prison I
feel happy knowing that I am only occupying a cell intended
for others whose morality is below mine, and whose consciences
can make them nothing but cowards.

I believe in God. I believe in a final judgment of the soul.
I am satisfied to wait until then to face my accusers and con-
demners and may the Lord have mercy on their souls.

If the white man's God is not a myth, I wonder how some of
the race will face Him? Is He a God of moods, prejudices and
passions? If He is not, then whiteman, where do you expect
and intend to spend Eternity? Probably Mr. Bryan will tell
us when he has completely disarmed the evolutionists. But
whether this God exists in reality for the white man or not,
there is an Eternity, and I intend to take no chances with not
getting there right. Resting on my conscience I defy a world
to make a criminal of me, and I am more satisfied to rest in the
honor and cleanliness of my own soul and character, than to
merit the good will of the agents of injustice and corruption.

A District Attorney once had condemned and subsequently
electrocuted an innocent man charged with murder. His skillful prosecution and brilliant effort to convict the accused on
manufactured and circumstantial evidence were with the eye
of creating a reputation for future success in his profession.
Subsequently the innocence of the electrocuted man was discovered, but the Attorney had already built up a large practice
and made his reputation through the case. Oh! for the repu-

tations that have been made and built upon the dead bones **and** the wrecked lives of innocents. What **man** can look his fellows in the eye having made his name and reputation by stealing the characters of others? What place can such an individual find in society when at every turn the graves of his victims rise before him and the shadows of the wrecked lives, like Banquo's ghost, haunt him? To take success thus attained is to forfeit every impulse of manhood. I would rather be a hangman!

HOW ALLEGED CRIMES ARE DISPOSED OF.

(Reproduced from the "Atlanta Constitution," Atlanta, Georgia, Wednesday, July 16, 1925.)

Only Few Acquitted in Federal Courts.

"The United States district court for the northern district of Georgia tried 1,189 criminal cases during the fiscal year ending July 1, 1925, and in these cases only 127 were acquitted according to the annual report of Capt. W. Hager, United States district attorney, made public Tuesday. The convictions amounted to 89 per cent. of the cases tried, which is the best record yet made by the district attorney's office."

Let fools who do not understand the ways of modern society laugh as they may. Crime is what you make it. The prison doesn't always hold the biggest criminals. They are criminals in our day who have no influence, no money, no powerful friends,—no one to reach the seat of temporal power; and those who steal from the innocent, ignorant and the public are **good citizens,** because they are above temporal reproach.

Satisfaction though, will come for those who are punished unjustly by the laws of man, when, by the arrangement of Deity, Dives and his lord are ushered in before the Common Judge who is not color or class blind, who is not of a party nor for a party, but for **Justice** to all mankind.

I dismiss from my mind the thought of crime. I laugh at my accuser, and to him who thinks evil, I say, man, purge thyself.

> "Should you feel inclined to censure
> Faults you may in others view,
> Ask your own heart, ere you venture,
> If that has not failings, too."

BROTHERLY LOVE, CHARITY AND GOD

The unreasonable of the white race prate about the inferiority of the Negro. They tell us historically, biologically, ethnologically, economically, politically and generally, that the black man is inferior, incompetent, and by himself unable to contribute much to human progress; yet, when a black man shows himself determined to prove the race's ability, they grab hold of him, harass him, make a monkey out of him, and, if he persists, they either club him to death by trickery, sinister designs, or incriminate him and send him to prison. If he rises up in the West Indies, they so environ him that he is bound to die of starvation; if he rises up in America they employ others of his race to discredit him, and, if that is difficult, frame him and send him to prison for imaginary crime. If he rises up in Africa, he is undermined and murdered or exiled from his native hearth. And still the white man boasts of his superiority through brute force of shot, gas and shell. Give the Negro fifty years of unhampered or unmolested freedom of action and in less than that time he will prove to the world that he is the greatest genius Nature ever fashioned and the most liberal and charitable of God's creatures. Give the Negro a chance and he will teach the white man the way to Justice, Charity, Brotherly Love and God.

THE IDEALS OF TWO RACES

A Message to the Negroes of Harlem introducing Mr. John Powell of the Anglo-Saxon Clubs of America.

October 28, 1925.

Fellow Members and Friends of the Universal Negro Improvement Association:

As you are aware our Association stands for the highest and best in human effort. We desire for ourselves a fixed and permanent place in the affairs of the world—fixed and permanent from the viewpoint of autonomous recognition. Our longing cry has been for a "Free and Redeemed Africa"—a home where our scattered race might assemble itself in the exclusive promotion and development of those things that are dear and precious to the human heart, and representative of the loftiest in progressive ideals.

In our desire to achieve greatness as a race, we are liberal enough to extend to others a similar right. We are not selfish in desiring all to the exclusion of others. We believe in the doctrine of "Live and let live." To others, not of our race, we extend the heartiest of best wishes, and in so doing we feel that there are others who also wish us well.

In the great American confusion of races it is hard to discern our friends, but as a people we have not been entirely friendless. When I speak of friendship I mean that which is sturdy, honorable and sincere. Such a friendship I desire to apprise you of in the introduction of Mr. John Powell, of the Anglo-Saxon Clubs of America.

Mr. Powell represents a body of men and women for whom I maintain the greatest respect because of their honesty and lack of hypocrisy. They represent the clean-cut and honest section of the white race that uncompromisingly stands for the purity of their race, even as we unhesitatingly and determinedly agitate and fight for the purity of the Negro race. All races should be pure in morals and in outlook, and for that we, as Negroes, admire the leaders and members of the Anglo-Saxon Clubs. They are honest and honorable in their desire to purify and preserve the white race even as we are determined to purify and standardize our race.

Mr. Powell and his organization sympathize with us even as we sympathize with them. I feel and believe that we, the two organizations, should work together for the purpose of bringing about the ideal sought—the purification of the races, their autonomous separation and the unbridled freedom of self-development and self-expression. Those who are against this are enemies of both races, and rebels against morality, nature and God; for acting to the contrary, no good or ethical purpose can be served, but a continuation of world confusion, immorality and sin.

I unhesitatingly endorse the race purity idea of Mr. Powell and his organization, and I have pledged my moral support to their program in that direction, expecting of the honorable and honest of his race the same regard and support for ours. We do not ask more than we will give. We want a free and independent nation of our own, with the right to make our distinctive contribution to civilization, and for this we offer no apology.

I am asking you, my friends and co-workers, to hear Mr. Powell, whom I have invited to speak to you. Extend to him and the Anglo-Saxon Clubs the courtesy and fellowship that is logical to the program of the Universal Negro Improvement Association.

With affectionate regards and best wishes, I have the honor to be,

Your Obedient Servant,
MARCUS GARVEY,
President-General,
Universal Negro Improvement Association.

AN ANSWER TO THE APPEAL TO WHITE AMERICA

Speech delivered by Mr. John Powell of the Anglo-Saxon Clubs of America, at Liberty Hall, New York City, U. S. A., on the 28th day of October, 1925.

(Reprint from Negro World)

Mr. Chairman and members of the Universal Negro Improvement Association, I have never in my life been more touched and more moved, than by the cordial reception you have given me and my friends tonight. I wish I were an orator so that I might give adequate expression to the feelings and the thoughts that are moving in me.

I would like to tell you how it was that I came to know more about your organization, and the purposes for which it stands. Major Ernest Sevier Cox, a man who spent six years of his life traveling all around the world in order to study racial problems in various parts of the world, wrote a book called "White America." Major Cox was for several years in Africa; he worked in the mines in South Africa; he went through the whole length and breadth of Africa from the Cape up to Cairo, studying the various problems that came under his observation. He wrote this book, "White America," the purpose of which was to find a real and ultimate solution to that great problem which has vexed the mind and heart of all America now for 200 years and more. His book was very violently criticised by certain newspapers which I believe, are under the influence of the National Association for the Advancement of Colored People. So it was a great surprise as well as a great pleasure to Major Cox when he received a letter from a member of the Garvey organization in St. Louis. his letter told Major Cox that its writer had seen a copy of "White America," had read it and felt tremendously encouraged to find that there was a white man advocating essentially the cause of the Garvey movement. He wrote that there were many things in that book which he could not approve of, as his point of view was different, but it was a great joy to the members of that Chapter of the Universal Negro Improvement Association to find that there was a white man who was seriously advocating those very purposes for which Marcus Garvey stood.

Major Cox's Letter

He requested Major Cox to write a letter to be read before that branch of your organization. Major Cox wrote a very strong and very moving letter, which was read by Mr. Ditto before his organization, and he wrote back to Major Cox and said, "I wish you could have been here to have seen the enthusiasm with which your letter was received; our members are reading and studying "White America," and many of the members have said that "White America" should be in every Negro's home along with the Bible." Major Cox was naturally very pleased with this, and later when Mr. Ditto asked if he might publish the letter Major Cox suggested that he enlarge on the letter. The result of that was a little pamphlet which Mr. Cox wrote and published, entitled "Let My People Go." It is a message from white men who wish to keep the white race white to black men who wish to keep the black race black; and it is dedicated to Marcus Garvey, that great leader who has sought to do for his own race what the greatest of white Americans sought to do for that race and to encourage the race to do for itself—none other than Abraham Lincoln.

With Marcus Garvey at Atlanta

This pamphlet was brought to the attention of your great leader and he corresponded with Major Cox, and last· June when I went down to Georgia to address the Georgia Legislature in favor of a bill for the preservation of racial integrity, I went to the prison to see Marcus Garvey. I expected to see a man with bowed head; I expected to see a man depressed and unhappy and embittered, because in the meantime I had read his "Appeal to the Soul of White America," and it had touched me to the heart. When I saw him I saw a man with head erect, with eyes open and clear, unashamed and unafraid, free from all bitterness, free of rancor; not one word of complaint escaped his lips, not one word of bemoaning; his one thought was for you—his people and his loyal followers. And as we discussed these matters I found that in every essential principle the ideals and ideas of Marcus Garvey were identical with those of the organization which I have the honor to represent—the Anglo-Saxon Clubs of America.

There was nothing that Marcus Garvey could not say frankly and freely to me without danger of misunderstanding; there was nothing that I could not say to Marcus Garvey openly and frankly and freely without danger of misunderstanding; and I realized that I was in the presence of a man of the highest idealism and the noblest courage and the profoundest wisdom; a man dedicated to a noble and a sacred cause—the cause of the independence and integrity of his race.

On my return to Richmond at the next meeting of the Anglo-Saxon Clubs, I reported the result of my conference with your leader. The newspapers were represented at that meeting and the Richmond Times-Dispatch (white) published an account of my talk. In the next issue of the Norfolk Journal and Guide—a Negro newspaper—there were large headlines spread across the top of the page "Garvey In Prison Forms New Alliance." The readers of the Norfolk Journal and Guide were reminded that Garvey had formerly been a member of the Ku Klux Klan, and that his association with the Ku Klux Klan having been cut short by his imprisonment, even in prison he had taken occasion to ally himself with other enemies of the race, namely, the Anglo-Saxon Clubs of America. That article was copied in the Negro Press all over the country, and unfortunately, I am afraid, caused a great deal of ill feeling and ill will.

Garvey did not hesitate to assume full responsibility for everything that he had said to me and for every assurance that he had given to me and Major Cox. As a result of that, the wife of your great leader came to Richmond about that time. I introduced a resolution at the meeting of the Anglo-Saxon Clubs of America, that our organization write a message of sympathy and of confidence to the Richmond Chapter of the Universal Negro Improvement Association, expressing our indignation at the injustice that had been meted out to Marcus Garvey, expressing our approval of his activities for the integrity and independence of his race, and requesting that our sentiments be communicated to his wife, who was to be the guest of honor on that occasion, and requesting that if it were possible that arrangements may be made by which members of our organization could attend that meeting. The chairman of the Richmond Chapter at once replied cordially and courteously inviting us to attend the meeting. We did attend the meeting, and never in all my life have I heard speeches of greater force, of greater power than I heard that night, and it is as a result of that night that I was asked to appear before you tonight.

The Negro Is Awake

One more thing: A member of your organization in Detroit got in touch with Major Cox and asked him to send out 50 copies of "White America." Major Cox sent the copies out. A few days later he received a letter saying that before the package was opened all the copies were disposed of; please send 250 more. Major Cox did not have 250 copies to send but sent what he had. A few days later he received a letter from Detroit saying that there were several Negroes acting as book agents in Detroit selling "White America" to white people in Detroit. Within two weeks 17,000 copies of Major Cox's pamphlet were used in Detroit. Think of what that means! It means that the Negro in the United States is today awake; he is aroused; he listens no longer to the flattery and the blandishments of the politician; he is beginning to look facts in the face. It means that at least in Detroit, and I believe over the whole length and breadth of this land, the Negro is beginning to show more clearly the way towards a real solution of this problem than the white man who considered himself so wise.

It was a joy to me to realize that there were such men as the members of your organization in St. Louis and Detroit. It was a bitter mortification to me to realize that the members of your organization were doing spontaneously what I have been laboring for ten years to get the people of my race to do. And I want to congratulate you from the bottom of my heart for the courage and independence that you are showing in facing those facts and seeing them clearly and distinctly. And I speak to you not merely as a white American; I speak to you as a Virginian; I speak to you as the descendant of slave owners.

The South Does Not Hate the Negro

I want to say to you tonight that there is no decent white man in the South who can hate the Negro race; no decent man, no sane man who can have aught in his heart but feelings of kindliness and of gratitude towards the Negro race. As you have heard before, your people did not come here willingly; they were captured by force and violence; they were thrust in between decks in the horrible pest ships; they were brought to America, and when they thought they were going to breathe the free air of God's blue heaven and see God's green earth they found themselves still shackled in the chains of slavery. And why? There were forests to be cut down; there was land to be tilled; there was work of all kinds to be done, and the white man wanted the work done but did not want to take the trouble to do it himself. Your ancestors did that work; it is owing to their muscle, to their brawn, to their industry, to their good-will that this country made the progress in a few years that otherwise would have taken hundreds of years.

Not only that; but there never was a people who under hardship and oppression showed the spirit of kindliness and forgiveness which your people have shown. At a time when the armies of the South were fighting in a great war between the States— a war which was being fought on the part of the North to free you and your ancestors; at that very time, your people in the South stayed on the plantations, protected the women and children, raised the crops and sent the food to the front to the army that was fighting to keep them in slavery. And white people in the South know that; and white people in the South know what it means, and they are not insensible to feelings of gratitude and of thankfulness. We know what we owe you; we know it, and we intend that the whole world shall see that we appreciate this debt and pay it not only justly but generously. (Applause.)

The Negro Not Yet Free

And what is this situation that faces us? It is not a new situation; it has come up again and again in the past; we see it in various parts of the world today. What is this situation? The Civil War was fought that the slaves in America might be free, that war was won, the Emancipation Proclamation proclaimed them free; the 13th Amendment to the United States Constitution secured that freedom; the 14th Amendment made them citizens of this country, and the 15th Amendment provided penalties on any State that should attempt to take the right of suffrage from any man on account of his race, color or previous condition of servitude. The great war; three constitutional amendments, and is the Negro in America today free? (Cries of No! No!)

In the South, honest people will tell you, the Negro does not get a square deal in any court of justice; any honest man will tell you that the Negro is not allowed to vote freely in the South. In the South he is treated legally and politically with less consideration than if he were some alien born beyond our shores, who had lived in this country for a few years and taken out naturalization papers. No one denies the unfairness and the injustice of that; I least of all. In spite of the fact that the Emancipation Proclamation and these amendments to the Constitution exist, there is slavery today in the South and a worse slavery than that which existed before the war of secession. At that time the slave at least was the property of his master, and it was to the master's interest that his property be well taken care of. Today in sections of the South they have something worse than chattel slavery; they have peonage where the people are slaves, but are not the property of masters, and it is not to the advantage of the man who is getting the benefit of that slavery to see to it that his workers are properly housed, properly fed, properly clothed and properly looked after.

The Peonage System

Such conditions exist in some parts of the South that would make your blood run cold. The story I am going to tell you I have from a former governor of Georgia—a man whom many of you at one time learned to hate, but a man who sacrificed his whole political career in order that he might break up peonage in the State of Georgia. He told me of the case of this farmer who had gone into the court; he wanted labor; certain Negroes were brought in this court for trivial offenses. You see, they arrest them for vagrancy; if they do not happen to have a job, they arrest them and make it a crime not to have a job. They are brought into court and fined. This poor fellow cannot pay the fine and is to be put in prison. The farmer steps up and pays the fine, and then the prisoner is turned over to him to work until his labor has paid back the amount of the fine. That sounds pretty fair because anybody would rather work on a farm than to rot in jail. But let us see how it works out. The poor fellow is taken on the farm; he has got to eat; he has got to have clothes; he is not allowed to go into some market and buy his food and clothes; no, he buys them from the farmer and the farmer keeps the account, and by the time that poor devil has worked for that farmer for two years he is more in debt to him than he was at the start; if he tries to get away they put the blood hounds after him and shoot him.

Now there was a farmer who had a lot of those peons and they began to get restless; they wanted to get away and the farmer got frightened because he had a guilty conscience. And this is what he did: He took eleven men out to his field in broad daylight—4 o'clock in the afternoon, and started them digging a pit, until they had a wide ditch deep enough. He took his gun and shot number one of his eleven laborers in the head and kicked him over in the ditch, and the other ten covered him up; when he was covered up he shot number two and the other nine covered him up; and so he went on down the line and shot the eleven, and kicked the last one over the ditch and covered him up himself.

"Hugh Dorsey's Sacrifice"

That happened in America; our America, free America. But Hugh Dorsey determined that these things should not be, and he attempted to break up that hideous custom, with the result that he did not break it up entirely but he did improve conditions tremendously, and he was kicked out of office and will never again hold political office in the State of Georgia as a result. Many people whom you have been taught to regard as your enemies are really your friends, and Hugh Dorsey is one of them who has sacrificed his whole political career to attempt to stop that injustice. It did not stop there; they began soon to make peons of white people too. You all know of the case down in Florida where they had white peons. The Legislature heard of it and they had something to say about it and things have been cleaned up a little bit since then.

You cannot be unjust to one member of your citizens without endangering the liberty of all your citizens. If there is going to be justice in America there has got to be justice for the colored man as well as the white man. (Applause.)

The South Offers No Social Equality

Now, my friends, in the South we do not offer social equality; we do not offer you political equality. You know why. You have heard the reasons for that expounded by your great leader, Marcus Garvey. I have given you some idea now, if you did not know it before, as to how your people are treated in the South. But in the North and West they do offer you political and social equality. Let us see how you are treated in the North and the West. How many of you have heard of Springfield, the home of Abraham Lincoln, where hundreds of your people were shot down like cattle? How many of you have heard of East St. Louis, where the only fault of your people was that they were willing to work when the white people wanted to live and get higher wages for loafing. How many of you have heard of

Chicago, where the fault of your people was that they wanted decent houses to live in, in decent communities. Not only did they shoot your people down by the hundreds, they looted your houses; they burned the roofs off over your heads ;and in Pennsylvania a few years ago the Mayor of Chester, Pa., got his police force and rounded up every Negro in Chester—there were about 600 of them—and marched them down to the southern border of that town and said, "Go back South where you belong; we won't have you here." More recently the mayor of Johnstown, Pa., said that no Negro should live in the town and tried to send all the Negroes out of town.

Has the Negro a Chance in America?

Yes, we do have horrible things in the South. We have lynching, we have peonage, but you never heard of any such thing happening south of the Mason-Dixon line. Worse things are done to you in those parts of the country where they claim they are going to give you social equality, and many people really believe they are going to get it. If worse things happen to you there than happen to you in the South, what chance is there for you here in America?

Now, there is no use being sentimental; there is no use being visionary; we live in a practical time and we are practical people, and we have got to face facts; and the fact of the matter is that there is not a Negro in the United States of America today who is free; not one. The war did not make you free, and constitutional amendments did not make you free and the N. A. A. C. P. has not made you free. Why aren't you free? Let us go right down to the rock bottom of it. Why aren't you free? You have got magnificent people here in this country—people of learning, people of intelligence, people of culture, people of courage; yes. We are the first people to proclaim it to the world. Why is it that you are not free? What I am going to say to you is nothing new to you.

You are not free because the civilization that you are living under is not your own. (Applause.) That man would indeed be bold, who would deny to the Negro the possibility of the development of a higher order of civilization. Perhaps the Chinese may do it. Your civilization goes back 6,000 years. That white man (whose ancestors were going either naked or clad in skins through the jungles three thousand years ago) would be indeed bold who would assert that it was impossible for the Negro to develop his own civilization and his own culture. But it is perfectly sure that you will never do that in America. In America you have the position of intellectual and cultural parasites. No race can develop, no race can evolve unless it is standing on its own feet, and is supported by its own backbone.

The Indians did everything to stop mixed marriages; their whole legal system was based on this idea of caste; their religion was based on this idea of caste; their politics was based on this idea of caste; their whole civilization was based on it; everything was based on it. It was the most ironclad system that human wit has ever devised. They even went so far as to authorize the soldiers to slay all illegally mixed persons and they did not stop it. Nothing has ever stopped it. Watch a man smoking a cigarette. You see the smoke go up in circles, curling and mixing in the air around you; diffusion, yes; and it is a law of physics that no two fluids whether local or gaseous can come in contact without diffusing, and that diffusing widens until a state of equilibrium is reached and you have a uniform fluid. What is true of fluids is true of races. As surely as God is in His heaven any two races that live side by side for any length of time are going to mix.

Well, now, it does not necessarily mean that either of these races is a bad race, because you want to prevent that mixing. Here are two chemicals; this chemical is a beneficent chemical; it is a good thing; it is fine for you; it does you a lot of good; and here is another that is splendid; it is a harmless, good chemical; but mix them together and you may get a deadly poison.

The Danger of Mixed Races

Now it is not a question of whether this race is higher or lower or the other race is higher or lower; that is not the point at all. The danger does not come from one being higher and the other lower. The danger comes from their being different, and it is not to say that either of two races is evil or injurious, but realize that the mixture of these races may produce something that may be tremendously harmful and hurtful to both races. Now, if you people stay in America, you are going to mix with the white people and the white people outnumber you eight to one. What will that mean, my friends? That will mean the death of your race. If you stay here willingly it will mean the suicide of your race.

Yes, I know the white people that want to keep you here—those white people who go around saying, "Yes, the Negro birth-rate is decreasing, and the Negro death rate is increasing, and at the end of 300 years there won't be a Negro living in America." That is what they are saying. "We will keep them here and

use them and let them die out." That is what most of them are
saying at inter-racial conferences, and they are saying that to
your people to try to cajole you. Are you going to stay here and
let yourselves be used? By a decreasing birth rate and an increasing death rate if you stay here it means the death of your
race—the suicide of your race. There is no use deceiving yourselves and there is no use our deceiving ourselves, with all the
good will in the world, with all of the understanding in the world,
we cannot do away with conditions that make America a place of
toil and trial and tribulation for you. People cannot help their
instincts; they cannot help it to save their necks, and some of
the wisest and best people are very often the people who are
most filled with prejudice and with bigotry. You have seen that
yourself and we cannot help it; we cannot take it out of people.
What we can do is to realize, as President Coolidge said the
other day, "That we are in the same boat."

Preserving the Races

Now your people and our people are in the same fix; you want
to preserve your people; and don't want the Negro race to die
in America and I want to preserve my people. I do not want
the white race to die in America. We have that interest in common. In addition to that, you have labored nobly and generously
to help us here in America, and it is up to us to realize what you
have done for us, what you have meant to us, and to see to it
that in any solution of this problem you get not only what is coming to you, but get the tribute and the glory that grateful hearts
should pour out in abundance to you.

A Miscarriage of Justice

My friends, I had hoped tonight that another Southerner would
be here with me and address you; I mean George Gordon Battle,
the attorney for your great leader. Several weeks ago I was
asked to prepare an article on Garvey and his movement, and I
wrote to Mr. Battle telling him what I wanted to do and asked
him to give me some facts to write a book. He sent me Garvey's
appeal to the President of the United States for a pardon; he
told me that every word of that appeal was genuine and sincere,
and this morning when I called him to get his final answer as
to whether or not he could be with us tonight, he told me it was
a great distress to him; that this was his very busiest week in
the year, and he did not have a moment, and it was quite impossible to get away; but he authorized me to say to this meeting tonight that, in his opinion, the trial of Marcus Garvey was

the greatest miscarriage of justice; that there was no testimony —no evidence which could fairly have convicted him of that of which he was accused, and that he believes that it was only a matter of time when that injustice will be atoned and Marcus Garvey will be pardoned. (Applause.)

And I want to say to you that in my opinion and belief, if the white people in the South of this country realize that Marcus Garvey was standing not only for the salvation of his own race but for the salvation of the white race as well—if they realize that he had been railroaded into prison merely because he did not have a white face—if they realized what he stood for and what he meant, I believe that the South would rise to a man and demand that your great leader be released and restored to you. (Great applause.) There are some of us down there who realize that, and we are going to leave no stone unturned to spread that. Your enemies in your own race have the help and support of white people; white people give them money; white people go and flatter them and hold out false hopes to them and hob-nob with them, and offer them social equality and put up money to help them; and some of those white people are people of great wealth and influence. I want to tell you this: that man for man we can match them; we will raise up for you and for your organization, man for man, as many as your opponents have among the whites of this country and they won't be whites who stay around in one district of the country; they will be whites from the North, from New England, from the Middle States; from the Southern Atlantic States, from the Gulf States, from the Middle West, from the Pacific Coast, from the far Northwest. It is coming and you will see it.

I noticed when I came in, the first things that struck my eye were some tags which all of you are wearing, and I looked at them and I saw "Let him go." I want to offer an amendment— free him; we don't want to let him go; we want to keep him here to do this work. (Thunderous applause.) And, my friends, if there is any honor in the American nation, I can promise you that when Marcus Garvey is free he shall not be deported.

THE NEGRO AND HIS LATENT POWERS

To Bless All Humanity

Nature is yet to be fully explored and conquered. The mysteries of Creation and the wonders of man's creative instinct are still to be revealed. Hidden truths are still to be unfathomed. Civilization is but a small and meagre achievement to what is still possible of man by his mastery of, and ascendency over, the mysteries that surround us. The ingenuity of man is not completely explored. When black Africa awakens, brushes his latent intelligence and stretches out his hand to achieve through the impulse of his God, as he is gradually doing, in spite of the opposition of the Caucasian world, there will come the true realization of the power and genius of man. Our race once partially uncovered the mysteries of the Universe, then, drunk with power and success, we went to sleep for thousands of years. Like Rip Van Winkle we are rising from our slumber of the ages and shortly we shall bless mankind with the wonder and greatness of life as revealed to us through God from the sleep of countless centuries. We once handed down a civilization through the ages that has been claimed, exploited and abused by a morally weaker people, who, like ourselves, in the past, are forgetting their God and making a mockery of Him. Our sins lead us astray and into bondage, but the time is near at hand when our Princes will rise to bless and glorify the true and ever living God. Surely the Negro shall put the world to wonder in the revelation of God through the race.

PART III

THE REPUBLIC OF LIBERIA

and

THE UNIVERSAL NEGRO IMPROVEMENT ASSOCIATION

———— ——

Blessed are ye, when men shall revile you, and persecute you, and shall say all manner of evil against you
falsely, for my sake.—Matt. v, 11.

THE PLOT

For the information of the innocent white and black millions who do not know of nor understand the ways and methods of modern intrigue in State craft, and the means adopted by statesmen, their hirelings and servants, dictated by the influence over public opinion of the rich Capitalists who control Government in behalf of their personal and corporate interests, the following plot, to discredit me, in the leadership of the Negro race, and to destroy my influence among the natives of Africa, is revealed:

Scene, Africa: The second largest continent; the richest of all the continents; yet fully un-explored. Promises to become the centre of the world's wealth and resources. Originally the native home of the blacks. Stolen from them by the crafty nations of Europe, namely, Portugal, Belgium, Spain, Italy, England, France and Germany, (the latter losing its share in the World War) under the guise of Christianity and humanity. The European powers have decoyed the innocent natives, robbed them of their patrimony and possessions, and reduced them to abject dependence. From this continent the Europeans removed millions of the black natives into slavery in the Western World. This slavery continued for 250 years. Through the agitation of liberal white men the blacks were emancipated.

Scene, America: The emancipated and enlightened Negroes, under my leadership, are endeavoring to regain possession of their native land, for the purpose of re-establishing the national independence of the race, and to honestly bring all the native blacks under the influence of true religion and bless the world with the reign of peace, justice and human love. The selfish whites, who mean no good to Africa or the black race, oppose the idea, revealing the farce and lie of their Christian professions. I go ahead and agitate and propagate the question of Negro nationalism, preaching the doctrine of "Africa for the Africans, those at home and those abroad" even as the whites agitate and propagate the appeal of "A White America," "Europe for the Europeans," "A White Canada," and "A White Australia."

Scene, Europe and America:

At the start of my agitation, white statesmen and capitalists, holding investments, directly or indirectly, in the diamond, rubber, ivory, wool, cotton, gold, palm oil and other interests in Africa, instructed their newspapers, such as "The New York Times," of New York City; "The Manchester Guardian," of Manchester, England, and their other continental and colonial organs and associated syndicate, to cast ridicule upon the idea and portray me as a clown, buffoon, ignoramus, cheat and impossible person. For the first few years of my effort the Capitalists' press made every effort to impress the public, especially Negroes, that I was a big fool or an ignorant black clown. They ridiculed my appearing in a robe, of ordinary European or American collegiate pattern,—distinguishing my rank of office in the large organization of which I was head. They called me all kinds of names, for wearing, on demonstrative occasions only, this robe, that is commonly worn by their college or university presidents, professors, graduates, church and legal dignitaries and millions of persons of their race, to show collegiate, academic or other distinctions. I was elected President General of my Association. Just as the Pope is head of his Church, or the Archbishop of Canterbury head of his faith, and called His Holiness or His Grace, the people designated that the person who held my office within the organization should be referred to as His Excellency. This was a source of amusement and further ridicule for the white press, forgetting that in Germany, England, Italy and other countries in Europe such titles are applied by their race and used by the millions, and that in America there is only a mild departure from the custom, but that there are large numbers of the best people of white society who go to Europe annually to attach themselves to royalty and nobility, even though I made no pretence to such rank or office. Subsequently, I was elected Provisional President of Africa, and wore a uniform, on celebrations or demonstrations only, as a mark of office. The white press ridiculed this and inspired Negroes and the public to laugh the idea to scorn, and held me up as a buffoon for wearing an ordinary uniform of office, yet they said not a word of the uniforms and trappings of their Czars, Emperors, Kings, Princes, Presidents, Nobles, Generals, Admirals, and millions of men and women of affairs of their race, as well as the millions who wear such uniforms in their fraternal societies. In spite of this ridicule, I continued to impress millions of Negroes with the reasonableness of African nationalism and Negro Independence. This further annoyed and surprised them. They found out that ridicule alone would not drive Negroes away from me, nor from the ideal. They added "villain" to my denunciations in a more spirited and scientifically arranged propaganda against me.

Scene, The Power of Government:

They used the power of Government to intimidate me in my business efforts, started with the purpose of raising the necessary funds with which to execute the plans of real race emancipation. They inspired disloyalty and dishonesty among my Negro employees. If I had a dishonest employee accused for crime, he is freed. I am subsequently sued by the individual for false imprisonment. A heavy judgment for several thousand dollars is returned against me. Other employees are encouraged thereby to steal with impunity from the organizations. By such, reverses in business come, as would be natural, under these circumstances; they now become more bold in publishing that I am a villian, robbing the "poor colored people." They have me indicted, convicted and imprisoned. The news is flashed across the continents, to every nook and corner, and particularly to every village, town and hamlet in Africa. They influence my first wife to be unfaithful, and, after divorce, supply her with money and protection to do harm to my name and reputation. She openly boasts of it. They employ other Negroes to go from place to place, among the race, preaching about my supposed dishonesty or "robbing the poor colored people" with the purpose of driving away from me the following that they feared would make my dream of nationalism in Africa come true.

Scene, British:

The British method of discrediting feared "native" leaders is unique. When ridicule is not successful enough in dealing with them, they make criminals of them and then hold them up to the public as such. They train the "natives" (all dark people) to look down upon any one who has been to prison, so by that method they defeat the marked individual. During the trial of my case in New York (the plot which was skillfully laid), the British interests had their special correspondents in attendance. The testimony was retailed out that one of the ships of the Black Star Line was formerly a yacht owned by the American multi-millionaire H. H. Rogers. The yacht was used in the great world war as an auxiliary cruiser, after which it was purchased by the Black Star Line and converted into a passenger boat for inter-colonial trade. On one occasion I was to have travelled on this boat to visit the West Indian and Central American divisions of the organizations as a passenger like any other passenger. The boat was delayed in leaving New York and I sailed to my several destinations on ships of other lines. Subsequently, I met the boat in Cuba (stranded as by arrangements of the enemies). I removed the boat to Kingston, Jamaica, for repairs, to continue its voyage with its passengers. The British interests, for propaganda, among the African natives, through a Manchester paper and other London journals with their African connections, gave out the following false news to the blacks of the continent: "That I was an immoral libertine, who had taken the black people's money, and partly from the natives of Africa, and fitted up a palatial yacht, (private) with the most elaborate Eastern decorations and costly furnishings, with a perfumed saloon adorned with Persian rugs, carpets and Egyptian hangings and that I had aboard a harem of fifty young colored women who danced and performed before me in this elaborately perfumed saloon as I reclined on an exquisite couch upholstered with the most costly of Eastern materials. That I drank myself drunk with the most costly wine in a debauch with the women of the harem, etc. These lies were retailed among the natives of Africa to prejudice their minds, and especially the cause I represent. That failed to stir the natives; then after my conviction they broadcasted everywhere that I was convicted and now a criminal in prison caused by my robbing the Negroes of Africa. It was more effective then to say "Africa" to stir native prejudice and hate. This also did not help them much in discrediting me as a large number of the natives were already educated by my effort, to expect anything by way of lies from those who wanted to keep them enslaved to methods of exploitation. Several educated and wide awake natives who knew the truth assumed the leadership of the native people after my imprisonment. To win back the Africans to their state of insecurity and religious watchful waiting much was done by the interests.

Scene, Africa:

His Royal Highness, the Prince of Wales, went on a trip to Africa, and visited all the native dependencies of England, including the Union of South Africa. The following bit of news from South Africa speaks for itself:

Johannesburg, S. A.—A Garvey paper published here and known as the African World, has created a furor among the whites.

Its platform of "Africa for the Africans" has created consternation both here and in England. The government has been asked to suppress it. The Sunday Times here had the following to say about the African World recently:

"A more treacherous, inflammatory, deluded and deluding publication it is difficult to imagine. In any but a British country those responsible for its publication would instantly be dealt with in swift and certain fashion,

"The avowed aim of The African World is to 'free Africa from the incubus of European control,' and to 'instill the psychology and traits of Zaghlul Pasha in the African race.' In its third issue, published on June 13, it has the barefaced impudence to refer to 'the imperishable message of His Highness Marcus Garvey, Potentate of the Universal Negro Improvement Association. Every well-informed native knows Marcus Garvey to be an unprincipled rogue and swindler who is now serving five years in prison for cheating the Negroes of the United States out of huge sums of money.

"It was poisonous propaganda of the type openly reached by, and permitted in, this seditious native organ that the Prince of Wales warned the Bantu races against when he advised them to beware of "tendencies to mistrust those in authority or to turn to those whose smooth promises have yet to be translated into performance."

"To detect and demolish the specious fallacy of the 'Africa for the Africans' argument is child's play to the European mind. Left to themselves, the natives would die of drought or wipe each other out in tribal warfare. Enlightened native opinion on the subject is scarcely less emphatic. Two years ago the Natal native paper, 'Ilanga ase Natal,' stated (concerning Garvey):—

" 'A leader of natives who tells his people that they will be able to take back the land of their fathers by force of arms, and who contends that the native is the social equal of the white, we have no use for, and we will give him a wide berth. The truth must be told to the native, and the truth is that the white man is here to stay; that he is very strong, far stronger than the native, especially in his well-developed brain; also that the native can attain the same height, but only along the same difficult path, and in no other way. It will do our cause no good at all to impress upon the native that he is as good as the white man, for this cannot be demonstrated in practice'."

World Talks

The African World, white, a European weekly, says:

"In the 'Negro World,' of July 11, which is the official organ in the United States of the Garvey organization, we notice an editorial gloating over the birth of the new 'African World' at the Cape, under the heading 'We Two.' We would tender both the 'Negro World' and its latest offspring in South Africa, which has quite illegally assumed our name, a grave warning, in their best interests, to abstain from any interference in native affairs south of the Equator.

No Garveys Needed

"South Africa knows how to deal with its own problems better than anyone else, and Marcus Garveys are not needed either there or anywhere else to teach us our own business. Liberia, the Negro Republic of the West Coast, arrived at the same conclusion when Garvey delegates arrived at Monrovia last year by promptly deporting them on the immediate drastic orders of its enlightened ruler, President King. We hope to hear similar good news ere long from the Cape, where the machinations as suggested by the latest native journal will probably not be permitted to exist much longer."

Scene, New York and Other American Cities:

In 1919, after the wonderful success attending the organizing and fostering of the work of the Universal Negro Improvement Association by me, and the complete defeat of the Negro political opposition in New York City and the elimination of one Samuel Duncan, the head of a rival faction of the organization that broke away in 1918, the said Duncan, who was a close friend of one W. A. Domingo who was once employed by me as an editor of the Negro World,—started a series of letter writing, of the most vile and wicked nature, to the British, French and Italian Home Governments and the Colonial Governments of these Nations, stirring up their hatred for me and the work of the Association. His letters to these Governments stated that I was a dangerous character who had planned the downfall of all these Governments, and that the Universal Negro Improvement Association was the Agency through which this gigantic feat was to be accomplished. That the Negro World was the medium of circulation among the people of these countries and colonies, and that the Governments were to immediately suppress the paper. Domingo had already been dismissed for writing socialistic and allied propaganda for the Negro World, contrary to the policy of the paper; but skillful Duncan must have preserved some of his friend's articles and forwarded them with the communications. After Domingo had been dismissed, I personally assumed the editorship of the paper which jumped in circulation by seventy-five thousand copies. This aggrevated the group that was out, and more so, to see the growing prosperity of the organization and its auxiliary the Black Star Line. The Governments were also warned by Duncan that Garvey was sending out ships with propagandists to visit all these colonial outposts. The Imperial and Colonial Governments immediately passed laws forbidding the circulation of the Negro World. In certain places the punishment to be seen with a Negro World was imprisonment for five years, some life imprisonment and in French Dahomey the penalty was death. The paper had a circulation in English, Spanish and French. Some of the enlightened West Indian Colonies that knew there was no truth in the wicked information of Duncan, passed no seditious laws against the paper. Such countries like Jamaica and British Honduras still receive the Negro World, and, since its circulation from 1918 up to the present, no disturbances between the peoples and those Governments have happened, while in places where the Negro World has been suppressed there have been skirmishes and hatred between the peoples and the Governments. The Negro World is suppressed in such places like Trinidad, British Guiana, Barbadoes, etc., in the West Indies and all the French, Italian, Portuguese, Belgian and some of the British Colonies in Africa. The suppression of the Negro World by the White Governments in Africa and the West Indies is a gallant testimony to their real meaning of the statement of the racial inferiority of the blacks. Superior beings do not go out of even the ordinary way to mingle into the affairs of lesser creatures; but we find that the whites lose no opportunity to suppress the intelligence of "native races." They fear the Negro World edited by a black man, much more than they do "The London Times," "LeMatin," "The New York Times," "Manchester Guardian," "New York World," or "Chicago Tribune" of the white race. So much for the inferiority of the Negro. The Light Negroes, in the different cities of America, formed themselves into a syndicate to write and contribute to the white magazines, journals and periodicals. One would write to a certain magazine or paper either against me or boosting their own class interest. The articles would be published, then the other members of the group, from far and near, would write complimentary letters to the Editors, praising the articles and writers and boosting the particular Journals or Magazines. By this artful method, these writers get their articles in the several papers, and in many cases they influence several Sunday Editors and Daily papers to attach members of this group to their papers as special writers on race subjects. The light Negro has fooled the white man in America into believing that he represents the best of his race. This is so common a belief that whitemen themselves write of it as such. The very light Negroes have an artful method of undermining the darker elements of the race to the former's advantage.

Letter of Samuel Duncan to Colonial Governors.

March 4, 1920.

"The West Indian Protective Society of America.

"Main Office 178 West 135th Street, New York, N. Y.

"His Excellency the Governor of St. Lucia.

"Sir: I beg to convey to you confidentially the following information and suggestions to the end that peace and good feeling shall continue between His Majesty's white and colored subjects within the British Empire, and especially in the British West Indies.

"There is in this city an organization known as the Universal Negro Improvement Association and African Communities League, at the head of which is one Marcus Garvey, a Negro, a native of Jamaica. This organization is not only anti-white and anti-British but it is engaged in the most destructive and pernicious propaganda to create disturbance between white and colored people in the British possessions.

"This organization employs as a medium through which to carry on its propaganda a newspaper published in this city and known as the Negro World. So inciting and inflammable and purposely colored are the news and editorial articles in this paper that the authorities in several of the islands have been compelled to take energetic action to deny it admittance to those islands and prevent its circulation among the colored people thereof. It was the known radical attitude and friction creating policy of the Negro World that was responsible for the drastic newspaper ordinances recently enacted in British Guiana, St. Vincent and other West Indian islands.

"Another medium for carrying on the propaganda of the Universal Negro Improvement Association and African Communities League is the Black Star Line which owns the steamer "Yarmouth" (soon to be known as the Frederick Douglas) of greater importance to Garvey and those associated with him in pushing this world-wide pro-Negro and anti-white and anti-British propaganda than the making of money through freight and passengers is the effect and impression that the presence of this ship of the Black Star Line is expected to exert on the colored people of the islands when it calls at their ports.

"Yet another and perhaps the most effective way of carrying on its propaganda is through the members of the Universal Negro Improvement Association and African Communities League and stockholders of the Black Star Line who leave this country for the West Indies, and who are expected to stealthily work among the natives and stir up strife and discontent among them. These members and stockholders of the above named organization faithfully perform the work that the suppressed Negro World cannot do, and thus sow seeds of discontent among the natives of the island to which they go. The recent bloody strikes in Trinidad, when several persons were killed and wounded, and much injury caused to shipment and other industries can be traced to the subtle and underhand propaganda work of the agencies above referred to.

"I venture to suggest that Your Excellency would be serving well the cause of the empire and contributing in no small way to the promotion of peace and good feeling between the white and colored people in the West Indies should you cause to be carefully scrutinized and precautionary measures taken in the case of all colored persons coming into the colony from the United States and the Panama Canal with a view of ascertaining whether such persons are members of the Universal Negro Improvement Association and African Communities League, subscribers to and readers of the Negro World, stockholders of, or in any way connected with the Black Star Line, and upon affirmatively establishing any of these facts to exercise your official discretion as to their admission into the colony.

I have the honor to remain,

Very truly yours,

Samuel Augustus Duncan.

"Executive Secretary of the West Indian Protective Society of America. The only society in the United States looking after the interests of colored people of foreign birth."

The above letter reveals the malice and hate of the writer, Samuel Duncan, a friend of W. A. Domingo.

Duncan was the president of the New York Branch of the Universal Negro Improvement Association when it was first organized in 1918, and from whom the Association had to be rescued as explained in my article, "The Negro's Greatest Enemy." He is a naturalized American Negro citizen of St. Kitts, British West Indies.

After he was dislodged from the Universal Negro Improvement Association in 1918 he formed the imaginary "West Indian Protective Society of America," which he falsely states is "looking after the interest of colored people of foreign birth." True to type and form, he dealt dishonorably with those who were decoyed and intrigued into believing in the merits of his imaginary society; in consequence of which he had to leave New York. His society never materialized, while the Universal Negro Improvement Association had grown into an organization of world-wide importance.

Consequent on the writing of the above letter, to all the Colonial Governments and the Overseas Dominions; the office of the British Consul General in New York, questioned and refused passports to all West Indian Negroes who applied to them for permission to return home, either on business or pleasure. Passports were issued only to those who voluntarily denounced me, or would volunteer imaginary information against me or against the organization. Orders were sent by the Smut's Government of South Africa not to allow any Negroes from America or the West Indies to depart for Africa.

This letter of Duncan's, a West Indian Negro, reveals the same character and disposition, as that written by the eight American colored persons and proves conclusively that the so-called "intellectual" Negro, whether of the tropics or America, is a danger and a stumbling block to the progress of his own race. He is jealous and envious and will resort to any extreme "to down" or destroy his fellows, if they attempt to rise above him either in service to race or personally.

The following is a letter received from one of the Colonial Governors of the British West Indies in answer to one I had forwarded to them (copy of which unfortunately is misplaced), in order to correct the false statements of Samuel Duncan:

Reply of Governor of Jamaica to Marcus Garvey.

Colonial Secretary's Office

Jamaica, April 19, 1920.

"Sir: I am directed by the Governor to acknowledge the receipt of your letter of the 10th ultimo, drawing attention to the fact that one Samuel Duncan of New York is said to be communicating with Colonial Governments and misrepresenting the aims and objects of the Universal Negro Improvement Association and the steamship line controlled by them.

"2. I am in reply to say that, as your association is aware, this Government has treated the Black Star Line precisely in the same manner as other steamship lines have been treated, and to point out that this equality of treatment is what may be termed a "positive act" because it means that the regulations whereby the port of Kingston is safeguarded from coal famine, are enforced without any unjust discriminations.

"I am, Sir,
        "Your obedient servant,
    (Signed)   H. Bryan,
                                    "Colonial Secretary."

Marcus Garvey, Esq.,
    Universal Negro Improvement Association,
    Universal Building, 56 West 135th St.,
    New York, U. S. A.

Scenes, Liberia, West Africa and America:

In 1920, I arranged to dispatch to Liberia a delegation of Negroes, (consisting of W. H. Eason, a native of North Carolina, then American Leader of the Universal Negro Improvement Association, a mulatto, who subsequently drifted into the camp of the enemies; Herbert Harrison, a black Negro, native of the Virgin Island, an American, who was then connected with the Negro World, the official organ of the Association, who, being a socialist, drifted out of sympathy with the organization, claiming that it was capitalistic, etc., and Elie Garcia, an octoroon, formerly connected with the Haytian Government) to confer with the Liberian Government on colonization of that country by Negroes from the Western world.

Owing to the lack of steamship accommodation, only the Secretary of the delegation, Garcia, arrived in time. He was then designated as a commissioner, with full powers to negotiate with the Liberian Government. He was received most cordially by the Government, presided over by President C. B. D. King and Edwin Barclay as Secretary of State, two black Negroes who formerly hailed from the West Indies directly or through their parents, Barclay going from Barbadoes, and King, the son of a Jamaican West Indian soldier, who had been sent with his black regiment, under white British officers, from the West Indies, by the British, to wrest away from the African natives their lands and possessions in the Ashanti, Zulu and Basuto wars. The Liberian Government, through King as President, and Barclay as Secretary of State, entered into the following understanding and agreement with the Universal Negro Improvement Association, as by letter of the Secretary of State to Elie Garcia, the Commissioner of the organization then in Liberia:

LETTER FROM COMMISSIONER GARCIA TO PRESIDENT KING

Monrovia, Liberia, June 8, 1920.

To His Excellency the President of the Republic of Liberia,
Executive Mansion,
Monrovia.

Honorable President:

The Universal Negro Improvement Association and African Communities League, Inc., is an organization with a membership of three million members scattered in the United States of America, South and Central America, the West Indies, Great Britain and Africa.

This organization was founded for the following purposes:

"To establish a Universal confraternity among the race; to promote the spirit of pride and love; to administer to and assist the needy; to assist in civilizing the backward tribes of Africa, to assist in the development of independent Negro nations and communities; to establish commissionaries and agencies for the representation and protection of all Negroes irrespective of nationality; to promote a conscientious spiritual worship among the natives of Africa; to establish universities, colleges and academies for the racial education and culture of the people; to conduct a world-wide commercial and industrial intercourse for the good of the people; to work for better conditions in all Negro communities."

The Universal Negro Improvement Association controls the Black Star Line Steamship Corporation, capitalized at ten million dollars in the United States of America, as also the Negro Factories Corporation, capitalized at one million dollars under the laws of the United States.

For the successful accomplishment of the program above outlined the Universal Negro Improvement Association is extremely desirous to transfer its headquarters to the City of Monrovia or any other convenient township of Liberia.

Owing to the rumors prevalent in the United States with respect to the unfriendly attitude of the people of Liberia to persons of other Negro communities, a statement which my organization had great reason to doubt, it was thought best to approach the Government of Liberia on the subject of lands before settling our future program.

Therefore, as commissioner of the great organization, I beg on its behalf to make the following request:

"That in case its objects as stated above are approved by the

Liberian Government, it would give me a written assurance that it will afford us every facility for procuring lands for business, agricultural or industrial purposes and that government will do everything in its power to facilitate the work of the Association along those lines.

"In return it is the intention of the organization with its membership of three million members to lend financial and moral assistance in building and subsidizing institutions for the higher education of Liberia, for improving generally the international prestige of the country by organizing outside of the country developing corporations backed by the entire membership of the U. N. I. A.

"The Universal Negro Improvement Association would be prepared to do anything possible to help the Government of Liberia out of its economic plights and to raise subscriptions all over the world to help the country to liquidate its debts to foreign governments.

"It is the intention of the Universal Negro Improvement Association to establish a trade route between America, the West Indies and Liberia through line of steamers of the Black Star Line Steamship Corporation.

"All these things will be unselfishly done in the interest of the people of Liberia and those who may seek future citizenship under her flag.

"It is the intention of the U. N. I. A. to encourage immigration by Negroes from the United States of America, South and Central America and the West Indies to develop Liberia.

"It is the intention also of the U. N. I. A., with the transfer of its headquarters to Liberia, to bring with it a well equipped medical and scientific unit for the development of higher sciences of Liberia, to build hospitals, sanatoriums and other institutions for the benefit of the people of Liberia.

"Trusting that Your Excellency will give due consideration to my request, I am Your Excellency's

"Most obedient servant,

"UNIVERSAL NEGRO IMPROVEMENT ASSOCIATION AND AFRICAN COMMUNITIES LEAGUE, INC.

"ELIE GARCIA,
"Commissioner."

REPLY OF SECRETARY OF STATE FOR LIBERIA
(Liberian Seal)
Document 2
Department of State
Monrovia, Liberia,

248-L   June 14th, 1920.
Sir:

The President directs me to say in reply to your letter of June 8th, setting forth the objects and purposes of the Universal Negro Improvement Association, that the Government of Liberia, appreciating as they do the aims of your organization as outlined by you, have no hesitancy in assuring you that they will afford the association every facility legally possible in effectuating in Liberia its industrial, agricultural and business projects.

I have the honor to be,
Sir,
Your obedient servant,

EDWIN BARCLAY,
Secretary of State.
Elie Garcia, Esqr.,
Monrovia.

The agreement to colonize Liberia was further confirmed and approved by additional documents and agreements made and entered into by the Liberian Government with Gabriel Johnson, then titular head of the Universal Negro Improvement Association, who was elected its Potentate at the convention of the organization held in New York City, 1920, and who was then Mayor of the City of Monrovia, Capital of Liberia, and General in the Liberian Army, George Osborne Mark, the Deputy Potentate of the organization, a native of Sierre Leone, West Africa, formerly a civil servant of the British Government and Cyril Critchlow, Secretary to the legation of the Universal Negro Improvement Association in Liberia, a naturalized American citizen born in Trinidad. It was rumored that after the elevation of Johnson to such a prominent position among Negroes, a jealousy sprang up on the part of King, due to the fact that Johnson was referred to as the first Negro in the world at a State banquet, given in his honor, on his return from the United States to which place he was sent as a delegate, to attend the convention of the Association, when he was elected as the titular head of all the Negroes of the World. Johnson is a quadroon born in Liberia of American parents who first settled in Liberia after its establishment, by the American Colonization Society, (white), and where he appeared at the banquet in his stately robe of office (quite in contrast to that of the President's) as the first Negro in the World, and a toast was thus proposed by a Mr. Cassell, President of the College of Liberia. In rising to drink in response to the toast the President of Liberia, in jealousy and humiliation and with irony, lifted his glass and responded, "I drink to the health of the Mayor of Monrovia." From that time onward, it is alleged, the President, through jealousy, started to double cross and obstruct the plans of the organization. He had it circulated that the Mayor could not serve his own Government and that of another, when in fact he knew the Universal Negro Improvement Association was not a Government, but an organization. Even though he was a son-in-law of Johnson, the jealousy continued, and, to relieve Johnson of the surpassing honor of being titular head of the Negroes of the world, he maneuvered to make him Consul General of Liberia for Fernando Po,—the most lucrative of all the foreign Liberian posts,—he was influenced to accept this position and relinquish his office as Potentate of the Universal Negro Improvement Association. This however, did not affect the agreement between the Liberian Government and the Association to colonize the country. All preparations were being made by the Association in America to carry out the plan of colonization. With that aim in view, the Black Star Line was formed for the transportation of the people. The enemies of colonization in America, (the very light Negroes, lead by W. E. B. DuBois, the Negro politicians and those of the white race who wanted to discredit and imprison me to please their Negro political wards and foreign powers) tried to make the plan unpopular and unsuccessful. See DuBois' writing in the "Crisis," (the organ of his organization), articles contributed to white magazines and articles written by Seligman (white) Director of Research of the National Association for the Advancement of Colored People, in the New York Sunday World and "Cincinnati Inquirer." "These oppositions and general warfare against me, along with other agencies, brought about my indictment for the Black Star Line. All plans were near completion, in spite of the indictment, for carrying out of the colonization program, starting with the actual leaving of the colonists in October of 1924. A new steamship company was formed by the name of the Black Cross Navigation and Trading Company, to transport the colonists. The

Second group of officials and first group of experts sent to Liberia in 1921. Bottom row (left to right):

Association dispatched to Liberia in December of 1923, another delegation to finally concrete all arrangements for the work of colonization. The delegates comprised Robert Lincoln Poston, then Secretary General of the Universal Negro Improvement Association, a native of Kentucky, as Chairman. (He died at sea, aboard ship, from pneumonia, on the eve of landing in New York, on his return from Europe and Africa, in February 1924), Henrietta Vinton Davis, fourth Assistant President General of the Association, a native of Washington, D. C. and J. Milton Van Lowe, an attorney of Detroit, Michigan, who acted as Secretary of the Delegation. The delegation was to work in conjunction with the Association's Attorney in Liberia, Arthur Barclay, called the Nestor of Liberia, and sometimes the "Grand Old Man," ex-president of the Republic and leading legist, and the other resident representatives of the Association in Monrovia.

LETTER TO PRESIDENT OF LIBERIA INTRODUCING DELEGATION

56 West 135th St.,
New York City, N. Y.
December 5, 1923.

His Excellency, Hon. C. B. D. King,
President of Liberia,
Monrovia, Liberia.

May it please Your Excellency:

This letter serves to introduce to you Hon. Robert L. Poston, Secretary-General of the Universal Negro Improvement Association; Attorney J. Milton Van Lowe of Detroit, Mich., and Lady Henrietta Vinton Davis, Fourth Assistant President-General of the Universal Negro Improvement Association, who have been sent as a delegation from the Universal Negro Improvement Association to interview you and your good government, in continuation of the proposition undertaken with you in 1921 for the furtherance of the plan to assist in the development of Liberia, industrially and commercially, by the settlement in some parts of the country of a large number of American and West Indian colonists who desire repatriation to their native land, Africa, for the establishment of permanent homes.

The spirit of kinship has ever lingered with us on this side, and now, more than ever, millions of people are looking homeward, as the only solution of their grave problem and condition.

Mr. Poston is Chairman of the Delegation and Mr. Van Lowe

its Secretary. They are charged by the Universal Negro Improvement Association, representing six million Negroes, to confer with you for the purpose of arriving at some amicable arrangement by which the Association and the people at this end can help in the settlement of industrial groups in Liberia, as above stated, for the commercial and industrial development of the country, and for the advancement of their own peace and happiness.

Your visit to America has brought you into close touch with the race problem, which presses greatly upon our people, causing a great dissatisfaction, which leads large numbers of them to feel that the only place where they could have permanent happiness and peace is Africa, their Fatherland. There are thousands of families now awaiting the word from you and your good government that they will be welcomed, to settle in some part of the country, to help in its rebuilding. These families that are ready for settlement, as soon as arrangements are reached, will go out not as charges, but as persons of independent means. In this respect we can guarantee the repatriation to any part of the country you may designate, according to previous talks with you in 1921, between twenty and thirty thousand families in the first two years, starting, say, from September, 1924. The worth of each family would be roughly estimated at $1,500.00 each, the multiplication of which would make such colonists more helpful to the country in revenue, and through other resources.

It is felt that our intention has been grossly misrepresented to you by our enemies and outsiders, who have sought on so many occasions to embarrass us in our good intention toward you and Liberia, but, as you must realize, reform movements like that of the Universal Negro Improvement Association, will always be misrepresented, and no one more than you could better appreciate the difficulties such movements have to undergo in the beginning. We have had to spend the last five years organizing sentiment in the West Indies and America toward the appreciation of the plan of economic and industrial interest in Africa by Negroes, in that for a long while the Negro has been trained at this end to absorb and become entirely a part of the civilization around him, and to ignore the creation of an independent existence that would lend honor and prestige to the race. Because of that, we have had an up-hill fight for the last five years, which has caused us to have encountered many bitter enemies, who, no doubt, have tried to influence you and your good government in prejudice against us, but you know well the situation, and can, as above stated, appreciate our trying position.

As you know, Mr. King, the race has been practically divided against itself through color and other prejudices. In America and the West Indies we have had a tremendous fight of the lighter element against the darker ones, and that is accountable to a great extent for some of the bitterness that exists against the Universal Negro Improvement Association at this time, but when it is considered that we can only succeed by being a united people, you will further appreciate our effort to bring about such a result.

Our earlier work in Liberia was handicapped, because of misunderstanding and bad representation. The men, Crichlow and Garcia, whom we sent out did a great deal of harm with their indiscretions, which caused us to have delayed, and in other words suspended, the efforts we started to make in the carrying out of our industrial program in Liberia. The setback was chiefly due also to certain unforeseen circumstances, but it is felt that no prejudice will be harbored against us in Liberia because of that, in that you can all well appreciate the difficulties we had to encounter. We are now starting in real earnest with the backing and support of a stalwart membership and if your good government will help as you promised to do in 1921 by the grant of lands in certain parts and especially around the region of the River Cess or any other part that you may designate to the delegation, we feel sure that in another twelve months from the first settlement, that we will be able to show wonderful improvement in helping in the development of the country.

The people at this end are uncertain of their future, and large numbers of them who are fairly independent are desirous of permanent home settlement, and these people are now anxiously awaiting word from you that would satisfy them in making up their minds to make Liberia their future home. We can see nothing else but a bright future for Liberia in this direction, and if you will enter into the spirit with which we are desirous of helping, there is no reason why you and your government could not become in a few years the Saviour of our wandering people.

It is for us to state that our program for the industrial development of Liberia and its settlement by Negroes from this part is supported by a large number of influential friends, who will be willing to do anything to help us along, with what we are able to do ourselves, but there must be an assurance that there is appreciation for what we are endeavoring to do from your side, which could be made manifest in the granting to us of the accommodation for the people who are desirous of settling.

We need not discuss with you in this letter the many evil and wicked misrepresentations that have been made against us, but suffice it to say that the heart of every real member of the Universal Negro Improvement Association is with Liberia in its higher industrial and commercial development.

We would like to see Liberia become one of the first powers of the world, and anything that we can do economically and industrially shall be done unstintingly.

As you know, the Black Star Line, one of our early ventures, was temporarily suspended because of disloyalty and dishonesty on the part of some of the people we engaged in our earlier venture, but on a favorable report from the delegation, the Association intends to have two large ships equipped between September and December, 1924, for permanent trade between Liberia and America. We are now laying plans for the carrying out of this project.

Our bigger work is still ahead of us, and if we are given a fair chance and opportunity, we shall be able to carry it out more successfully to the good and betterment of Liberia and those concerned.

We are therefore asking you to give the delegation, as our representatives, the consideration necessary, so as to enable us to make the kind of report by which the people will be encouraged to take advantage of settling in the country for its development.

Anticipating a favorable understanding, we shall work assiduously to bring about an era of prosperity for Liberia and our people, starting in the year 1924.

With very best wishes for a successful administration and for the progress of your country, I have the honor to be, your obedient servant,   MARCUS GARVEY,
President-General,
Universal Negro Improvement Association.

The delegation arrived, was accorded a public reception, attended by leading officials and citizens. They met the President and an additional agreement reached whereby a local committee of Liberians, consisting of his Vice President, the Chief Justice, two ex-presidents, several officials of the Government and the Comptroller of Customs, Mr. Dixon Brown as Secretary, were to be the local committee of reception for the Colonists who were to settle in the country. All these gentlemen, and others they would add from time to time, with

Group of Commissioners of U. N. I. A. sent to Liberia in 1924 in company with local Liberian Committee at Monrovia. Front row—W. Dennis and Ex-President Howard (whom King succeeded). Second row—Van Lowe, Lady Davis, R. L. Poston and Chief Justice Dossen. Rear—Ex-President Barclay, Comptroller of Customs; Dixon Brown and D. C. Carranda (a government employee).

the approval of the Universal Negro Improvement Association were to receive the colonists on their arrival in 1924. The following plans were also suggested by the committee and signed by themselves.

Committee's Suggestions:

Document 3

Suggestions of Local Liberian Committee Appointed by President King.

The directors and management of the business of the U. N. I. A. in Liberia so far as it relates to emigration shall be entrusted to an Advisory Committee consisting of seven Liberians, viz: Hons. Arthur Barclay, D. E. Howard, J. J. Dossen and Messrs. W. F. Dennis, Dixon B. Brown, D. C. Carranda and H. T. Wesley who shall have the power to increase their number as the circumstances may require.

This committee shall co-operate with the parent body of the U. N. I. A. in New York, in formulating plans for the establishment of new settlements in Liberia for emigrants sent out by the association as colonists, and in locating them in said settlements and in directing the general affairs of said association in Liberia.

The following plan is hereby submitted for the consideration and approval of the executive committee of the parent body in New York:

(a) We advise that preference shall be given to emigrants of the age of fifty years and under of strong physique and a fixed determination to become citizens of Liberia and remain in Liberia.

(b) That preference also be given to agriculturists and men of industry.

(c) That all emigrants shall possess at least one thousand five hundred dollars cash to each family and every single person not connected with a family five hundred dollars.

(d) That emigrants shall be sent out in groups of not more than five hundred at a time and shall be assigned to such new localities as the advisory committee may suggest. Ample notice must be sent to the advisory committee in Liberia of the intended dispatch of any body or group of emigrants.

(e) That every emigrant before leaving America shall subscribe to an oath that they will respect the established authority of the Liberian government.

(f) The first settlement shall be established on the Cavalla river in Maryland County, near Cape Palmas. We advise that such machinery as saw mills, motor trucks, motor cars and other road equipments be sent along with the colonists. That the subjoined list of patent drugs which have been found useful in this climate be brought along with the emigrants. Also fishing nets, sporting and hunting rifles and accoutrements.

(g) We advise the establishment of a hospital at Cape Palmas and the dispatch of doctors and drugs along with the first group.

(h) We strongly recommend that preparation, such as cottages and receptacles be provided for the emigrants before they are sent out and lands surveyed and plotted in each community. The association to see to it that a sufficient quantity of farming implements be sent along and that food for at least six months be provided for each and every group. Prospectors and mineralogists should be advised to join the emigrants coming out.

(i) We further advise that such settlements be provided with chapels, schools and workshops.

The attention of emigrants might be called to the cultivation of coffee, cocoa, kolanuts, sugar-cane, ground-nuts and the oil-palm. The time most appropriate for the dispatch of emigrants to Liberia is between October and May.

We recommend that for the present ships be chartered for the transportation of emigrants.

Signed at the city of Monrovia, Liberia, this sixteenth day of February, 1924.

ARTHUR BARCLAY,
     Monrovia, Liberia.
D. E. HOWARD,
     Monrovia, Liberia.
JAMES J. DOSSEN,
     Harper, Md. County, Liberia.
H. TOO WESLEY,
     Harper, Md. County, Liberia.
WILMOT F. DENNIS,
     Monrovia, Liberia.
DONGBA CARMO CARANDE 2d,
     Monrovia, Liberia.
DIXON BROWN.

———

List of patent drugs that have been found useful in West Africa:
Radway's Ready Relief.
Indian Root Pills.
Sloan's Liniment.

Castor oil.
Dr. Jayne's Household Remedies.
Pond's Extract.
Ammonia.
Cuticura soap and ointment.
Peroxide (in liquid form, for cuts, bites, etc.).
Quinine.
Castile soap.
Epsom salts.
Fruit salts.
Senna and salts.
And other known remedies.

DIXON BROWN,
Secretary to Advisory Committee.
Monrovia, February 16, 1924.

REPLY SENT TO PRESIDENT KING

56 West 135th St.,
New York City, N. Y.
March 31, 1924.

His Excellency C. B. D. King,
President of Liberia,
Monrovia, Liberia.
May it please Your Excellency:

We beg to inform you that the delegation of three persons, consisting of the Hon. Robert Lincoln Poston, Lady Henrietta Vinton Davis and Mr. J. Milton Van Lowe, who were sent to Liberia to negotiate for the emigration to that country of American and West Indian Negroes, who desire to settle in Liberia and to become a part of its citizenry, returned Monday, the 17th inst., and made a report to us of their stay in your good country. Unfortunately, the chairman of the Delegation, the Hon. Robert Lincoln Poston, died at sea at 5 a. m. on the passage home. His death was mourned by the entire world-wide membership of our association and millions of citizens in America.

The other members of the delegation laid before us certain suggestions of the local committee, consisting of the Hons. Arthur Barclay, D. Howard, J. J. Dossen, Dixon Brown and Messrs. W. F. Dennis, H. T. Wesley and D. C. Caranda, which fit in splendidly with the plans of our association, and which we are pleased to adopt, and to inform you of same. A copy of the suggestions is hereto attached.

The delegation has further inspired us with the great need for quick action in helping in the industrial, agricultural and educational development of Liberia. They spoke highly of the country and its possibilities, and we are satisfied on their recommendation, and from what knowledge we ourselves possess, that serious active steps should be taken by us to help your good country.

Simultaneous with the arrival of the delegates in America, there has been published news purporting to be from one Butler, Limited, of Liberia, that you refused to see the delegates and that American and West Indian Negroes are not wanted in Liberia. This bit of news has been circulated by the unfriendly Negro press, and has also been circulated in the Crisis, the magazine of the National Association for the Advancement of Colored People, in the report of Dr. Du Bois.

We have not contradicted the statement and do not intend to do so, because we did not want to create any controversy over the matter that may be embarrassing in any way. We quite appreciate the position taken by you, and for the best interest of Liberia we have always refrained from saying or doing anything that would create any misunderstanding involving the interest of the country. You and your good government may rest assured that the Universal Negro Improvement Association and its representatives will at no time say or do anything that would embarrass you and your good government.

Officially, we beg to accept, also, the following plans, for which we ask your approval and co-operation:

1. That the Universal Negro Improvement Association be granted by your government five (5) or six (6) different sites of land in Liberia, located at different points in the neighborhoods of the Cavella River, Maryland county, Sinoe, Grand Bassa and Cape Mount, in areas of eight (8) square miles each or more, for the purpose of building townships for the settlement of colonists as citizens and natives, for the development of Liberia, and that said townships be developed under the plan laid out in the suggestions of the local advisory committee.

2. That we approve and agree to the suggestions of the local advisory committee that the first settlement of colonists be established on the Cavella River, in Maryland county, near Cape Palmas, and to inform you that we are making arrangements for the first group of colonists of about four hundred (400) or five hundred (500), to sail from New York on or about the 15th of September, 1924, consisting of the class of people as mentioned in the suggestions of the local committee. Preparatory to their sailing away from America, however, the Association

shall send to the place designated through the advisory committee a small contingent of experts, who will survey the settlement and inaugurate such preparations as are necessary for the accommodation of the colonists who are to arrive in October.

3. We shall send out and establish at Cape Palmas, as suggested by the committee, a hospital, with doctors and units, for the medical accommodation of the colonists and the people of Liberia.

To repeat, we shall carry out all the suggestions made by the advisory committee, with the amendments to two paragraphs submitted by us, as per attached memorandum; but we further ask, if your government will be good enough to grant the Association in the immediate neighborhood of each settlement (granted under the arrangement of holding in trust for the colonists), an additional plot of land of five thousand (5,000) or more acres, each for the exclusive development of the Association agriculturally or industrially, as a source of revenue by which the Association may be able to meet some of its current expenses in its development plans for the good of the country and its citizens.

Should you and your good government acquiesce in the proposition herein outlined, we ask that an agreement be drawn to embody said plans, and that our attorney and representative, Hon. Arthur J. Barclay, sign same in our behalf, copies of which will be forwarded to us at our headquarters for certification

With very best wishes, we have the honor to be
Your obedient servants,
UNIVERSAL NEGRO IMPROVEMENT ASSOCIATION.

President-General.
Secretary-General.

Suggested amendments to the first and second paragraphs of suggestions by local advisory committee, by parent body, Universal Negro Improvement Association, New York.

That the words, "with the approval of the parent body, Universal Negro Improvement Association," be added to the last word "require" of the last line of the first paragraph, which paragraph shall read as follows:

The directors and management of the business of the U. N. I. A. in Liberia, so far as it relates to emigration, shall be entrusted to an advisory committee consisting of seven Liberians, viz.: Hons. Arthur Barclay, D. E. Howard, J. J. Dossen and

Messrs. W. F. Dennis, Dixon B. Brown, H. Too Wesley and
D. C. Carranda, who shall have the power to increase their number as the circumstances may require, with the approval of the
parent body of the Universal Negro Improvement Association.

The following additions are suggested for the second paragraph: That the words "assisting and co-operating" be added
after the word "and" in the fourth line of the second paragraph,
preceding the words "in directing," which paragraph would read
with addition, as follows:

This committee shall co-operate with the parent body of the
U. N. I. A. in New York in formulating plans for the establishment of new settlements in Liberia of emigrants sent out by
the Association as colonists, and in locating them in said settlements and assisting and co-operating in directing the general
affairs of the Association in Liberia.

The foregoing additions or amendments are requested to the
suggestions of the local committee, acceptance of which would
satisfy completely the Universal Negro Improvement Association in its approval and adoption of the suggestions made by the
said committee under date of February 16, 1924, submitted to
the delegation representing the Universal Negro Improvement
Association, consisting of Robert Lincoln Poston, Henrietta
Vinton Davis and J. Milton Van Lowe.

Acting on the agreements reached from 1920 to 1923, both
written and oral, the Association in America and the West
Indies, purchased, through the Black Cross Navigation and
Trading Company, the S. S. General George W. Goethals, from
the Panama Railroad Company, a subsidiary of the American
Government, a ship of over 5,000 tons, of class 1A. In the
meantime, according to arrangements with the Liberian Government, local committee and people in Liberia, the advance
guard of the colonists were dispatched. The Association sent
away a group of technical and mechanical experts to lay out
and build the first four Concentration Camps for the colonists
who were to sail from New York in October, 1924. The Experts
sailed away from America in June, 1924, including engineers, mechanics and secretaries. The men were under the
direction of William Strange, mining and civil engineer of over
thirty years practical experience. The pioneers were all responsible men, of families, with one exception. Contracts involving
years of service had been entered into with them. Some were
taken from responsible positions with Governments, for their
fitness to perform the pioneering work of construction. Plans
of cities were already drawn and requisitions for materials

placed. Strange was Directing and Supervising Engineer. He gave up large business opportunities in America to help in the undertaking. Goods, materials and machinery to the extent of fifty thousand dollars were ordered, the gross part of which was shipped to Liberia in July, 1924, from New York on the ships of the Bull Line to meet the men on their arrival who had sailed via Europe. Hundreds of thousands of dollars of other materials and machinery were about to be shipped out with the Colonists, aboard our own ship, the General Goethals, in October, 1924. It was all arranged with the local committee in Liberia and the Government and people that the first of the four colonies we were to start building in Liberia, was to be at Harper, the County of Cape Palmas, where the Chief Justice of the Republic, James Jenkins Dossen, lived. As a further proof of Dossen's love for his race, interest and sincerity in the project, the following letters from him are annexed:

Monrovia, Liberia,
West Africa,
February 28, 1924

The Hon. Marcus Garvey,
New York, N. Y.

Dear Sir:

I trust that before this letter reaches you, your delegates sent to Liberia will have reached you and reported the whole-hearted reception received in Monrovia.

It was a pleasure to the friends of emigration to note the general enthusiasm shown by our people in the program to send to Liberia, colonists of the race in other lands, to help build up this nation as well as to give an opportunity to Negroes aboard to enjoy the pure atmosphere of manly freedom. It is sincerely hoped that you will not fail to put over your great program. We have organized an Advisory Committee of some of our best men, who will take care of the movement on this side, and they have drawn up a Plan, which I think will prove very useful and valuable to you on that side. if followed. I gave the delegation a copy of an oration which I delivered some time ago, and which contains many historic and other data about Liberia, etc.

You will see that we have recommended that the first settlement be established on the Cavalla River This locality offers many advantages to traders, miners, farmers, and other men of industry. Besides, the climate there is healthy. Please con-

vey to my good friend, John E. Bruce, my kindest regards, also
Rev. Ellegor.

Wishing you and your movement all success,
I remain,

Yours truly,
JAMES J. DOSSEN.

———

Judiciary Department,
Supreme Court of the Republic of Liberia,
Chief Justice's Chambers.

Monrovia, West Africa,
May 2, 1924.

The Universal Negro Improvement Association,
New York.

Dear Sirs:

I am in receipt of your letter of April 3, together with a copy
of the Amendments made by you to our suggested Plan for
which I thank you very much. The Secretary has not yet received your letter but as soon as it comes to hand the necessary action will be taken thereupon. I may state however, that
your Amendments appear to me to be all right.

I am glad to learn that you are busy working out our Plan
and that you hope to dispatch your first colonists in September,
next. We shall stand ready to co-operate with you on this side,
in putting over the enterprise successfully.

We entertain great hopes that working upon this line, you
will accomplish much good in promoting the growth and industrial development of the Republic of Liberia, and securing the
Liberty, Independence and Protection of the millions of Negroes
now under foreign domination.

I handed your delegation, when it was here, a pamphlet containing on oration by me on the "Origin, Rise and Destiny of
Liberia." I believe this would be interesting reading to all
concerned in Liberia, and serve as a propaganda in your emigration enterprise. I told them that they might have a few
thousand copies printed and sold at about twenty cents per
copy, and after paying the cost for printing to remit me the
balance together with 500 copies for circulation out here.

I may state that this oration has been a stimulus to Negroes
every where who have read it; and even among the Whites, it
has aroused greater interest in the potential natural resources
of Liberia, than anything else which has appeared in print for
many years. They promised to lay this before your Executive

committee, which I trust they have done.

Yours faithfully,
JAMES J. DOSSEN.

During the time all these arrangements were being made in America, and made public, W. E. B. DuBois, of the National Association for the Advancement of "Colored," "Light" People got himself appointed as Ambassador Extra-ordinary of the United States, to attend the second inaugural, in Liberia, of "Black" President King. At the same time Mrs. Helen Curtis (octoroon), wife of a late Consul General to Liberia, and an active member of the National Association for the Advancement of Colored People, who had recently completed a campaign of raising funds from the whites for the Association, under the designation of "The Crusaders," sailed also for Liberia. On her arrival she was installed in the Executive Mansion as a guest of President King. DuBois was the guest of other parties. What transpired then against the interest of the Universal Negro Improvement Association can be imagined. On the arrival of the experts and engineers of the Universal Negro Improvement Association in Liberia, to carry out the work of preparing for the colonists, they were immediately seized by the instructions of President King, and deported against the protest of the Liberian people and members of his Government. He terrorized and threatened the members of his own Government, who were solely depedent upon his good will for their positions and livelihood because they murmured at the outrage. The following week, after the deportation of the men from Monrovia, the first shipment of supplies and materials from the United States arrived at Cape Palmas, in care of Chief Justice Dossen. The Government allowed the materials to land, and a couple months after, without any warning or advise to the Association in America, sold parts of the materials to pay official salaries. Salaries of the officials of the Republic were over-due then for several months. Strange, the very day on which the ship arrived in Liberia, the Chief Justice died at Cape Palmas. It is rumored that "there was a hand of State in it," although the Chief Justice was a sufferer from diabetes. Some persons claimed that he died from lack of proper attention and medical care, for policy of "State." It was also rumored that if the "powers" in Monrovia, the seat of Government, had allowed the contemplated progressive colonies to be built by wide awake American and West Indian Negroes in the county presided over by the Chief Justice (politically) he would have become the

logical candidate for the next presidency of the Republic, which
was not in keeping with the plans of the Monrovian group that
had planned to indefinitely perpetuate itself.

The ruling group of the country is related by blood. When
one brother is out of the Presidency, a son-in-law takes it, or
nephew or cousin and so the group constitutes itself the
reigning power of the country. However, the Chief Justice,
the most loyal patriot of all Liberia, "passed away." Immediately on the publication in the New York World (daily
white paper) of the plans of outlay of the cities and townships to be built by the Association in Liberia, the forces of
opposition in America and Europe, got in touch with the Liberian President, and in a couple of days after, the Liberian Consul General in America, at Baltimore, one Ernest Lyons (another Negro of miscegenationistic tendencies, being himself a
hybrid, originally of British Honduras), was instructed, according to his own statement, to file with the State Department, at
Washington, a protest against the Universal Negro Improvement Association, sending out American Negroes to Liberia,
and that he was instructed not to vise their passports—
an act most villainous and treacherous after all the agreements and arrangements arrived at between the Liberian Government and people and the Universal Negro Improvement Association. This act of treachery has caused a great estrange-
ment between King and the people of Liberia, who live under
the terror of his despotism.

The proposed plans for colonization work in Liberia were contained in a full page advertisement which appeared in the New
York World under date Wednesday, June 25, 1924, as follows:—

COLONIZATION OF AFRICA BY NEGROES AS SOLUTION OF RACE PROBLEM

**Universal Negro Improvement Association Working to Develop
Colonies in Liberia as Peaceful Homes for Negroes—
Similar to Homeland in Palestine for Jews**

Over a hundred years ago the white friends of the Negro in
America, known as the American Colonization Society, helped
establish the Black Republic of Liberia with the hope that it
might become the home of those Negroes who wanted to live
among themselves. After great sacrifice and with much difficulty the early settlers of the republic have perpetuated the government until it stands out today as the most serious attempt of
the race to help itself.

The Universal Negro Improvement Association, organized under the laws of the State of New York, aims at assuming the responsibility of helping to develop Liberia as a natural home for Negroes. Toward this end several missions have been sent to Liberia for the purpose of arranging for the repatriation of as many Negroes as desire to go to that country to settle and to help in her industrial, agricultural and cultural development.

The following plans have been decided on by the Universal Negro Improvement Association: That the Association is to build four colonies in the Republic, the first on the Cavalla River, for which a group of civil and mechanical engineers have been sent to start preparatory work for the accommodation of the first batch of colonists, who will sail from New York during the Fall of the present year and following years.

The Association is raising a fund of $2,000,000 to bear the cost of constructing and establishing the first colony. The building plan for each colony is as follows (all Government buildings to be under the control of the Liberian Government):

BUILDING PLANS

Government

1. Court House and Post Office.
2. Town Hall
   a. Public Safety
      1. Police Station
      2. Fire Protection
      3. Hospital

Community Interest and Entertainment

1. National Theatre
2. Churches (2)
3. Large Public Hall
4. Public Park

Public Education

1. Public Library
2. Public Schools (2)
3. Public High School (1)
4. Colleges of Arts and Sciences
5. Trade School and Engineering Works

Public Utilities

1. Electric Light and Power Plant

2. Water Filtration Plant
3. Sewerage System and Sewage Disposal Plant
   a. Transportation Facilities
      1. Roads, Streets and Pavements
      2. Wharf and Dock and Water Front Improvement
      3. Railroad, 4-15 miles
   b. Commissaries (2)
   c. Dormitories (2)

This Is the Best Solution of the Negro Problem

All those who desire to help the Negro under the auspices of the Universal Negro Improvement Association in developing himself, are asked to subscribe to the fund of two million ($2,000,-000) dollars now being raised for the promotion of the Cavalla Colony.

Address your donation to the "Treasurer, Colonization Fund, Universal Negro Improvement Association, 56 West 135th Street, New York, U. S. A." Bankers: Chelsea Exchange Bank, Harlem Branch, 135th Street and Seventh Avenue.

The Fund

Marcus Garvey	$100.00
Mrs. Marcus Garvey	50.00
William C. Ritter	25.00
New York Division, U. N. I. A.	250.00
Mrs. Leola Warden, Columbus, Ohio	5.00
G. E. Barnes and others, Victoria de Lastunas, Oriente, Cuba	25.65
Mrs. P. S. Watterhouse, New Orleans, La.	15.00
Mrs. Peter Jackson and others of the Milwaukee Division Universal Negro Improvement Association	93.10
Friend of U. N. I. A. Francisco, Province Camaguey, Cuba	100.00
Mrs. Lucy Johnson, Cincinnati, Ohio	4.00
Other donations	2,734.87
Motor Corps, Unia, Pittsburgh, Pa.	11.00
Mrs. Malinda Hopkins, Chicago, Ill.	5.00
Laura Lee Div., No. 450, Lumberport, Va.	15.00
New Orleans Div., New Orleans, La.	15.00
Richmond Div., No. 193, Richmond, Va.	7.50
Mrs. Mary Belgrave, Boston, Mass.	8.00
Blue Island Division, Blue Island, Ill.	15.00
Holdenville Div., Holdenville, Okla.	51.00
Mrs. Annie Darden, Columbus, Ohio	5.00
J. W. Green, Seattle, Wash	5.00

E. A. Nibbs, Seattle, Wash............................	2.50
N. W. Hudgins, Seattle, Wash......................	1.00
A. M. Brown, Seattle, Wash........................	1.20
C. D. Cristman, Seattle, Wash.....................	1.00
J. B. Martin, Seattle, Wash.........................	1.00
Nellie E. Brown, Seattle, Wash....................	1.00
Mr. Rufus A. Reid, Seattle, Wash..................	1.00
H. Maitland, Seattle, Wash.........................	1.00
Mattie L. Maitland, Seattle, Wash.................	1.00
W. A. McLine, Seattle, Wash.......................	1.00
S. P. Moore, Seattle, Wash.........................	1.00
Joseph Lynch, Seattle, Wash.......................	1.00
Sarah Lynch, Seattle, Wash........................	.50
A friend, Seattle, Wash.............................	.20
Marie Jones, Seattle, Wash.........................	.25
Wilford Edwards, Seattle, Wash....................	.50
Frank C. Williams	.50
James Moore, Seattle, Wash	.50
J. D. Nelson, Seattle, Wash........................	1.50
E. Chambers, Seattle, Wash........................	1.00
Jennie Ellis, Seattle, Wash.........................	1.00
Geo. F. Carter, Seattle, Wash......................	1.00
Nannie R. Webb, Seattle, Wash....................	.50
Maude Keizer, Seattle, Wash.......................	1.10
Joseph Keizer, Seattle, Wash.......................	1.00
Thomas McPherson, Seattle, Wash.................	.25
Mary Costello Moore, Seattle, Wash...............	.50
Rachel Famber, Seattle, Wash......................	.50
Wm. Famber, Seattle, Wash........................	.50
Victoria Bean, Summit, N. J........................	25.00
Will Ford, Detroit, Mich............................	25.00
Geo. Brothers, South Bend, Ark....................	2.00
Walter Estes, N. Edmonton, Canada................	15.00
Mr. and Mrs. Manfield Sterkes, Farrell, Pa..........	5.00
C. W. Davis, South Bend, Ark......................	2.00
Chas. Carter, Carbon, W. Va.......................	10.00
Mrs. P. S. Waterhouse, New Orleans, La............	15.00
Milwaukee Division, Milwaukee, Wis...............	93.10
Danville Division, Danville, Ill.....................	15.00
Lucy Johnson, Cincinnati, Ohio.....................	4.00
Laura Palmer, Gary, Ind............................	12.23
Victoria de Lastunan Div., Prov. de Cuba............	25.65
Jean Gillman, Dover, N. J...........................	10.00
Boyd Timmons, Dover, N. J.........................	10.00

Leola Darden, Columbus, Ohio.................... 5.00
Mary McDonald, Gary, Ind........................ 5.00
Embry Darden, Gary, Ind......................... 5.00
William Patterson, Colp, Ill.................... 10.00
Frances Frederick, Hartford, Conn.............. 2.10
Francisco Division, Camaguey, Cuba............. 100.00
Morales Division, Morales, Guatemala........... 100.00
George Smith, Brooklyn, N. Y................... 5.00
J. S. Patterson, Portland, Oregon.............. 20.00

Total.. $4,086.20

Signed:

UNIVERSAL NEGRO IMPROVEMENT ASSOCIATION.
MARCUS GARVEY, President.
WILLIAM SHERRILL, 2nd Vice-President.
RUDOLPH SMITH, 3rd Vice-President.
HENRIETTA VINTON DAVIS, 4th Vice-President.
G. EMONI CARTER, Secretary.
CLIFFORD BOURNE, Treasurer.
LEVI F. LORD, Auditor.
G. O. MARKE.
THOMAS W. ANDERSON.
PERCIVAL L. BURROWS.
JAMES O'MEALLY.
NORTON G. THOMAS.

Immediately after King so suddenly and rudely repudiated the agreements with the Universal Negro Improvement Association to build up Liberia, he gave away, for 99 years, the same tracts of lands to be occupied by the association, to the Firestone Rubber Company (white) of Akron, Ohio, for rubber prospects and exploitation. He immediately conscripted the natives to build roads, for the convenience of this concession, without pay or shelter. The press in Liberia that supports King,—and none dare oppose him,—suddenly shifted from praising the effort of the Universal Negro Improvement Association to help Liberia, to tooting for the Firestone Rubber Company, hoping that millions of dollars would be spent by them, beyond the ability of the Universal Negro Improvement Association, out of which the governing class would profit. The Firestone people, however, are keen business men, who see the dollar, and not humanity, and up to now they have not started to scatter the dollars as the Liberian officials expected. King suppressed the entry of the Negro World into Liberia, and also opened all communications addressed to and sent by the Universal Negro Improvement Association. He has been accused by his own countrymen of pilfering their mail, and there is now an action pending against him, instituted by one of his countrymen, for intercepting and reading his mail. His suppression of the Negro World is caused through his fear of public sentiment against him. The people of Liberia being poor and helpless have to bow to his tyranny. Immediately after he repudiated me and the Universal Negro Improvement Association, he was made a Cavalier of the Legion of Honor of France and was honored by the English, by their sending to Monrovia, a battleship, to convey himself and his family on a visit to Sierre Leone, where he was reared. It is understood that the Universal Negro Improvement Association was inveigled by these enemies, into spending these large sums of money in the interest of the country, then repudiate all the agreements, so as to inflict unredeemable financial loss upon the Association, thereby proving the incompetence of my leadership and my general denunciation for fraud. How well the plot has succeeded the American public will judge. Suffice it to say, that at the time when Ernest Lyons filed his protest with the State Department, thousands of American and West Indian Negro families of substantial means and good industrial purpose, scattered all over the United States and the West Indies had already prepared themselves for departure to Liberia, then to them, the land of hope, peace and racial justice, and this group included people of the race of all shades of color, from black to octoroon. Again the Negro has defeated himself but his spirit is not dead.

Scene, New York and Liberia:

PETITION TO THE SENATE AND HOUSE OF REPRESENTATIVES OF LIBERIA, MONROVIA, LIBERIA.

From Four Million Negro Members of the Universal Negro Improvement Association of the United States and Millions of Negroes in Other Parts of the World, Through Their Representatives Attending the Fourth Annual International Convention of Negro Peoples of the World

Dated, August, 1924.

May it Please the Honorable House:

We, the deputies and delegates of the Fourth Annual International Convention of the Negro Peoples of the World, assembled in Liberty Hall, New York City, United States of America, from the 1st to the 31st of August, 1924, under the auspices of the Universal Negro Improvement Association, beg to submit this our appeal to your Honorable Body asking for such considerations as you may give in helping to remedy a wrong that has been inflicted upon the Universal Negro Improvement Association, and incidentally upon millions of Negroes of America and the West Indies who originally planned to make Liberia their permanent home and of which country they had hoped to become citizens in keeping with the constitution framed and made law by your illustrious fathers and amended by your honorable selves.

As you may know, the Universal Negro Improvement Association represents the Negro masses in America and the West Indies. For six years this association has carried on a continuous system of education among its people to the end that they be organized into one great movement looking forward to their return to Africa, from whence their forefathers were taken centuries ago, and to there rehabilitate themselves and once more possess themselves of the land, of which they were original owners. With this end in view, it was decided that the most convenient way of their being able to help their native land—Africa—was through assisting the Republic of Liberia to establish herself as a successful nation through her higher industrial, agricultural and commercial development, thereby proving completely the Negro's undisputed ability for self-government.

Being mindful of the fact that Liberia was established over one hundred years ago to offer such an opportunity for the race to demonstrate itself in the higher sphere of government, and that, you and your fathers have so nobly demonstrated this ability, and knowing that we at this end possess material, financial and other resources that we could place at your disposal in helping to further develop the country, we sought the good graces of your government in 1920, through the offices of His Excellency, President Charles King, and the Honorable Edwin Barclay, Secretary of State, requesting that the Universal Negro Improvement Association be admitted into the country and be given such rights, concessions and facility to work as would enable us to assist in the development of Liberia, as per document No. 1 attached hereto, and answer, document No. 2, signed by the Secretary of State, the Honorable Edwin Barclay. After an understanding had been effected in 1920, as above referred to, the association was again assured in 1921 by the Honorable Edwin Barclay, Secretary of State, acting as President in the absence of President King, who was on his way to the United States of America, that every facility would be granted to the association to carry out its program; and again in February, 1924, the Association sent to Liberia a third commission, headed by Sir Robert Lincoln Poston, which commission was received, after proper representation on the part of our attorney in Liberia, the Honorable Arthur Barclay, to the President, His Excellency, Charles B. King. At the meeting attended by the Honorable Arthur Barclay, the late Honorable Chief Justice J. J. Dossen and the delegation consisting of Sir Robert Lincoln Poston, Lady Henrietta Vinton Davis and the Honorable J. Milton Van Lowe, the President, His Excellency, Charles B. King, outlined a program of operation for the Universal Negro Improvement Association in Liberia, in keeping with the original agreement of 1920 and the endorsement of 1921, and subsequently appointed a committee consisting of prominent citizens of Liberia and members of the government, namely, Vice-President Wesley, the late Chief Justice, J. J. Dossen, Honorable Arthur Barclay, ex-President Howard, Honorable D. Carranda, Honorable W. Dennis and the Honorable Dixon Brown, as a committee to assist the Universal Negro Improvement Association in carrying out the plan of colonization. We received from the committee certain suggestions, embodied in document No. 3 hereto attached, which suggestions we attempted to carry out to the very letter, to the extent that we dispatched from America, in June of the present year and July, two shipments of materials to the Cavalla region at Cape Palmas, materials which are now on the spot, and an expert group of engineers—civil and mechanical—to start immediate operation in preparing homes for the first group of colonists which would leave America in October, according to the suggestion of the committee, for whose conveyance we had already secured by purchase a steamship of 5,300 tons, as well as signed contracts involving two million dollars ($2,000,000) for further materials to be shipped away to the Cavalla colony.

After all this was done in keeping with the suggestions of the committee and previous understanding with the government as per documents attached and referred to, we were most rudely informed through the public press in America, without any previous notification from the government in Liberia, that passports of members of our organization would not be vised by Liberian consuls in America and elsewhere, and that no one under the auspices of the Universal Negro Improvement Association be allowed to land in Liberia; that we were not wanted in the country and reports of that evil nature.

All this was broadcast through the white and colored papers by the Consul General of Liberia, the Honorable Ernest Lyons of Baltimore, without any offense on the part of the Universal Negro Improvement Association or without any previous intimation that there was anything wrong or unpleasant affecting the understanding that existed between the government and the Universal Negro Improvement Association and the Universal Negro Improvement Association and the local committee appointed by President King in February, 1924.

Adding further insult to our already good intentions, we were informed by cable from Liberia, that our expert engineers, who included some of the best men of America and the West Indies, whom we had sent out under contract at great sacrifice, were rudely deported and not allowed to land. We also sent our Sir James O'Meally, High Commissioner General of our Association, a highly cultured and educated gentleman, and he also was not allowed to land, but had to seek refuge in Lagos, British West Africa, until he was able to communicate with us for his immediate return to the United States. Some of the men we sent out had large families at this end whom they separated themselves from, others had resigned government positions in the West Indies and America to take up the appointments with us in Liberia. Two of these men were not American citizens but British subjects, and under the quota for British subjects coming to the United States of America, on their return, were

Group of experts sent by the U. N. I. A. to Liberia in June, 1924, to start construction work in building concentration camps and laying out townships and surveying and laying out farms for the colonists who were to have sailed from America aboard the S. S. General Goethals in October, 1924, in keeping with agreement with Liberian Government. Special Committee of Reception for the Colonists appointed by President King, and the Liberian people.

Top row: (1) William Strange, Supervising and Directing Mining and Civil Engineer. (2) James C. Roberts, Electrical Engineer. Middle row: (1) James N. Walcott, Shipwright and Builder. (2) James A. O'Meally, Commissioner. (3) Reginald Hurley, Carpenter and Builder. Bottom row: (1) J. Nicholas, Mechanical Engineer. (2) Rupert Christian, Secretary and Paymaster to Colony.

not allowed to land, but had to be sent back to Holland, from whence they had trans-shipped from Liberia and again we had to remove them from Holland back to their original homes in the West Indies and leave their families in the United States, whom we also have to ship out to them.

All this humiliation has been heaped upon us by the act of your good government for absolutely no just cause, because up to the present we have not been officially notified or informed that we have done anything displeasing to the government or in violation of the understanding that existed.

The above complaint is not the only one that we have to lay as touching the action of the government, but on the 26th of August of the present year, the Associated Press (white) of the United States, circulated through the white papers all over this country and abroad the following:

LIBERIA DENOUNCES GARVEY PLAN—URGES U. S. TO CHECK BLACK HEGIRA

Policy of Negro Improvement Association Declared Incendiary in Note to Washington—Opposes It in Principle and in Fact

---

Washington, August 26 (Associated Press)—The Government of Liberia, in a formal communication delivered by Ernest Lyon, Consul General, has advised the Washington Government that it is "irrevocably opposed both in principle and in fact to the incendiary policy of the Universal Negro Improvement Association, headed by Marcus Garvey."

The note, signed by Edwin Barclay, Secretary of State of Liberia, says:

"The Government of Liberia, irrevocably opposed both in principle and fact to the incendiary policy of the Universal Negro Improvement Association headed by Marcus Garvey, and repudiating the improper implications of its widely advertised scheme for the immigration of American Negroes into the republic under the auspices of this association, which the Liberian Government, believes does not appear to be bona fide and has in addition a tendency adversely to affect the amicable relations of the republic with the friendly states possessing territories adjacent to Liberia, 'desire to place on record their protest against this propaganda so far as it relates to Liberia, and to express their confidence that the Government of the United States will neither facilitate nor permit the emigration under the auspices of the Universal Negro Improvement Association of Negroes from the United States with intent to proceed to Liberia.'"

A similar communication was published in the Daily London Telegraph and other London papers, which again reveals that the Secretary of State of your good government and your President have undertaken to carry on a propaganda in foreign countries against the interest of the Universal Negro Improvement Association, without first giving the Universal Negro Improvement Association, with whom they have had an understanding, a chance or opportunity to defend itself against any imaginary departure from the original and only representation that we have made to your good government in our intention to help the country.

It is for us to state that bewteen 1920 and 1924 all our representations to the government through President King and the Secretary of State have been wholly to the point of assisting to develop the country industrially, agriculturally and commercially, and at no time have we ever suggested anything contrary to these intentions. The communications bearing date of 1924, the last communications sent to the President of Liberia, hereto attached and marked 4 and 5 respectively, further explain our position and intention, and, therefore, leaves us at a loss to know that, while we at this end entertained the most friendly and helpful intention and spirit toward Liberia, that the President and Secretary of State should so endeavor to wound our feeling and try to hold us up to public ridicule.

It is in this wise that we petition your honorable body to take steps to right the grievous wrong because we believe in the honor and integrity of the Liberian people. We feel that you are blood of our blood and flesh of our flesh, and that you would not willingly on your own initiative attempt to do us such injury and work upon us such harm that even a white government, unfriendly though they may appear to be, would not do.

We beg to draw to your attention that while our own black republic of Liberia deported, humiliated and disgraced our own men sent there to help the country, that the British government allowed our men to land on their territory in Africa and treated them most cordially until they were able to book passage back to the United States. We also beg to inform you that our representatives in France are most courteously welcomed and treated by the French, while on the other hand, we have been treated so discourteously and humiliated by our own.

We further petition you to intercede between the Secretary of State and the President to withdraw the unholy restriction and discrimination that they have made against the members of the Universal Negro Improvement Association and millions of Negroes in America and the West Indies from returning to Liberia to help in the development of that country. We, on this side, are aggrieved because there is national discrimination in our society, where our race is discriminated against by members of the white race. It is that discrimination that caused our fathers and your fathers to settle in Liberia, and it was freedom from such that caused you to adopt the motto: "The love of liberty brought us here," yet the same liberty is to be denied other members of our race by your good government, quite contrary to the spirit of the constitution of good Liberia.

We ask, therefore, for your immediate action in this matter. Is it necessary that we call the attention of your most honorable body to Section 8, Article 1, of the Bill of Rights of the Constitution of the Republic of Liberia?

"No person shall be deprived of life, liberty, property or privilege but by judgment of his peers or the law of the land."

We beg to submit that there has been no judgment under such section of any violation of principle, privilege or rights of the Universal Negro Improvement Association in its relation with the government.

Again we beg to draw your attention to Sections 12 and 13 of Article 5 of the constitution:

"Sec. 12. No person shall be entitled to hold real estate in this Republic unless he be a citizen of the same. Nevertheless this article shall not be construed to apply to colonization, missionary, educational or other benevolent institutions, so long as the property or estate is applied to its original purpose."

"Sec. 13. The great object of forming these colonies being to provide a home for the dispersed and oppressed children of Africa and to regenerate and enlighten this benighted continent, none but persons of color shall be admitted to citizenship in this Republic."

Amended by Section 6 to read that Article 5, Section 13, be made to read:

"That none but Negroes or persons of Negro descent shall be eligible to citizenship in this Republic."

Must we understand that the Constitution is set aside especially to operate against the Universal Negro Improvement Association and the millions of Negroes who are members thereof?

We feel that your honorable body will not so discriminate and thus nullify the constitution of the only free black nation in the world. We are asking you, as above stated, for consideration and redress, and trust that you will act immediately, so as to enable us to carry out our good intentions toward the republic and the race. We are still prepared and ready to give all aid to Liberia and to its people, in helping to make her a first-rate nation. We have absolutely no political designs. We are a peaceable, law-abiding group of people in America, where we operate, and for the last six years we have been recognized by the government, received by the State and Federal authorities and by the President on several occasions, and it is alarming to us to learn that, while white governments treat us with respect and decency, our own should act in the manner complained of.

This petition must not be regarded as an insult to His Excellency the President and the Secretary of State, nor an attempt to hold them up to impeachment or anything of the kind, but we desire to state the facts and ask for your help and good services in restoring the friendship and fellowship that we desire to exist between all parties concerned. After the publications by the Liberian Consul-General in America and by the broad publicity engaged in by the Secretary of State, we have had to make one or two statements through our paper, the Negro World, for the purpose of clarifying our position and preventing public condemnation when we were not at fault. These, we trust, you will not interpret to mean any attack against the President or Secretary of State, but only statements made to justify our position at this end and save us from the condemnation of the public, who were made to believe that we were not in earnest in what we were attempting to do in helping Liberia and to settle with colonists from this part of the world—the country that we love.

We also beg to draw to the attention of your honorable body the great danger that lurks in the future through the granting to the Firestone Rubber and Tire Company of certain concessions, which we do hope have not yet been ratified by you. Whilst it is not in our province to interfere with your legislation, we beg to point out to you the motives generally underlying white capitalists when they seek entry into the countries of weaker peoples. It is our firm belief that the Firestone concessions in Liberia will lead them ultimately to seek the usurpation of the government, even as has been done with the black Republic of Haiti after similar white companies entered there under the pretense of developing the country. It is generally known that certain members of the white race do not humor a government by darker and weaker peoples, and it is our belief that as time goes on the Firestone Rubber and Tire Company's interest will seek to further tighten its hold upon the republic, with ultimate aim of superseding its government and placing it in the hands of the white race. We are asking you, therefore, if it is possible, not to ratify the concessions and to guard most jealously the freedom and integrity of your dear country.

We, your petitioners, further ask that your honorable body make provision to guarantee to the Universal Negro Improvement Association that a commissioner or advocate be sent to plead before your honorable body, or before any proper tribunal, or before the officials of the government, the cause of the Universal Negro Improvement Association, that he shall be admitted to the country to make such representation, and that no judgment be passed upon the Universal Negro Improvement Association or its membership at large until such plea has been made before your honorable body or before a responsible tribunal appointed by the government.

We also beg to request of you that you pay no attention to the representations of the man W. E. B. DuBois, his agents or representatives, who may, directly or indirectly, by anonymous and other harmful letters or communications, endeavor to prejudice you against the Universal Negro Improvement Association to the end that no honest assistance be given Liberia by Negroes who are in earnest to build it up by and for themselves, but that Liberia and the race be exposed to the designs of those who desire to exploit and humiliate them, for which Negro agents in America and elsewhere are being used.

For these and other considerations we, your petitioners, do humbly pray.

SIGNED for the five thousand delegates and deputies attending the Fourth Annual International Convention of the Negro Peoples of the World, representing eleven million members of the Universal Negro Improvement Association and others of the Negro race.   MARCUS GARVEY,
Speaker in Convention.
Secretary of Convention.

The following letter written by Ernest Lyon, Liberian Consul General in America, reveals beyond the shadow of a doubt the disposition of the present clique, called the Liberian Government (King and Barclay) to subvert the purpose for which the country was founded by the philanthropic and far-seeing white people of the American Colonization Society, and make it a "close corporation" or a country run in the interest of a few unworthy Negroes, who have skillfully "grabbed" the government of the country by questionable election methods and political fraud.

The high and lofty purpose the country was founded to serve, and which the Universal Negro Improvement Association seeks to carry out in the repatriation of American and West Indian Negroes is to be defeated by graft and clique interest. The letter speaks for itself:

LIBERIAN CONSULATE GENERAL

In the United States of America.
828 North Carey Street
Baltimore, Md.

October 26, 1925.

Mrs. ....

....

....

My Dear Madam:

I have yours of the 23rd instant asking for necessary provisions relative to your desire to visit Liberia to which I am replying.

1. Secure passport from the Washington State Department certifying that you are an American citizen.

2. Make affidavit before a Notary declaring that you are not connected with the Garvey Movement.

3. Send your American passport and affidavit to be vised by me at the Consulate General in Baltimore, No. 828 N. Carey Street.

4. Inclose fee and return postage amounting to five dollars and fifty cents ($5.50).

(Signed)

ERNEST LYON.
Liberian Consul General.

ROBBING THE NEGRO'S VALUES

The selfish and heartless capitalist of the white race conspires to rob Negroes of their land and values in many instances by employing and using the conscienceless and disloyal members of the race who happen to be removed from the majority by intelligence, to betray the people into a false sense of feeling of security. In some instances, entire countries are thus stolen with their mineral, agricultural and other wealth; in others the people's investments and interests in banks, insurance companies, real estate holdings, including private dwellings, churches, corporation stocks and allied financial undertakings are pilfered with the concurrent and conniving consent of these so-called "intellectual" Negroes. The method is a selfish and shameful one and the honest and liberal-minded whites should, for the sake of decency, history and better understanding of the future and their generations seek to prevent this, in conjunction with the loyal, race-patriotic and unselfish, intelligent New Negro who is endeavoring to save his race from the greed and graft of the old school. A new case in question is the stealing of the rubber values of Liberia from the race through the connivance of selfish Negro officials of that country.

SCENE: ABOARD SHIP (FRENCH LINER "PARIS") NEW YORK HARBOR:

Barclay interviewed by "The New York Times," enemy capi-

---

talist paper against Marcus Garvey, August 13, 1925:

LIBERIA WOULD BAR GARVEY, ENVOY SAYS

Republic, However, Welcomes Any Other Settler From America, Minister Asserts

---

HERE ON UNOFFICIAL VISIT

Is Met on the Paris by State Department Representative—

"The Honorable Edwin Barclay, Minister Plenipotentiary for the Republic of Liberia, arrived yesterday on the French liner Paris, on an unofficial visit to this country. Henry Carter, special representative of the State Department, met him at Quarantine. The Liberian Minister will go to Washington after spending a few days in New York.

"Mr. Barclay is 43 years old and has been in the service of his Government seven years, part of the time as Attorney General. He speaks English with scarcely any accent and said he had been educated at the old college of Liberia in Monrovia, the capital of the republic.

"Are you coming here to negotiate a loan?" he was asked.

"No," replied the Minister with a smile. "We do not need to borrow money from the United States just now, but later, perhaps, a loan may be asked for to develop the railroad system in Liberia. My mission in this, my first visit to America, is to endeavor to cement the friendship between the two countries."

"What about the rubber concessions?" he was asked.

"The Firestone Rubber Company has a concession of one million acres and can have as much more land as it desires," he replied. "Rubber is thriving well in Liberia, and there will be a good crop this season. Fifteen hundred acres, planted by the Firestone concern as an experiment, have turned out a success, and 20,000 acres are now under cultivation.

"Labor is very cheap in Liberia and strong, healthy men work for 25 cents a day. The language of Liberia is English. It is a country for young men, and any of the colored people who wish to go there from America to live will be heartily welcomed, and given grants of land to cultivate."

"Do you include Marcus Garvey and his aides in this invitation?"

"No," the Minister replied in decided tones. "Neither Garvey nor any of those who have been identified with him would be received in Liberia."

Listen to the language of the selfish, "ignorant intellectual" heartless black Negro, exploiter and "Statesman" from Liberia, typical of the King Administration of that country:

This man is without any apology an agent and subject of the new slavery imposed upon African natives, whose labor is sold by this type of the race for twenty-five cents and less per diem for producing rubber, etc., for a white exploiting corporation—another Belgian Leopold outrage.

Can you see the reason why Barclay and King and their kind in Liberia hate and oppose me? They can sell the labor of "husky" black men and women for twenty-five cents and make the profits.

Garvey sought to standardize the wages of the black race and dignify the social life of the people. They sought to exploit the people and keep them in "their places" for themselves and the unreasonable capitalistic systems of Africa. Must the two million blacks of Liberia perish at the hands of such men? Must wide-awake and right thinking American and West Indian Negroes, be kept out of Liberia and prevented from helping in the honorable development of their ancestral country?

Barclay and King want the ignorant of the American and West Indian Negroes who will join the hosts in Liberia at twenty-five cents a day, so that they could continue to exploit them, but opposed to the intelligent and wide-awake members of the Universal Negro Improvement Association who seek to lift the standard of the people to the common level of civilization. Oh, Government! how many crimes are committed in thy name?

In Liberia the Negroes of the Barclay and King type treat the natives like dogs, and with greater inhumanity than some of the most selfish whites. They keep the natives poor, hungry, shelterless and naked, while they parade themselves in the tropical sun in English frock coats and evening dress. They work and tax the natives to death while they, themselves, impugn the dignity of labor and pay no taxes. Do you wonder why such Negroes want to keep Marcus Garvey and his aides out of Liberia? Such Negroes are afraid of me, for they realize they have no colleague in me to exploit the labor of the unfortunate blacks and build up class distinction, based on an education of the wrong sort; but a foe to special privilege and an enemy of selfishness intended to injure Negroes.

When those Negroes found out that my intention was to really help the country and not to particularly enrich them; that my desire was to properly and honestly advance the cause of Liberia as a real Negro nation with the assistance of Chief Justice Dossen, they deported my representatives.

Will the honorable white men of America support that kind of a thing in Liberia, and perpetuate the miseries of the natives, and keep back the solution of the race problem?

Read the history of the Colonization Society of America (white) and don't allow King, Barclay and their group to throw dust into the eyes of white America and discourage good, black, American citizens who want to go to Liberia and help in the development of the country as a creditable Negro nation.

GOOD (?) CHRISTIANS AND THEIR RELIGION

TAKING LIBERIA FROM THE NEGRO

This chapter was intended as a commentary and further explanation of the Firestone coup in Liberia and its resultant effect on the Negroes of Africa and the Western World, but the mailing of this document was not allowed, being against the rules of the Atlanta prison.

The document is, therefore, on file at the prison.

Scene: A Confidential Report on the True Conditions in Liberia by Commissioner Garcia to Marcus Garvey: Elie Garcia's Liberian Report dated August, 1920.

ECONOMICAL AND MORAL CONDITIONS

"Liberia although a very rich country in natural resources is the poorest place on the face of the earth and actually the people are facing "starvation."

This condition is due to many facts, first the strong repulsion of the Liberians for any kind of work. There is no cultivated land in the Republic and RICE which is the National food is imported from England and other places and sold at a fabulous price, although it can be produced in enormous quantities there.

Class distinctions—This question is also a great hindrance to the development of Liberia. There are at this present time two classes of people; the Americo-Liberians also called "sons of the soil" and the natives. The first class, although the educated one, constitutes the most despicable element in Liberia. Because of their very education, they are self-conceited and believe that the only honorable way for them to make a living is by having a "Government job." The men of this class having been most of them educated in England or other European places, are used to life, which the salaries paid by the Government do not suffice to maintain. Therefore, dishonesty is prevalent. To any man who can write and read there is but one goal, a Government office, where he can graft.

"For the same reason, they are absolutely hostile to "immigration" by American or West Indian Negroes, that is, if said Negroes show any tendency to take part in the political life of the Republic. This fact is of great importance and I dare suggest that words must be given to any one going to Liberia in the interest of the U. N. I. A., to deny firmly any intention on our part to enter into politics in Liberia. This attitude will remove any possible idea of opposition and will not prevent us after having a strong foot-hold in the country to act as we see best for their own betterment and that of the Race at large.

"The policy for the present must be to limit our program to Commercial, Industrial and Agricultural developments.

The Liberian politicians understand clearly that they are degenerated and weak morally and they know that if any number of honest Negroes with brains, energy and experience come to Liberia and are permitted to take part in the ruling of the nation, they will be absorbed and ousted in a very short while.

"Another important fact is the attitude of the Americo-Liberians towards enlightening the native tribes. This intention of the U. N. I. A. must be kept quiet for a while. As it is the Americo-Liberians are using the natives as slaves, and human chattel slavery still exists there.

"They buy men or women to serve them, and the least little insignificant Americo-Liberian has half a dozen boys at his service—for he, himself will not even carry his own umbrella in the street, said article has to be carried by a boy, and so, for the smallest parcel. While in Monrovia I went to a store and bought 7 yards of khaki to have 2 pairs of trousers made. The merchant wrapped the khaki and gave it to me. As I was stepping out of the store my companion (an Americo-Liberian) said to me: "Why I don't suppose you are going to carry this bundle yourself?" "Why not?" said I, "it is a very small parcel." He answered that it was not the custom in Liberia for any gentleman to carry parcels, therefore the usefulness of having slaves.

"It is also deplorable to state that the highest Liberian official lives in a state of polygamy, which is highly detrimental to the improvement of morality among the natives as well as to social development among themselves.

It is unavoidable in a place where a young girl can be bought for 2 or 3 pounds (sterling) and become one's possession. To conclude, the Liberians are opposed to any element which may be instrumental in bringing to an end their political tryanny, their habits of graft and their polygamic freedom.

FINANCES, DEBTS AND ROADS

"It is said by competent persons that the total revenues of Liberia—Customs duties, taxes and others—amount to a little over 4 millions of dollars a year. Of this supposed amount only a little over 2 millions are usually accounted for. The other 2 millions being divided between the high officials and some subordinate employees. This statement does not seem exaggerated, if considering the salaries received by some officials, one would venture to investigate their expenses and ways of living. The total debts of Liberia amount to the sum of $1,700,000.00, the interest of which can hardly be kept up owing to the misappropriation of the funds. It may be well to say that the Republic of Liberia is a concern bringing returns to a few individuals including the three foreign receivers.

"There is not a mile of road in all Liberia and in Monrovia

which is the Capital, not a street worthy of the name. Bush grows in front and around the Executive Mansion.

Yet with all this backwardness to his account the average Liberian is as proud as a peacock and boasts of being a citizen of a free country. I was a silent witness to a discussion between a West Indian Negro recently arrived in Monrovia and a prominent Liberian. The West Indian was trying to show him —without malice—the tremendous work which had to be done before Liberia can be made an up to date place. The Liberian got vexed and in his rebuke said "that he never sang in the cornfield" alluding to the slave ancestors of the West Indian, but, the latter answered him, that it would be impossible for him to do so as there was no cornfield to be seen in hungry Liberia. He was dismounted by the answer and departed. I could not help thinking that the answer was well deserved and very appropriate.

FOREIGN RELATIONS AND FOREIGN INFLUENCE

"If Liberia ever needed help it is at this present time, when the small Republic is the object of a close contest between America, England and France.

I understand that there was great hope among the Liberians that America would be their best friend, and that they would be prevented from having any dealing with their great neighbors, France and England. Representatives of both countries were making an active propaganda, until my arrival against the American Loan and both have made it publicly known, that their Governments are ready to help Liberia with any amount of money. It would seem very philanthropic from generous France and proud England if one did not know that the settlements of said help, will sooner or later, bring a loss of territory for insolvent Liberia, if not the loss of her national autonomy. When my arrival was made known in Monrovia, and also what was the aim of the U. N. I. A. Br . . . propaganda did not spare the U. N. I. A.

"On the contrary the attitude of the French was rather friendly or apparently so. I was informed that the F. C. had received orders previous to my arrival not to allow the Commission to sail from the West Coast without visiting all of her colonies. For what purpose? I will not venture to say.

While these propaganda were going on, the Liberians were still expecting much from the U. S., until the famous memorandum was presented to them early in June.

I have read the original document signed by the American Charge d'Affaires and I will say, that from beginning to end, it is the most insulting and humiliating document ever presented to a free people for ratification.

"According to the terms of this Memorandum, if Liberia wants to use the amount of five millions open to her credit by the U. S. she must first;

Submit to the U. S. (Secretary of Treasury) a financial statement of all her debts and interest due on same. After said debts have been investigated by the U. S. and found correct and binding upon the Republic, the Secretary of Treasury of the U. S. will pay them. For the rest of the amount, a Receiver General is to be appointed by the U. S. who will collect all revenues of the Republic, of any source whatever and disburse them without the intervention of any Liberian Official.

"All his help,—Assistant, Commissioner and others to be appointed by the President of the U. S.

The financial budget of the Republic, before its presentation to the Senate, must be submitted to the Receiver-General, who shall have the power to increase or decrease some expenses for salaries or others without interference from the Government. The Receiver and whatever help he may require is to receive salaries adequate to their range from the revenues of the Republic. These salaries to be fixed by the President of the U. S. The Receiver-General shall have the power to dictate all measures necessary to the improvement of the country and such dictations to be enforced by the Government without modifications.

"The Senate shall have no right to grant any concession or vote any contract, without submitting same for approval to the Receiver-General. The Receiver-General shall also have the power to investigate the workings of all Government offices and to introduce better systems. Once a year, the Receiver-General will give to the Government a report of his administration, financially and otherwise.

All public works, sanitary improvements to be directed and controlled by the Receiver-General or his deputy. The interest and principal of the loan to be paid in gold.

These are only a few of the terms that I can remember from the voluminous document of 53 pages.

The adoption of this contract for ten years if signed by the Government will mean the election of a white king over Liberia, and will be a great inconvenience to the U. N. I. A.

"This memorandum has caused a great consternation in Liberia to the great satisfaction of British and French, who are endeavoring more than ever before to extend their influence in Liberia, which is already too large. The British Bank of West Africa and Elder Dempster Co., make night day in Liberia and because of the presence of this only bank, British currency is almost the legal tender of the country. Poor Liberia is hard up against three strong white Nations determined to choke her. Who will have the best chance at it? This is the problem. May God help her! For as it is any one of the three will be harmful to her later.

"The Senate has been called for an extraordinary session to deliberate about the memorandum, which it is hoped will be refused. Meanwhile I was given a tip that the gentleman sent to the states as Delegate to the Convention was secretly empowered by the Government to see what help could be gotten from the U. N. I. A. My cipher cablegram was to put you wise in the case. However, the American memorandum, though insulting as it is, proves that the U. S. is well informed of the unreliability of the Liberians to handle money. I make this statement to impress you—Mr. President—with the fact that in whatever financial help to be given by the U. N. I. A. to the Government we must keep an eye wide open on the use made with the help so given and even manage to have a voice in the disbursements, otherwise it will be only fattening the purses of a few individuals.

COMMERCIAL AND AGRICULTURAL POSSIBILITIES

"The possibilities along those lines are so broad that they can hardly be enumerated. Liberia is a new field, new in every sense of the word. But it is necessary to say that before any large commercial or agricultural venture can bring adequate returns, large sums of money must be spent to build roads and other means of conveying the produce to sea ports.

The three things most urgently needed in Liberia are: a little railroad, a coast wise line of steamers and about 100 miles of decent road. I have heard that it was the intention of the Liberians to petition the Black Star Line for the establishment of a coast line running between Cape Palmas and Freetown.

I sincerely believe that it would be of great advantage to the Company to do so, not only financially but also inasmuch as it would win the inalienable devotion of the Liberian people and of the people of the West Coast in general.

There is no communication between the ports of Liberia, except when it pleases the Elder Dempster to dispatch a boat to some of the ports. The people are entirely at the mercy of this company.

"I believe that two or three little steamers from 600 to 800 tons trading along the coast will bring enormous profit. If any information is desired on the matter I will furnish the company with data and figures taken on the spot. At all events I suggest that the Black Star Line will think seriously of establishing something of the kind at the earliest opportunity.

In so far as the railroad is concerned I have obtained from the Auditor of the Sierra Leone Railroad some information on the cost of the railroad by mile.

Thirty or forty miles of railroad will be quite sufficient for the present.

It costs, including surveying, clearing, grading, ties, and laying of tracks, purchase and cost of rails, pikes and tools, rolling stock, repairs, shops and so forth, a little over nine thousand dollars a mile.

A corporation with $400,000.00 can successfully undertake the work.

IMMIGRATION BY NEGROES

"Starving Liberian has no accommodations at the present for any large number of persons. Immigration and establishment of Negro concerns and corporations if successfully carried out will bring the necessary developments to induce immigration in large numbers.

While in Monrovia, eight carpenters and masons came from Freetown to do some work for E. D. Co. For two days lodging could not be found for the men, neither somebody to board them.

CONCLUSIONS

"As a fact and a true one, the people of Liberia welcome sincerely the U. N. I. A. and expects much from it.

Liberia being in urgent need of help, it could not be otherwise. They fear only—political domination—from their helpers—blacks or whites.

The article of the Constitution dealing with the powers of the Potentate and some references in the Negro World, in regard to the election of a ruler for all black people have been a troublesome night-mare to them.

But, with diplomacy, and also modesty and discretion on the

part of those who will represent the U. N. I. A. in Liberia, our work is bound to be successful along all lines."

Respectfully submitted,

ELIE GARCIA,

Commissioner to Liberia.

NEGRO LEADERSHIP AND WHAT IT MEANS

I would not exchange two five-cent cigars—even though not a smoker—for all the Colored or Negro political leaders, or rather mis-leaders, of our time. The fraternity is heartless, crafty and corrupt. They exist for themselves only, and give no honest thought to the future, nor the condition of the people, except to exploit the said condition to their political benefit.

The leaders of the race are visionless and selfish. They think of none but themselves.

Among the whites, we have a few political charlatans and crooks, but that race can well afford, under the circumstances, to tolerate them, because they are surrounded and circumvented by Statesmen and race Patriots who are ever vigilant and on guard in protecting the rights of their people. Among us Negroes, there is no relief from such a class, because they monopolize our politics and obstruct our outlook. The only tempering hope is religion, and that is like dry bones, we have to wait a long while for them to come together in the Valley.

To use our present political leaders there must be a conversion and reformation in head and heart. I believe it to be impossible with the inviting system of graft, therefore I suggest that leadership be assumed by our uncorrupted youth, with a program clear, positive and determined, counting well the cost of opposition and persecution, which generally leads to the Bastile and the Guillotine.

Scene: The League of Nations, Geneva, Switzerland

In the forward step to establish colonies in Africa, the Association sent a delegation to the League of Nations at Geneva, in 1922, to present to that body a petition asking for the turning over to the Organization all of the late German African Colonies, which were taken from them during the war by black soldiers, and which were claimed by France and England. I sent special instructions to Sir Eric Drummond (British) Secretary-General of the League, explaining the object of the Delegation, and asking that they be seated as representatives of the Negro Peoples of the World. The delegation consisting of G. O. Mark, Chairman, William Le Van Sherrill, James Augustus O'Meally and Jean Joseph Adam, Secretary and interpreter, was received and seated unofficially at the session. The Petition was presented by the Persian delegation at the League on behalf of our delegates. This opened the eyes of, and no doubt offended the British, French and big colonial powers and at a later session of the League, in 1923, a rule was adopted that nationals can only bring their grievances and submit petitions for consideration through their own governments. This rule affected the petition of 1922 and it is assumed that the rule was the scheme by which the plans of the Association were to be defeated at Geneva. The delegation of 1923, got no favorable consideration and up to the present we have not been officially notified of the final disposition of the petition, although I have been "finally" put away in jail, which no doubt may be interpreted as the "offiicial" answer.

Scene: Harlem, New York, Largest Negro Center in the World,
Philadelphia, Chicago, Pittsburgh, Baltimore and
Other Large Negro Centers

To break up the solidarity and nullify the strength and cohesiveness of the Universal Negro Improvement Association, agents of governments, organizations, corporations and individuals, interested in the exploitation of Negroes operated among the membership, and officers of the Association in several cities, namely, New York, Chicago, Pittsburgh, Philadelphia, Baltimore,. etc. Special persons were detailed to approach each and every executive officer of the Association and by decoy, gather from him the detail of what was supposed to be discussed by the executive council of the Association. Twelve hours after the holding of an executive council's meeting, I would receive information from my secret service department just what went on, and what did not, through certain of the said executive officers retailing the news to persons employed to gather it from them. In the major cases, women and money lenders were used to decoy the executive officers. A friendship was trumped up with these executive officers by the agents, they were offered loans of money "to tide them over," invited to homes, parties, receptions and dinners by the ladies or men and thus made to "talk it out," what they knew and did not know. Other agents were employed to follow them up and work on their fears. They were told that they were such "good fellows," that they (the agents), their friends, would like to tip them off of what is going to happen, etc. "If I were you I would take all I could get, and leave. They will hold Garvey, and he will have to shoulder the responsibility, you get yours and go, because if you remain, you will be punished with him. They are going to imprison and hang that nigger. You better look for yourself. I have a lot of friends who will help you. If they owe you any money, sue them, you are bound to win. Take my advice and do that, gather in all the money you can for yourself and make it hard for that Garvey." With propaganda of this kind and repeated approaches from different directions, according to the organization of the agents, the morale of these officers was broken. They succumbed to the influence of misconduct, some resigned of themselves, and others had to be forced out before they were quite ready to go. After these executives left the Association, they sued the Association for large sums of money for imaginery salaries, and in every case they received judgments. Some sued for fifteen thousand dollars, some for ten thousand, others for smaller amounts.

In the different cities, Negro newspapers were influenced and subsidized to conduct propaganda against me, and against the Association, because of the tremendous confidence the people had in me, and their willingness to financially support my efforts on their behalf, I incurred the jealousy and enmity of prospective Negro business men. They calculated that if they could turn the financial support the people were giving the organization to their own private business they would be able to build up private fortunes for themselves. They therefore joined in the attack upon and against me for the purpose of switching the membership to their enterprises. They would hold out to the members promises of great possibilities. Some of the members switched to them and bought stock in their propositions, of real estate, banking enterprises, insurance companies, chain restaurants, etc. These enterprises never lasted longer than six to nine months, when they and their promoters disappeared. From such sources most of my public vilification has come.

THE BETRAYAL OF A STRUGGLING RACE

Why Garvey Was Double-Crossed and Imprisoned.   The Mighty Influences at WORK to Discredit HIM

Since closing the many chapters and statements, bearing on the Liberian situation, in relation to the Universal Negro Improvement Association and myself, the following happenings have occured to confirm every prediction and statement of mine, through my speeches and writings, exposing the reasons why the Liberian Government, under King and Barclay, double-crossed me in my effort to help build the Black Republic.

My many statements of 1924, made before the Fourth International Convention of the Negro People, at Liberty Hall, New York, and my subsequent petition to the Liberian Congress, presented in December, 1924, on behalf of the entire Negro race, warning the Government against the designs of the Firestone Rubber Company and other selfish white capitalistic concerns, to ultimately subvert the Government of Blacks and establish, through well planned and sinister manoeuvres, a military or naval dictatorship over Liberia, with the idea of protecting their interests, as is being done in Haiti, by the banking interests of New York, are fully justified.

All well informed and keen business men and statesmen knew years ago, that the re-action in the immediate rubber industry would come, bringing a sudden change in the supply and markets, affecting the whole world, and especially America, with its limited and circumscribed field of supply. This afforded Liberia a wonderful chance to have pushed herself forward, and, by proper co-operation and management among Negroes, force an entry into the rubber market and practically corner the trade, the revenue from which could have been used for national development and for placing the Country in an enviable position among the progressive nations of the world.

We of the Universal Negro Improvement Association knew that Liberia would have become a coveted rubber center; that designs by English and American white capitalists would have been fostered to rob the Country of its rich assets and other resources of natural wealth, and ultimately its autonomy, having to deal only with the dull, ignorant, selfish, narrow and racially unpatriotic group, headed by King and Barclay, that run the country.

With this knowledge and intelligence of the whole affair we

did everything that was humanly possible, under the circumstances. We sought to help the country for the race and develop it to a standard among other nations to the everlasting credit of the black man.

After entering into agreements and understandings, as heretofore related in other chapters with the Liberian Government, officials and people, and after launching out, practically, with the expenditure of large sums of money to start our work of reclamation with our men and machinery on the spot, the dishonorable, racially unpatriotic officials of the country, were, no doubt, influenced to double-cross us, as they did, and give away the concessions and country to white exploiting capitalists and thus deprive the race of the opportunity and glorious chance to make good under its own direction; and now come with the effrontery, through Barclay, offering American Negroes the opportunity to go to Liberia to work at 25 cents per day under a white exploiting company. This treachery to the race out-does that of Benedict Arnold. It is only because of Barclay's vile statement in the New York Times and other newspapers why the private report of Garcia is published. It was our intention to promote the rubber and other industries on a competitive basis for the absolute good of Liberia and the Negro race. Our Association had laid the foundation in America, in the West Indies and Central America, through years of careful and proper organization work, for placing at the industrial and national disposal of Liberia fully 10% of the accumulated wealth of the Negroes of these regions, aggregating in gross $2,500,000,000. But the King and Barclay group in Liberia had no confidence in their race and had no patience in our "getting there." They were, no doubt, dazzled by the glittering and attractive Gold Dollars of the Firestone Rubber Company, and as Lucifer—they fell. The following news items speak for themselves.

One of the major causes of Garvey's troubles:

FIRESTONE LEASE OF RUBBER LAND NEARLY CONCLUDED
(Atlanta Constitution, 1925)

"Akron, Ohio, August 19 (A.P.)—Negotiations for the lease by the Firestone Tire and Rubber company of one million acres in Liberia to be devoted to rubber raising have been virtually concluded.

This became known tonight following a two-day conference between Harvey S. Firestone, president of the Company, and Edwin Barclay, Liberian Secretary of State. Mr. Firestone was assured his proposition would be accepted.

While no official announcement could be obtained it was learned from authoritative sources that a $100,000,000 corporation will be formed shortly to operate the plantation on a scale which will assure American manufacturers an adequate rubber supply."

LIBERIAN SECRETARY AT FIRESTONE PLANT
(Afro-American, August 20, 1925)

"Akron, O.—Edwin Barclay, Liberian Secretary of State, arrived this week to go over the plans of a proposed Liberian loan with the Firestone Tire and Rubber Company. He is expected to visit Baltimore and Washington later.

Asked about rubber concessions, Mr. Barclay said:

"The Firestone Rubber Company has a concession, 1,000,000 acres, and can have as much more land as it desires. Rubber is thriving well in Liberia, and there will be a good crop this season. Fifteen hundred acres, planted by the Firestone concern as an experiment, have turned out a success, and 20,000 acres are now under cultivation."

Hitting Garvey for Firestone:
LIBERIAN MINISTER ARRIVES TO PUSH TRADE RELATIONS
(Pittsburgh American, 1925)

"New York, August 20 (P. N. S.)—Edwin Barclay, Minister Plenipotentiary from Liberia, arrived on the French liner, Paris, Wednesday and was met at Quarantine by Henry Carter, special representative of the State Department. The Liberian representative said his visit has nothing to do with loan negotiations, but was chiefly to further commercial relations between his country and the United States. He will be at the Hotel Ambassador for several days before proceeding to Washington.

Mr. Barclay is forty-three years old and speaks English fluently. He said that Liberia was a country for young men and that if he were asked to speak to American Negro organizations relative to Negroes from the United States going to his country he would be pleased to do so. Referring to Marcus Garvey, he said that neither Garvey nor any one identified with him would be welcome to Liberia.

Asked about rubber concession, Mr. Barclay said:

"The Firestone Rubber Co., has a concession, 1,000,000 acres, and can have as much more land as it desires. Rubber is thriving well in Liberia, and there will be a good crop this season.

Fifteen hundred acres, planted by the Firestone concern as an experiment, have turned out a success, and 20,000 acres are now under cultivation."

LIBERIAN RUBBER PROJECT BACKED

Mr. Hoover Approves Firestone Plantation Plan

(Special from Monitor Bureau, 1925)

"Washington, August 22—An important factor in the Administration program for combating the high price of crude rubber, due to the British export restrictions, is the potential field for production of crude rubber in Liberia, by American interests, it was indicated by Herbert Hoover, Secretary of Commerce, who is much interested in the efforts of American producers and manufacturers of rubber products to find new fields for rubber production.

Mr. Hoover gave his approval to pending proposals of American interests to follow the lead of Harvey Firestone, who is contemplating the establishment of extensive rubber plantations in Liberia, said to offer ideal conditions for such development. He said that he hoped American manufacturers would undertake rubber raising.

Although the recent Commerce Department report on the possibilities of rubber growing in the Philippines was favorable to such development, Mr. Hoover has found there is no immediate prospect of American interests going into that territory, to any great extent, due to the restricted ownership of land and to uncertainties as to the future of the Philippines. Liberia, he indicated, offers a more immediate prospect for the growth of American plantations which in seven years from time of planting, would begin to return substantial crops.

The land laws passed by the Philippine Legislature prohibit more than 2,500 acres of land being held under one ownership, and this is a serious obstacle to potential American growers, it was pointed out."

Will the great Government of the United States—the Country of Washington, Lincoln, Madison, Grant, Monroe, and Jefferson; the noble men and women of the American Colonization Society, and broad minded and liberal white Americans, who really desire a solution of the Negro problem, sit supinely by and allow a few selfish, heartless and inhuman Capitalists of their own race, and ignorant, crafty and unpatriotic members of our race, to blight the hopes and destroy the future of the Negro in his urge and look toward Nationhood? Forbid it, Almighty God. In the name of God and Justice, we call upon you the good white people of America to act and act quickly.

I believe that there are honorable and honest White men and women in America who will now come to the rescue of the Black race, with all the danger it entails, and save us from the unholy designs and wicked influences of the crafty and corrupt of our civilization and time. Help the Negro save himself from the hand of the heartless white exploiter, who has ruined our race for centuries, who brought us into slavery, who tortured our fathers and mothers and corrupted the morals of our generations; save us, dear white friends, from a repetition of the horrors of the Congo and Peru. Oh, God, touch the heart of white America and let the people hold the hand of a selfish and vicious Capitalism that seeks, in company with others, to wreck the rights of the darker races. Oh, God, help the Black Man and rescue him from the outrage!

White men and women of love and justice who believe in your God, remember Cain and his brother, Abel. Oh, when God calls upon us to give an account—What will you say? What will your answer be when asked to give an account of your brother, Abel? We the blacks "are the children of Abel," why slay us, when there is so much for everybody? Will the God of Justice and infinite love uphold you in the vile onslaught upon the black race of Africa and the universal exploitation of the people everywhere? Surely not, for if in the sin of injustice and corruption you continue, even His vengeance shall visit you to the third and fourth generations. You, whitemen, have taught us the love of God, you have had us to see Him in all goodness and perfection; is He a mockery to you? He must be something real. Must we by your actions deny His goodness and love for us and seek and search for the God of Africa, the Allah most high, noble and Almighty?

GOD AND HIS HOSTS

My advice to all friendly whites—Keep out of Africa and Asia. Leave South Africa alone. Go to North and South America and Australia. Stay in Europe, but, remember, give Africa a long berth, for one day God and His hosts shall bring "Princes out of Egypt and Ethiopia shall stretch forth her hands."

WHITE AMERICA

By

EARNEST SEVIER COX

White America traces the contact of the white race with colored races during the past six thousand years. It shows that the American Negro Problem is but part of an age-long and world-wide color problem that has never been solved and cannot be solved except by separating the races or mixing them.

———

This book has received support from America's outstanding authorities in ethnology and allied sciences. Donations from Northern and Southern men were made to place a special "Congress Edition" of White America in the hands of members of Congress.

———

The author of White America is also the author of "Let My People Go," a small volume dedicated "To a black Negro making herculean effort to do for the Negro what the greatest of white Americans sought to do for the Negro and encouraged the Negro to do for himself—To Marcus Garvey, a martyr for the independence and integrity of the Negro race."

———

The book, "White America" (price, $2.00), by Earnest S. Cox, and the little book, "Let My People Go" (15 cents per copy, five dozen for $3.00), are issued by the White America Society, Richmond, Va. Write for them.

AFRICAN FUNDAMENTALISM

A Racial Hierarchy and Empire for Negroes

Negro's Faith Must Be Confidence in Self
His Creed: One God. One Aim. One Destiny

The time has come for the Negro to forget and cast behind him his hero worship and adoration of other races, and to start out immediately to create and emulate heroes of his own. We must canonize our own saints, create our own martyrs, and elevate to positions of fame and honor black men and women who have made their distinct contributions to our racial history. Sojourner Truth is worthy of the place of sainthood alongside of Joan of Arc; Crispus Attucks and George William Gordon are entitled to the halo of martyrdom with no less glory than that of the martyrs of any other race. Toussaint L'Ouverture's brilliancy as a soldier and statesman outshone that of a Cromwell, Napoleon and Washington; hence he is entitled to the highest place as a hero among men. Africa has produced countless numbers of men and women, in war and in peace, whose lustre and bravery outshine that of any other people. Then why not see good and perfection in ourselves? We must inspire a literature and promulgate a doctrine of our own without any apologies to the powers that be. The right is ours and God's. Let contrary sentiment and cross opinions go to the winds. Opposition to race independence is the weapon of the enemy to defeat the hopes of an unfortunate people. We are entitled to our own opinions and not obligated to or bound by the opinions of others.

If others laugh at you return the laughter to them; if they mimic you return the compliment with equal force. They have no more right to dishonor, disrespect and disregard your feeling and manhood than you have in dealing with them. Honor them when they honor you; disrespect and disregard them when they vilely treat you. Their arrogance is but skin deep and an assumption that has no foundation in morals or in law. They have sprung from the same family tree of obscurity as we have; their history is as rude in its primitiveness as ours; their ancestors ran wild and naked, lived in caves and in branches of trees like monkeys as ours; they made sacrifices, ate the flesh of their own dead and the raw meat of the wild beast for centuries even as they accuse us of doing; their cannibalism was more prolonged than ours; when we were embracing the arts and sciences on the banks of the Nile, their ancestors were still drinking human blood and eating out of the skulls of their conquered dead; when our civilization had reached the noon-day of progress, they were still running naked and sleeping in holes and caves with rats, bats and other insects and animals. After we had already unfathomed the mystery of the stars and reduced the heavenly contellations to minute and regular calculus they were still backwoodsmen, living in ignorance and blatant darkness.

The world today is indebted to us for the benefits of civilization. They stole our arts and sciences from Africa. Then why should we be ashamed of ourselves? Their modern improvements are but duplicates of a grander civilization that we reflected thousands of years ago, without the advantage of what is buried and still hidden, to be resurrected and re-introduced by the intelligence of our generation and our posterity. Why should we be discouraged because somebody laughs at us today? Who to tell what tomorrow will bring forth? Did they not laugh at Moses, Christ and Mohammed? Was there not a Carthage, Greece and Rome? We see and have changes every day, so pray, work, be steadfast and be not dismayed.

As the Jew is held together by his religion, the white races by the assumption and the unwritten law of superiority, and the Mongolian by the precious tie of blood, so likewise the Negro must be united in one grand racial hierarchy. Our union must know no clime, boundary or nationality. Like the great Church of Rome Negroes the world over must practice one faith, that of Confidence in themselves, with One

PHILOSOPHY AND OPINIONS

God: One Aim: One Destiny: Let no religious scruples, no political machination divide us, but let us hold together under all climes and in every country, making among ourselves a Racial Empire upon which "the sun shall never set."

Let no voice but your own speak to you from the depths: Let no influence but your own rouse you in time of peace and time of war. Hear all, but attend only to that which concerns you. Your allegiance shall be to your God, then to your family, race and country. Remember always that the Jew in his political and economic urge is always first a Jew; the white man is first a white man under all circumstances, and you can do no less than being first and always a Negro, and then all else will take care of itself. Let no one innoculate you with evil doctrines to suit their own conveniences. There is no humanity before that which starts with yourself. "Charity begins at home." First to thyself be true, and "thou canst not then be false to any man."

God and Nature first made us what we are, and then out of our own creative genius we make ourselves what we want to be. Follow always that great law. Let the sky and God be our limit, and Eternity our measurement. There is no height to which we cannot climb by using the active intelligence of our own minds. Mind creates, and as much as we desire in Nature we can have through the creation of our own minds. Being at present the scientifically weaker race, you shall treat others only as they treat you; but in your homes and everywhere possible you must teach the higher development of science to your children; and be sure to develop a race of scientists par excellence for in science and religion lie our only hope to withstand the evil designs of modern materialism. Never forget your God. Remember, we live, work and pray for the establishment of a great and binding racial hierarchy, the founding of a racial empire whose only natural, spiritual and political limits shall be God and "Africa, at home and abroad."

Eyes to My Soul: The Rise or Decline of a Black FBI Agent. Tyrone Powers. ISBN 0-912469-33-1.

The Progress of the African Race Since Emancipation and Prospects for the Future. Tony Martin. ISBN 0-912469-35-8. (pamphlet)

Reflections on Our Pastor: Dr. Martin Luther King, Jr. at Dexter Avenue Baptist Church, 1954-1960. Wally G. Vaughn, Ed. ISBN 0-912469-34-X.

Best Poems of Trinidad. A. M. Clarke, Comp. ISBN 0-912469-36-6.

Song: Poems. Paloma Mohamed. ISBN 0-912469-38-2.

The Economic Future of the Caribbean. E. Franklin Frazier and Eric Williams (Eds). ISBN 0-912469-37-4.

A Man Called Garvey: Fully Illustrated Children's Book on the Life and Work of Marcus Garvey, by Paloma Mohamed. ISBN 0-912469-40-4.

Caribbean Mythology and Modern Life: Five Plays for Young People on Caribbean Issues and Mythical Characters. By Paloma Mohamed. Contains original illustrations and glossary. ISBN:0-912469-42-0.

The Selma Campaign, 1963-1965: The Decisive Battle of the Civil Rights Movement . Wally G.Vaughn and Mattie Campbell Davis (Eds). ISBN 0-912469-44-7.

Order from: The Majority Press, Inc., 46 Development Road, Fitchburg, MA, 01420, USA. Tel: 1-978-829-2521 . Fax: 1-976-348-1233. Email:orders@pssc.com. For administrative and editorial matters: Email: tmpress@earthlink.net. Website:www.themajoritypress.com.